THE GREAT CONSPIRACY TRIAL

THE GREAT CONSPIRACY TRIAL

An Essay on Law, Liberty and the Constitution

by JASON EPSTEIN

 Random House · New York

For Barbara

Contents

THE GREAT CONSPIRACY TRIAL

1

The Haymarket Statue

ON THE NIGHT of October 6, 1969, a cast-iron statue, about twelve feet high, of a Chicago policeman was dynamited from its pedestal, and fell to the ground in Haymarket Square. Metal from its shattered legs landed on the John F. Kennedy Expressway some hundred feet distant. But the helmeted head and the body, together with the upraised right arm, were carried off by the police to their garage on Cermak Road, an undistinguished thoroughfare of commercial buildings and small factories. Cermak Road was named for the unfortunate mayor of Chicago who was killed in 1932 when a bullet probably intended for Franklin Roosevelt, with whom he had been attending a rally at the time, struck him instead.

The destruction of the statue, according to Mayor Richard Daley, was "an attack on all the citizens of Chicago." On the following morning he announced that these "citizens collectively would now take part in the rebuilding." By the next day, however, the citizens of Chicago had other things to think about than the mayor's hyperbolic commitment of their resources to repair a statue which most of them had probably never seen and of which the city's officials had thought so little as to have moved it twice from its original site to make way for new roads and buildings.

What had diverted the people of Chicago were excited accounts in the papers that a ragged army of perhaps a thousand young radicals had come to Chicago that day determined, they said, "to tear Pig City apart" and "to bring the war in Vietnam home to Chicago." This little army—the inflamed residue of the frustrated radicalism of the sixties or, in its own view, the American vanguard of a world-wide revolution which would eventually destroy the American empire—called itself Weatherman, having chosen its name from a line of a popular song: "You don't need a weatherman to know which way the wind blows." No matter how they might be beaten by the Chicago police, of whom some 2,000 had been mobilized to defend the city against them, these Weathermen believed that the wind blew in their favor. It was the same wind, they said, that had blown in favor of the 50,000 Chinese Communists in the 1920's, even though fewer than a thousand of them survived the Long March, and that had also blown in favor of those Cubans who had sailed on the ship *Granma* to liberate their country, and of whom only fifteen of the original seventy-five had survived.

Though the police have yet to find who dynamited the Haymarket statue, it was clear to them that the bombing was meant to have symbolic meanings. According to Sergeant Barrett, president of the Chicago Police Sergeants' Association, the attack on the statue was "an obvious declaration of war between the police and the SDS and other anarchist groups." But in this, Sergeant Barrett was mistaken, for the violence that the Weathermen brought to Chicago marked not so much the declaration of a new war as the continuation of an earlier one.

The Haymarket statue had been erected, according to a worn inscription on its limestone pedestal, "in memory of the seven Chicago police officers martyred in the anarchist riot of May 4, 1886." This epitaph, however, reflects the bias of its author, for it remains unclear to what extent the Haymarket Riot had, in fact, been caused by the anarchists who had held a meeting in the square that night, or by the police who had provocatively arrived as the meeting was about to disband and unnecessarily ordered the anarchist speakers and the handful of their followers who remained in the square to leave. All that is known with certainty is that as the police marched up to the anarchists and asked them to disperse, someone threw a dynamite bomb, which burst spectacularly in the rainy night. One policeman was killed instantly and in the battle that followed between the police and the workingmen, many of whom were armed, sixty more police were wounded, of whom six later died. Many workingmen also died, but how many is unknown.

Whoever threw the bomb was never discovered. Within the month, however, eight anarchist leaders were indicted for conspiracy to commit murder, and brought to trial. Though most of the jurors admitted prejudice against the defendants, Judge Gary, who presided at the trial, denied arguments by the defense to disqualify them. Their oath that they would hear the evidence and decide the case impartially was enough, he said, to provide a fair trial. The defendants were thereupon found guilty and the judge sentenced seven of them to hang. As for the eighth, there had been so little evidence against him that even the prosecutor, a man named Grinnell, asked the judge to be merciful in his case. For this reason Judge Gary sentenced the eighth defendant to fifteen years in the penitentiary. Four of these defendants eventually were executed. A fifth blew his head off with a blasting cap which his girl friend had smuggled into prison.

As soon as the defendants were sentenced, an appeal was undertaken before the Illinois Supreme Court. For this

purpose the original lawyers were joined by Leonard
Swett, a friend and former law associate of Abraham Lincoln. But feeling against the anarchists was high in Chicago.
Mayor Harrison, running for reelection, said, "My fear is
that we will have some terrible trouble in this city in the
next two years if the Supreme Court gives the anarchists
a new trial." In this atmosphere the appeal failed, as did a
later appeal before the United States Supreme Court.

Nevertheless, there was considerable sympathy for the
doomed men. In England George Bernard Shaw solicited
Oscar Wilde, among others, to sign a clemency petition
to be brought before Governor Oglesby of Illinois, and
William Morris asked Robert Browning to sign a similar
appeal. In America William Dean Howells fought vigorously to save the anarchists. He tried to recruit the support
of the poet John Greenleaf Whittier, a Quaker pacifist, but
Whittier turned him down, saying that the defendants
"were more dangerous than other murderers." Even in
Chicago many businessmen and lawyers argued for clemency, but Marshall Field, the department-store owner, ordered his spokesman, who happened to be the same Mr.
Grinnell, to tell the Governor to go ahead with the hanging,
in the belief that to show mercy would encourage further
anarchy. As a result, Field's fellow businessmen withdrew
their support from the defendants. To oppose Field, one
businessman said, "might injure [us] socially and in business." At the last moment, however, Field relented in the
case of two anarchists who renounced their revolutionary
beliefs and these the Governor agreed to spare.

Thus three of the eight defendants survived, and in 1893,
Governor Altgeld, who had studied the trial record with
care, granted these three full pardons. Altgeld concluded
that the judge had "conducted the trial with malicious
ferocity . . . that every ruling throughout the long trial on
any contested point was in favor of the State and further,
that page after page of the record contains insinuating

remarks of the judge . . . with the evident intent of bringing the jury to his way of thinking." But it was unnecessary, Altgeld said, to consider these improprieties in order to find that the Haymarket Trial had been a judicial disgrace. "Until the state proves from whose hands the bomb came," he wrote, "it is impossible to show any connection between the man who threw it and the defendants." The charge that the anarchists had "conspired" to throw the bomb was insufficient to convict them, Altgeld said, and he added that "no judge in a civilized country had ever before laid down such a rule" as the one that Judge Gary presented to the jury when he said that it was sufficient for a finding of guilt "to believe that there was a conspiracy to overthrow the existing order of society and that the defendants were party to such a conspiracy and that the policeman was killed by a bomb thrown by a party to the conspiracy."

Immediately Altgeld was assailed by the Chicago press for siding with the anarchists. The *Tribune*, which had urged that a public subscription of $100,000 be raised to reward the jurors who had found the anarchists guilty, declared that "Altgeld has apparently not a drop of true American blood in his veins . . ." a reference to the fact that Altgeld's parents had brought their son to America from his native Germany when he was three months old. *The New York Times* suggested that Altgeld may have been a secret anarchist himself, while Theodore Roosevelt said that Altgeld wanted "a red government of lawlessness and dishonesty as fanatic and vicious as the Paris Commune." But despite such attacks Altgeld left the Governor's office, according to the Chicago *Inter Ocean*, a paper which normally opposed him, "the most influential Democrat in the West and with his bitterest opponents conceding his personal honesty and his political strength." Once they were released, the three anarchists abandoned Socialism and simply disappeared.

The defendants in the Haymarket Trial considered themselves communists with respect to economic matters and anarchists where the state itself was concerned. Just what this might have meant in practical terms had their program ever come to pass is, however, unclear. Followers of Kropotkin and Bakunin, Marx and Nechayev, inspired by the Paris Commune of 1871, and embittered by the great American Depression of 1873–8, which destroyed for many of them the hopes of reconciliation and progress which had accompanied the end of the Civil War, these revolutionaries, who were loosely associated with the radical International Working Peoples' Association, urged the few thousand workingmen who followed them to arm themselves against the police and the Pinkertons, and advocated a society based on their ideas of common sense and the rights of man. In their manifesto they declared: "The political institutions of our times are the agencies of the propertied class; their mission is the upholding of the privileges of their masters. . . . Since we must rely upon the kindness of our masters for whatever redress we have, and knowing that from them no goodness may be expected, there remains but one recourse—FORCE. It is your right, it is your duty to arm."

Their program included "the destruction of the existing class rule by revolutionary and international action; the establishment of a free society based upon cooperative organization of production; the free exchange of equivalent products without commerce and profit mongery; the organization of education upon a secular, scientific basis, with equality for both sexes; equal rights for all without distinction of race or sex; and the regulation of all public affairs by free contracts between autonomous and independent communes resting on a federalistic basis."

One way in which the anarchists of the IWPA meant to bring this program about was through "propaganda by deed," what the Weathermen and other contemporary

radicals call "exemplary actions," or what Kropotkin himself called "insurrectional deeds [by which] the anarchists
seek to awake in the people the popular sentiment and
initiative for the violent expropriation of property and the
disorganization of the state." It was with this awakening
in mind that the Chicago anarchists of the 1880's advocated
the use of dynamite. "Dynamite! Of all the good stuff, this
is the stuff," wrote a contributor to the *Alarm*, a radical
paper edited by the anarchist leader Albert Parsons, whose
family had come over on the second voyage of the *May-
flower*, whose grandfather had fought in the American
Revolution, and who was later to hang as one of the Haymarket defendants. "Stuff several pounds of this sublime
stuff into an inch pipe, plug up both ends, insert a cap with
a fuse, place this in the immediate neighborhood of a lot of
rich loafers who live by the sweat of other people's brows
and light the fuse."

Such advice, however, hardly inflamed the workingmen
of Chicago as the advocates of propaganda by deed had
hoped. Workers who had survived the Depression of the
seventies and had just emerged from the Depression of
1883–1885 were not interested in destroying the American
economic system, but hoped it would stay afloat, no matter
how precariously, and provide them a living. No doubt
some of the more sanguine workers hoped for more. By
the 1880's Chicago had spawned from its stockyards and
factories, its department stores and railroads, a swarm of
new millionaires who had begun to build their gray stone
castles along the lake shore. Their luxurious example must
have competed powerfully in the souls of ambitious workingmen with the claims of brotherhood and community
urged by the radicals. Many skilled workers and craftsmen
had, by this time, joined the Knights of Labor, a conservative brotherhood that strongly opposed the anarchists and
other agitators. "Let it be understood," the manifesto of

this organization declared, "that the Knights of Labor have no affiliation, association, or sympathy for the band of cowardly murderers, cutthroats and robbers known as anarchists, who sneak through the country like midnight assassins, stirring up the passions of ignorant foreigners, unfurling the red flag of anarchy and causing riot and bloodshed. They are entitled to no more consideration than wild beasts."

The continental frontier was closed. From Henry George's immensely popular book *Progress and Poverty*, hundreds of thousands of Americans learned that economic progress in America—by which George meant the completion of Westward expansion, combined with a financially centralized industrial economy—deprived those Americans who had been left behind of economic opportunity. But from the boisterously growing economy of Chicago there emerged a new frontier, still more challenging and even richer than the old one. The opportunities offered by the city's swelling industrial and commercial enterprise were temptations which only the noblest or most indolent spirits could resist, while the threat of poverty and the loss of respectability suggested horrors which must have intimidated all but the bravest. To maintain a surplus of workers the industrialists had brought immigrants to Chicago by the thousands from Eastern Europe so that by the eighties these workers would gather before dawn outside the factory gates and the packing plants pleading for whatever work they could get at whatever wages the owners cared to offer. Though skilled workers had begun to join trade unions, and thousands of them belonged to such conservative associations as the Knights of Labor, these unskilled immigrants were, as a rule, helpless. Their attempts to form unions were met with dismissal and beatings. When these tactics failed, black strikebreakers were imported from the plantations of the rural South.

Thus the anarchists, finding their potential followers distracted on the one hand by the lure of wealth and respectability, and on the other by the fear of starvation, were left to sustain themselves mainly by their own oratory, which appealed not so much to workers as to intellectuals and reformers like themselves. From time to time, however, as occasions arose, they would attach themselves to issues that seemed likely to agitate the workers, and that might lead to frustrations by which the workingman could be convinced that his only hope lay in revolution.

By the 1880's such an issue had arisen in the form of a demand by workingmen throughout the country for an eight-hour day. Parsons himself had been an early advocate of this Eight Hour Movement and had urged his followers in the Socialist Labor Party, of which he had once been a leader, to avoid violence: "The great principles of Humanity and Popular Sovereignty," he said at the time, "need no violence to sustain them." The goals of labor, he argued, could be achieved through legal means, principally the ballot. But by 1886 Parsons had abandoned these views and become a revolutionary. Until the workers control their own wages and hours, he wrote in the *Alarm*, "they will remain in economic bondage and wage slavery." He therefore refused to support the general strike which the present leaders of the Eight Hour Movement had called for May. Such a strike, the anarchists felt, was merely reformist. The correct position, they said, was "to take over the whole damned system and change it." Yet the anarchists could hardly afford to dissociate themselves from a cause that 300,000 workingmen had joined. Despite their principled objection to a compromise with the wage system, the anarchists ended, as May 1 approached, by supporting the general strike, though they took no active part in organizing it.

Throughout the country on May 1, thousands of workers left their jobs. In Chicago itself, the center of the Eight

Hour Movement, 80,000 walked out. For the most part the demonstrations were peaceful, but the Chicago papers had prepared their readers for the worst. "The socialist agitators," according to the Chicago *Inter Ocean*, "have boasted that they would turn the demonstration . . . to good account. . . . There will be in Chicago today some of the shrewdest wire-pullers of the socialist movement. . . . There is one standing admonition that the wage workers should keep in mind—Kick them out."

The *Daily Mail* went further. "There are two dangerous ruffians at large in this city; two sneaking cowards who are trying to create trouble. One of them is named Parsons; the other is named Spies [who was to hang along with Parsons] . . . These two fellows have been at work fomenting disorder for the past ten years. They should have been driven out of the city long ago . . . [They] have been engaged for the past six months for the precipitation today. They have taken advantage of the situation to bring about a series of strikes and to work injury to capital and to honest labor. They have no love for the Eight Hour Movement. These fellows don't want any reasonable concession. They are looking for riot and plunder . . . Keep them in view. Hold them personally responsible for any trouble that occurs. Make an example of them if trouble should occur."

Though the leaders of the strike had urged their followers to avoid trouble, the police had been alerted, partly by the inflamed press. So had the militia, whose officers had been given copies of the War Department "Manual for Riot Tactics," a pamphlet prepared after the labor violence of 1877.

On May 1 some 30,000 strikers paraded in an orderly way through the streets, and that night, under the auspices of the Trades and Labor Assembly, they held a tremendous ball. The next day, too, was peaceful. On May 3, however, a fight broke out on Black Road near the McCormick harvester plant, which had been shut down earlier in the year by its owners when a number of workers, insisting on their right to form a union, had struck. The plant soon reopened, staffed this time by strikebreakers, and the fight on May 3 broke out when these strikebreakers left the plant at the end of the day and encountered a group of McCormick strikers who had been meeting at Black Road. The police soon arrived, and in the confusion one worker was shot and killed.

August Spies, the anarchist whom the *Daily Mail* had described, along with Albert Parsons, as a "cowardly fellow," had gone to Black Road as a reporter for the *Arbeiter Zeitung*—today it would be considered part of the underground press. He concluded, as had a number of other spectators, that the bloodshed had been considerably greater. The next day he and the other anarchist leaders called for a mass meeting of workingmen to be held in Haymarket Square to denounce "the latest atrocious act of the police, the shooting of our fellow workingmen yesterday." A few of the handbills announcing the meeting urged the workingmen to arm themselves, but when Spies saw these words he demanded that they be deleted. Most of the 20,000 circulars that were distributed did not carry this advice.

Though Haymarket Square was much larger in those days than it is now—large enough to accommodate 20,000 people—hardly more than a thousand turned up that night to hear the anarchists. By ten o'clock the rain had begun and, with only a few hundred people left in the square, the revolutionaries proposed that the rest of the program be moved half a block away to Zepf's Hall, where Parsons and his family had already gone. But Sam Fielden, a former Methodist minister and the last speaker of the evening, who, along with Parsons and Spies, was later to be sentenced to death, but who later recanted and was eventually pardoned by Altgeld, insisted that he was about to conclude his speech and asked for only a minute more. "I tell you," he said to the few listeners who clustered around the wagon which he used as a platform, "war has been declared upon us and I ask you to get hold of anything that will help resist the onslaught of the enemy. People have been shot. Men, women and children have not been spared by the capitalists. You are called upon to defend yourselves. What matters it whether you kill yourselves with work or on the battlefield resisting the enemy?"

At this moment—it was about twenty past ten—a force of 180 policemen entered the square and formed a line only a few feet from the wagon from which Fielden was speaking. The police captain, a notorious head-cracker named Ward, ordered the crowd to disperse and the speaker to step down from the wagon. As Fielden, rain dripping from his beard, began to comply, the black-powder bomb exploded in a flash of blue and orange light.

A curious aspect of the affair is that, while the police had been expecting trouble all day in the aftermath of the violence at the McCormick plant, Mayor Harrison, a hearty fellow whom the revolutionaries liked to denounce for the silk underwear he wore, but who was in fact not unsympathetic to labor, had left the Des Plaines Street police station near Haymarket Square at about ten o'clock, and had gone home. "Nothing is likely to occur to require interference," he told Captain Ward. Why the police entered the square twenty minutes later is therefore as much a mystery as the origin of the bomb itself.

Throughout their trial the eight defendants sat quietly, in the hope that their peaceful demeanor might help to convince the jury of their innocence, but when the verdict was finally given and they were allowed to speak in their own behalf before sentencing, they abandoned this pos-

ture. To expect mercy from Judge Gary, who had throughout the trial shown such prejudice against them, was
pointless.

August Spies was the first to speak and he spoke for
several hours. He accused the State's attorney of conspiracy to commit murder—a charge which, as events were to
show, made rather more sense than the government's charge
against the eight defendants. Then he told the judge
". . . you may sentence me, for I am an anarchist. I believe
that the state of castes and classes—the state where one
class dominates over and lives upon the labor of another
class—is doomed to die and make room for a free society,
voluntary association or universal brotherhood, if you like.
You may pronounce sentence upon me, Honorable Judge,
but let the world know that in 1886 in the State of Illinois,
eight men were sentenced to death because they believed
in a better future . . ." As for the conspiracy charge itself,
he replied that he had seen his friend Louis Lingg (who
was later to bite the blasting cap and blow himself up in
his cell) only twice before at meetings of the Central Labor
Union. He had never spoken to him. With Engle, another
defendant, he had not been on speaking terms for years,
and Fischer, still another defendant, "used to go around
making speeches against me."

Lingg himself, who had arrived in America from Swit-
zerland only a year before, addressed the court in German.
Short and handsome with a well-shaped beard and "slate
gray" eyes, he was the subject of much romantic speculation on the part of the spectators. At the time of the trial
he was twenty-two years old, the youngest of the defendants. "I repeat," he said, "that I am the enemy of the order
of today and I repeat that with all my powers so long as
breath remains in me, I shall combat it. I declare again,
frankly and openly, that I am in favor of using force. If
you cannonade us, we shall dynamite you. You laugh. Per-

haps you think, 'you'll throw no more bombs,' but let me assure you that I die happy on the gallows, so confident am I that the hundreds and thousands to whom I have spoken will remember my words; and when you shall have hanged us, then mark my words. They shall do the bomb throwing. In this hope I say to you, I despise you. I despise your order, your laws, your force-propped authority. Hang me for it."

A monument to the Haymarket defendants was unveiled in the Waldheim Cemetery in a western suburb of Chicago in the same week that Governor Altgeld pardoned the three surviving anarchists. This monument, which includes a figure of Justice crowning a fallen worker, soon became a sort of shrine to which workingmen in considerable numbers were to pay homage, encouraged, in later years, by the Communists who had an interest in keeping alive the infamous memory of Judge Gary and the innocence of his victims.

It is not inconsistent with whatever honor is due the memory of Louis Lingg and his fellow apostles of dynamite that the Weathermen, when they came to Chicago on October 8, 1969—the anniversary of the death of the Che Guevara—chose to pay their respects not at the shrine in the Waldheim Cemetery, assuming they knew of its existence, but to blow up, if indeed it was the Weathermen who did it, the statue of the Chicago policeman which had been erected in 1889 by a group of Chicago businessmen and which had been rededicated in 1966 by Mayor Richard Daley.

On the night of October 8, while the Haymarket statue lay on the floor of the police garage on Cermak Road, the Weathermen gathered in Lincoln Park, some three miles north of the Loop, near a statue of Garibaldi. The plan was to assemble there to pay their respects to Che Guevara as well as to Nguyen Van Troi, a Vietnamese who had been shot by a firing squad for having tried to kill former Secretary of Defense Robert McNamara. They would then march out of the park and begin to "tear Pig City apart." Dressed in what they called "full street-fighting gear," including helmets, goggles, heavy jackets and boots, their wrists taped and arms padded, they marched in groups or "cadres" of six or seven into the park. "It's amazing," one of them reflected, "that in a couple of hours I might be dead." Another was surprised and frightened by how few Weathermen had turned up, since the attack on "Pig City" was supposed to be a national action, and Weathermen had promised to come from all over the country. Nevertheless, they chanted the name of Ho Chi Minh, and by nine o'clock speakers had begun to address them. One of these announced that "this revolution is slowing down. We've got to fasten it up." Another speaker was Tom Hayden, who had arrived in the park with Abbie Hoffman and John Froines, defendants, along with five others, in the Chicago Conspiracy Trial, which had begun two weeks earlier in Chicago's Federal Building down in the Loop.

"People have been saying that the Chicago 8 are against this demonstration," Hayden told them. "This is not true. While there are some differences among the 8, we are all united in the need to intensify the struggle and end the war. We are glad to see people back in Lincoln Park. We are glad to see the militancy of Chicago increased." Several months later, however, Hayden spoke differently about the Weathermen. "There was," he said, "something deeply wrong in what [they had done] in Chicago. It was random violence. To ourselves revolution is like birth, blood being inevitable, but the purpose of the act is to create life, not to glorify the blood." Rennie Davis, another defendant, told reporters a few weeks after the Weathermen had left that he "wholeheartedly disagreed" with their tactics, though on the day the statue had been dynamited, he expressed enthusiastic approval.

The Weathermen had come to Chicago in a spirit of defiance and revenge. Many of them had fought and been beaten by the Chicago police in Lincoln Park and in the Loop at the time of the Democratic National Convention fourteen months earlier. The object of their rage, however, was not Chicago itself but what they called the American empire of which Chicago was, in their view, the bloated and malevolent heart. To destroy what they considered this monstrous organism, which, they felt, fattened on the lives and spirits of the world's poor and which thought nothing of killing whichever people it could not profit from, whether in its own ghettos and prisons or in the villages of Vietnam, justified, in the eyes of these Weathermen, whatever violent actions they might be capable of. In this respect, they differed from Hayden and the other defendants who were on trial in the Federal Building on charges of having conspired with the intention of inciting a riot at the Democratic Convention.

The Conspiracy defendants were part of an older generation of radicals. Many of them had gone South to take part in the nonviolent civil-rights activities of the early sixties. David Dellinger, the oldest of the alleged conspirators, a man in his fifties, was a famous pacifist, a disciple of Gandhi and the successor to A. J. Muste as the leader of nonviolent opposition to American militarism. The militancy of these defendants, no matter how extreme it might appear from conventional perspectives, arose from moral commitments which many nonradicals might find intelligible. They were against the war in Vietnam, against racism, against an economy committed to profit, and which had become dangerous to man and nature. Because they saw these evils not as correctible flaws within a generally healthy and benign culture, but as symptoms of a deep and

perhaps incurable sickness—as a kind of cultural insanity—
they engaged in radical criticism of American institutions
generally. What these militant leaders and many of their
followers called for, in their various ways, was a profound
and revolutionary reconsideration of the values by which
America and the other industrial nations had come to live.
By the time of the Democratic National Convention in
1968, most of them had begun to call for revolution itself.
But for all their aggressive manner and the frequent violence of their speech, their attack was essentially rhetorical:
verbal, theatrical, even, at times, academic. Their aim was
not to destroy America, as the Weathermen said they
wanted to do, but to persuade their followers to reclaim it,
divest it of its empire, and restore it to its primitive ideals,
as they conceived them; a position consistent, generally,
with the manifesto of the Haymarket anarchists who had
attempted to fuse certain ideas of Jefferson and Tom Paine
with those of such European radicals as Marx and Kropotkin.

The Weathermen, on the other hand, were determined
not to argue with a dying culture but, no matter how feeble
their present means, to try to kill it. Their talk conveyed
a kind of terminal feeling. It returned again and again to
the idea of death. "Dig it. First they killed those pigs," said
Bernadine Dhorn, a leader of the Weathermen, at a meeting
two months after the destruction of the Haymarket statue.
Miss Dhorn, who had graduated a few years earlier from
law school, was referring to the murder in Hollywood of
the actress Sharon Tate and her friends. ". . . then [the
killers] ate dinner in the same room with them; then they
even shoved a fork into a victim's stomach. "Wild!" said
Miss Dhorn.

Perhaps Miss Dhorn intended no more by these remarks
than to illuminate the hypocrisy by which a society deplores
the violent murder of an actress, while collectively it mur-

ders Vietnamese and brutalizes its own poor; so that Miss
Tate and her friends, being white Americans, got no more
than they deserved, in Miss Dhorn's view. But her celebration of murder also reflects another concern of the Weathermen: that their instinctual sources of aggression have been
illegitimately taxed by a culture that has perverted and col-
lectivized these energies and converted them to purposes of
mass killing, leaving its individual members psychologically
feeble and thus unable to confront their brutal culture with
sufficient force. Hence the echo in Miss Dhorn's manifesto
of the passion with which such writers as the Marquis de
Sade and D. H. Lawrence attacked the institutions of sexual
repression within their own cultures. Like these enthusiasts
for sexual self-determination, Miss Dhorn and her followers
may feel that society has stolen from its members an important part of their instinctual capital, and that to regain
these resources is essential not only to their personal survival,
but to the survival of the species.

The violence of Miss Dhorn's rhetoric suggested a quan-
tum leap beyond the wild hair, the primitive expletives, and
the shabby clothes by which the main body of radical youth
mean to dissociate themselves from their country and its
customs. Her morbid perspective is a quite different matter
from what the Conspiracy defendants seemed to have in
mind when they came to Chicago with their sanguine proposals for an alternative politics in America, an end to the
war in Vietnam and to the suffering in the ghettos.

Yet the defendants and the Weathermen were linked not
only by the presence of the latter in Chicago, who had come
there partly to protest the trial; they were also con-
nected in the way that later developments within a continuous process reflect earlier ones. The Weathermen had
splintered off a year earlier from Students for a Democratic
Society, the organization that Tom Hayden and Rennie
Davis had helped to found in 1962. "Many of this year's
Weathermen were disillusioned by the way legal and peace-

ful protest was smashed in the streets of Chicago last year,"
the defendants wrote the day after the rally at the Garibaldi
statue. "As we warned at the end of the 1968 Convention
here, these strong arm police methods would not intimidate
young people but instead would turn them into warriors.
Chicago will, as will America, reap what it sows." Though
Thomas Foran, the United States Attorney who prosecuted
the alleged conspirators, was later to describe such statements as this as endorsements of the Weathermen by the
defendants, the actual relationship was more ambiguous.
What the Weathermen represented for the defendants was
a tactical and ideological dilemma, not unlike what the defendants themselves presented to the liberal generation of
which they were in turn the frustrated and bitter heirs.

By ten o'clock on the night of the eighth the Weathermen assembled by the Garibaldi statue had other things to
think about than what their presence in Chicago may have
meant to the eight defendants. Their numbers had grown to
about three hundred, hardly enough to confirm the revolutionary visions with which they had boarded their buses for
Chicago, but enough to give the impression that an army
had in fact gathered to do battle. So intense had feeling
grown among these Weathermen by this time that one of
them was later to write, "I could hardly concentrate on any
of the speeches." Then suddenly one of the speakers announced, "We are going to see Judge Hoffman. Let's go."

"Before the absurdity of going through with the action
sunk in my head fully," a Weatherman later wrote, "three
or four hundred people started running toward the Park's
exit . . . within a minute or two, right in front of my eyes,
I saw and felt the transformation of the mob into a battalion
of three hundred revolutionary fighters . . . Yes. We were
out to smash the totality of this imperialist social order: we
were really out to fight. Each one of us felt the soldier
in us."

Julius J. Hoffman, the seventy-four-year-old judge who

presided at the trial of the Chicago Conspiracy, lives with his wife in a two-bedroom apartment on the twentieth floor of the Drake Towers, one of Chicago's more opulent residences, about a mile south of Lincoln Park on Lake Shore Drive. Though he was to suffer many insults before the Conspiracy Trial ended, his sleep was not disturbed by the Weathermen on the night of the eighth. Within a dozen blocks of his shadowy tower, its name, in Gothic letters on a huge electric sign, visible through the fog, the march of the Weathermen was stopped by a line of police. As if prepared for such obstruction, the marchers deployed themselves westward, away from the lake, and ran along Goethe Street, chanting the name of Ho Chi Minh alternately with a version of Mao Tse-tung's admonition, "Pick up, pick up, pick up the gun." Soon they found themselves in the elegant presence of Chicago's most expensive dwellings, amid those dozen or so streets between the lake and State Street which the guidebooks call the Gold Coast, and where the city's thrones and powers live—the very center of the enemy citadel. With stones taken from construction sites to supplement the long staves they carried, the Weathermen smashed the windows and glass arcades of these buildings as they passed. They so alarmed some diners who observed this mayhem through the curtained windows of one of the smart restaurants in the area that they asked the waiters to bolt the entrances. Then, turning into State Street and finding there a row of well-lit shops, the Weathermen proceeded to smash these windows too until, at last, the police formed a line across Division Street, arrested what Weathermen they could, and dispersed the rest.

In the mild evening the residents of the neighborhood gathered along the sidewalks to consider the damage that had been done. One such group, having returned an hour before from the Adlai Stevenson Institute, where a liberal journalist had lectured to them against the war in Vietnam, stood and watched while a man and woman swept up the glass that had once been the window of their shop—a curious sort of place, a hairdresser's as well as a shop for dresses and personal ornaments. Within the bare frame of the shopwindow, dresses still hung, arranged in a diminishing perspective to entice the passer-by; but now, proximity having exposed their mystery, they seemed as pathetic as the bewildered shopkeepers bent over their brooms.

The next day and for some days thereafter, this window and the others along either side of State Street were to remain boarded up while scraps of revolutionary posters blew in the wind. This small part of Chicago did indeed briefly look as if a kind of war had come to it. Throughout the winter, as the Conspiracy Trial dragged to its troubled end, infusing the neighborhood around State Street with a disconcerting self-consciousness so that arrangements for dinner were made and broken according to how people felt about the proceedings in Judge Hoffman's courtroom, the night of broken glass returned to the mind as a kind of puzzle on whose surface there was no clear sign, but in whose depths there was the hint of an ominous political mutation, of an unfathomable future discord.

For the Weathermen themselves, however, who gathered at the end of their week in Chicago around the naked base of the Haymarket statue, the events that they had precipitated offered no such concern. "In the last four days," one of them said, "we have learned some important lessons. We have learned that the spirit of the people is greater than man's technology . . . We are small but we have stood in the way of history." Louis Lingg's poor ghost had returned at last.

Though the Weathermen had not torn Chicago apart— nor were they likely to do so—the broken windows along State Street foreshadowed the gathering storm in Judge Hoffman's courtroom. This storm, by the time the trial ended, was to do damage to far more than a few shopwindows. It would tear at the dry roots of the old democracy itself—a democracy that had grown brittle and vulnerable since the time when Judge Gary and his jury, together with the Supreme Courts of Illinois and the United States, along with Mayor Harrison and Marshall Field, to say nothing of the newspapers and the people themselves, had failed it in the preceding century.

2

Judge Campbell's Grand Jury and Representative Cramer's Bill

THE UNITED STATES District Court for the Northern District of Illinois, where the Chicago Conspiracy Trial was held, occupies several floors of the new Federal Building on Dearborn Street, between Adams and Jackson, in Chicago's Loop. Of this thirty-story structure, made of steel and green glass, and designed by the late architect Mies van der Rohe, the Chicago Art Institute has said, "The commitment to order everywhere present is translated into an authoritarian and heroic presence . . ." There is no "recourse to historical vocabulary." Except for a colored photograph of Richard Nixon, which sits upon the ground-floor information booth, the building lacks all adornment. In normal times a carillon somewhere within plays popular and patriotic tunes, which can be heard ordinarily in the lobby and on the surrounding streets; but during the Conspiracy Trial the carillon was silenced and armed guards stood at each of the four revolving doors. Pasted on the glass wall beside each entrance were notices, to which were affixed official seals and signatures of the court, proclaiming that while the trial was in progress no photographs were to be taken from the streets or plaza adjacent to the building and that people without proper business should keep out. The guards at the doors were ordered to search purses and brief cases and to question visitors whose manner seemed to them unusual.

These regulations were imposed by William Campbell, chief judge of the district; and when, in the course of the trial, a Chicago lawyer named Oliver presented a petition, signed by thirty-five fellow lawyers, complaining that such unusual precautions created an atmosphere "in which detached, dispassionate deliberation had been made impossible," Judge Campbell ordered him to explain to the court why he should not be punished for commenting openly on pending litigation, a violation of a rule of the court.

Oliver was eventually reprimanded by a panel of three judges, including Campbell himself. But had Judge Campbell's colleagues been genuinely scrupulous in enforcing the rules of the court, instead of merely compliant with the angry whim of their chief, they would have reprimanded Campbell too: for more than a year the chief judge had openly made the prosecution of the demonstrators at the Chicago convention his personal business, an interest that he made abundantly clear to the press as well as to his fellow judges. Thus he had violated not only the rule of his own court concerning comment on pending litigation, but legal decorum of considerably more ancient standing as well.

On the afternoon of September 9, 1968—a week after the Democratic National Convention—Judge Campbell, an expressionless man of sixty-four, with a receding chin, an abundant nose, and eyes that had begun to sink into their pouches, who looked, at a glance, as if he had been too loosely assembled, like a moose in judicial robes, entered his courtroom. He was about to convene a new grand jury of twenty-three members, as he did at the beginning of every month. These jurors are chosen by lot from lists of voters within the federal judicial district, and it would be their duty, the judge explained to them, to hear evidence presented by the United States Attorney and to vote indictments accordingly. The unusual presence of newspapermen in the court suggested that the swearing in of this September grand jury was to be a special occasion.

The judge began by explaining the history of the grand jury, which represented, he said, "the oldest legal institution in America," one that derived, in fact, from Magna Carta. Before that time, he told the jurors, the King "could order anyone's arrest and imprisonment and there he waited until the Crown decided to prefer charges against him, if it did. If it didn't he stayed there anyway." The grand jury had been conceived, he explained, to take this awful power away from the King and place it in the hands of his subjects. "Therefore, there is no greater power than yours." If sixteen of you "feel that there is insufficient ground to prosecute, you vote what is called a no bill and there is no prosecution."

"You are not," the judge added, "to consider questions of guilt or innocence . . . yours is entirely a one sided hearing. You don't hear the party accused. You are to judge [only] whether there is sufficient ground to put him on trial . . . If sixteen or more of you feel there is reasonable ground . . . you then return an indictment, and the party named is arrested, a trial date is set and then the government has the burden of proving him guilty beyond a reasonable doubt. . . ." Since the people under investigation by the grand jury are presumed to be innocent, Judge Campbell concluded, the deliberations are to be kept secret.

The account that Judge Campbell presented to the grand jurors seated before him was largely fiction. The discretion which historically belongs to the grand jury in practice belongs to the prosecutor and his staff—in this case, the United States Attorney for the Northern District of Illinois and his various assistants. These men present the cases they want to try, and the grand jury, which seldom has independent access to the evidence, votes as the government attorneys suggest. There was nothing in the appearance of the grand jurors seated before Judge Campbell—a typical "redneck" grand jury, according to a government lawyer who later met with them—to suggest that these jurors, once they began their deliberations, would challenge the usual procedure. But Chief Judge Campbell, for reasons that were to become clear in the course of the afternoon, chose not to proceed in the usual way.

As the judge completed his general history of the grand jury and its function, Mr. Foran, the United States Attorney for the Northern District of Illinois, entered the courtroom, but the judge, instead of turning the jurors over to him, as is customary, asked him to take a seat. "I have one or two specific items," he explained to Foran, "so if you will just sit down there, please."

"Ordinarily," the judge continued, "two days a week are enough to do the regular business of the grand jury in this district, but in view of the charge I am going to give you, you will probably have a little more to do." The judge then proceeded to outline for the jurors four possible indictments, three of which they eventually handed down. This was an unusual intrusion by a judge into the deliberations of the grand jury; especially since, as was later to become known, Judge Campbell's plan was that he himself would preside at the trial which was to follow from the first of these indictments.

"I find from reading the newspaper," he told the grand

jurors, "that various people are accused by various other people of interstate conspiracy to promote riot and civil disorder in violation of federal law." There is also, he added, "a second category of charges . . . that the police in quelling riots and preserving order . . . are accused of violating the civil rights of the people they were confronting." Then he named a third set of charges which he hoped the grand jury would look into. These had to do with "some television networks [which] are accused of engaging in interstate conspiracy to violate civil rights and provoke riot and disorder and to unduly influence the elective rights of people in violation of the Federal Communications Act." Finally there was a fourth category of violations, in which the television media may have violated the wiretap provisions of the Federal Communications Act.

What Judge Campbell meant by this last item was that a reporter for one of the networks had been caught bugging a hotel suite where some convention delegates had been holding a secret meeting. For this the reporter was subsequently indicted, pleaded no contest, was found guilty, and placed on probation. But what mainly interested Judge Campbell were the first three sets of charges: those concerning the demonstrators, who were said to have conspired to cross state lines in order to promote riots; those concerning the police who, "in quelling" these riots had been accused of violating the civil rights of the people who took part in them; and those concerning the networks.

Only with respect to the third category of charges was the chief judge to be disappointed by what he was later to call "my grand jury." But these charges were most unreasonable, according to the networks themselves, who angrily complained to the Federal Communications Commission, which had begun an investigation of its own into these alleged provocations. Though Judge Campbell, together with his old friend Mayor Daley, may have felt that the networks contributed to the trouble in Chicago, a Federal Communications Commission Report on March 2 rejected this theory, as the networks had urged. The networks, according to the FCC, had given "a reasonable opportunity for presentation of contrasting viewpoints." Nothing more was heard of the matter.

That the chief judge suggested the substance of the indictments, three of which the grand jury was later to hand down, may have puzzled some of the jurors, as it did several Chicago newspapermen; for the judge had explained less than a half-hour earlier that the grand jury is supposed to reach its conclusions independently, without external influence. The Court's function, he had told the grand jurors, is to protect this independence. But these were not, as Judge Campbell then made clear, normal circumstances. What made this situation special, he explained, was that certain "self-appointed" agencies were investigating "these various alleged federal offenders which are purely the province of this grand jury to investigate." What Judge Campbell wanted to make certain was that none of these other agencies would interfere with the authority "vested by the Constitution" in this grand jury.

The self-appointed agency that Judge Campbell was most afraid would usurp the Constitutional authority of his grand jury was none other than the Justice Department itself. "We find the Attorney General of the United States," Campbell told the grand jurors, "quoted in the press as investigating criminal charges in a criminal division of his office. [Another] of the articles I [have] read said that the Civil Rights Division of the Attorney General's office had another investigation going. It seems one of them is investigating the actions of the police and the other is investigating the actions of the mob. Well, if either one of them did anything wrong in violation of [the law] that is something you should find out."

What Judge Campbell had apparently read in the press was that the Attorney General, Ramsey Clark, had begun an investigation of his own into the Chicago disorders. He was also planning, so it had been rumored, to appoint a Chicago lawyer named Daniel Walker either as special prosecutor, in place of Mr. Foran, to present evidence to the grand jury or, failing that, to make Walker chairman of a special investigating committee of the President's Commission on Violence to consider the causes of the turmoil during convention week.

But Judge Campbell probably knew more than he had been able to read in the papers, for it had become a subject of much concern in the White House as well as in Mayor Daley's office, in the days following the convention, that Clark did not feel it to be a federal responsibility to prosecute the demonstrators, the "various people," according to Judge Campbell, who had been "accused by various other people of interstate conspiracy to promote riot and civil disorder."

It was not, as Clark later explained, his view that the job of the federal government was to prosecute people who may have broken local laws against rioting or inciting to riot. These were, he felt, matters to be dealt with in local courts—an argument that he had also made more than a year earlier, when Congress had been debating what was later to become the so-called Stokely Carmichael bill. This bill made it a federal crime to cross state lines with the intention of causing a riot, the crime with which Campbell had suggested the grand jury might charge the demonstrators. Clark had argued against this bill that there was plenty of local law to protect communities against advocates of violence. Furthermore, as Clark had said on this earlier occasion, ". . . a law which requires you to prove the state of mind (i.e., the intentions) of an individual when he travels in interstate commerce, is very difficult to [enforce] . . ."

But if Clark was dubious of the federal anti-riot statute, he was also "under enormous pressure," as Fred Vinson, Jr., the chief of his Criminal Division, was later to admit, "to step in and prosecute the [demonstrators]," pressure that came not only from Congress, which had passed the federal anti-riot act, despite Clark's objections, by a vote of 347 to 70, but from Mayor Daley's office, and especially from President Johnson. Thus Clark sent Frank Taylor of the Criminal Division of the Justice Department to Chicago to see if there were any grounds on which to prosecute the convention demonstrators under the new anti-riot statute.

Clark's main concern, however, as he later explained, was with the Chicago police. For, while he felt that the prosecution of the demonstrators was properly a local matter, he also felt that the federal government had the obligation, under various civil rights acts, to protect American citizens who might have been subjected to summary punishment by local authority. This issue had increasingly concerned the Justice Department in the South but had seldom, in Clark's view, arisen seriously in the North until the Chicago convention. Accordingly, Clark sent to Chicago, along with Taylor of the Criminal Division, Robert Owen of the Civil Rights Division of the Justice Department.

It was to these representatives of the Justice Department that Judge Campbell referred in his instructions to the grand jury. He then went on to assure the grand jurors that "there is no agency, State or Federal, not even this Court, that has the primary and complete authority, [the] right and duty that vests in this grand jury. [You] possess the only authority that exists anywhere . . . there is no authority higher than yours . . . and you are responsible to no one except your own conscience. I would appreciate it, [therefore] if the [Attorney General] would assemble and send to this grand jury any and all information he has. . . . This [grand jury] is the only body who can examine [the evidence] authoritatively under oath and can determine what, if any, violation of federal law has occurred within this district and to act accordingly."

Thus Judge Campbell added to the pressures on Clark from the White House and the mayor's office the weight of his own influence with the grand jury, an influence which, at this point in the afternoon, had quite undermined the theory of the grand jury's sovereignty which he had expounded an hour earlier. Taylor and Owen thereafter functioned not so much as representatives of Ramsey Clark but, insofar as they were permitted to function at all, as assistants to Foran. Furthermore, Judge Campbell was, later in the month, to order both Justice Department men removed from the grand jury proceedings entirely, an order which angered the Attorney General, and which he overruled. As for Daniel Walker, it had now become impossible for him, with Tom Foran in charge of the grand jury, to serve as special prosecutor, assuming Clark had had such a proposal in mind. Both Walker and Clark later said that this scheme had never been contemplated, but Judge Campbell may have believed differently, given the abundant rumors that circulated at the time: hence his haste to foreclose the possibility by putting Foran in charge of the jury on September 8.

By October the jurors had heard some three hundred FBI reports of police violence. Accordingly they voted, under a Reconstruction statute which makes it a crime for local officials to interfere with the civil rights of American citizens, to indict eight policemen, the only ones, according to the FBI, who could be identified by name.

The grand jury did not, however, make these indictments public until the following March, at which time it had also voted to indict eight demonstrators who it charged had violated the anti-riot provision of the Civil Rights Act of 1968, the law which finally encompassed the "Stokely Carmichael" bill that had been approved by the House a year earlier, and which Ramsey Clark felt should not have been passed.

When Clark left office in January there remained, however, some question about how the grand jury would deal with the demonstrators, and Clark was asked by a reporter whether he had changed his mind on the subject of their possible indictment. "No," he said, "and if the new administration does prosecute them, that will be a clear signal that a crackdown is on the way." When the indictments finally were handed down, some two months later, John Mitchell had become Attorney General, and it was he who ordered Foran to proceed with the prosecution of the alleged Chicago conspirators, even though, as Clark said at the time, "the same lawyers in the Department who [told] me that proceedings against the demonstrators could not be justified must have told the same thing to him." As for the curious fact that eight demonstrators had been indicted along with eight policemen, Clark said that this was "politics pure and simple. The eight-to-eight balance makes this clear."

Yet if it was Mitchell who finally approved the indictments under the new Republican Administration, and who also agreed to let Foran, a Democrat, remain in office long enough to prosecute the case, it was Campbell who first introduced the grand jurors to the charges. He hovered over their deliberations, and later reluctantly disqualified himself from sitting as the judge at the trial of the demonstrators because it had become clear, as the lawyers for the defense charged and as everyone in the Federal Building knew, that his personal interest in the matter made it most unlikely that he could maintain an impartial appearance.

A year later, Edwin Robson, Campbell's successor as chief judge, was to say that one of his most important tasks would be to swear in each month's grand jury. "They are charged to be independent," he said. "I want strongly to preserve that independence," an allusion perhaps to the vigor with which his predecessor had pursued an opposite course. The source of this vigor, it was commonly assumed by the Chicago newspapers as well as by the gossips around the courthouse, had been Judge Campbell's affection for Mayor Daley, a frailty which is often invoked to explain the eccentricities of Chicago officials. But this explanation may be superficial. The passions that appeared to move the chief judge may have been more personal than those likely to be inspired merely by affection for an ancient political ally.

William Campbell graduated from Loyola Law School in 1926 and entered the general practice of law the following year. Like many graduates of Loyola, including, for example, Thomas Foran, he combined his interest in the law with an involvement in Democratic politics. Before long he had made himself known in Washington as a sort of emissary or nuncio to Franklin Roosevelt on behalf of the liberal Chicago bishop Bernard Shiel. According to a contemporary, he had managed to enhance himself in the eyes of the President by emphasizing his friendship with the bishop, while he improved his situation with the bishop by implying a similar friendship with the President. Soon thereafter, he was put in charge of the National Youth Administration for the state of Illinois, and by 1938 he was appointed United States Attorney, the post now held by Mr. Foran. Two years later he became a federal judge, and by 1959 he was made chief judge.

Nothing in his career suggests that he was unusually qualified for these high positions. He was an ordinary student of the law. His career as a public servant was distinguished by nothing more than a diligent regularity. On the bench he was remarkable neither for wisdom nor learning. He was, however, a loyal Democrat and an energetic partisan of the Catholic Church, whose hierarchy dominated Chicago's Democratic political machine in the years before World War II. Above all, according to his contemporaries, Campbell was a grateful citizen of Chicago.

He was born in moderate circumstances on the city's West Side—which has since become a black ghetto—but now lives more elegantly on Lake Shore Drive. These domestic comforts he owes partly to his wife's successful real estate investments. But her investments may also have embarrassed the judge when a local newspaper revealed that one of Mrs. Campbell's main collaborators in her profitable speculations had been the proprietor of gambling casinos in Las Vegas, a man who had been introduced to the judge and his wife by a Chicago promoter in whose favor Judge Campbell had once decided a bankruptcy proceeding. When Campbell was asked about these dealings he said that "Neither my wife nor I were ever owners of any of the buildings in which [the gentleman from Las Vegas] had any interest." This was, at least, technically true since, as the newspaper then pointed out, Judge Campbell's wife had owned only a five percent interest in two buildings in which the casino operator owned a similar share.

There is nothing, of course, illegal or necessarily irregular in any of this. As Campbell himself explained, such investments are particularly appropriate for a federal judge, since litigation concerning local real estate speculations is unlikely to come before the federal court. The judge neglected to mention that other litigation that might concern Mrs. Campbell's fellow speculators could, indeed, come before the federal court. What is clear, however, is that in the tight little citadel that encloses those Chicagoans who understand the city's rules and customs and who are loyal to them, Judge Campbell occupies a particularly snug corner. It is not inconceivable that the judge, in such hermetic circumstances, with his fortune made and the year of his retirement in sight, might even have wandered so far in imagination as to contemplate still further judicial or political advancement by virtue of the esteem in which he and the mayor held each other and of the mayor's special relationship with President Johnson.

In these circumstances, Campbell may have needed no special stimulus from his friend the mayor to direct his vengeance toward the leaders of the protest that descended upon Chicago during the Democratic National Convention. Not only had these "outside agitators" contributed with such effect to the collapse of President Johnson's career, but they had shattered the illusion of civic harmony by which the leaders of the city of Chicago sustain their personal and political power. Furthermore, they had challenged the liberal political principles by which Judge Campbell must not only have supported his self-esteem but advanced his career.

It is, at any rate, arguable that his own anger had led him to keep the September grand jury in session until the following March, by which time Ramsey Clark, with his preference for limited federal authority, would be safely out of office and a new Administration—whether Humphrey's or Nixon's, it hardly mattered—would have been installed. Should Humphrey be elected, his obligation to Mayor Daley, together with his own memories of the Chicago demonstrations, would perhaps override whatever residual objections he might have had to the constitutionally dubious provisions which had so disturbed Ramsey Clark in the federal anti-riot law; while if Nixon were to be elected, there could hardly be any question how his Administration would deal with the radicals whose fate was being deliberated by Judge Campbell's grand jury.

But neither Judge Campbell nor Attorney General Mitchell would have been able to indict the eight Chicago demonstrators under federal law had not the United States Senate, eleven months earlier, passed the Civil Rights Act of 1968, a bill which President Johnson signed on April 11 of that year, partly as a memorial to Dr. Martin Luther King, who had been assassinated a week earlier. This Civil Rights Act included not only a provision for open housing that made it a federal crime, under certain conditions, for the owner of a house to refuse to sell his property to a qualified buyer of whatever race; it also included the federal anti-riot law, which made it a crime to cross state lines with the intention of inciting a riot. Without this anti-riot law Judge Campbell would have had to leave the punishment of the Chicago demonstrators entirely to the state courts of Illinois, which had, in fact, already begun to consider a number of indictments against the demonstrators under various local laws.

The federal anti-riot law had boiled up from the South in response to the growing militancy of the civil rights movement in the 1960's. "There is a great demand for this bill," said Representative Colmer of Mississippi, Chairman of the House Rules Committee, on July 19, 1967, a week after the Newark riots. "Seventy bills on this subject were introduced to the Judiciary Committee since this Congress convened . . . and 132 resolutions were referred to the Committee on Rules requesting that the bill be brought to a vote. This is unprecedented in my service in the House. But there is an even greater demand among the people at home for this legislation. Let me say this to those who are thinking of voting against this bill. What are they going to say when they go back home and meet with their policemen and firemen and the municipal authorities and the mayor who have been through the holocausts and who have risked their lives? I know what you ought to do with this bill and that is to pass it unanimously, to let those people up in New Jersey know that Congress is trying to do something."

But it was not to impress the people in New Jersey alone that Representative Colmer wanted to show how vigorously Congress could respond to these acts of violence. Later in the debate his fellow Southerner, Representative Thompson of Georgia, produced a list of riots that had occurred throughout the country since the previous September. This list included riots in San Francisco in which "several hundred Negroes set fires, broke store windows and threw rocks at police cars," after a white policeman had shot a Negro youth; in St. Louis, where "rioting Negroes threw rocks and smashed store windows, looted, started fires with gasoline bombs and assaulted passers-by after the arrest of a Negro woman for a traffic violation"; in Clearwater, Florida, where "400 Negroes engaged in vandalism," after a white policeman had attempted to break up a fight between two Negro men; and in Tuskegee, Alabama; Nashville, Tennessee; Louisville, Kentucky; Houston, Texas; Tampa, Florida, and several other cities where, after white policemen had attempted to make arrests, blacks had rioted. According to Representative Colmer, it was not, however, the blacks alone who were responsible for these riots.

"The great majority of Negro people," Colmer argued, "are good, law abiding citizens. But we are dealing here with an organized conspiracy, backed by the Communist Party. They are the people who have the most to gain from this kind of anarchy and unlawfulness." This view was supported by Representative Cramer of Florida, the sponsor of the anti-riot bill. He cited the authority of Mayor Daley, who had said after the rioting that followed Martin Luther King's attempts a year earlier to organize a campaign for open housing in Chicago and its suburbs, that "outsiders are responsible for fomenting the unrest that has led to violence and looting on Chicago's West Side."

It was not so much King, however, who disturbed the Congressmen; it was Stokely Carmichael who would come, according to Representative Colmer, and "leave in his wake thousands of Negroes whose blood was simmering, waiting for the instance, certain to occur in any large city, when a felon is arrested or shot. Charges of police brutality ring out and, like turning up the flame under a cauldron of simmering oil, the boiling point is quickly reached. The riot is under way. The viciousness of Carmichael's public utterances makes one shudder to think what he tells his adherents in private meetings."

The substance of these private conversations had been suggested to the House Committee on Appropriations on February 16 of the same year by J. Edgar Hoover, who had gone to Congress in his usual way to request a larger budget for the FBI. According to Representative Colmer, Hoover had "discussed the Communist influence in racial matters and had pointed out that Stokely Carmichael had been in frequent contact with Max Stanley, a field chairman of the Revolutionary Movement." The man Hoover had in mind was actually Max Stanford of the Revolutionary Action Movement, a faltering black militant group, which Hoover described to the Appropriations Committee as "a highly secret, all Negro, Marxist-Leninist, Chinese Communist oriented organization, which advocates guerilla warfare to obtain its goals. Communists and other subversives and extremists," Hoover added, "strive ceaselessly to precipitate racial trouble and to take advantage of racial discord in this country. Such elements were active in exploiting and aggravating the riots, for example, in Harlem, Watts, Cleveland and Chicago."

Though the House passed the anti-riot bill later that day by 277 votes, a number of Northern liberals, including Celler and Ryan of New York, had argued strongly against it. Celler, the chairman of the Judiciary Committee, who said that he too "loathed" Stokely Carmichael, nevertheless introduced into the record a statement by the American Civil Liberties Union which attempted to show that the bill was unconstitutional on several grounds, particularly that it threatened the First Amendment rights of speech and assembly. Even more important, according to the ACLU, the bill violated the due process clause of the Fifth Amendment, since it did not require that the intent to incite a riot and the actual commission of the overt act of incitement must occur at the same time in order for the crime to have taken place. The same objection was later raised by Representative Edwards of California. "This bill," he said, "makes it a crime to cross a state line with the intent to incite a riot. Sometime later, even months or years, if an individual after crossing a state line commits some overt act that could be construed as encouraging or promoting a riot, he will have violated the law. I don't know if the sponsors deliberately intended this separation by time of specific intent and overt act. If they did, this bill violates one of the fundamental concepts of criminal law, that intent and the crime must be contemporaneous."

It may be assumed that Representative Cramer and his Southern colleagues did, in fact, have such a "separation by time" very much in mind. Had the law been written so that an outside agitator's mischievous intentions and his overt acts of incitement were required to occur at the same time, as Representative Edwards said was demanded by due process, then he would be guilty of no more than a local crime, committed in a particular place at a particular time. For the Southern Congressmen to prove to the people of Newark, as well as to those of Mississippi and Florida, that Congress could do something about black riots, it was essential that Carmichael's intent occur on one side of a state line, while his overt act of incitement occur on the other—otherwise there could be no federal jurisdiction.

In a later brief on the anti-riot act, the ACLU returned to this question of due process. For a true crime to occur, the brief argued, the criminal intent and the criminal act must be simultaneous. This, the ACLU said, is a matter of "black-letter law." Otherwise, how could the law deal fairly with a man who intended to kill his enemy on Monday, but changed his mind on Tuesday, while on Wednesday he is attacked by this very enemy whom he then kills in self-defense? The inference of intent from the overt act, the ACLU argued, would be contrary to the presumption of innocence on which Anglo-American law rests.

To these arguments Representative Smith of California replied that it is not the business of Congress to think about such problems. "The courts are the ones charged with the responsibility of determining whether or not a certain piece of legislation is constitutional. To try to determine whether a [pending law] is or is not constitutional is not necessarily a function of this body at the present time." Nor, said Congressman Sikes of Florida, should the First Amendment interfere with the efforts of Congress to halt black riots. "Those who incite to violence should be punished," he said, "whether or not freedom of speech is impaired. Once a federal law is enacted making it possible to arrest and punish individuals who incite others to violence, those who wish to express themselves freely on controversial questions will find ways of doing it in an orderly and non-provocative fashion."

It was not only such liberals as Edwards and Celler, however, who opposed the bill. A year earlier, when similar legislation had been before the House, John Doar, chief of the Civil Rights Division of the Justice Department, had been sent by Ramsey Clark to the Judiciary Committee to argue that the pending legislation might be constitutionally invalid. Doar's objections, however, were not so absolute as those suggested by the liberal Congressmen. Doar felt that with certain modifications the anti-riot bill could be made constitutional. He advised that Congress take a more cautious approach to possible violations of the First Amendment, that the terms "riot" and "incitement to riot" be more narrowly defined, and that the link between the intention to incite and the actual acts of incitement be more sharply drawn. What Doar proposed was that "the internal structure of the bill might be simplified in such a way as to avoid constitutional problems and at the same time effectuate the purposes of the sponsors," a compromise which, according to the ACLU, could not logically be made. Yet as one of his former colleagues later explained, Doar presented his objections to the bill in the form of constructive criticism partly because it would have been impolitic for the Executive branch, given the mood of the country at the time, to have opposed it outright. With one ghetto after another in flames, the Executive branch, he said, "was not about to come out in favor of riots."

Nevertheless, Ramsey Clark, in a television interview three days before the Congressional debate in the summer of 1967, attacked the bill with considerably more vigor than Doar had done a year earlier. Clark argued that the bill would not be effective, that in view of the abundant local legislation concerning incitement to riot it was unnecessary, and that furthermore he disagreed with Mr. Hoover: "Of course there are many people traveling all the time in the general area of black power and other movements but we find very little evidence that they are directly responsible or even indirectly responsible for these riots."

Clark, however, was hardly the man to influence these Southern Congressmen, for in their view he was scarcely less dangerous than Carmichael himself. Shortly before the vote was taken that afternoon Congressman Abbitt of Virginia rose to criticize a "high government official" who had explained the day before "that riots are the inevitable consequence of decades of neglect, discrimination and privation. This is not true," Abbitt said. "Riots are more likely the consequence of statements like these, which tend to give a segment of our population the idea that the government is behind them in their lawlessness. The Attorney General has had his agents at work in the Southern states to 'prevent violence' but nowhere have I seen or heard of the agents of the Justice Department making arrests and pressing charges in Newark or Plainfield or Cairo. Some sort of double standard evidently exists where violence is concerned, depending upon who commits the act, against whom and where it is committed.

"Nothing will stop lawlessness as quick or as sure as a demonstration that violations of the law will bring swift and sure arrest," Abbitt continued. "For too long have we permitted the lawless element to run roughshod over innocent citizens simply because high government officials have looked the other way. A majority of the rioters are hoodlums, looking for trouble, seeking a living without working for it and demanding something for nothing from the government. It is time for the good people of America to say that this has gone far enough, that they will charge the people in responsible positions to see that the law is carried out, that order is restored. Our police must be assured that government is behind them and that they are not expected to stand idly by and be kicked by lawless hoodlums. Every time law enforcement officials arrest these rioters the cry raised is 'police brutality' and some bleeding heart will rush in and want to investigate the police rather than the hoodlums. We must put a stop to this."

Once the House bill was passed, it then went up to the Senate where, according to newspaper accounts, it would presumably be defeated, as similar legislation had been defeated a year earlier. Throughout the fall the anti-riot bill languished in the Senate Judiciary Committee. President Johnson, in his State of the Union message on January 17, indicated that he would not support federal anti-riot legislation. He agreed with his Attorney General that riot control was a local problem and that federal law would be redundant as well as ineffective. On the following day, however, Representative Cramer stood up in the House to attack the President. "I regret to say," Cramer said, "that the President in his State of the Union message last night performed a national disservice by suggesting that the federal government had no responsibility to provide federal criminal laws to combat riots and civil disorders that are reducing sections of America's greatest cities to ashes. I was shocked at what amounts to encouragement through federal non-action to riot leaders who have already threatened to burn down parts of America without federal penalties."

Three weeks later Johnson reversed himself. In his Crime Control Message, which he delivered to Congress on February 8, the President said, "I propose the Federal Anti-Riot Act of 1968," which would "punish any person [who] incites or organizes a riot after having traveled in interstate commerce with the intention of doing so." This would be a narrower bill, the President said, than the one proposed by Congress, but it would "give the federal government the power to act against those who might move around the country inciting or joining in the terror of riots." The President, according to *The New York Times*, had asked the Justice Department to draft the appropriate legislation. Why Johnson changed his mind remains unclear. No doubt the public interest in law and order, which Congress had recognized as an unusually lively political issue, influenced him, especially in view of the forthcoming November elections. It was also rumored that the President was reluctant to offend influential Southern legislators, whose continuing support he needed for his military program in Vietnam. For their part, the Southern leaders wanted his support against the Senate liberals, in order to give their constituents federal protection from black militants.

There remained, however, the problem of getting the

bill through the Senate, which had defeated Congressman
Cramer's similar bill the year before. The solution was to
attach it to the pending Civil Rights Act of 1968, which
was bogged down by the threat of a Southern filibuster.
Originally this act was to include only a provision that
would grant federal protection to civil rights workers, but
at first even this limited proposal found little support among
the Senators. Nevertheless, Senator Mansfield, the Democratic leader, and Senator Dirksen, the Republican leader,
agreed to work on a compromise that a majority of the
Senators could accept. They went ahead even though the
voters appeared to have lost interest in civil rights legislation and seemed, as the summer of 1968 approached, to be
concerned mainly with crime prevention. As for the civil
rights leaders themselves, they were divided on the useful-
ness of further rights legislation. Some of them had taken
the position that the important problems were economic,
and that the further extension of civil rights legislation,
though it remained important, was secondary. To the surprise of the liberal Senators, however, a compromise version
of the protection bill proposed by Senator Ervin of North
Carolina was defeated by a large majority. Many of the
Senators who voted against Ervin's bill wanted a stronger
law. This encouraged the liberals to think that a major
civil rights act could be passed in 1968, despite the nation's
apparent apathy. Thus a group of Northern Senators led
by Javits of New York and Hart of Michigan introduced
an amendment to the pending Civil Rights Act which
would make it a federal crime for certain property owners
to refuse to sell their houses to black buyers.

To pass this open-housing bill, however, would require
that the prospective filibuster be closed off, and this could
be done only by a two-thirds vote of the Senate. The first
attempt to end the filibuster failed by a margin of six votes,
but on the second attempt Senator Dirksen agreed to sup-

port the liberals, provided that the open-housing bill was substantially diluted. To this the liberals quickly agreed. The Dirksen compromise would exclude single-family houses and certain other small properties from the act, a modification which removed about 30 percent of the housing units in the country from federal jurisdiction. But even with Dirksen's support for a weakened bill, the second attempt to end the filibuster failed, this time by a margin of four votes. By the following Monday, however, a third attempt to end the filibuster succeeded by a single vote. It was rumored that in order to accomplish this, Dirksen and the other sponsors of the Civil Rights Act had arranged a further compromise, though it was unclear, at the time, just what this compromise might have been.

The next day an anti-riot bill, substantially the one the House had adopted in July, was introduced by Senator Thurmond of South Carolina and Senator Lausche of Ohio as a further amendment to the Civil Rights Act. Vice President Humphrey attempted unsuccessfully to block this amendment on procedural grounds, arguing, as President of the Senate, that it was not germane to the act under consideration. But Humphrey's efforts failed and the Thurmond-Lausche amendment was passed later that day, by a vote of 82 to 13. Javits, Hart, and the two Kennedys voted against it, but several other liberals voted for it, perhaps for fear that the open-housing provision, which they had so precariously brought to the floor, could not be passed if the Civil Rights Act did not also include an anti-riot chapter. Another factor in the large liberal vote for the anti-riot bill appears to have been that Senator Long of Louisiana had indicated that on the following day he would introduce even more drastic anti-riot legislation. Long's proposal was that rioters be subject to federal penalties whether they crossed state lines or not, a proposal that might answer the question raised by the separation in time between the intention and the overt act, but that would also call for a federal police force.

Thus there was considerably less debate over the anti-riot bill in the Senate than there had been in the House. Senator Lausche argued, "It is time to make good the promise of American democracy to all citizens. I want an anti-riot bill." Senator Holland of Florida said, "I think riots are the things that excite the whole nation into the present state of mind, that we need to pass legislation and it is anti-riot legislation they are talking about." Senator Cooper of Kentucky urged the anti-riot bill on the grounds that it was stronger than the one passed by the House.

But Javits and Hart objected. "I think I sense the feeling in the Senate," Javits said. "I will do my utmost along with [Senator Hart] to get the best [anti-riot] measure possible." What Javits meant was that he would not vote for the Thurmond-Lausche amendment. Instead, he wanted the Senate to wait for the President's proposed version of the anti-riot bill, which was due to be delivered from the Justice Department later that day.

The President's bill arrived late in the afternoon, shortly before the vote was taken; but the Senators paid little attention to it. It was accompanied by a letter from the Attorney General which said that the President's proposed bill would make it a crime "to incite or organize a riot, after having traveled in interstate commerce with the intention to do so, if the riot occurs or is [furthered] by the person's activities." Though the Attorney General said that this bill was "carefully drawn" and would not impede speech or assembly, its effect, Clark implied, would be the same as that of Cramer's bill. Clark said "this proposed legislation would reflect the federal government's commitment to do its full part to prevent and control riots."

Clark's version did, however, propose an interesting and subtle technical modification. In Cramer's bill the essence of the crime was the defendant's intention when he crossed a state line. This intention the jury would presumably infer from the defendant's overt acts of incitement. The overt acts themselves, however, do not have to be criminal, in Cramer's version. They may be as innocent as handing out a leaflet, organizing a rally, or making a speech, all of which acts are protected under the First Amendment. But in the Attorney General's version, the prosecutor would have to show that the overt act of incitement, as well as the defendant's intentions, had been criminal. Given the broad permissiveness of the First Amendment, this would require a far more rigorous proof than Cramer's bill demanded. Under the Attorney General's version, the prosecutor would have to prove not only that the defendant intended to cause a riot, but that he literally caused it: his evil intentions alone would not be enough. In practice, however, this requirement would not necessarily impede an eager prosecutor or an unfriendly judge, much less an antagonistic jury, whose members might ignore the distinction intended by Clark's modification, especially if a hostile judge and prosecutor chose not to clarify it for them. Furthermore, there still remained the problem of linking intentions held on one side of a state line to acts committed on the other side. Clark's bill, like Cramer's, ignored the case of the interstate traveler who changes his mind from one side of a state line to the other.

In his letter to the Senate, Clark said nothing to suggest that he had been wrong in his original objections to federal anti-riot legislation. Evidently he had submitted his proposed anti-riot bill not because his personal commitments had changed but because he felt the same political pressures that Javits had felt in the Senate and that his fellow Senators felt in the country itself.

Clark's proposed bill also differed from Cramer's in its definition of a riot. The House bill defined a riot as a public disturbance involving acts of violence by one or more persons in a group of three or more that threaten the safety or property of another person. This is the definition which the Senate accepted. The definition proposed by the Attorney General would have required a minimum of twenty people whose conduct must be tumultuous as well as violent, a distinction more appropriate to lexicography than to the law. Though the Attorney General said in his letter that this bill would not do much to stop riots, he did say that it would "prove helpful in deterring those who might otherwise consider crossing state lines to incite or organize a riot."

The Civil Rights Act of 1968, with its weakened open-housing law, together with the Thurmond-Lausche anti-riot provision, was passed by the Senate on March 11. Voting for the bill were the two Kennedys, Hart, Javits, Ribicoff, McGovern, and Mansfield, even though the anti-riot provision was substantially the same as the one that the liberal Congressmen had warned a year earlier would violate due process as well as the First Amendment, and even though some of its critics argued that is was conceived as a bill of attainder against such "outside agitators" as Martin Luther King, who would be murdered only three weeks later. Eugene McCarthy was absent from the Senate when the vote was taken, but he told Senator Byrd of West Virginia that had he been there he would have voted in favor. Byrd himself voted for the act, though with reservations. He thought the open-housing provision was too strong and the anti-riot provision too weak. The other Southern Senators voted as a block against the act. Though they lost, some of them at least must have been gratified that their Northern colleagues, in passing the anti-riot bill, had accomplished on their behalf what they could never have accomplished by themselves. As for the liberal supporters of open housing, none of them felt that the disadvantages of the anti-riot chapter might outweigh the presumed benefits of the open-housing law and that therefore the entire act should, perhaps, be voted down. By the time the Civil Rights Act finally came to a vote, only Senators Thurmond and Stennis continued to speak against it. Thurmond's objections were the same as those Ramsey Clark had made a year earlier when the anti-riot bill was being debated in the House. "Our system of government," Thurmond argued, "and our constitutional heritage called for the maintenance of law and order by the states. This bill attempts to bring into the Federal sphere a portion of law enforcement which should be left with the states," a principle which Thurmond applied, of course, only to the open-housing provision, not to the anti-riot law.

Once the Civil Rights Act was passed, the Senate liberals proceeded to congratulate themselves. Senator Javits said the Act "would be a landmark in American history." Senator Mansfield praised Senator Dirksen for "having played a vital role in shaping the measure. His motives," Mansfield said, "were simple and straightforward. He urged an effective bill simply because it was the right thing to do." A report in *The New York Times*, however, suggested another motive. According to the *Times*, Dirksen was afraid, after the Ervin compromise had been defeated, that his opposition to the Civil Rights Act would hurt him in his forthcoming campaign for reelection. Senator Hart said, "Today I have never been prouder to be a member of the United States Senate." Only Senator Spong of Virginia mentioned the anti-riot law. He said that he had opposed the civil rights bill because he didn't believe in open-housing, but that he thought the anti-riot law would help "our nation to deal with the serious problem of civil disorder." Thus the tributes of the Senators were concluded.

On April 11, 1968, President Johnson signed the Civil Rights Act into law. He spoke with pride of the open-housing passage, said nothing about the anti-riot bill, and eulogized Dr. King. Though Mrs. King and Ralph Abernathy, King's successor as head of the Southern Christian Leadership Conference, were invited to the ceremony, neither showed up. The President, however, may have been too busy to be troubled by this. On the same day he authorized a force of 549,500 troops for Vietnam—the highest of the war—and called up 24,500 reserves. Secretary of Defense Clifford said that hereafter the responsibility for fighting the war could gradually be turned over to the South Vietnamese.

Eleven months later, on March 20, 1969, Judge Campbell's grand jury indicted the eight Chicago demonstrators for having begun to "combine, conspire, confederate and agree together on or about April 12, 1968 . . . to travel in interstate commerce with the intent to incite, organize, promote, encourage, participate in and carry on a riot . . . and thereafter to perform overt acts for the purpose of inciting . . . a riot . . . in violation of section 2101 of Title 18, United States Code."

By the time these indictments were handed down Nixon had been in office for two months. Four days later, Representative Cramer rose once more to speak in the House. "It is with a sense of solid satisfaction," he began, "that I note the recent action of the Justice Department in securing indictments under the 1968 anti-riot act against eight individuals charged with instigating riots and violence at the Democratic National Convention last year.

"As author of the anti-riot act, I naturally had been concerned over the apparent recalcitrance of the previous Attorney General to enforce its provisions. It is my belief that had the Justice Department made known its intention to prosecute individuals traveling in or using the facilities of interstate commerce to incite riots before the August convention, at least some of the individuals under indictment today may have been discouraged from traveling in the first place and much bloodshed might have been avoided. The eight indictments are evidence that the Nixon Administration will not permit our sacred institutions to be debauched and other people's property to be reduced to ashes. I am therefore highly gratified that the present Justice Department is enforcing the anti-riot act and I commend the President and Attorney General Mitchell for implementing the first essential step toward restoring tranquility to the United States."

3

Black Radicals

By the time of the Chicago convention, Stokely Car-michael, with whom the Southern Congressmen who sup-ported the anti-riot bill had been so concerned, had lost some of his influence, especially among the more extreme black militants. His decline was partly the result of harass-ment by the FBI, whose agents followed him not only to the campuses where he gave speeches, but even home to New York when he visited his mother. This surveillance somewhat limited his freedom of movement and may have intimidated some of his potential followers. In addition, a number of factional disputes had arisen within the Student Non-Violent Coordinating Committee—called SNCC and pronounced "snick"—of which Carmichael was chairman. Furthermore, Carmichael himself seemed by this time to have lost some of his earlier confidence in the power of his movement to improve the condition of black people in America. Thus within a year he would remove himself to Africa; from there he would issue occasional criticisms of other black activists, but would himself take little part in political agitation. What he hoped to achieve, he said, was a pan-African Union, which would include Afro-Americans as well. Such a union, centered in Africa, would, he said, supply the necessary "land base" for a successful attack on American racism.

But the main factor in Carmichael's decline was a growing militancy within the civil rights movement itself—a shift of emphasis which accompanied the diminishing effectiveness of nonviolent tactics in the South and which coincided with and to some extent perhaps helped to stimulate a political intensification among white radicals as well. Among blacks, the most explicit embodiment of this new emphasis was the Black Panther party, which had been founded two years earlier in Oakland, California, by Huey P. Newton, a former law student, and Bobby Seale, an Air Force veteran who had recently quit the Revolutionary Action Movement, the organization which according to J. Edgar Hoover had been supplying Carmichael's Marxist-Leninist, Chinese Communist ideology.

Of the two founders of the party, Newton became the leader, an arrangement which Seale happily accepted, since he recognized that Newton's gifts as a radical organizer were superior to his own. The ideology of the Black Panther party was largely Newton's creation, and it differed significantly from the positions taken by Carmichael and his followers.

Carmichael's program, which had evolved from the frustrations of the civil rights movement in the South in the early sixties, was based on the idea of Black Power, an essentially separatist principle, by which blacks were to take over and run their own communities and institutions. Black people, he wrote, "must redefine themselves and only *they* can do that. [They] must assert their own definitions, reclaim their history and culture and create their own sense of community." From within their separate enclaves they would then fight for a greater share of social and economic power. They would also reform or, as one of Carmichael's followers said, "modernize" the institutions which they took over, but they would leave the essential forms of American enterprise fundamentally intact. What Carmichael wanted was an end to the racist exclusion of blacks from the potential benefits of American life. This meant that blacks should be free to establish and control institutions of their own, particularly those, like the police and schools, that directly concern their own communities. "American racism," Carmichael said, "only mouths its preference for a free competitive society, while at the same time forcefully and even viciously denying to black people the opportunity to compete."

To achieve their goals, Carmichael felt, blacks would first have to overcome in their own minds the feelings of inferiority that they had inherited from having lived so long amid their white oppressors. Thus Carmichael's program depended not only upon militant and often violent rhetoric, which was meant to help his followers combat their feelings of weakness, but upon the idea that black culture is superior, aesthetically as well as morally, to the racist culture of the whites—an assertion that the Southern Congressmen who debated the anti-riot bill felt was an attempt by Carmichael to inspire his followers with anti-white feelings: to leave them, as Representative Colmer had said, "with their blood simmering."

Though the Panthers did not reject the idea of Black Power nor, at first, oppose Carmichael himself, whom they named Honorary Prime Minister of the Black Panther party, Newton's program was considerably more radical than Carmichael's. It responded not mainly to conditions in the rural South, but to those in the Northern ghettos, and it recognized that a further extension of civil rights legislation would make little difference in the lives of urban blacks, who could vote but who could not make a living. Thus Newton's program addressed itself as much to the question of class as to race, and it did not hesitate to make the inevitable Marxist call for class struggle. A writer whom Newton greatly admired was the revolutionary Marxist Frantz Fanon, the black theorist of the Algerian revolution who had influenced Carmichael, too. Like Carmichael, Newton also read Mao Tse-tung and Malcolm X. But the idea that he developed from these writers was different from Carmichael's. Carmichael argued that American blacks were an oppressed colonial minority, held captive within "the mother country." To free themselves they must create a culture and economy of their own. But Newton felt that black revolutionaries should not let their blackness separate them from potential white allies, and thus become, as the Panthers said of certain Black Power advocates, "cultural nationalists." Instead, they should become a vanguard of "revolutionary nationalists," and lead the poor and oppressed of whatever race toward revolutionary socialism; hence the Panther slogan "All Power to the People," by which the Panthers meant not simply power to black people but to all oppressed people. Carmichael and his followers, so the Panthers argued, would probably be content with American society, provided that they could purge it of its racism and participate in its benefits as equals or better. Newton's view was that the present system was fundamentally rotten, that racism was merely a symptom of its deep corruption, and that there could be no peace for anyone, no matter what his personal circumstances, until American society and its institutions were not simply "modernized," but fundamentally changed along Marxist lines. "Capitalism," Newton said, "deprives us all of self determination. Only in the context of socialism can men practice the kind of self determination to provide their freedom."

Carmichael had said, "before a group can enter the open society it must first close ranks," but such assertions of Black Power, the Panthers argued, would lead at best to elitism and at worst to political isolation—most likely to a

little of the first and a lot of the second. Furthermore, Carmichael's position was racist. Thus, while Carmichael's idea
of Black Power attracted its strongest support among black
college students—among people much like Carmichael himself, who had attended a New York City high school for
gifted students and then graduated from Howard; the
Panthers looked for their support in the ghetto. As Newton's ideology evolved, he hoped that the Panthers would
one day take their program into the factories, where they
would urge black workers as well as whites to take control
of the means of production. "The revolutionary national-
ist," Newton said, "sees that there is no hope for cultural or
individual expression, or even that his people can exist as a
unique entity, as long as the bureaucratic capitalists are in
control."

Thus the Panther program recalls not only some of the
aims of the Haymarket anarchists, who were among the first
American radicals to urge that the workers, blacks included,
should destroy the American system of monopoly capitalism; but of their agrarian cousins, the radical Populists,
whose platform for the elections of 1892 included a bill of
particulars which might as easily have been written for the
Panther newspaper.

"We meet," the populist platform began, "in the midst
of a nation brought to the verge of moral, political and
material ruin. Corruption dominates the ballot box, the legislatures, the congress and touches even the ermine of the
bench. The people are demoralized . . . The Newspapers are
largely subsidized or muzzled, public opinion silenced . . .
and the land concentrates in the hands of the capitalists. The
urban workers are denied the right to organize for self protection, a hireling standing army, unrecognized by our
laws, is established to shoot them down. The fruits of the
toil of millions are boldly stolen to build up the colossal
fortunes of a few, unprecedented in the history of mankind;

and the possessors of these, in turn, despise the Republic and endanger liberty."

What the Panthers advocated as a means to cope with the current expression of these evils was a radically oriented coalition of poor whites and blacks—the more poorly paid factory workers, the unemployed, and what Seale called the street people. This constituency was not unlike the biracial coalition of tenant farmers and defeated small businessmen that Tom Watson, the leader of the Southern populists, had put together in the 1890's, and which, until it was destroyed by electoral fraud, murder, and racist agitation, briefly fluttered the chieftains of the Democratic party—the grandfathers of the Colmers and Cramers in the South. In urging Southern whites to join forces with blacks, Watson had said: "You are kept apart in order that you may separately be fleeced of your earnings. You are made to hate each other because upon that hatred is rested the keystone of the arch of financial despotism which enslaves you both. You are deceived and blinded that you may not see how this race antagonism perpetuates a monetary system which beggars both. . . . The accident of color can make no difference," Watson said, "in the interests of farmers, croppers and laborers," in their struggle against the Democratic oligarchs, the industrialists and the businessmen of the new South. Though Newton may have known nothing of this earlier attempt at a coalition of poor blacks and whites, his own revolutionary instincts led him to revive the old populist strategy. To this cause he added his version of Fanonist class struggle and sought his followers primarily among the urban "Lumpenproletariat." Though Marx had no faith that this class would advance the cause of the revolution, Newton felt differently.

The slogan of Watson's populists was "Keep the avenues of honor free. Close no entrance to the weakest, the poorest, the humblest." What the Panthers wanted for the poor was

"land, bread, housing, education, justice and peace." Like
the populists, they saw the ballot as one way to win their
program, but like the more radical populists they were also
ready to defend themselves with guns against public officials
or anyone else who might try to prevent them from organizing their communities.

Clearly, if Mr. Hoover and Representative Colmer had
been alarmed by Stokely Carmichael's secret conversations
with the mysterious "Max Stanley," then the overt Marxism
of the Panthers, and their armed presence on the streets of
Oakland—a display that Stanford's Revolutionary Action
Movement said was rash and dangerous—must have excited
them almost beyond endurance. Inevitably, Hoover turned
his attention from Carmichael to the Panthers. By the time
the Nixon Administration had been installed, Hoover called
them "the greatest threat [among black militants] to the
internal security of this country." Attorney General
Mitchell had hardly settled into his new office before he
assigned a Justice Department official named Worheide to
organize an investigation of the Panthers—or, as the
Panthers later said, to destroy them.

The Panthers had probably first attracted the serious attention of the FBI when about a dozen of them went to the
San Francisco Airport in February 1967 to meet Betty
Shabazz, the widow of Malcolm X. Their plan was to escort her into the city, where she would appear on the following day at a ceremony arranged by the various black
militant factions in the Bay Area to commemorate Malcolm's death. What distinguished the Panthers that day was
not simply that they entered the airport wearing their uni-
forms—black leather jackets, black trousers, jaunty berets,
and brightly polished shoes—but also that they were armed
with shotguns, rifles and pistols.

As Bobby Seale recalls the episode, a plain-clothes policeman walked up to the group and said, " 'What are you
doing with those guns?'

"Newton replied, 'What are you doing with your gun?'

"Then another officer asked, 'Is that gun loaded?'

"Newton answered, 'If I know it's loaded, that's good enough.'

"The officer replied, 'Well, you can't go into the airport.'

" 'We're going into the airport,' Huey answered. 'This is public property and you can't deny us our constitutional rights just because we've got guns. We're going in whether you like it or not. I'm going to exercise my constitutional rights and the Panthers here are going to exercise their constitutional rights and that's all there is to it. This is public property,' Newton added.

" 'No, it's private property,' the officer replied.

" 'Even if it is private property,' Huey said, 'if it accommodates more than 200 people at a time, then any citizen can exercise his rights on it. So get out of our way. We're going inside whether you like it or not, swine.' "

Thus the Panthers carried their guns into the airport and formed an honor guard for Malcolm's widow at the boarding gate. The next day the San Francisco newspapers carried the story of the episode, and the Panthers, of whom there were hardly thirty at the time, were suddenly famous, at least in the Bay Area.

When Betty Shabazz stepped off the plane, the Panthers escorted her past the baffled airport police and the surprised onlookers, and then drove her into the city where she was to meet Eldridge Cleaver at the offices of *Ramparts* magazine. Cleaver had been a staff writer for *Ramparts* since his release on parole a few months earlier from Soledad Prison, where he had written an admiring article about Malcolm, whom he called "the universal hero of black prisoners." For this reason, among others, Malcolm's widow wanted to meet him. As Cleaver describes this episode, the armed Panthers filed into the *Ramparts* office, waited for the interview to be over, and then proceeded to escort Betty Shabazz back to her car, which was waiting downstairs. On the way to the sidewalk a television cameraman approached the group. Newton ordered him to leave. The cameraman refused, and in the confusion that followed the police, who had been attracted to the area by the presence of the Panthers, began to assemble menacingly. One officer, a "big beefy cop," according to Cleaver, "undid the little strap holding his pistol in his holster and started shouting at Huey" to put his gun down. But Huey threatened to shoot if the officer reached for his pistol, and the terrified officer was forced to back away. Cleaver was so impressed by this episode that he thereafter became one of Newton's followers and contributed, through his writings, to the further reputation of the Black Panther party.

The Panthers financed the purchase of their weapons partly by selling copies of Mao's *Little Red Book* on the Berkeley campus, a capitalistic expedient that Newton had proposed to his small band of followers the summer before. Thereafter, the guns and the *Red Book* became part of the Panther's essential paraphernalia. From Mao's book, Newton derived the Panther slogan: "We are advocates of the abolition of war; we do not want war; but war can only be abolished through war; and in order to get rid of the gun it is necessary to pick up the gun." Thus the Panthers carried their guns not simply for self-defense but for ideological purposes as well. Their weapons were to be the symbols as well as the means of Newton's projected revolution.

Newton's reading was not limited to Mao, Fanon, and other contemporary revolutionaries. According to Seale, Newton carried his guns on the front seat of his car and his law books on the back seat. His knowledge of the law and especially of the Constitution, which he regarded as a sacred document—an Excalibur with which to disarm the police—affected Seale greatly. The epigraph to Seale's book, *Seize the Time*, an evangelical history of the Black Panther party and its legendary leader, includes the following quotation from Newton, a version of Mao's injunction to "pick up the gun," supported by Article II of the Bill of Rights: "I'm Minister of Defense of the Black Panther Party. I'm standing on my Constitutional rights. I'm not going to allow you to brutalize me. I'm going to stop you from brutalizing my people. You got your gun, pig. I got mine. If you shoot at me, I'm shooting back."

For Newton and Seale the Constitution was a document born out of revolution. Its Bill of Rights was for them, as it had been for Jefferson, created to protect the rights of free men "against every government on earth, general or particular, and what no just government should refuse or rest on inference." It was, as Newton and Seale knew, the Constitution as much as the guns themselves that had humiliated the police in front of the *Ramparts* office. Seale's respect for this document as a revolutionary instrument was inseparable from his devotion to Newton himself.

A month after the episode at *Ramparts* an Oakland legislator introduced a bill to modify the California fish and game laws concerning the use of firearms. Newton concluded that this bill was directed against the Panthers. Thus a group of his followers, led by Seale but not including Newton himself, went with their guns to the state capitol at Sacramento to demonstrate against the pending legislation which, they felt, threatened not only themselves but the sacred Constitution as well. Seale's plan was to read a statement to this effect on the floor of the capitol. As the Panthers entered the building, "One or two white people," Seale later wrote, "stopped and looked at us and had questions on their faces of 'What the hell are those damn niggers doing with those goddam rifles?' But I didn't pay a bit of attention because I knew our Constitutional rights to have guns. The Second Amendment of the Constitution says that no police or militia force can infringe upon that right. It states that specifically."

The presence of the Panthers in the state capitol resulted

in still further publicity for the party, but Seale and Cleaver were arrested for a technical violation of the firearms law, which prohibits the display of guns in public buildings. Because Cleaver had gone to Sacramento, with the permission of his parole officer, as a reporter for *Ramparts*, and had carried a camera, not a gun, he was released. Seale, however, served five months in prison. But the invasion of the state capitol by the armed Panthers made the party known to black militants throughout the country. By the fall of 1968 the Panther party was to have chapters in several Northern cities and more than 2,000 members, all of whom were required to read the *Little Red Book* and acquaint themselves with the use of firearms. By September the Panthers were to claim that the circulation of their weekly newspaper exceeded 100,000 copies, and though the party's membership remained marginal, its fame and influence had grown greatly.

As a result of this notoriety, the police became increasingly aggressive. Not only did they follow the Panthers wherever they went, but they began openly to provoke them. Nevertheless, the Panthers, under Newton's guidance, continued to embarrass the Oakland police in matters of law as well as tactics; accounts of these humiliations were printed defiantly in the Panther paper. As Cleaver was later to write, "Malcolm X prophesied the coming of the gun, and Huey Newton picked up the gun, and now there is gun against gun," a fact of which most radicals in America and many policemen had by this time been made aware by the Panther newspaper.

Early on the morning of October 28, 1967, several Oakland policemen who had been following Newton's car stopped him. A shoot-out followed, and an officer named Frey was killed. Newton and another officer were seriously wounded. Newton was arrested and placed in a prison hospital. Soon thereafter, a grand jury, having deliberated for thirty-six minutes, charged him with murder and attempted murder. The prosecutor did not, however, show the murder weapon to the jurors, a detail that suggested to the Panthers and other observers that Officer Frey may have been killed not by Newton's gun but perhaps accidentally by the gun of a fellow officer.

The shooting and subsequent indictment marked a new level in the continuing program of police harassment which, in the next three years, would result in the arrest and shooting of hundreds of Panthers, not only in Oakland and San Francsico, but in Los Angeles, Chicago, New York, and several other cities. But the indictment further stimulated the growth and enhanced the reputation of the party among radical groups, particularly white radical groups. By the new year, a vigorous campaign to "free Huey" had been organized, and throughout the country radical organizations had begun to decorate their quarters with posters showing Huey Newton, a beret cocked over his right eye, seated in a large, fan-backed wicker chair, a gun in one hand, an African spear in the other. Furthermore, the time had come for the Panthers to act on Newton's principle that where black and white radicals had a common interest they should not let the accident of color separate them.

To broaden the base of their campaign for Newton's defense, the Panthers, early in 1968, formed a tentative alliance with the Peace and Freedom party, a loose coalition of West Coast radicals, mainly white, who had run a few candidates for local and national office in 1966. Though Cleaver had met some of the leaders of the Peace and Freedom party at *Ramparts*, and had come to trust them personally, he also made it clear what the conditions of the alliance were to be. "If Peace and Freedom calls itself revolutionary, or even radical," Cleaver said, "and not a product of traditional American politics, it should realize that the revolutionary fervor comes from the most oppressed class—which is black

people. Any political party which is supposed to be revolutionary or radical and not just on vacation from the Democratic party would support the vanguard of the oppressed,
which is what the Panthers are."

The terms that Cleaver proposed to the Peace and Freedom party were that the whites would look after their
constituency and interests and the blacks after theirs. However, the two groups would cooperate where it appeared to
be in their joint interest to do so. What this meant in practice was that the Panthers would help the Peace and Freedom candidates secure black signatures for their nominating
petitions for the forthcoming elections, while the Peace and
Freedom party would lend the Panthers their sound trucks
and give them money for Newton's defense.

Carmichael, when he heard of these arrangements,
strongly opposed them. He said that whites could not be
trusted and predicted that they would betray the Panthers
as soon as it was in their interest to do so. In the alliance
that Cleaver had made, Carmichael said, the whites would
get the votes, but the blacks would do no better than get
shot. He reminded the Panthers that Tom Watson, the
Georgia populist who had once solicited black support,
later endorsed a constitutional amendment to deny the vote
to blacks when he discovered that most blacks who voted
supported the Democratic machine. "The history of the
period," Carmichael wrote, "tells us that the whites—
whether Populists, Republicans or Democrats—always had
their own interests in mind. The black was little more than
a political football, to be tossed and kicked around at the
convenience of others whose position was more secure."
This, he said, was how the Peace and Freedom party would
treat the Panthers once the elections were over. Most Black
Power advocates agreed with Carmichael and kept their
distance from the Panthers as well as from their white allies.

But Carmichael's analogy proved to be incorrect. The
Panthers, unlike the Georgia blacks of the 1890's, turned

out not to be victimized by their alliance with the white radicals, but to dominate it. In the following months it was to be the Panthers and not the Peace and Freedom party who would lend their revolutionary vocabulary and much of their ideology to white radical groups throughout the country. It was, for example, from the Panthers that white radicals not only learned to call the police "pigs" but soon came, in certain extreme cases, to abjure their own so-called "white-skin privilege." What some of these white radicals wanted was to prove the authenticity of their own revolutionary ardor, and at the same time to discover in themselves new degrees of revolutionary feeling, by exposing themselves to the same risks that the Panthers had taken when they confronted the police on the streets of Oakland.

Thus the Weathermen, when they rampaged in the streets of Chicago during the early days of the Conspiracy Trial, meant not only to do what damage they could to the city but to force the police to treat them with the same brutality that they had shown to the Panthers. What the Weathermen had in mind was a kind of revolutionary psychotherapy by which they hoped not only to inspire in themselves the right revolutionary attitudes toward violence, but also to purge themselves of any remnant of the middle-class idea that the police are the protectors of society and not its enemy. The Panthers found such tactics absurd, adventurist, and suicidal, and rejected an appeal by the Weathermen to join their Days of Rage in Chicago. Nevertheless, by this time it had begun to seem that the Panthers might have become the revolutionary vanguard for some white middle-class radicals—if not for the majority of blacks or for the white working class—that Newton had hoped for three years earlier. As for the Peace and Freedom party, it nominated Eldridge Cleaver for President and Huey Newton for Congress. After the election the party more or less dissolved.

A more lasting and significant alliance with whites resulted from the Panthers' choice of Charles Garry, a sixty-year-old, white San Francisco lawyer, to defend Newton. Garry, who had been recommended to the Panthers by Beverley Axelrod, the lawyer who had helped arrange Cleaver's parole from Soledad, was chosen by the Panthers over several black lawyers who had offered their services because, as Seale later explained, "Garry was a better lawyer. We looked at his record, the number of people he had kept off death row, the number of murder cases he had won and those in which he had actually proven people innocent. From all this and because of our concern for brother Huey, we felt it was Garry who was needed."

There was, in addition, a political factor in the Panthers' choice of Garry. The black lawyers who had offered their services saw Newton's defense, according to Seale, as an opportunity to enhance their standing in the black community, presumably, as Seale surmised, in order to strengthen their negotiating power on other matters with the white power structure. But Garry, according to Seale, had "been viciously attacked by the cops in the past when he fought for the labor unions and a lot of people in the power structure didn't like him. . . . The way Garry explains it," Seale said, is that "the institutions are being used by big money and the rich businessmen who control them and he doesn't want to be a puppet for any of that. He said that he made up his mind a long time ago about whether he was going to do his fighting in the streets or go ahead and work for the people in the courtroom. We always respect the fact that he made the decision [to become a lawyer] because we need someone like Charles R. Garry to be able to come forth and stick up for people when he sees things going wrong and to defend the underdog. That is something that we know Charles Garry has dedicated his life to. I have never seen a person like that, even in the Black Panther Party."

Newton's trial began on July 16, 1968, and lasted until September 9. The Panthers had promised that if Newton were found guilty of murder and sentenced to the gas chamber, "the sky [would be] the limit." What they were threatening, as Seale later explained, was not only violence but that the Panthers would appeal the case to the Supreme Court, an interpretation of which the majority of Seale's comrades had probably been unaware at the time, to say nothing of less intimate observers. By the time the trial ended, however, the Panthers were in a mood to celebrate. Garry had destroyed the government's first-degree murder case and left the question of who shot whom so thoroughly entangled in conflicting testimony that the jury could do no better than find Newton guilty of voluntary man-slaughter, despite the rulings of a judge who repeatedly favored the prosecution. Newton was sentenced to a maxi-mum of fourteen years, but the gas chamber had been avoided. Thus Garry became a hero to the Panthers and, in Seale's estimation, "The Lenin of the Courtroom."

Thereafter, when Black Power advocates criticized the Panthers for their alliances with white radicals, Seale would remind them of Garry's defense of Newton and would argue: "We will not fight capitalism with black capitalism; we will not fight imperialism with black imperialism. Rather, we will take our stand against these evils with a solidarity derived from a proletarian internationalism born of socialist idealism." As for Garry's influence on the Panther political program, Seale wrote that, "sometimes he can almost see us making a mistake on some specific thing or situation, but he doesn't interfere with our politics. He doesn't try to run them or anything like that. Sometimes we find out that our political relationship with some organization was slightly off key and didn't work out. Often it would be something Charles had run down and told us we were making a mistake about. It's good to have a person around who will tell you

you are making a mistake and if you don't agree with him, he's willing to let you learn and still be a beautiful friend and comrade who is dedicated to defending you and who knows you are right."

While Newton's trial was in progress, white radical leaders from all over the country had begun to gather in Chicago to plan the demonstrations that were to take place at the Democratic National Convention in August. Of the many problems facing the organizers of the convention protests, one of the most troublesome was the reluctance of blacks to participate. There were several reasons for this, of which the most vexing to the white radicals was an ideological one. The great majority of black militants wanted nothing to do with activities organized by white radicals. These blacks shared Carmichael's view that in alliances with whites, blacks typically were exploited. It was this position, for example, that led the black radicals who had attended a meeting of the National Conference for a New Politics in Chicago a year earlier to form a separate black caucus. Not only were the blacks who attended this meeting reluctant to accept decisions voted by the white majority, but the issues which blacks faced were different, they insisted, from those facing whites. There was no common ground, they argued, for the national radical coalition of blacks and whites that the white sponsors of the New Politics conference hoped to achieve. By the summer of 1968 this split, despite the efforts of the whites, had grown wider.

But there were also practical considerations which kept the blacks aloof from the plans of the Chicago demonstration leaders. The most important of these was the tension in Chicago that followed the West Side ghetto riots after the assassination of Martin Luther King in April. Houses were burned. stores were looted, and four days of bitter violence passed before the city returned to normal. Mayor Daley, who liked to think of his city as an island of calm in a sea of trouble, was enraged and frightened. At the height of his agitation he called Tom Foran into his office and asked him to telephone Ramsey Clark for federal troops. Foran called, but Clark refused. Though much property had been destroyed, there was no evidence that troops were needed to reenforce the local police, Clark said. Furthermore, he continued, should it appear that federal troops were in fact required, then Daley himself, and not Foran, should request them. What Clark later assumed was that Daley had asked Foran to make the call because the mayor might have been reluctant, for political reasons, to admit that the Chicago police were unable to protect the city. If federal troops were to be sent, Daley wanted it to appear that the initiative had come from Washington.

Presumably it was to avoid the risk that his police would seem inadequate the next time trouble occurred that Daley, on April 15, gave his famous order to Superintendent of Police Conlisk to "shoot to kill arsonists and shoot to maim looters." This order, in effect, told the Chicago police to ignore the constitutional guarantee that "no person shall be held to answer for a capital or otherwise infamous crime unless on a presentment or indictment by a grand jury." What Daley intended was to suggest to the Chicago blacks that his patience had been exhausted, and that due process was not to apply in the case of black troublemakers.

An April 27, the Chicago Peace Council, a loose federation of antiwar groups, sponsored a peace parade in the Chicago Loop. This parade was part of a nationwide demonstration against the war, sponsored by the New Mobilization Committee to End the War in Vietnam, the same group that was later to organize most of the demonstrations at the Chicago convention. The Peace Council was not granted permits by the city of Chicago for this parade, and the police relied upon this detail to show that they were prepared to carry out the mayor's order. Though none of the

6,500 peaceful marchers was shot, twenty were injured by the police and eighty arrested. Not only had the Chicago police behaved with brutality reminiscent of the Haymarket episode, but a local investigating committee concluded that they had been ordered to do so by high officials. (A similar finding had been made by a citizens' committee after the Haymarket affair.) Mayor Daley had said, "there will be no trouble in Chicago this August," and his police evidently understood the means by which he expected them to maintain order.

Thus, by the week of the convention the various black militant groups in Chicago had withdrawn from sight. The leaders of the Blackstone P Rangers, the most formidable of these groups, had left the city for the weekend and warned their followers to stay away from the convention. The antiwar protests were no concern of blacks, they said, a conclusion with which the organizers of the Chicago protests bitterly disagreed. The war in Vietnam and racism at home were inseparable expressions of the same moral corruption, the white radicals told the few black leaders who still listened to them, but to no avail.

Only the Panthers agreed to support the Chicago demonstrations, a fact which pleased the demonstration leaders, but which had also come to the attention of the Intelligence Division of the Chicago Police. In a memorandum of August 21, Thomas J. Lyons, director of the Intelligence Division, told his superior, Deputy Superintendent John Mulchrone: "The Black Panther Party of California allegedly has plans for the Democratic National Convention. These plans include: the creation of incidents in Negro areas and involvement of white policemen to initiate complaints of police brutality; to create diversionary tactics to draw law enforcement officials away from the Amphitheatre; to employ the use of incendiary devices; and to employ prostitutes to solicit delegates to the Democratic National Convention.

None of these plans may ever materialize; however, the possibility does exist. This conclusion is based on one fact," Director Lyons wrote. "Thomas Hayden, Special Project Director for the New Mobilization Committee to End the War in Viet Nam, (and a Communist, according to the Chicago police files) is also the campaign manager for Eldridge Cleaver, leader of the Black Panther Party, who is running as a candidate for President of the United States under the banner of the Peace and Freedom Party of California. In the event that the Chicago area gangs are persuaded to join the Black Panthers, a serious situation could develop during the Democratic National Convention."

Director Lyons' warning of such elaborately planned turmoil may have been based partly on the advice of Earl Good, a writer for the financial weekly, *Barron's*. Early in August, Good had visited David Stahl, Chicago's deputy mayor, and told him, among other things, that the National Mobilization Committee was going "to send men into the Negro areas to breed disorder," a warning that Stahl passed on to his superiors, who in turn presumably gave it to the police. But much of Director Lyons' theory probably came from the FBI, which had come to be fascinated by the activities of the Panthers, and which had notified Chicago officials in July that Panther offices in Oakland, Cleveland, Atlanta, and New York had been advised to send their members to the convention. In the preceding April, an FBI agent named Ryan had visited the Chicago police and presented similar warnings of Panther violence.

What in fact had happened was that Hayden, on behalf of the New Mobilization Committee—or Mobe, as it is called—had invited Cleaver and his wife Kathleen to speak in Chicago on Tuesday, August 27. Cleaver accepted, but his parole officer refused him permission to leave the state. Thus Bobby Seale, the National Chairman of the Black Panther party, offered to go in his place.

On the morning of August 27, Seale was followed into the San Francisco International Airport by Deputy Sheriff Bill H. Ray of San Mateo County. Mr. Ray watched while Seale, accompanied by "two Negro males," bought his ticket with money that one of his companions kept in a paper bag. Under Ray's scrutiny Seale boarded the plane and that afternoon arrived in Chicago. Whether he intended, as his plane crossed from one state into another, to incite a riot that night can be known only to himself. Tom Foran, however, was apprehensive. Presumably on the basis of the same information that Director Lyons had passed on to Deputy Superintendent Mulchrone, he had gone before the August federal grand jury to present evidence concerning a Panther plot not only to disrupt the convention, but to assassinate the candidates.

4

The Conspiracy

TUESDAY, AUGUST 27, was an uncommonly sparkling day for Chicago in late summer. A lively breeze blew in from Lake Michigan. The temperature was in the fifties. A stranger to the city would have seen little to suggest that in Lincoln Park the night before the police had clubbed and gassed some 3,000 angry demonstrators, gathered there not only to protest the Democratic National Convention and the Vietnam war, but also to defy Mayor Daley and the other Chicago officials who had refused to grant them permits to hold their rallies and marches.

That morning in Lincoln Park knots of four or five demonstrators sat or slept on the grass. A broken bench, a line of parked cars with flattened tires were the only visible remnants of the turmoil the night before. Some of the demonstrators beat softly on small drums. Police drove their three-wheeled motorcycles slowly past them, stiffly apprehensive, affecting indifference. Rumors of further violence flew everywhere in the city.

In the crowded lobby of the Conrad Hilton down in the Loop, delegates to the convention found on the front pages of the morning papers pictures of Czech students battling Soviet tanks in Wenceslas Square. Across Michigan Avenue, facing the hotel, lines of blue-helmeted police stood in the sun. Behind them in Grant Park small groups of demonstrators slept or sat, their radios tuned to news of the fighting the night before. On the grass were scattered signs denouncing the war and the Democratic candidates. Meanwhile, the candidates themselves were preparing to address the California delegation, which was theoretically uncommitted since the murder of Robert Kennedy. Everyone, however, knew that Hubert Humphrey, the choice of Mayor Daley and President Johnson, would win the nomination.

Seale arrived in Lincoln Park at about seven that evening. Throughout the afternoon demonstrators had been gathering there, some of them to hear Seale, but most of them to show by their presence that the police clubs and tear gas the night before, far from having established the rule of law, had merely made them more resolute than ever. Some of the long-haired young demonstrators carried broken tiles to be used later that night as weapons, should the police attack again; but in the early evening these tiles were used instead as improvised castanets, which made a brave and puzzling music.

In the crowd as Seale arrived stood a tall, unshaven man in his late twenties, wearing the costume of a biker or motorcycle gang member—helmet, black-leather vest that left his arms bare, black trousers and boots. Though he called himself Bob Lavin, his real name was Robert Pierson. He was an undercover Chicago policeman. His job was to pose as bodyguard for Jerry Rubin, a demonstration leader who was later to become one of the Conspiracy defendants, and who that night was to join Seale on the platform with a speech of his own.

When he appeared as a witness, Pierson reconstructed a version of Seale's remarks—his memory refreshed perhaps by a recording which the government had made of Seale's speech. In court—his beard shaved, his hair cut and combed back in a glossy pompadour—he testified that Seale had said, "The time for singing We Shall Overcome is past. Now is the time to act, to go buy a 357 magnum, a carbine and an automatic and kill the pigs. We've got to break up into small groups and create guerilla warfare everywhere. We can no longer be arrested in large groups or be killed in large groups. We've got to break into small groups and surround the pigs."

It was upon Officer Pierson's testimony, together with the testimony of the San Mateo County deputy sheriff who had seen Seale buy an airplane ticket on the morning of the twenty-seventh in the San Francisco Airport, that the government based its charge that the Panther chairman had crossed state lines for the purpose of inciting a riot. As for the complex disruptions of which Director Lyons had warned Deputy Superintendent Mulchrone, the government, when it came to trial, presented no evidence either against Seale himself or against Tom Hayden, the "communist" who was supposed to have inspired the plot.

Pierson's summary of Seale's speech was superficially accurate, but misleading. By the time he had arrived in Chicago, Seale had condensed the Panther ideology, for such polemical purposes as the Lincoln Park speech, to a few formulas, more or less epigrammatic, in the manner of Mao's *Little Red Book*. Though Pierson's testimony implied that Seale's speech had been a direct call for an attack upon the police, this was not true. The speech expounded the policies and tactics of the Black Panther party, which rejects such unprovoked and desperate violence as useless and dangerous. Newton had said, "The nature of a panther is that he never attacks. But if anyone attacks him or backs him into a corner, the panther comes up to wipe that aggressor out." The speech Seale gave was one he had given many times before, often with more vehemence than he displayed that night in Lincoln Park.

He began with the idea that the corrupt American power

structure sustains itself only by force of arms. "We must understand," Seale said, "that as we go forth to try to move the scurvy, reprobative pigs, the lynching Lyndon Baines Johnsons, the fat pig Humphreys, the jive double lip talkin' Nixons, the slick talkin' McCarthys—when we go forth as human beings to remove these pigs, these hogs in the power structure, murdering and brutalizing people, not only here in the confines of racist, decadent America, but murdering and brutalizing and oppressing people all over the world—And when we go forth to deal with them, that they're gonna always send out their racist, scurvy, rotten pigs to occupy the people, to occupy the community, just the way they have this park occupied. There's a lesson the Minister of Defense, Huey P. Newton teaches: that whenever the people disagree with the political decisions that's been made upon their heads, the racist power structure sends in guns and force to see that the people accept these political decisions. But we're here as revolutionaries to let them know that we refuse to accept those political decisions that maintain the oppression of black people."

Seale's next point was that the people have the right to defend themselves against such illegitimate authority as he had just described. "If a pig comes up to you and you sit down and start talkin' about slidin' in, and rollin' in, jumpin' in, bugalooin' in, dancin' in, swimmin' in, prayin' in and singing We Shall Overcome, like a lot of these Toms want us to do—we jivin'. But if a pig comes up to us and starts swinging a billy club and you check around and you got your piece—you gotta down that pig in defense of yourself. You gonna take that club, whip him over his head, lay him out on the ground and then this pig is acting in a desired manner."

The crowd in Lincoln Park, which had grown by this time to perhaps 2,000—mostly white, long haired, the boys in jeans and tee shirts, the girls dressed much the same—

cheered this advice warmly, but Seale quieted them. He had a third point to make: It was wrong for the people to attempt to defend their rights individually. First they must organize. "Now listen here," he said, "if you gonna get down to nitty gritty, brothers and people, and you don't intend to miss no nits and no grits, you gotta have some functional organization, not only to make one individual pig or a number of pigs act in the desired manner but to make this whole racist, decadent power structure act in a desired manner." He then went on to explain the coalition between the Peace and Freedom party and the Panthers as an instance of such organization.

Political organization by itself, however, is not enough. What we need, Seale told his listeners, is direct political action. "Too many times in the past the people sit down around tables. When they sit down around these tables they get to arguing about whether or not this white racist wall that black people are chained against is real or not. They want to come talking about some molecular structure of the wall. And the molecular structure shows that the wall is really ninety percent space. So," he asked, "is the white racist wall that we're talking about real or not? You're damned right it's real. Because we're chained against this wall and when a few black people start popping a few of the spikes that hold them, that is when black rebellions [will] start tearing across this country. Make sure, if you want to coalesce, work, functionally organize, that you pick up a crowbar. Pick up a piece. Pick up a gun. And pull that spike out of the wall. Because if you pull it out and you shoot well, all I'm gonna do is pat you on the back and say, 'Keep shooting.' "

Pulling the spike out of the wall, however, he explained, requires not only picking up the gun or the crowbar, but avoiding the undisciplined rioting in which blacks succeed only in destroying their own property and losing their lives. "Now there are many kinds of guns," Seale said, "many, many kind of guns. But the strongest weapon that we have, the strongest weapon that we each individually have is all of us. United in opposition. United with revolutionary principles. What we gotta do is functionally put ourselves in organizations. Get every black man in the black community with a shotgun in his home and a 357 magnum and a 45 and an M-1 rifle. Then I want to say this. On the streets stop running in large groups. That ain't the right tactic. Large groups are wrong. We should run in groups of fours and fives—all around. Spread it everywhere. That way the man can't shoot down forty, wound a hundred and put 3,000 warriors in jail. We cannot continue using these tactics. So we want to start running in threes and fours and fives. Small groups, using proper revolutionary tactics. So we can dissemble those pigs who occupy our community like foreign troops."

What Seale had in mind, as Pierson testified, were the tactics of guerrilla warfare against a stronger enemy. But it was part of the Panther program that these tactics were not to be used offensively against the police, but only in self-defense to protect the political organization from attacks by the authorities. Political organization is the primary objective of the party; it is "the strongest weapon we have," Seale said. Later, when Seale himself testified at the Conspiracy Trial, he explained that what he had had in mind when he advised his listeners to form small groups to "dissemble the pigs," was that they should canvass in small groups to organize their neighbors to vote for community control of the police. "To dissemble the pigs," he testified, "is directly related to decentralization of police, which is a year-old program of the Black Panther party."

The government tried to convey a more sinister interpretation. In his cross-examination of Seale, Richard Schultz, the assistant prosecutor, asked, "When you said small groups using proper revolutionary tactics to dissemble the pigs, you were talking about shooting at the pigs with M-1 rifles in self-defense, were you not?" To this, Seale replied that "small groups also refers . . . to small groups of people selling papers and circulating petitions which is a functional program for the Black Panther party to get the police voted out." As for the weapons he had talked about, he told Schultz that "there's a law that states that black people or anybody else have the right to have a weapon and pick up a gun to go and defend friends against unjust attack."

Perhaps there were some in Seale's audience in Lincoln Park on Tuesday night who, like Officer Pierson and Mr. Schultz, interpreted his remarks about forming small groups to "dissemble the pigs" as a direct invitation to attack the Chicago police, of whom several hundred had by that time gathered in the park. In this case, had some of his listeners acted then and there upon this interpretation, Seale might have been responsible for having incited a riot; though the further question of his intentions as he flew across the country that morning would have remained unclear. Though Seale said nothing in his speech to incite an immediate attack upon the police, it is also true that the alternative meaning of his remarks that he supplied later from the witness stand could hardly have been inferred by listeners otherwise unfamiliar with the Panther program. On the other hand, listeners who were familiar with the program must have recognized in Seale's speech not an incitement to riot in Lincoln Park, but the Panther call for organized revolution, together with an outline of a specific revolutionary program to be implemented in the ghettos, partly by means of armed self-defense and partly through a form of guerrilla political organization.

"The thing we have to understand," he said, "is this. The pig power structure is using every tactic it can to survive.

We know that the Republican and Democratic party especially, got to have five or six or seven thousand troops
guarding their convention. It's not even a convention. It's
a giant pig pen. With some hogs in it. The city itself is
flushed with pigs everywhere. Every time you turn around,
there's the pig. So I'm saying this here: that we are tired—
sick and tired—tired of being sick and tired. Black people
are saying we're lost: we seem to be lost in a world of white
decadent racist America. I'm saying that we have a right
to defend ourselves as human beings, and if some pig comes
up to us unjustly, then we have to bring our pieces and start
barbecuing some of that pork."

Pierson, in his testimony, took this reference to pork to
mean that Seale wanted his listeners to kill the police, presumably the very officers whose blue helmets and shirts
could be seen at the fringes of the crowd. But what Seale
actually said was, "We hope that you can begin to set up a
few things organizationally to deal with the situation in
a very revolutionary manner. So Power to All the People.
Black Power. Power to the Black People. Panther Power.
Even some Peace and Freedom Power. Power and free
Huey. Thank you."

Seale left the park as soon as he had finished his speech.
He was followed to the microphone by Jerry Rubin, who
said, "We whites have been suppressed as blacks have for
the past 100 years. We're going with the blacks. We'll take
the same risks as blacks take. If they try to keep us out of
the park we'll go into the streets. They bring out the pigs
to protect the pigs they nominate."

Rubin then suggested that the crowd go to the Chicago
Transit Authority garage to show support for the black
bus drivers who had struck for equal recognition by their
union. About four hundred people, nearly all white, left
for the garage. Others marched south on Lasalle Street,
but this march soon dispersed. A third group went to Grant

Park opposite the Hilton. Among these marchers no guns or crowbars were visible, nor were there police reports of such weapons.

That evening the more loyal Democratic politicians gathered at Soldier's Field to celebrate President Johnson's birthday. They sang Happy Birthday and the Battle Hymn of the Republic, and by ten-thirty returned to their hotels. For fear of the angry crowd, Johnson himself did not come to Chicago for this ceremony. Meanwhile about four thousand demonstrators had gathered at the Coliseum, a shabby arena at the edge of the Loop, to celebrate an un-birthday party for the President. In the crowded and noisy hall they heard, among others, the folk singer Phil Ochs, the novelists Jean Genet and William Burroughs, and David Dellinger, the leader of the Mobe and one of the chief organizers of the demonstrations. Allen Ginsberg, the poet, was at the Coliseum too, but his efforts to calm the crowd the night before in Lincoln Park by humming Buddhist chants had irritated his throat, so he couldn't speak.

By eleven that night, a group of clergymen from the Lincoln Park area had gathered on the little hill in the park where the violence had been at its worst the previous night. They brought with them a large wooden cross, about nine or ten feet high, taken from one of the neighboring churches. This they erected, and then gathered in a circle around it. Their plan was to protest not only the behavior of the police but the enforcement by the city of an eleven o'clock curfew, which had been the pretext for the police attack on Monday night. The park, they said, belongs to the people, not to the politicians or the police. By the time the clergymen had settled themselves around the cross and begun their singing, several hundred protesters who had been at the Coliseum had also arrived in the park. Some of these did not approve of the nonviolent tactics proposed by the clergymen. These tactics had not worked in the

South, an angry helmeted girl said, and they wouldn't work here. Nevertheless the clergymen continued to sing, while the police, who had gathered under the brow of a small hill some two hundred yards away, were preparing to attack if the park were not cleared by eleven-thirty. By twenty past eleven, the more experienced demonstrators were handing out wet rags to the few hundred people seated around the cross. In many cases the response to these precautions was incredulous. Why would the police attack a peaceful group of priests and ministers who were doing nothing more than singing and debating the question of nonviolence?

Then suddenly the crowd began to stir. First one then another arose, and then they all began to run through the darkened park toward the street, where another line of police stood under the streetlights. Over the brow of the hill where the main body of police had been waiting, floodlights glared yellow through a great cloud of red and orange tear gas. Then it could be seen that these lights were mounted upon a truck, the same one that was dispensing the gas as it rolled slowly through the center of the gas cloud. In the glare, helmeted and masked police, some running, others crouching low, were silhouetted in a skirmish line. The cross was forgotten as everyone, including the clergymen—some clutching their guitars—fled, choking, out of the park. Enraged demonstrators ran through the neighboring streets smashing windows and streetlights. Police cars were everywhere, their beacons flashing blue; but the officers, having terrorized the crowd, were powerless to stop its rampaging.

Before long, some of these demonstrators had penetrated to the neighborhood known as the Gold Coast, a mile or so south of the park. There the police, in an effort to disperse them, fired a few canisters of tear gas. Soon the gas began to filter through the streets and into the buildings. Diners in the Pump Room, the most pretentious of Chicago's restaurants—where black waiters, dressed as Nubian slaves, carry swords of flaming meat to the tables—abandoned their dinners. Along State Street—where a year later the amazed residents were to watch the assault of the Weathermen upon their dress shops and grocery stores— the gas had begun to seep into the houses. Soon the children were awakened by the fumes. Choking, and in their bathrobes, they joined their puzzled parents along the sidewalks, where some young Democrats, who were leaving a party, had also gathered. A solicitous police sergeant explained to these spectators that the trouble had all been started by the communists; he knew because the Intelligence Division had the information in its files.

The next morning Seale made another speech, much like the first, but shorter. He spoke in Grant Park, adjacent to the Loop and opposite the Hilton. Then he returned to San Francisco, where the trial of Huey Newton was still in progress.

It was for having made these two speeches that Seale was charged, seven months later, by Judge Campbell's grand jury, under the Civil Rights Act of 1968, with having traveled to Chicago "in interstate commerce from outside the State of Illinois . . . with the intent to incite, organize, promote and encourage a riot, and thereafter, on or about August 27, 1968, at Lincoln Park he did speak to assemblages of persons for the purposes of inciting a riot; in violation of Title 18, United States Code, Section 2101." The maximum penalty, should he be found guilty, would be five years in jail and a fine of $10,000. It did not matter that no riot occurred until much later that night—or that the police appeared to have caused it. Under the anti-riot law, the intention is the essence of the crime, and the alleged acts of incitement—in this case, Seale's speeches— are sufficient evidence from which the jury may infer what the defendant's intentions had been.

But Seale was also indicted on another count. Along with

five other defendants who had been charged with having
intended to incite the riots, and two who had been charged
with teaching the use of incendiary devices, Seale was indicted for conspiring with these others to engage in crimes
for which each of them had been charged separately. Like
the others, he was subject to an additional five years in jail
and another fine of $10,000, should he be found guilty of
this conspiracy.

That a person can be charged not only with having committed a crime, but also with having conspired to commit
that same crime is, at first glance, puzzling. In such a double
indictment, the defendant becomes liable for having committed two crimes, when logically he appears to have committed only one—if in fact he committed any at all. Such
double prosecutions would seem, for example, to offend
the constitutional provision that no person shall be "subject
for the same offense to be twice put in jeopardy of life and
limb," an argument made by the defense in a motion to
dismiss the indictments. Judge Hoffman, however, did not
accept this argument and denied the motion. Conspiracy
charges would also seem to offend the principle of "black-
letter law" cited by Representative Edwards of California
—that for a true crime to take place, the criminal intent
and the criminal act must concur. But under conspiracy
law, the substantive crime need never take place at all. The
so-called illegal agreement itself becomes the crime even
if the harmful acts agreed upon are never carried out.
Thus, while it is a crime to commit murder, it is a separate
crime under conspiracy law for two or more people to
enter an agreement to commit murder. Even if it cannot
be proven that the defendants carried out their plans, they
can still be found guilty of conspiracy and sentenced as
heavily as if they had actually been shown to have killed
someone.

A still more curious aspect of conspiracy law is that a plan to commit a harmful act when it is devised by an individual is not illegal, but such a plan becomes illegal when two or more people are involved. Though this peculiarity of the law cannot be explained logically, it can be understood historically.

The origins of conspiracy law are to be found in the British Ordinance of Conspirators of 1305, which made it a crime for two or more people "to confederate or bind themselves by oath, covenant or other alliance" to bring false witness against innocent people. Under this ordinance the conspiracy was not held to be a crime until the falsely accused person had been acquitted, thus showing that the accusation had been false. By the seventeenth century, however, the doctrine of conspiracy was no longer primarily concerned with defending the innocent from unfair indictments, but with protecting the king from plots against his rule. The Poulterer's Case, decided by Star Chamber in 1611, held that an agreement to commit a crime was itself illegal, whether or not the crime was actually committed. It was no defense against the charge of conspiracy that the illegal agreement had no practical outcome. The plot itself was presumed to endanger the king's peace and was therefore a crime. A further development of this doctrine held that a conspiratorial agreement could be illegal even if its objectives were not. By the nineteenth century the theory of conspiracy in American law came to include "concerted actions to accomplish some criminal purpose or to accomplish some purpose, not in itself criminal, by criminal means."

These provisions of conspiracy law quickly became attractive to zealous prosecutors, for it was unnecessary in conspiracy trials for the government to prove that the defendants had actually done anything harmful. Conspirators could be convicted simply for having made an agreement, even if what they had agreed upon never came to pass or could not be proven in court to have been done by the defendants themselves. What prosecutors wanted, and what Star Chamber supplied, was the power to protect governments against combinations of any kind which threatened their authority. The assumption of the courts was that collective action presents a greater threat to authority than acts performed by individuals.

In modern times conspiracy law came to be applied widely in England and America against trade unions and other workingmen's associations. It evolved still further in the twentieth century under various anti-trust and price-fixing statutes that made it a crime for businessmen to combine in restraint of trade.

Under the anti-trust laws the elements of conspiracy law were expanded. It became a crime for two companies to combine so as to discourage competition, for example, by setting prices in order to force a competitor out of business —an action which would be not only legal but normal if it were undertaken by an individual company. The illegality of such a combination in restraint of trade derives from the greater strength of the combination to damage its competitors and gain its harmful objective. The combination, in other words, becomes the essence of the crime, and its necessary condition. In such cases as these, the government does not have to prove that the illegal combination actually produced harmful effects. The illegal combination in itself is presumed to be sufficient to discourage competition and restrain trade.

At this point the illogical aspect of most conspiracy indictments becomes apparent, for in their haste to win convictions, prosecutors have seized upon the expansion of conspiracy theory derived from anti-trust law, and yoked it to crimes which do not depend upon an illegal combination for their completion. What these prosecutors have done, according to the late Justice Jackson, is to expand the principles of conspiracy law to "the limits of their logic." A murder or burglary can, for example, be carried out by one or more persons, whether or not an illegal agreement has been made beforehand. In such crimes the substantive act, not the prior agreement, is the essence of the crime. The criminals can, in theory, meet at the scene of the crime and conceive and carry out their illegal acts then and there; or each of them can have a separate relation to the crime. This would be the case if the leaders of opposing political factions each spoke at a public meeting that then erupted in violence. In such circumstances all the speakers might then be charged with inciting to riot; but an assumption of conspiracy would clearly not follow from the evidence of their similar behavior at the rally, nor would a prior illegal agreement among them have been necessary in order for the riot to occur. The riot might have broken out if only one of them had spoken, or it might have happened spontaneously. Such a case is hardly parallel to a conspiracy in restraint of trade, whose harmful effects are the direct and necessary result of a prior illegal agreement, and could not have occurred otherwise.

Nevertheless, prosecutors tend to bring indictments for conspiracy in cases where two or more defendants are involved, on the theory that if evidence is lacking to prove the substantive crime, the government can rely upon the law of conspiracy to show the jury that whether or not the defendants actually committed the crime in question, at least they planned to do so. Thus conspiracy indictments are commonly brought in political trials in which the crimes charged are often vague, and usually less threatening to the authority of government than the existence of the alleged conspiracy that is said to have planned them. In such cases as these, the substantive crime charged against the defendants is often a pretext for the prosecution of the hostile political group to which the defendants belong.

As Star Chamber had decided in the Poulterer's Case, it

is the plot itself, not its outcome, from which the government seeks protection. Frequently in such cases the substantive crime cannot be shown to have occurred at all. In the Haymarket Trial, for example, the prosecutor was unable to produce either the murder weapon or the name of the person who used it; thus there was no way for the government to show that the defendants had been implicated in the act of murder itself. In the absence of the dynamite bomb and the identity of the person who threw it, there was technically no proof that a murder had actually been committed. The officers who died might have been carrying the dynamite in their own pockets and blown themselves up. The prosecutor, however, was able to show that some of the defendants had, at least, boasted that they were prepared to use dynamite against the propertied class, that several of them had been in the square at the time of the bombing, and that each of them was known to the others and shared more or less the same revolutionary views. A finding of guilt could be made upon such evidence of a conspiracy, Judge Gary instructed the jurors, who convicted the defendants accordingly. Thereupon the judge sentenced seven of them to death as if they had been guilty of murder itself.

The principle established in the Poulterer's Case—that the substantive evil need not be proven, that an illegal agreement is sufficient for a finding of guilt—was also applied in the trial of Ethel and Julius Rosenberg, who were convicted not for having stolen atomic secrets, but for having conspired to do so. The five defendants in the Spock Case were also charged not with substantive crimes, but with a conspiracy to aid and abet draft resistance. It was the prosecutor in this case, a man named Wall, who was asked by the Justice Department to complete the draft of the conspiracy indictment against Seale and his seven co-defendants.

Under this conspiracy indictment Seale was charged with having entered a criminal agreement to cross state lines with the intention of inciting a riot, as he had been charged under his separate indictment. But he was also charged with having conspired, along with his seven co-defendants, "to teach and demonstrate the use, application and making of incendiary devices," to "commit acts to impede, obstruct and interfere with law enforcement officers and firemen," to cause "large numbers of people to march on the International Amphitheatre even if permits to do so were denied," to encourage "large numbers of people to remain in Lincoln Park even if permits to do so were denied," to encourage "large numbers of people to break windows, set off false fire alarms, set small fires, disable automobiles, create disturbances in the Loop for the purpose of disrupting the city of Chicago and causing the deployment of military forces, and to cause large numbers of persons on August 28 to occupy and forcibly hold the Conrad Hilton Hotel."

Such a list of accusations must have been greatly disconcerting to Seale, whose knowledge of the law derived mainly from the majestic simplicity of the Constitution. Not only had most of the crimes listed in the indictment never occurred, but Seale had been in Chicago for only a few hours, made two speeches, and left. As for his co-conspirators, Seale had never known or spoken to any of them before he arrived in Lincoln Park; and there he met only one of them. This was Rubin, to whom he said no more, according to his recollection of the event, than "Hi, Hello." He was not to meet the others until the day of his arraignment, the following April. Furthermore, the speeches that he had given had been legal in themselves according to the First Amendment, and so had the assembly of people before whom he had spoken.

Under an indictment for conspiracy, however, the ordinary constitutional protections do not necessarily apply. A defendant may be found guilty of conspiracy, even if the acts of which he is accused are themselves perfectly legal, provided the purpose of the conspiracy is not. For example, it is not a crime to buy gasoline, nor is it a crime for a second person to buy a match or for a third to hold an insurance policy on a house that then burns down. But if a prosecutor can convince a jury that the defendant who bought the gasoline had guilty knowledge of the intentions of the defendant who bought the match, and that they shared this knowledge with the defendant who collected the insurance on the burnt building, then the jury may find that all three were guilty of a conspiracy to burn the house down, even though the actual arsonist is never brought before the court. In the Chicago case, the government's plan was to link Seale's statements about barbecued pork and M-1 rifles to acts and statements of the other defendants, so as to prove by the combination of these acts and statements that the defendants as a group had conspired to come to Chicago for the purpose of committing the crimes listed in the conspiracy indictment.

Under the law, each member of a conspiracy is responsible for the words and actions of all the other defendants, so that testimony given against one defendant may be used against them all. In a conspiracy trial, the usual restrictions against hearsay evidence are thus suspended. If the jury finds that a conspiracy did, in fact, exist, then each defendant who is found to have been part of the conspiracy may be found guilty on the basis of testimony given against the other conspirators. In a conspiracy trial guilt is not personal, but collective—like the crime itself. Nor does it matter that Seale had not known any of his fellow defendants before his arrival in Chicago on the twenty-seventh of August. Under what is known as the doctrine of "conscious parallelism," the existence of a conspiracy may be inferred by the jury from the similarity of purpose suggested by the overt acts of the defendants, unless the defense convinces the jury of a less sinister interpretation. Under this doctrine the defendants need not have met in advance to plan their crime, nor have known each other personally, nor need their arrangements have been made in secret. A conspiracy may be entirely public and it may include large numbers of people. Furthermore the government is under no obligation to indict all the members of an alleged conspiracy, but can choose as defendants whom it will from among those whose behavior seems consciously to have paralleled that of the other alleged conspirators.

When the indictments were handed down in March, it was at first unclear to the other defendants why Seale, of all the radicals who had been involved in the Chicago demonstrations, was included. Not only had he had nothing to do with planning the protests, but it was clear from the Panther newspaper that the party had no interest in national politics in the summer of 1968. Cleaver's candidacy was meant to publicize the party, not to affect the November elections. The Panthers' argument was not with the Democrats, or even with the war in Vietnam. It was with the American system as such. Much as the Haymarket radicals had at first held themselves aloof from the Eight Hour Day movement, on the ground that it was merely reformist, while what was needed was "to change the whole damned system," the Panthers were indifferent to the various efforts to reform the Democratic party. Furthermore, the Panthers were opposed to large public demonstrations, despite the contrary assumption of the Intelligence report issued by the Chicago Police Department. Not only were such actions futile, according to the Panthers, they were unnecessarily dangerous, especially to blacks. In the summer of 1968 the Panthers were mainly interested in Huey Newton's trial and the free-breakfast programs for ghetto children that the party had begun to organize. The Panthers wanted Huey out of jail, or at least out of the gas chamber, and they also wanted to get on with the organization of their revolutionary party based in the ghetto.

Of the other seven defendants charged with conspiracy by Judge Campbell's grand jury, five had been centrally involved with planning the convention demonstrations. Thus they might more logically than Seale be found to have conspired together with the intention of inciting a riot, provided the government could prove that their joint intention in coming to Chicago was not merely to organize demonstrations against the war and the politicians responsible for continuing it, but to disrupt the convention by violent means. One of the five was Dave Dellinger, Chairman of the National Mobilization Committee to End the War in Viet Nam, a loose coalition of a hundred or more antiwar groups. This coalition had been brought together originally by Dellinger and the late A. J. Muste to organize the antiwar demonstrations in New York and San Francisco in April 1967; it had then served to coordinate the protests at the Pentagon on October 21 of the same year. Working with Dellinger as Mobe project directors for the Chicago demonstrations were Tom Hayden and Rennie Davis, founders of the radical students' organization Students for a Democratic Society, known as SDS. The two other alleged conspirators who had been involved in planning the convention protests were Jerry Rubin and Abbie Hoffman, leaders of the so-called Youth International Party, or Yippies. Though the rather bureaucratic style of the Mobe leaders was sharply different from the Dionysian style of the Yippies, the groups worked together in the months preceding the convention to bring their supporters to Chicago and to secure permits for the various demonstrations that they were planning to hold. It was assumed, however, that at the convention itself the followers of these groups, though they might share a common objective, would pursue different tactics. But the Panthers were not interested in either group, or in their common objective, at least insofar as this objective related to the convention itself.

The Justice Department, on the other hand, was interested in the Panthers—considerably more so under John Mitchell than it had been under the previous Administration. So were Tom Foran and the Chicago Police Department, who had been expecting the Panthers to invade their city at the time of the convention. By the time the indictments were handed down, Mr. Worheide's Special Panther Unit had begun to work closely with local police departments to bring charges against the Panthers. By the end of spring 1969, more than a hundred Panthers throughout the country had been put in jail. In May, when Jerris Leonard, who had replaced John Doar as head of the Civil Rights Divsion of the Justice Department, was asked by the Director of the Illinois branch of the ACLU the reason for Seale's indictment, he replied, "The Panthers are a bunch of hoodlums. We've got to get them."

On April 9 the eight alleged conspirators arrived in Chicago to be arraigned. By this time Judge Campbell had withdrawn from the case, but his spirit hovered over it in the person of his colleague Julius J. Hoffman, a punctilious little man of seventy-four, with a reputation for handing out harsh sentences and then refusing bail while the defendants appealed. According to official sources, Hoffman was chosen for the Conspiracy Trial by lot, which is the normal procedure; but according to the courthouse gossips, he was chosen by Campbell himself, especially for his notorious ferocity.

Seale, accompanied by his lawyer, Charles Garry, entered the Federal Building for the arraignment, and proceeded to the twenty-third floor, where Judge Hoffman held court. The corridor outside the courtroom was filled with spectators, many of them Chicago Panthers. Federal marshals were posted at the courtroom doors to search whoever entered. Seale agreed to be searched, and took his place at the defense table facing the bench, but Garry refused to let himself be touched by the marshals. "I am one of the lawyers here," he told them, "and you're not going to destroy my integrity in Court." The marshals then refused to admit him.

In the midst of this contretemps, Jerry Rubin approached the courtroom door, accompanied by Abbie Hoffman, who was wearing a Chicago policeman's shirt. No sooner had the marshals completed their search of Rubin, than Rubin began to search the marshals, a prank which greatly amused Seale, who observed it from his place at the defendants' table. Then Seale was distracted by Garry's presence at the other end of the room. He and the other defense lawyers had been allowed to enter through the judge's own door, without being searched—a concession by Judge Hoffman to the dignity of the defense, of which there would be few other examples once the trial itself got under way.

The federal indictment which brought the defendants together for the first time in Judge Hoffman's courtroom on April 9 transformed them, if not into a conspiracy, at least into a group with a common political strategy for the duration of the trial. Thereafter, the defendants were to call themselves the Conspiracy. Rubin would occasionally come to the trial in an orange sweatshirt with the word Conspiracy printed across his chest, a costume which the wives and women friends of some of the other defendants would also affect from time to time. However, the irreducible political and personal differences among the defendants remained sharp throughout the trial. Occasionally they produced animosities that could not be hidden from the spectators in the courtroom. Yet the common purpose shared by the defendants expressed itself, as the trial wore on, not only in an approximate, if temporary, political convergence, but in a shared hostility toward the courtroom proceedings. This attitude they then conveyed to their radical sympathizers by means of the underground press and their own speeches.

Though Judge Hoffman was to insist repeatedly during the trial that nothing more than a criminal indictment was before his Court—that this was not, as he pronounced the word, a "po-lit-i-cal" trial—the defendants refused to accept his interpretation, which they described as both stupid and dishonest. Not only did the defendants know that Seale been thrown together with them as the result of a political decision by the Justice Department to "get" the Panthers, but that the federal indictment itself was consistent, they knew, with Nixon's campaign promise to restore law and order to the country. They also knew that Judge Campbell's eagerness to try the defendants in federal court was consistent with Mayor Daley's desire, as Ramsey Clark had also interpreted it, to vindicate the city of Chicago for the convention disturbances by the majesty of a presumably disinterested federal prosecution.

That Campbell and Daley, together with the Justice Department, wanted a political trial was made especially clear to the defendants by the fact that only one of them had been indicted separately under local law in the state courts of Illinois, where the cases of hundreds of other less prominent radicals involved in the Chicago disorders were to be heard. Though the federal anti-riot law provides that there can be no federal prosecution if the state courts choose to prosecute first, the Illinois courts declined to act in the case of all but one of the radical leaders. Only Rubin was indicted under Illinois law. The charge against him, however, was not inciting to riot, which would have excluded him

from the federal indictment had the state courts chosen to
try him first, but solicitation for mob action, a similar but
technically different charge. Thus the defendants concluded that what the government wanted was a political
confrontation, much as Daley had wanted such a confrontation, they believed, when he incited his police to
violence after the riots in April 1968, and as the Southern
Congressmen had wanted when they passed the anti-riot
act in 1967. From the defendants' point of view the government had chosen to use the courts not as an instrument
of justice but as a weapon with which to destroy a political
adversary.

At the arraignment, Judge Hoffman read the indictment
to the defendants assembled before him. For Rubin the
occasion was, as he later said, "The greatest honor of my
life. I hope I am worthy of this great indictment, the Acad-
emy Award of protest. It is the fulfillment of my childhood
dreams." But this was largely bravado. Two months earlier
Rubin had complained that "from the Bay Area to New
York we [radicals] are suffering the greatest depression in
our history. People are taking bitterness in their coffee, not
sugar. . . . It is 1969 already, and 1965 seems almost like a
childhood memory. Then we were the conquerors of the
world. No one could stop us. We were going to end the
war. We were going to wipe out racism. We were going
to mobilize the poor. We were going to take over the uni-
versities . . . [but] America proved deaf and our dreams
proved innocent. Scores of our brothers have become inac-
tive and cynical . . . [we are being destroyed] by the
American Way [which] is to pick one off here, one there
and scare the others into inaction." What was required in
order to revive the radical energies which had recently
subsided was "collective identification" with a revolutionary cause that could bring the disaffected radicals together
again. Such a cause, he said, might be "an offensive against

the courts." This would be "the most immediate link that the white movement could possibly make with blacks and poor whites," who are so often victimized by the law.

When he wrote these words, Rubin did not seem to have much hope that such a "collective identification" would emerge from the sullen political atmosphere which surrounded Nixon's inauguration. Probably he underestimated the interest that the forthcoming conspiracy indictments— then being processed by the Justice Department, which Rubin assumed would include himself—would generate among his fellow radicals. By the time Judge Hoffman had completed the arraignment and set the trial date for September 24, the ground had been established for the "offensive" that Rubin hoped would arouse the radical movement from its apathy. As Seale was later to say, this ground would be "fertilized by the repression supplied by the small minority of people who control this wealthy society."

Judge Hoffman often seemed to encourage the illusion that he was part of such a ruling class. "I am solvent," he was later modestly to confide to a reporter, a reference to the considerable and visible wealth he enjoyed by reason of his marriage to the former Eleanor Greenebaum (nee Bensinger), an heiress to a Chicago fortune derived from the manufacture of pool tables and bowling alleys. In Chicago, Judge Hoffman was known not only to be rich but, according to lawyers who knew him, to identify with the government in the cases that came before him. "Julius has always regarded himself as the embodiment of everything federal," a Chicago lawyer said of him. "He sees the defense in any criminal case as the enemy and he thinks it's his duty to help put them away."

Perhaps it was for this reason that when Judge Hoffman moved his courtroom from the old white marble Federal Building on the other side of Dearborn Street to the new one designed, as he liked to remind the defendants and their

lawyers, by the late Mies van der Rohe, he took with him
a pair of green glass library lamps that had once belonged
to Kenesaw Mountain Landis, a former federal judge for
the Northern District of Illinois. These lamps he placed
at either end of his bench. Though Landis is best remem-
bered for having been the first commissioner of baseball
when the post was established in the aftermath of the Chicago Black Sox scandal of 1919, he was perhaps even better
known to Julius Hoffman as the judge who had presided
in 1918, when Hoffman was himself an aspiring young
lawyer of twenty-three, at the extraordinary trial of 113
members of the IWW.

The Wobblies had struck the Western lumber camps and
copper mines. Their employers, together with the army,
had urged the Justice Department and President Wilson to
put an end to their disruption, in the interest of winning the
war. Thus the leaders of the movement were charged with
sedition, sabotage, and subversion, among other crimes.
Judge Landis ruled that the proceeding would be conducted as in any criminal trial, and ordered that evidence
of working conditions in the Western camps and mines
could not be presented to the jury. Nevertheless, the defense called as witnesses a number of Wobbly stump speakers who energetically harangued the jury with accounts of
the misery that the workers suffered. But these efforts to
sway the jury were in vain. When at the end of the four-
month trial the judge sent the jurors out to deliberate, they
returned within the hour, having found all the defendants
guilty on all counts. Thereupon Landis sentenced thirty-
five of the defendants to five years, thirty-three to ten
years, and fifteen to twenty years. Among those sent to
prison was a Harvard sophomore who had not even belonged to the IWW. In addition to these prison terms,
Landis fined the defendants a total of $2,000,000. Thus the
IWW—which had been formed in Chicago thirteen years

earlier at a convention where the widow of Albert Parsons was one of the speakers—was, for all but ceremonial purposes, destroyed. A national magazine at the time congratulated Judge Landis and agreed "That we should show as little mercy to internal agitators caught committing these acts as the Huns who destroy women and children and who seek to annihilate democratic civilization."

After their arraignment the conspiracy defendants sustained their spirits partly by reflecting on Judge Hoffman's comical appearance. They thought that he resembled the cartoon character Mr. Magoo, or a puppet whose stiffly held head perched atop the black robes seemed to be manipulated by a giant hand from beneath the bench. But they also knew that the wizened judge who glared at them from between Judge Landis' lamps saw them, as the Chicago lawyer had said, as "the enemy," much as Judge Gary had seen the Haymarket defendants, and Landis the Wobblies, and that he would do whatever he could to put them away.

As the date of the trial approached, Abbie Hoffman wrote, "The Chicago Eight are probably the most non-conspiring conspiracy ever hatched and yet we are going down. It's all a question of intent, the judge will say, and the jury will look over at us nasty eight and come down hard, for the jury will have a difficult time drawing a line between intent to overthrow the government, intent to incite riot, intent to be black, intent to help the Vietnamese keep their land, intent to give LSD to everyone who wants and intent to live in a family of man. At times I think I'll just scream out something like 'Guilty Due to Sanity.'"

5

Preliminaries

THE GOVERNMENT's original plan had been to indict the defendants on March 11. Accordingly, Jerris Leonard arrived in Chicago during the first week of March to help put the indictments in final form. Not only was there the question of the case against Seale for Leonard to consider, but there was also a problem in connection with evidence the government had gathered against the defendants by means of illegal wiretaps. The Supreme Court had before it at that moment a case whose outcome would determine the admissability of evidence obtained by such illegal means, and the Department of Justice was much concerned with what the Court would decide. The defendants too were interested in the Court's decision. They knew that part of the case against them would depend upon transcripts made by the government of telephone calls some of them had made to Cuba and other communist countries or their embassies. These transcripts had been mentioned a year earlier in a film made by the city of Chicago to rebut charges of police brutality. The film attempted to show, among other things, that the demonstrators had been manipulated by communists and so, presumably, deserved to be beaten.

On March 10 the Supreme Court ruled, in what has since

become known as the Alderman decision, that when the government engages in illegal wiretapping it must turn all such taps over to the defendants. A defendant has the right, the Court said, to know which of his conversations the government may illegally have overheard so that he can object during his trial to evidence derived from or tainted by the illegal surveillance. On the following day the Attorney General petulantly announced that in view of the Alderman ruling he was thinking of dropping the Chicago case entirely. The Justice Department, he said, might prefer to let the radicals go free rather than be forced by the Court to reveal the extent of its electronic surveillance, especially of foreign embassies. In an interview printed on the front page of *The New York Times*, Will Wilson, Chief of the Criminal Division of the Justice Department, declared, "We don't want the Communists to know we have them tapped," a comment that struck Abbie Hoffman, among others, as odd. "Pig Nation," Hoffman wrote, "says it doesn't want to admit that it is bugging a certain foreign embassy that we call from time to time to check on the sugar crop. It's weird because it's admitting it right on the front page of the New York Times!" As for the Alderman ruling, Hoffman added, "Nobody understood what the Supreme Court decision meant, but everyone thought without the wiretap evidence we'd beat the conspiracy indictments about to come out of Chicago."

Hoffman, however, misunderstood the purpose of Mitchell's threat to drop the charges. What the Attorney General wanted, according to several newspaper accounts, was to provoke an expression of public outrage against the Court for jeopardizing the case against the Chicago radicals. Though no such response occurred, the government revealed that it would go ahead with the indictments anyway, thus defeating the defendants' brief hopes that the Justice Department had decided to leave them alone.

The Justice Department also petitioned the Court for a rehearing in the Alderman case, but on March 24 the Justices in rather sharp language rejected this petition. Thereupon the Attorney General decided to ignore the Court's ruling. In a brief signed by Tom Foran but prepared by the Justice Department, the government argued, "The question whether it is appropriate to utilize electronic surveillance to gather intelligence information . . . in order to protect the nation against . . . possible danger . . . is one that properly comes within the competence of the executive and not the judicial branch."

Under a strict interpretation of the Constitution, such invasions of privacy come within no one's competence. The Fourth Amendment provides that "The right of the people to be secure in their persons, houses, papers and effects, against unreasonable searches and seizures, shall not be violated, and no Warrants shall issue, but upon probable cause, supported by oath or affirmation, and particularly describing the place to be searched, and the persons or things to be seized." Mitchell's argument was that in the interest of national security this amendment can be ignored. A person's private conversations, if not his more tangible effects, can be searched for and seized on the basis of no more legitimate warrant than official suspicion of a threat to national security.

Like the First Amendment, the fourth has been subject to much abuse of the sort that Mitchell advocated, especially in times of political stress—abuse that reflects the amendment's political origins. From medieval times, English law had prohibited arbitrary searches of private premises. But by the sixteenth century the Crown, responding to the emerging dissension over the Reformation of the English Church, had authorized the Stationers' Company—which had become the king's official censor—to search for and seize subversive and other dissenting documents wherever it felt such literature might be found. Though this authority was withdrawn in 1760, Parliament continued to permit such random searches in the colonies, particularly for contraband goods on which the colonists had refused to pay duty. Under general warrants or "writs of assistance" British revenue officers were free to rummage wherever they liked for such goods and whatever other evidence of colonial mischief they might incidentally find. It was the colonists' defiance of these searches that became, according to John Adams, "The first act of opposition to the arbitrary claims of Great Britain." The Fourth Amendment was drafted to assure that such casual invasions of private premises by public officials would not be resumed by the new American government.

Subsequently the Supreme Court came to interpret the Fourth Amendment to mean that public officials may legally search only for articles involved in the commission of a crime, for loot, for dutiable goods on which the tax has not been paid, and for other contraband. What the government may not legally search for is evidence to determine whether a crime may have been committed. Evidence of a crime must be known to officials beforehand and presented to a judge as probable cause for the issue of a warrant. This warrant then enables the police or other officials to search for evidence that may later legally be used in a prosecution.

But the invention of the telephone introduced an unlooked-for complexity into the Court's traditional interpretation of the Fourth Amendment. As early as 1895 the police had begun to tap telephones on the assumption that the Fourth Amendment did not protect private conversations. By the 1920's this practice had become widespread, mainly in connection with the activities of bootleggers. In 1928 in the case of *Olmstead v. United States*, the Supreme Court supported such surveillance by a vote of five to four, with Holmes and Brandeis dissenting. The majority ruled that

telephone conversations were not protected by the Fourth
Amendment. A tap, the majority wrote, was neither a physical trespass nor a seizure of tangible materials. But
Brandeis' dissent was vigorous. "As a means of espionage,"
he said, "writs of assistance and general warrants are . . .
puny instruments of tyranny . . . compared with wiretapping."

By 1934 Brandeis' position had become the basis for
Section 604 of the Federal Communications Act, which prohibited the interception and divulgence of private electronic
communications. In 1937 the Supreme Court interpreted
this law to forbid wiretapping of interstate calls and to prohibit from federal trials any evidence obtained by this
means. Nevertheless, by 1941 the Justice Department, ignoring federal law and the opinion of the Court, declared that
wiretapping was permissible, provided the overheard conversations were not divulged. It ruled that transmission of
wiretap evidence from a federal officer to his superior did
not constitute divulgence under Section 604. Franklin
Roosevelt also defied the Court's ruling and recommended
wiretapping in the interest of national security during war-
time.

This disregard of the Court persisted through the end of
the war and during the McCarthy period, but by 1957 the
Supreme Court returned to the issue. In *Benanti v. United
States* it ruled that state legislation permitting wiretapping
also conflicted with Section 604, a decision that New York
District Attorney Frank Hogan, among other local prosecutors, sharply criticized. Hogan, at the time, had authorized more than a thousand taps on the telephones of
suspected Manhattan gamblers and other shady figures. This
criticism from local law enforcement officials intensified, so
that by 1962 the Department of Justice under Robert Kennedy recommended that Congress permit wiretapping under
certain circumstances. Kennedy wanted such legislation

not only to accommodate local police officials, but for reasons of his own. His prosecution of James Hoffa, the Teamsters' leader, was based largely upon wiretap evidence, and he felt that electronic surveillance would be useful in gathering evidence against other criminal defendants as well, especially the Mafia. Congress, however, resisted these appeals. Meanwhile the Supreme Court continued to struggle with ways to enforce the prohibitions of the Fourth Amendment, while law enforcement officials persisted in their electronic survelliance, despite the Court's ruling to the contrary.

Finally in 1967 the Supreme Court, in the case of *Berger v. New York* overturned the Olmstead decision. In ruling against a New York State wiretap law, the Court stated that the Fourth Amendment "protected people, not places." Justice Brennan ruled for the majority that security from "police officers breaking and entering to search for physical objects is worth very little if there is no security against the officers using secret recording devices to purloin words spoken in confidence within the four walls of home or office. Our possessions are of little value when compared to our personalities and we must bear in mind that historically a search and seizure power was used to suppress freedom of speech and freedom of the press."

What the Court objected to in the Berger Case was the indiscriminate nature of wiretap surveillance permitted by the New York law. A warrant for legal electronic search and seizure, the Court ruled, must specify, as the Fourth Amendment requires, "the place to be searched and the persons or things to be seized." But the New York statute permitted a wiretap to be installed for a period of sixty days, with an unlimited number of sixty-day extensions thereafter. Such surveillance would inevitably result in the "seizure" of conversations well beyond the narrow specifications required by the Constitution. By implication, therefore, the Berger decision opened the way for future wiretap legislation, but required that such legislation provide for the issue of warrants only upon a precise specification of the time, place, and probable duration of the conversation sought. Six months later, in *Katz v. United States*, the Court refined its position further by ruling that the government could legally secure a warrant to intercept a particular conversation made from a specific public telephone at a given time. But such surveillance, the Court ruled, must be "so narrowly circumscribed that a duly authorized magistrate . . . clearly apprised of the precise intrusion . . . could constitutionally [authorize] with appropriate safeguards the very limited search and seizure that the government [desires]."

By 1968 the combination of the Court's rulings and the continued pressure from law enforcement officials for permission to wiretap prepared the ground for a new federal wiretap law. Under Title III of the Omnibus Crime and Safe Streets Act of 1968, Congress passed a law permitting electronic surveillance by officials of the United States government and by state officials as well, provided their own legislatures passed appropriate legislation. This new law permitted far greater surveillance than the Court had prescribed in *Berger* and *Katz*. In passing Title III, Congress also ignored the advice of Ramsey Clark, who had said of wiretap laws—as he had said of federal anti-riot legislation —that such laws do more harm than good. "With the rarest exceptions," he said, "we have found that electronic surveillance was unnecessary either in obtaining direct evidence or in developing leads."

Senator McClellan of Arkansas, one of the sponsors of the omnibus crime control act, argued differently. Title III, he said, would permit the federal government to help local officials control organized crime. But to Fred Vinson, Jr., the Head of the Criminal Division of the Justice Department under Clark, this argument seemed disingenuous. "Most policemen on the beat," he said, "know who the minor drug peddlers are, know who's running the numbers and who the guys on the lower rungs are. If city officials seriously wanted to wipe out syndicated crime they would look to their own police." But Senator McClellan had a further reason for supporting Title III. It would, he said, help local officials keep track of such black militants as Stokely Carmichael and his SNCC colleague Rap Brown. Thus he proposed that inciting civil disorder should be among the crimes for which courts may issue warrants authorizing wiretaps. A similar proposal had also been urged by the Southern Association of Intelligence Agents, an organization of police officials from nine Southern states. This association was formed to fight "subversion," by which the Southern police officials meant the efforts of "outside agitators" to promote integration, and later the black power programs of such militants as Carmichael and Brown.

Title III, as it was eventually passed, authorizes state and federal courts, upon application by a prosecutor or other law enforcement official, to issue warrants for electronic surveillance for periods of thirty days, and for as many additional thirty-day periods as the court may find appropriate. These warrants may be issued upon a showing of probable cause that evidence of certain crimes may be found. The crimes listed in the act range from murder to possession of marijuana, and include all offenses for which a defendant may be sentenced to a year or more. The law also provides that if an "emergency situation exists with respect to conspiratorial activities threatening the national security interest or to conspiratorial activities characteristic of organized crime," officials may eavesdrop for up to forty-eight hours without a warrant if they conclude that grounds for such a warrant can later be established. But neither the term "national security" nor the kinds of emergencies in which officials may eavesdrop without prior judicial approval are defined in the statute. Thus Title III grants unspecified powers of search and seizure similar to those given to the Stationers' Company in the sixteenth century, and which later aroused the colonists, according to John Adams, to take their first revolutionary steps.

It was perhaps with the excesses of this legislation in mind that the Supreme Court, on March 10, 1969, ruled in the Alderman decision that illegal wiretaps must be turned over to the defendants, and that evidence tainted by such taps cannot be admitted in court. The Justices did not, however, confront the constitutionality of Title III itself, which was not at issue in the Alderman case. It was obvious, however, that the vast scope of the new law far exceeded the narrow limits set by the Court in *Berger* and *Katz*, to say nothing of the views of Justices Brandeis and Brennan. Nevertheless, the Court made it clear that any taps made by federal agents before the passage of Title III in June 1968 were in conflict with Section 604 of the Federal Communications Act and thus inadmissable as evidence under the Alderman rule.

For this reason, the conspiracy defense filed a motion based on the Alderman decision asking the government to disclose its taps of any conversations of the defendants that had been overheard before the passage of Title III. The defense also asked that the government suppress from the evidence it would present during the trial whatever information had been derived from this illegal surveillance, and that the Court hold a hearing to determine the effect of the government's taps on the grand jury, and the likely effect on the evidence that would be presented during the trial itself.

Though the government replied promptly to several other defense motions on unrelated matters, it said that in the case of the wiretap motion it would withhold its reply until June 13. It gave as its reason for this delay that it was "undertaking an investigation to determine whether any of

the defendants in this case was ever the subject of electronic
surveillance." This was a puzzling excuse in view of Will
Wilson's assertion on March 11 that the Conspiracy Trial
would reveal to the communist embassies that their phones
had been tapped and that the indictments therefore might
have to be dropped.

A more plausible reason for the government's delay suggested itself to the defense on June 12, when the Justice
Department released tapes made illegally of conversations
between various New Jersey Mafia figures. The defendants
concluded from the release of these tapes that Attorney
General Mitchell hoped to inflame the public against the
Supreme Court by showing that the Justices had made it impossible for the government to prosecute the Mafia leaders
despite the presumably incriminating evidence supplied by
their overheard conversations. "With this announcement,"
the defense lawyers wrote, "the government again attempted
to mobilize a public sentiment of hostility to the courts in
order to create a smoke screen of support for the extraordinary and otherwise unjustifiable position it was to take in
Chicago."

That the government withheld its reply to the defense
motion on wiretap evidence until the day after it had released the Mafia tapes suggests some basis for the suspicions
of the defense lawyers. But whatever Mitchell's motives
may have been, he made it clear on the thirteenth that he
was not going to drop the charges against the Chicago
radicals because of anything the Supreme Court might have
decided. Nor was he going to release *all* the illegal tapes as
the Alderman rule required.

In its reply to the defense motion, the government
argued that "any President who takes seriously his oath to
'preserve and protect' and defend the constitution will no
doubt determine that it is not unreasonable to utilize electronic surveillance to gather intelligence information con-

cerning those organizations which are committed to the use of illegal methods to bring about changes in our form of government and which may be seeking to foment violent disorders"—a curious argument since it requires the President to "preserve and protect" the Constitution by transgressing one of its inviolable amendments.

The government brief went on to say that in matters of national security the executive branch, not the courts, makes the necessary interpretation of the law, at least where electronic surveillance is concerned, an assertion that also rests upon a novel interpretation of traditional procedure. A fundamental principle of American law, announced by Chief Justice Marshall in the case of *Marbury v. Madison* in 1803, holds that in matters pertaining to the validity of legislation the Court must make the final determination according to its reading of the Constitution. Marshall's ruling made no exception for matters of national security.

The government did, however, admit that five defendants had been illegally tapped. These were Seale, Rubin, Dellinger, Hayden, and Davis. Thereupon Foran turned over to the defense lawyers transcripts of some of their intercepted conversations. Foran also agreed to suppress from the evidence he would present at the trial any information derived from these illegal taps. However, he also petitioned the Court to issue a so-called "protective order" to prohibit the defendants from revealing what these taps of their conversations contained, a puzzling request with which Judge Hoffman nevertheless complied. In addition, Foran told the defendants that he would not turn over to them certain other transcripts of their conversations. The reason he gave was that to reveal these taps could jeopardize national security.

To this the defendants objected and asked Judge Hoffman to rule whether these transcripts could legally be withheld by the government on the grounds indicated by the United

States Attorney. The Alderman decision, the defense argued, ruled that *all* illegal taps must be given to the defendants. Judge Hoffman, however, refused to face this question until after the trial. "I have determined," he said in a ruling he made on September 9, "that the most appropriate method of procedure would be to conduct a hearing after the jury trial." He would then, he said, be more familiar with the evidence and better able to know which elements of the government's case derived from the electronic surveillance. Whereupon he ordered the withheld taps to be impounded until after the trial.

This ruling disturbed the defense greatly. It ignored the principle established in the Alderman Case that the defendants and their lawyers had the right to hear all the illegal taps and thus make timely objections during the trial to evidence that had been illegally gathered. The trial judge might then rule on the validity of each such objection, but he could hardly deny the defendants the right to make objections at all, a right which the Supreme Court intended them to have.

The reason that Judge Hoffman gave for withholding the transcripts was that to release them would not be in the interest of "national security." This ominous echo of the government's language convinced the defendants that at the end of the trial the judge would rule that the withheld taps contained nothing that the defense had a right to hear, and that he himself had determined that the prosecution had introduced no inadmissible evidence derived from them— a prediction which proved to be correct.

Thus the defendants and their lawyers approached the trial with a gathering sense of doom. Judge Hoffman's decision on the wiretap motion confirmed their feeling that he would not only do whatever he could to see that they were convicted, as the Chicago lawyer had warned, but that in doing so he would considerably exceed his constitutional authority, as well as the prescribed limits imposed on trial judges by the Supreme Court. What the defendants feared was that Judge Hoffman would hold himself as much above the law as his colleague Judge Campbell had done, to say nothing of Attorney General Mitchell and the authors of the anti-riot law.

By the end of the summer the defendants were prepared to argue that the real conspiracy was not the one with which they had been charged, but a far more ominous one which involved Judge Hoffman and John Mitchell in league with Tom Foran, Richard Daley, President Nixon, and the Southern Congressmen. The objective of this conspiracy was obvious to the defendants. It was to crush radical opposition to American racism and the war in Vietnam, and at the same time to intimidate the liberals who more cautiously opposed these betrayals of American democracy. From what they had seen of Judge Hoffman's court so far, the defendants concluded that its proceedings would be no more legitimate than the repressive government of which it was part.

Their obligations as committed revolutionaries were thus clear. Though each of them would interpret and act upon these obligations in his own way, none of them doubted that the trial would challenge his revolutionary convictions and his standing as a radical leader. No matter with what gloom the defendants might privately reflect upon the indictments, the trial would provide them an occasion, they felt, to confront their intolerable government in one of its most extraordinary transgressions—the shameless and unconstitutional manipulation of its own federal courts. It was a challenge that the defendants felt the Supreme Court would ultimately have to support. But they also had in mind an appeal to a court more formidable yet—"the people" themselves. No matter what the trial jury might decide, the defendants would take their case to a jury of their true peers—the disaffected youth of the country, the legitimate heirs to the power that the defendants felt had been so cruelly abused by its present trustees. Rennie Davis, when he was asked what he wanted from the trial, replied, "To get acquitted and to get Daley."

Discouraged as the defendants were by their first impressions of Judge Hoffman's court and the ordeal that loomed before them, they felt that sooner or later they would all get what Davis wanted. Thus they began to ready their defense.

6

Uniting the Front

As September 24 approached, Hayden wrote: "We need to expand our struggle to include a total attack on the courts. The court system is just another part of this apparatus that is passed off as 'open and impartial.' This is no reason for us to become submissive at the courtroom door." Though the defendants, by the end of summer 1969, were unsure of the tactics they would pursue in their attack upon the court, their strategy was self-evident. They would hold up to the actual practices of the judge and prosecutor the moral pretensions from which the judiciary and the legal system claimed their authority. In this way they would let the world decide who was innocent and who was guilty. Thus Hayden felt that the Conspiracy defendants could not lose. Should they be acquitted, their victory would be obvious. But should they be convicted, the court would stand accused of having railroaded them under an unconstitutional law augmented by Judge Hoffman's prejudiced rulings, of which the wiretap decision was a striking instance, and would soon, Hayden felt, come to be a typical one. Comparable moral dramas involving the pretensions of educators had been played out on hundreds of college campuses in recent years, while the defendants themselves had taken part in many similar confrontations with authority on the streets of Selma, Oakland, and Chicago itself, and even in the hearing rooms of Congress. A few months earlier five of the defendants—Dellinger, Hayden, Davis, Hoffman, and Rubin—had been called before the House Un-American Activities Committee, which they then denounced as a corrupt and foolish anachronism: Hayden and Davis by turning their testimony into an attack on the committee; Hoffman and Rubin by appearing in farcical costumes. Hoffman wore an American flag, and Rubin came as a guerrilla, naked to the waist, waving a toy gun.

The defendants' response to what they regarded as illegitimate authority derived not only from their own personalities and the political commitments to which these had led, but from their reflection upon three political trials which had immediately preceded theirs. Of these, the most instructive in a negative sense was the conspiracy trial of Dr. Spock and four other opponents of the Vietnam war that had been held in Boston a year earlier. The defendants in this trial had been charged, in an indictment personally authorized by Attorney General Clark, with having conspired to aid and abet draft resistance. Though their lawyers attempted to introduce an attack on the legitimacy of the undeclared war, Dr. Spock and his fellow defendants submitted respectfully to the Court when evidence to this effect was ruled irrelevant by the judge. Furthermore, each defendant had his own lawyer whose counsel he agreed to accept no matter how such advice might obscure the political objectives for which the defendants had risked punishment in the first place. To refute the conspiracy charges, these lawyers stressed the individual political motives of their clients. One of the defendants went so far as to testify that he thought his acts of resistance might actually have helped the government in its pursuit of the war. But as Hayden later wrote of himself and his co-defendants, "we could not be as respectable or as respectful, even if we tried." Furthermore, despite their good behavior, the efforts of a prejudiced judge had led to the conviction of the defendants in the Spock trial. Thus Hayden concluded that "good manners are no guarantee of acquittal," even had he and the others been willing to affect them. "We do not intend," he said, a defense like Spock's. "Their failure was political. Their courtroom testimony went unheard."

Garry's defense of Huey Newton three months later in Oakland was also legally conventional. Nevertheless, he and the Panthers succeeded in emphasizing the political aspects of the prosecution more forcefully than the cautious lawyers in the Spock case had been willing or able to do. Not only had the Panthers undertaken a dramatic and effective national campaign to "free Huey," but Garry managed throughout the trial to convey the idea that a kind of warfare had arisen in the ghetto between the police and the people. In subtle ways he attempted to tell the jurors that the police were an instrument of "colonial oppression"; that they represented what the Panthers call "the mother country," at war with the black colony trapped within its borders. An episode within this war, Garry argued, was the decision by the police to stop Newton's car, the act that provoked the incident in which one of them was killed. Thus, while Newton was on trial for a particular crime of violence, Garry and the Panthers were able to show that there was a political dimension to the prosecution as well. For Hayden, Newton's trial was "a great inspiration." For Seale, however, it was something more. It was a practical demonstration of the kind of political defense that he, as Newton's representative, would attempt to make at his own trial.

In January 1969 seven white radicals had gone on trial in

Oakland for conspiracy to commit certain misdemeanors during Stop the Draft Week a year and a half earlier. It is a peculiarity of California law that a conspiracy to commit a misdemeanor is a felony—a more serious crime than the misdemeanor itself. But it was not for this reason that the trial of the Oakland Seven, as the defendants called themselves, aroused as much interest as it did among white radicals. What stimulated this interest was that the Oakland defense promised to become a direct challenge to the Vietnam war, to the Oakland police, and to the government which persisted in the first and was kept in power—so the defendants claimed—by the second. Not only did the defendants come to court in the same casual or eccentric costumes that they wore on the streets, but Garry, who had agreed to defend them, introduced evidence of police brutality, the legitimacy of antiwar protest, and the right of self-defense against illegal police conduct. As a result, the Oakland Seven mounted a far more explicit political defense —which a mild-tempered judge did little to impede—than had been possible in the Newton case or had been congenial to the cautious lawyers in the Spock trial. This defense was amplified by press conferences, rallies, and demonstrations arranged by the defendants and their supporters, so that to a significant degree the trial took place not only in the courtroom but in the streets and on the campuses, where the legal issues were subordinated to the political confrontation. Despite their obvious disrespect for the government and the judge, whom the defendants called Piggy Phillips and described as a "good German," the Oakland Seven were acquitted. Their acquittal, Hayden said, caused "wild enthusiasm throughout the Bay Area." It also made Garry the obvious choice of the Chicago defendants to supervise their legal defense.

Thus the elements of the Chicago defense began to emerge as September 24, the date Judge Hoffman had set for the trial, approached. Unlike the defendants in the Spock trial, the Chicago defendants would minimize their political, personal, and ideological differences, emphasize their solidarity, and openly call themselves the Conspiracy. They would do whatever they could to call attention to the political nature of their prosecution, and would present themselves as political prisoners, not as criminal defendants. Furthermore, they would appeal to the people as a whole—not simply to the twelve representatives of the people selected to hear their case. As Hayden later wrote, "If we are acquitted by a jury of the people, then the government becomes the criminal, even if we are in jail." The Chicago defendants would also retain their identity in the courtroom. They would wear the same clothes, use the same language, and act upon the same revolutionary principles for which they felt they had been indicted. "We cannot," Hayden later said, "resist illegitimate authority in the streets only to bow to it in the courtroom . . . we must risk contempt of court where the court is brazenly in contempt of our rights."

As the summer wore on, the defendants were thus prepared for a political confrontation, no matter how unwelcome the occasion. They were apprehensive of the outcome, but they recognized that the government, in bringing them together as symbolic representatives of the main tendencies in American radicalism, had suggested the outlines of their defense. Yet for all their efforts to join forces in response to this challenge, the defendants were hardly of a single mind in planning their strategy. No matter how they might try to submerge their political differences for the sake of the trial, they were unable to hide the fact that their common political ground was barely enough to accommodate them all comfortably.

"When I appear in the Chicago courtroom," Abbie Hoffman wrote that summer, "I want to be tried not because I support the National Liberation Front—which I do—but because I have long hair. Not because I support the Black Liberation Movement, but because I smoke dope. Not because I am against a capitalist system, but because I think property eats shit. Not because I believe in student power, but that the schools should be destroyed. Not because I'm against corporate liberalism, but because I think people should do whatever the fuck they want and not because I am trying to organize the working class but because I think kids should kill their parents. I'm guilty of a conspiracy all right. Guilty of creating liberated land in which we can do whatever the fuck we decide. Guilty of helping to bring the Woodstock Nation to the whole earth."

Hoffman got the idea of Woodstock Nation from the Woodstock music festival held that summer in upstate New York and attended by several hundred thousand young people. From their long hair and colorful clothes, their open sexuality, free use of drugs, and sympathetic regard for their fellows, Hoffman concluded that the Woodstock people foreshadowed a climactic break not only with conventional American decorum—which he despised—but with Puritanism itself and thus with the Protestant habit of self-restraint, deferred gratification for the sake of future gain, and the subordination of nature—including one's own nature—to the accumulation of profits. Thus Hoffman extrapolated from the Oedipus complex the political imperative that children should kill their parents: that the new generation should break abruptly—even violently—with the old, and that the family, as the fundamental social institution, should be destroyed. When Hoffman took the stand to testify in his own defense, he gave Woodstock Nation as his place of residence, and when he was asked where this was, he replied that it was a state of mind. Thus he brought Woodstock Nation with him into the courtroom itself and spoke as its emissary.

Though to a disinterested observer the Woodstock event might have seemed no more than a midsummer frolic with no specific political meaning, *The New York Times* agreed with Hoffman that it had, in fact, been a "rebellion," and felt that its victim had been the old culture of self-denial, polite appearances, and fiscal responsibility. This "rebellion" was a "feverish" one, the *Times* complained, and an "outrage." The parents of "these freakish-looking intruders," must "bear a share of the responsibility for this episode." Like the *Times'* editorial writer, the more narrowly Marxist element among the young radicals was also enraged by the Woodstock festival. For them, Woodstock had been a self-indulgent refusal of political responsibility. The revolution, they said, can evolve only from a specifically political form of organization arising from the class struggle. The "celebration of life" which Hoffman found at Woodstock was, in the opinion of these puritanical Marxists, no more than a frivolous denial of political reality, an offense to the working class, and a willful descent into the tomb of capitalist luxury.

For the Panthers, too, the Woodstock festival was a troublesome political issue, and there were doubts among the defendants whether Hoffman and Seale, once the trial began, could reconcile their different political interests sufficiently to insure the solidarity that the defendants as a group hoped to display. Though Cleaver had proposed a year earlier that Jerry Rubin, Hoffman's Yippie collaborator, run with him as Vice Presidential candidate on the Peace and Freedom ticket, Cleaver was in exile by the summer of 1969, and the remaining Panther leadership had become suspicious of Yippie hedonism. So had Hayden, who had increasingly reconciled his own views with those of the Panthers. "Bourgeois life styles," he wrote in the summer of 1969, "will disappear only when capitalism is destroyed," a view much different from Hoffman's that such "life styles" had already begun to collapse through their intrinsic defects, a collapse that would sweep capitalism away as well.

To this, Hayden objected that "The cultural revolution can only begin, but never be carried through, without successful struggle against the institutions of the society. The fact is that we have been able to change our heads so far not through the magic of drugs—though drugs haven't hurt —but through the struggles we have fought and especially the struggles the Third World people fight on our behalf. . . . The idea that you should change your head instead [of struggling to change the institutions] is linked to a syrupy pacifism . . . The power structure [according to this idea] is only in our heads and if ignored will go away." Hoffman was wrong, Hayden said, to assume that "we will hollow out the fountains until the system peacefully falls."

But Hayden also objected to the "distorted proletarianism" of the orthodox Marxist faction that had arisen within the radical movement and which called itself Progressive Labor.

"The call to proletarianize ourselves," by which the Progressive Laborites meant that student radicals should cut their hair, identify with the working class, and shun most student demonstrations as "adventurist, diversionary and alienating to the working people," was, in Hayden's view, a form of "white, middle class, self-hatred which has bedeviled the left for so long . . . We are not weightless people from a vague 'intermediate layer,' " he wrote, "only able to have power when united with the working class." We are powerful in ourselves, Hayden felt, and "we will not build alliances by denying who we are . . . it is elitist to assume that workers need students to radicalize them."

For his own part, Hayden proposed, as an alternative to the hedonism of Woodstock and the joyless Marxism of Progressive Labor, an effort to extend "the revolutionary culture and politics" that had developed in Berkeley over the past decade, a city to which Hayden had gone to live the year before. Berkeley, he wrote, occupied "in the worried calculations of the ruling class . . . the same key subversive role in the international youth rebellion that, say, Peking does in the Third World Liberation movements"— a position that other radicals, as well as disinterested observers, may have found somewhat provincial. Hayden, however, gave in support of his thesis the long list of student uprisings that had occurred in Berkeley since the early sixties, and the growing hostility there between the officials and the students. From this, Hayden concluded that Berkeley represented the model for the future American revolution, in that it combined elements of the Woodstock cultural style with such specific revolutionary actions as the unauthorized construction of People's Park by militant students on a block of unused land owned by the university, and the unsuccessful defense of this "liberated" territory by the students in a fierce battle with the Berkeley police.

The fragmentation of radical youth into several factions by the summer of 1969 was the result, among other causes, of the maturity of their movement and of its expansion; or conversely, of the anguish born of a decade of frustration, and the dilution of the movement's original purposes by a variety of tributary interests, personalities, and sects. The spirit of rebellion had by 1969 come to embrace, in one way or another, a large part of American youth. A widespread and diverse sectarianism therefore arose from the variety of responses to the growing rigidity of American political and judicial institutions under the pressure of radical youth. Though this sectarianism was not enough to obscure the common enemy—the stifling culture and rapacious politics of the United States—it was sufficient to alarm the Panthers, who had come not only to welcome alliances with white radicals, but to feel that they required them in order to survive.

By the summer of 1969, the federal government had joined the local police in what appeared to be a general plan to destroy the Panther party. Vice President Agnew called the Panthers a "completely irresponsible, anarchistic group of criminals," and Mr. Worheide of the Justice Department's special Panther unit had spent the spring and early summer traveling from city to city to assist the police in preparing indictments against them. In April, twenty-one Panthers had been indicted by District Attorney Hogan of New York for allegedly having conspired to blow up several department stores, the Botanical Gardens, and a police station, among other buildings. Though no evidence of such a plot was produced at the time, nor had the police discovered the large supplies of bombs required for such an ambitious project, Mr. Hogan appeared on television to announce that the bombings were to have taken place the day after the Panthers had been arrested. The twenty-one Panthers were therefore held on bail of $100,000 each.

On May 22, eight party members were arrested in New Haven for the murder of Alex Rackley, a New York Panther. On June 4, the Chicago police raided the Panther headquarters there and confiscated a petition signed by 15,000 people demanding the release of Fred Hampton, the Illinois party chairman, who had been sentenced to two to five years in prison for allegedly having stolen seventy-one dollars worth of ice cream bars to be distributed to ghetto children. There were other raids in Detroit, Denver, Indianapolis, and Sacramento.

To publicize their difficulties and organize support in opposition to the government's policies, the Panthers on June 19 called for a United Front Against Fascism in America. The announcement was made by Seale and Garry, together with David Hilliard, a Panther captain. The United Front would be inaugurated, the Panthers said, by a conference to be held in Oakland from July 18 to 20. Representatives from more than 1,000 organizations had been invited. Seale said that the Panthers had formed temporary alliances in the past with white radical groups, notably the Peace and Freedom party, but these, according to Seale, had been only a beginning. "This time the Front will include all progressive people, you name it. We don't give a damn what the ideology of an organization is. If they're against fascism in America, they should join the Front."

The indiscriminate breadth of Seale's invitation was uncharacteristic. Not only was it hard to imagine that the Panthers could ally themselves with the largely middle-class multitudes who would assemble later that summer at Woodstock and who would appear, from the Panthers' point of view, to have been drugged and exploited by a ruling class that valued their passivity; but Progressive Labor had denounced the Panthers as counterrevolutionary. People are oppressed, these Marxists said, not as blacks or browns but as workers. In reply, the Panthers said that Progressive Laborites were traitors to Marxist-Leninism.

Progressive Labor's response was that the United Front had been suggested to the Panthers by an analogy at once decadent and false. "In calling for this conference," the Progressive Labor newspaper said, the Panther leaders, "have relied heavily on material from Georgi Dimitrov [a Bulgarian Communist of the 1930's and a leader of the Comintern who was later killed by Stalin]. Dimitrov's strategy in the thirties is the Communist Party strategy now. He said fascism was the open terror against the people by the most ruthless section of the ruling class. Therefore Communists must decide what are the 'most progressive capitalists' and unite with them. This is the tired out Communist Party line of everyone uniting against the 'ultra right.' We thought this old chestnut had died. We were wrong; it is being offered again by the Panther leaders."

From the perspective of the forthcoming Conspiracy Trial, however, the Panthers' choice of Dimitrov as their model was of much greater interest than the ideological objections of Progressive Labor to a United Front that might include non-Marxist elements. In 1933 Dimitrov was arrested in Berlin and charged with complicity in the Reichstag fire. The evidence against him consisted only of a waiter's testimony that he had seen him dining a week earlier with van der Lubbe, the simple-minded Dutchman who was found at the scene of the fire. The reason for Dimitrov's arrest was clear. The Nazis wanted an occasion to justify their suppression of the Bolsheviks, not only so that they could destroy a political enemy, but in order to rally the German center behind their own party as the indispensible protector of the state. To Hitler, the Reichstag fire seemed a "sign from heaven" that the suppression of the Bolsheviks could now begin. It was necessary only to link the communists to van der Lubbe—who had, in fact, once been a party member. For this purpose, the testimony of the waiter was, in the opinion of the Nazis, sufficient.

On the day after the fire, Hitler, as a "defensive measure against the Communist acts of violence endangering the state," demanded that President Hindenberg suspend constitutional guarantees of civil liberties. Thus the German government imposed "restrictions on personal liberty, freedom of speech and of the press, and the rights of assembly and association." It also declared that "violations of the privacy of postal, telegraphic and telephonic communications, as well as warrants for house searches and the confiscation of property" became permissible "beyond the limits otherwise prescribed by law." Immediately thereafter, communists, pacifists, and other opponents of the and killed. To accommodate the thousands of prisoners, the first concentration camp was opened in a suburb of Berlin. Hitler expected that the Reichstag trial would encourage sufficient anti-Bolshevik feeling to justify these excesses.

To the Panthers, the analogy with their own situation was clear. Not only had their headquarters been raided, their members jailed and beaten, and in some cases killed, but they were being brought to trial in one city after another on charges which, they insisted, had no merit, and which were meant only to justify the suppression of the party by the government. Thus the Panthers followed the example of the communists in 1933 who, in response to Hitler's attack on the German Bolsheviks and his indictment of the communist leaders as conspirators in the burning of the Reichstag, organized the original United Front against Fascism. Much of the success of this front, which gained abundant sympathy for the communists throughout the world, resulted from Georgi Dimitrov's decision not to let a German lawyer defend him, but to defend himself—a defense which he undertook with great brilliance.

Though the presiding judge did what he could to keep Dimitrov quiet, he was largely unsuccessful. The press reported the Bulgarian's interrogations extensively, and thus contributed to the failure of Hitler's anticipated justification of his suppression of the Bolsheviks. The Reichstag trial became a metaphor for German duplicity. Dimitrov's repeated question to government witnesses—"had not the Reichstag fire, in fact, been the signal for the destruction of the working class parties and a means of solving difficulties within the Hitler government?"—was widely understood to imply the actual basis for the prosecution. Often throughout the trial, Dimitrov was dragged from the courtroom when he insisted on repeating questions that the presiding judge ruled were inadmissible. On one notable occasion he provoked Goering—who appeared as a witness in his hunting costume—to shout at him: "I'll tell you what the German people know. They know that you are behaving disgracefully here, that you are a Communist scoundrel who came to Germany to burn the Reichstag down. You are a criminal who belongs on the gallows." Such episodes as these, widely publicized by journalists sympathetic to Dimitrov, if not necessarily to the Bolsheviks, added to the disgrace of the Germans.

Thus Dimitrov's example at the Reichstag trial was to serve the Panthers in a double sense. Not only did the communist response to the Nazis suggest to the Panthers that they too might benefit from a united front of "all progressive people," but Seale's eventual decision to defend himself at the Chicago trial may also have been suggested by Dimitrov's similar expedient.

The leaflet announcing the United Front that was to gather in Oakland on July 18 included a long denunciation of "incipient American fascism," written by Dimitrov two years after the Reichstag trial. He asked whether, in opposing this fascism, "the American proletariat can content itself with the organization of only its class-conscious vanguard," and his answer was "no." What he called for instead was a "mass party of toilers."

Among the sponsors listed by the Panthers, under Dimitrov's statement, were Charles Garry, Tom Hayden, and William Kunstler, one of the lawyers who had been chosen to work with Garry on the Chicago defense. But the names of no "toilers" appeared on the announcement, and few such people were present among the 3,000 radicals who attended the conference itself. According to Hayden, "The United Front conference was a disaster. Few liberals came and the white radicals felt legitimately insulted by the Panthers' criticism of hippies, anarchists and other elements of the white left." Meanwhile, Progressive Labor attacked the Panthers for having accepted the support of the Communist party, which had been supplying bail money to the Panthers. According to Progressive Labor, the Communists were a bourgeois party of reformers, no longer interested in revolution.

In the same spirit, Progressive Labor and other militant white groups chided the Panthers for their program to establish community control of the police. Seale argued on behalf of this campaign: "If a policeman's brutalizing somebody in the community and has to come back home and sleep that night, we can deal with him in the community." He urged white militants to undertake similar campaigns for community control of the police in their own neighborhoods. However, some white militants found this program less than revolutionary and denounced the Panthers accordingly. Others, including the Weathermen, thought that community control in white neighborhoods would simply legalize police racism in those areas. In reply to such criticisms, Seale insisted, "When you begin to develop a United Front you do not start off with a bunch of jive ideological bullshit." But Seale underestimated the sectarianism that divided his audience, and failed to suggest a program that could unite them. Thus the conference ended in squabbling, and the hope for a United Front faded.

A month later, on the night of August 20, Seale was returning to Oakland from San Francisco, where he had attended the wedding of a fellow Panther. His car was stopped by agents of the FBI. He was arrested and charged with having fled Connecticut to avoid prosecution in connection with the murder of Alex Rackley, the crime for which eight New Haven Panthers had been arrested on May 22, and for which six other Panthers, in various cities, had been arrested subsequently. Garry denounced Seale's arrest "in the guise of a fugitive" as "a lot of bunk." Seale, he said, had been available in the Bay Area since his return from New Haven, where he had given a speech at Yale on May 19. "If they wanted him, all they had to do was to ask me to produce him," Garry said. "They didn't have to go through all this garbage." On the following day Seale was charged with murder under a New Haven warrant and held without bail. Outside the courthouse where he was arraigned, several dozen pickets carried signs saying FREE BOBBY and FIGHT FASCIST OPPRESSION. Seale himself said of his arrest that it was "a clear case of fascism raising its ugly head in America."

At this time it also became known that Garry would be unable to attend the Chicago trial that was to begin the following month. His doctor had told him that his life would be in danger if he did not have his gall bladder removed. Accordingly the defense asked Judge Hoffman on August 27—the anniversary of Seale's Lincoln Park speech —to postpone the trial until November 15, by which time Garry was expected to have recovered. Judge Hoffman, however, denied the motion. Several other defense lawyers had joined the case, he said, and the defendants would be adequately represented whether Garry attended or not.

To this the defense replied that Garry was not simply one of their lawyers but "the head of our trial team." Judge Hoffman, however, said that in his courtroom a lawyer was a lawyer, and that he did not recognize "trial teams"—a term that he uttered with evident contempt. On September 9, Garry himself appeared before Judge Hoffman to request a postponement, and once again the judge denied the motion. The trial, he said, would begin on the twenty-fourth, with or without Garry.

Though it is within the discretion of a judge to deny such postponements in the interest of holding a prompt and orderly trial, the defense considered Judge Hoffman's denial in this instance a clear confirmation of his prejudice.

While Judge Hoffman was known to be proud of his court calendar, which was more current than that of any other judge in his district, judges routinely grant postponements in the case of illness and Hoffman himself was known to have done as much on many less urgent occasions. From his brusque and unusual denial of Garry's motion, the defendants added to their intuition of the judge's hostility the fear that his prejudice had arisen from a premature suspicion of their motives. This suspicion, they felt, would lead the judge to anticipate objectionable behavior where none was intended, and to exaggerate the significance of whatever defiant acts the defendants might deliberately commit in keeping with their political objectives. These fears did not, however, cause the defendants to modify their plans for a strong defense of their political interests.

Three days later, Judge Hoffman issued a writ of habeas corpus ad prosequendum, under which Seale was to be delivered from San Francisco to Chicago to stand trial. That evening, Garry visited Seale in the San Francisco County Jail and, as Seale recalls the episode, informed him, "They are going to move you tomorrow." Garry also said that his forthcoming operation would make it impossible for him to serve as Seale's lawyer. The judge, he said, had denied a postponement and there was no way for him to appear in Chicago on the twenty-fourth. Seale then said, "Look man, when I get to Chicago I'm not letting those cats choose a lawyer for me. Someone I've never spoken to. They don't have any right to do that. I think I'll be better off defending myself if you can't make it there."

To this Garry replied, according to Seale's account, "O.K., you have a legal right to do that."

The next morning Seale was chained and placed in a car between two other federal prisoners, each leg chained to a leg of one of his companions. Handcuffs on all three were attached to chains around their waists. Two federal marshals took turns driving, and that night the prisoners were kept in a jail in Reno. The next night they spent in Salt Lake City, where, Seale recalls, "The marshal went out and bought me a 79¢ box of chicken and a 20¢ milkshake with a few french fries thrown in." In Laramie, Wyoming, the next night, the prisoners slept in a "clean and roomy jail," and on the following night they stayed in Hayes, Kansas, where they had "fried chicken, peas and everything the jailer had." But on the following night they stayed in Springfield, Missouri, in the "dirtiest, filthiest jail" Seale had ever seen. "When I say filthy, you have to imagine what I'm describing," he recalled, "and I'm not exaggerating one pound." The following night they spent in St. Louis and the next day, Thursday, August 18, they arrived in Chicago, where Seale was lodged in the federal tier of the Cook County Jail.

Throughout his journey Seale was out of touch with Garry, who had not been informed of the route the marshals would take. Thus when it was learned that Seale had arrived in Chicago, Garry sent a telegram to Kunstler, who was in New York at the time, preparing for his prolonged residence in Chicago. He asked Kunstler to do what he could to get in touch with Seale. Kunstler then called the Panther headquarters in Chicago and suggested that Fred Hampton, the Illinois party chairman, visit Seale in jail in order to establish communications between the prisoner and his lawyers. On Friday, August 19, Hampton, accompanied by William Birnbaum, a Chicago lawyer who had agreed to assist the defense, went to the county jail, but Warden Moore refused to let Hampton see Seale. When Kunstler was informed of Moore's decision, he attempted to call Birnbaum, but was unable to reach him. Therefore he called Stuart Ball, a young law school graduate, who had also agreed to assist the defense, and asked him to prepare an emergency motion on Hampton's behalf, to be submitted to the court on the following day. Though the federal court is closed on Saturday, an emergency judge is assigned to hear urgent motions. In Kunstler's opinion, the presentation of the motion he asked Ball to prepare was such an emergency.

When Ball called the district court on Saturday morning he was advised to refer his motion to Judge Austin, the emergency judge assigned for that day. However, Judge Austin was not in the Federal Building, and when Ball called the judge's home he was told that the judge was playing golf and could not be reached. Thereafter Ball called Judge Hoffman's clerk, explained his problem, and was told that Judge Hoffman would hear him at 4:30.

At 4:45, Judge Hoffman arrived in the courtroom, and Ball presented himself. He wore a pointed beard, his reddish hair extended beyond the collar of his faded work-shirt, and he had on an old pair of blue jeans. "I think the court should know in the first instance," he explained, "that I am not a lawyer licensed to practice in this jurisdiction. I graduated from law school last June. I have taken the bar examination in Washington, D.C. I am awaiting the results." He then explained that he was present on behalf of Mr. Kunstler in the matter of Fred Hampton. Judge Hoffman said, "I will hear what you have to say not as a lawyer, but as a human being."

Then Ball repeated that on the advice of Mr. Birnbaum he was in court not as a lawyer but as Mr. Kunstler's agent, a confirmation of the understanding that he and the judge had reached a moment earlier. But at this point something appears to have gone wrong, presumably with Judge Hoffman's hearing.

"I say," he exclaimed, "you have disregarded [Mr. Birnbaum's] advice . . . You are not licensed to practice as a lawyer in the United States District Court here or anywhere else. Is that right?" Thereupon Ball was obliged to repeat once more what he had already told the judge twice before concerning his lack of credentials. The judge then agreed to hear his motion. When Ball finished, the judge asked Richard Schultz, the assistant prosecutor, to reply.

"I think it is absolutely incredible," Schultz argued, "that the defense in this case has in effect asked Your Honor to come down on a Saturday." Schultz also took exception to the description in Ball's motion of Hampton as a "legal investigator . . . I would like to inquire," Schultz said, "as to a number of things, if I may, to determine just what that means. May I be permitted?"

The judge, however, did not wait for Mr. Schultz's inquiries. "Well, it means for one thing," Judge Hoffman said, as he read through the papers that Ball had submitted to him, "that he is a convicted felon . . . so I can't blame the warden for not permitting him in there." Then the judge asked Ball, "Is this Mr. Kunstler's signature on these papers?" Ball replied that it was not. "Another legal assistant in this case," he explained, "was authorized [by Kunstler to sign his name]."

"I ask you, sir," the judge demanded angrily, "who forged Mr. Kunstler's name, because his name is appended to one page, two pages of this document, and then the document is signed by a man who concedes that he is out on appeal bond after conviction for robbery." The judge then denied Ball's motion, and ordered Schultz "to investigate the activities of this man Ball for coming into the United States District Court, getting a judge here from his home, and without a license to practice law." He then asked Ball, "Are you Stuart Ball's son."

"Yes," Ball replied, "I am."

"Well, you don't do credit to your father, sir. I am amazed. I have known your father for a long time. I consider him a professional and a personal friend. He would not approve, sir, of your coming in here in this manner."

The judge then repeated his instruction to the assistant prosecutor. "I want you to investigate the activities of this young man . . . who has come into this court and has undertaken to bring a judge of the United States District Court here from his home and to address the court. He had no right to address the court in the first place."

Mr. Ball's father, a distinguished Chicago attorney and a former president of Montgomery Ward, did not agree with Judge Hoffman's estimate of his son. Later in the trial, when the judge excluded Ball from the courtroom for allegedly having laughed at him—an impoliteness that Ball denied—the elder Ball came to court to argue on his son's behalf. "Everything my son has done in this case," he told Judge Hoffman, "he has done after counseling with me. There has been no act or conduct on his part of which I am ashamed." Ball was thereupon readmitted to the courtroom, but the bitterness remained.

On the twenty-fourth, the day on which the selection of the jury was to commence, Seale was told by his jailers that he would be taken to the Federal Building. As he was waiting to be processed, he saw Jerry Rubin, who was also in Cook County Jail, having been put there to serve the last twenty-five days of a forty-day sentence he had received in San Francisco for his part in an antiwar demonstration two years earlier. Together, Rubin and Seale were taken across Chicago to the Federal Building and placed in the lockup, one floor above Judge Hoffman's courtroom. There Kunstler came to visit Seale. As Seale recalls the meeting, Kunstler said, "I heard you were talking about firing all the lawyers unless you had Garry."

"Yeah," Seale replied, "because all you cats were supposed to do for me is file motions. As far as I'm concerned Garry is going to be my trial lawyer. He's always been my lawyer." Seale recalled that Kunstler then told him that if he fired the lawyers, "Judge Hoffman would appoint some kind of public defender. So I told Kunstler, well they can appoint a public defender, but I ain't working with no public defender. I want Garry . . . and if Hoffman tries to appoint you or anyone else as my lawyer, then I'm going to fire you cats anyway." He would, he said, defend himself.

Accordingly, Kunstler's colleague, Leonard Weinglass, petitioned the Court on the 24th to let Seale conduct his own defense. Judge Hoffman denied this motion. Meanwhile, Kunstler filed an appearance with the court—that is, indicated that he would serve as lawyer—for Seale, Rubin, Dellinger, and John Froines, a defendant who was charged with teaching the use of incendiary devices, as well as with having been part of the conspiracy. At the same time Weinglass filed appearances to represent Hayden, Davis, Hoffman, and Lee Weiner, who was also alleged to be part of the conspiracy and was separately charged with having planned to blow up the parking garage under Grant Park.

Why Kunstler filed an appearance for Seale despite Seale's objections remained somewhat of a mystery throughout the trial and thereafter. In the hectic two days before the trial began, the defendants, the lawyers, and the Illinois Panthers met and discussed at length the problem of Seale's legal representation. The Illinois Panthers were sympathetic to the defendants' wish to create an impression of unanimity at the trial, an impression that Seale's separate defense would jeopardize. At the defendants' request, Fred Hampton called Garry's office in San Francisco to discuss the problem, but Garry was already in the hospital and could not speak. One of his partners answered and said that, while he understood the defendants' predicament, he could not speak for Garry in his absence. Perhaps Kunstler, responding to the wishes of the other defendants, and sensing some uncertainty among Garry's partners, then decided to file an appearance for Seale.

That night, in Cook County Jail, Seale wrote a motion in his own hand asking the court to allow him to fire his lawyers and postpone his trial until Garry could defend him. The next morning, when he arrived in court, he told Kunstler he was fired. He then showed his written statement to the other defendants, one of whom, as Seale recalls, objected: " 'Man, that's going to make it look like all of the defendants are splitting.' "

Seale replied, "Man, the defendants aren't splitting. I'm not splitting from you cats. It's just that my situation is very different, man, in a lot of ways. These cats stuck me on the tail end of this indictment to try to railroad me to prison, so I need Garry here and everybody knows it. I'm not going to be letting Hoffman pick and choose my lawyer for me, when he knows that Garry is my lawyer."

To this the defendants said, "Well, O.K." Seale then proceeded, as he later wrote, "to exercise my constitutional rights." Accordingly, he submitted to the clerk of the court the motion he had written the night before, which began, "I, Bobby G. Seale . . . have been by motion denied the right to speak out on my own behalf [a reference to Weinglass' petition on the 24th]. . . . I submit to Judge Julius J. Hoffman that the trial be postponed until a later date where I, Bobby G. Seale, can have the legal council [sic] of my choice who is effective, Attorney Charles R. Garry, and if my constitutional rights are not respected by this court then other lawyers on record here representing me, except Charles R. Garry, do not speak for me or represent me as of this date, September 26, 1969. I fire them now until Charles R. Garry can be made available as chief council [sic] in this trial of so-called conspiracy to riot and in fact be my legal council [sic] of choice who is effective in assisting me in my defense."

According to the Sixth Amendment, "the accused . . . shall have the assistance of counsel for his defense," a right

which the courts have traditionally interpreted to mean
that if a defendant so chooses he may defend himself. Thus
the United States Code provides that "in all courts of the
United States the parties may plead and conduct their own
cases." Seale knew that he had this right. He also knew
that such a right had often been exercised in the past,
especially by defendants who felt that they were being
tried for their political views, and who wanted not only
to defend themselves but to use the court, insofar as rules
of procedure allow, as a political forum. Huey Newton,
for example, had defended himself in the municipal court
of Richmond, California, two years earlier, when his own
lawyer failed to turn up. Judges are expected to grant this
right, provided it is requested early enough in the trial so
as not to interfere with an orderly proceeding. Thus in two
Smith Act cases, the communists Eugene Dennis and Eliza-
beth Gurley Flynn defended themselves. So did ten of
fourteen Catholics, including several priests, who had gone
on trial in Milwaukee in 1968 for having destroyed draft
records. These defendants, too, had refused the services of
William Kunstler and a group of civil rights lawyers in
favor of defending themselves.

Judge Hoffman, however, denied Seale this right. He
reminded him that Kunstler, "a very able criminal lawyer
from New York," had filed an appearance to defend him,
and that this was why he could not defend himself—a
ruling that Kunstler called "narrowly technical." To this,
Seale replied, "If my constitutional rights are denied, I
can only say that you are a blatant racist." He then referred to his hand-written motion in which these sentiments also appeared, and in which he had insisted on
Charles Garry as "chief counsel." The judge, however,
repeated that he did not recognize the function of a "chief
counsel" or of "trial teams" in his court. "This is not a
baseball team," he said.

It was not only Seale who wanted Garry's services. So did the other seven defendants. Thus the defense lawyers felt that by refusing to postpone the trial on Garry's behalf the judge may have denied all the defendants their constitutional right to counsel of their choice. Foran dismissed this possibility in a conference with the defense lawyers; but he admitted to them that he was not equally sure that Seale's rights had not been violated. Accordingly, Foran reminded the judge on the afternoon of the twenty-fourth that not only were the defendants represented by Kunstler and Weinglass, as well as by Birnbaum and another local lawyer named Bass, but that four other lawyers had filed appearances for the defendants, but had never shown up. Foran wanted the record to show that all the defendants, including Seale, were adequately represented despite Garry's absence, and that if an error had been made, which might later become grounds for an appeal, it was the fault of these four absent lawyers.

Kunstler replied that the four lawyers had never intended to participate in the trial but had agreed only to prepare pretrial motions. Their work in this respect having been completed, their services were no longer needed. For this reason the four lawyers had notified the court by telegram earlier that week of their intention to withdraw. The judge, however, responded to Foran's tactic by issuing bench warrants for the arrest of all four lawyers. "My wishes," he said, "are that a lawyer respect this court. You cannot withdraw from a case in my court by telegram. I wish to have the four men brought here as expeditiously as possible. Bench warrants will be issued for their arrest."

Startled by this unusual order, Weinglass angrily asked the judge, "How about Mr. Garry, your Honor. Wouldn't you like him brought in too?"

"You take care of your orders. I'll take care of mine," Judge Hoffman replied.

On the night of September 25, one of the four lawyers, Michael Tigar, a professor of law at UCLA, was awakened by federal marshals, put on a plane, and found himself the next morning—having been fingerprinted and photographed—in the lockup on the floor above Judge Hoffman's courtroom. On the morning of the twenty-sixth, Tigar and Gerald Lefcourt, another of the four lawyers (who was later to defend the twenty-one Panthers arrested by District Attorney Hogan), stood before Judge Hoffman's bench. The judge announced that the keys to the county jail were in the pockets of the defense. By this Kunstler assumed him to mean that "if the defendants waived their right to counsel . . . with respect to Garry then the jailhouse door would open for these . . . attorneys." The defendants, however, described this tactic as "blackmail" and "ransom," and refused to accept the judge's offer. At a lunch-time press conference they said they would not drop their request for Garry's services—thus waiving the right they felt they had under the Sixth Amendment—in exchange for the release of the lawyers.

The contretemps that had begun with Judge Hoffman's refusal to grant a postponement for Garry's illness, threatened, by the third day of the trial, to become an impasse. At the end of the morning session the judge ordered Tigar and Lefcourt into the lockup, where they spent the lunch hour. It was unclear, in view of the position the defense had taken and the corresponding intransigence of the judge, how they were ever to be released.

7

Just Another
Brown Envelope

ON SEPTEMBER 26, when Seale accused Judge Hoffman of racism, the judge had replied, "Do you know you are addressing the judge who ordered the first desegregation of schools in the North?" Then he warned Seale not to repeat such criticisms. "I caution you," he said. "Your remarks are contumaceous," by which he meant that they could become the basis for a charge of contempt of court.

The desegregation order to which the judge referred involved the schools of South Holland, Illinois, a community whose board of education had, like most other Northern and many Southern school boards, ignored a ruling of the Supreme Court handed down in 1954, which held that separate school facilities did not provide equal educational opportunities and were thus unconstitutional. Judge Hoffman's order, which he issued in July 1968, was that South Holland must integrate its six elementary schools, of which four were largely white and two nearly all black. Throughout the Conspiracy Trial the judge would refer to this ruling as proof that he was "as good a friend of the black man as they have in this community." Visitors to his chambers, decorated with petit point that had once belonged to Disraeli, and with monogrammed blue and green towels in the lavatory, could see a framed editorial from the Chicago *Daily News* praising him for this decision, an accolade which hung on his wall beside a letter from President Nixon and a notice of appointment to the federal bench signed by President Eisenhower, of whom a small bust sat on an adjacent table.

The judge's sense of himself as a friend of the blacks was a conviction he seemed to hold most strongly. It not only angered him that Seale and the other defendants accused him of racism, but such accusations apparently puzzled him as well. He himself belonged to a much abused minority and, though he admitted that he was "lucky to be Jewish," since he thus became eligible for appointment "to the so-called Jewish seat on the court," he apparently chose to think of himself as someone whose own ethnic peculiarity had taught him to sympathize with the predicament of other minorities.

Thus in 1954, when he had been on the federal bench for only six months, he chided a lawyer who had called attention to the historic plight of American Negroes in an effort to show that his black client should be treated mercifully. This client, a janitor, the father of two children, and a veteran of the Korean war who had been decorated for his part in four battles, had cheated the Veterans Administration of a hundred fifty dollars. Though he had repaid fifty-five dollars of this amount and had been forgiven by the army, Judge Hoffman nevertheless sentenced him to jail for a year and a day. To the lawyer's plea for mercy the judge replied, "Please don't discuss this matter of race here. If there is any judge on the bench who looks after the underprivileged members of other races, it's me."

In a ruling he made in 1962, however, Judge Hoffman revealed that his solicitude for the underprivileged might not have been so great as his concern about other more practical matters that sometimes confront a federal judge. In the preceding year, twenty-two black parents had come before him to argue that their children were denied equal educational opportunities in the segregated schools of Chicago. Citing the Supreme Court ruling of 1954, they objected to the policy of the Chicago Board of Education that their children must attend schools closest to their homes in the city's South and West Side ghettos. What they hoped, according to their attorney, was that if Judge Hoffman ruled in their favor the city would have to undertake "massive transferring" of black pupils into white neighborhoods, a program that the Chicago Board of Education and the great majority of Chicago's white population strenuously resisted. Judge Hoffman ruled against the twenty-two black parents. They had not, he said, exhausted the local remedies available to them. Therefore, he would not hear their case. The black parents then took their suit to the Circuit Court of Appeals. A year later the Supreme Court ruled, in a similar case, that parents did not have to exhaust local administrative remedies before seeking relief in federal court. With this ruling in mind the Appeals Court ordered Judge Hoffman to hear the suit of the twenty-two black parents. By this time, however, the blacks had come under great political pressure to abandon their case, and nothing more was heard from them. A year later the ghettos erupted in the Chicago school boycotts of 1964. These resulted in the resignation of the schools' superintendent, but the schools themselves, like the neighborhoods they served, remained as segregated as ever.

Thus by the time the case of the South Holland school district came before Judge Hoffman in 1968, his decision was, in effect, preordained by the ruling of the Appeals Court. Furthermore, an order to desegregate the six elementary schools in South Holland, though it irritated the white majority in that small and distant community, hardly demanded of the judge such fortitude as he would have needed to order that black children be bused into the white neighborhood of Chicago itself, as the twenty-two black parents had demanded in 1962.

Nevertheless, Judge Hoffman admitted to a reporter that after the South Holland decision, "Bankers and other influential people stopped me in the street and asked, 'How in hell did you decide that case that way?' I told them that I didn't rule that a Negro walking down the street had the right to propose marriage to a white woman. Nor was the question of housing reached. All I did was apply the Supreme Court ruling which outlawed segregated education."

By the morning of September 26, the jury had been selected. Though in most state courts the opposing lawyers have the right to question prospective jurors through a process known as voir dire—an examination of prospective jurors or witnesses to determine their competence—in federal courts this procedure is left to the judge himself, on the theory that he will protect the interests of both parties. The adversaries, however, are invited to submit questions to the judge which he, in his discretion, may or may not choose to ask the prospective jurors.

Accordingly, the defense had submitted to Judge Hoffman a list of forty-four questions. Some of these pertained to the political attitudes of the prospective jurors, and others, suggested by Abbie Hoffman, were directed to their cultural views. Thus the defense proposed that the judge ask the prospective jurors whether they felt that "it is wrong for people who object to the war against Viet Nam, racism and economic inequality to travel from one part of the country to another to demonstrate"; whether they believed that "dissent is harmful to the country"; and whether they believed that "black people are free and equal in the United States." The defense also asked the judge to inquire whether, "if your children are female, do they wear brassieres all the time"; whether they "know who the Jefferson Airplane, Phil Ochs, and Country Joe and the Fish are"; and whether they "consider marijuana habit-forming."

The forty-fourth question reflected an interest of the lawyers. "At the conclusion of this case, would you be willing to disregard the instructions of the judge concerning the law and assert the primacy and independence of the jury by deciding the case on the basis of your own moral convictions, concerning the guilt or innocence of the defendants, in line with the accepted legal doctrine that the jury represents the ultimate moral authority of the community in a democratic society?" What the lawyers hoped to do was to challenge a convention that has been the rule in most United States courts since the 1840's: that the jury decides only upon the facts, while the judge interprets the law. Though the judge ignored this question—as he did the preceding forty-three—the lawyers for the prosecution were thus forewarned, as they later acknowledged, that the defense might attempt in the course of the trial to overreach the customary authority of the court, and argue the constitutionality of the law itself directly before the jury.

The panel of three hundred prospective jurors was assembled in a ceremonial courtroom larger than the one in which the trial itself would be held. Most were middle-aged, nearly all seemed to be middle class, and there appeared to be more women than men. About thirty panel members were black. Judge Hoffman chose to ask the prospective jurors only whether they could consider the evidence fairly and give an impartial verdict. Of the prospective jurors, about seventy felt they could not, and left the courtroom. Though many of these admitted to reporters that they were prejudiced against the defendants, one woman said that she had been bothered by the tone in which Judge Hoffman had read the indictment. He had done this, she said, with such vehemence as to make the grand jury's charges seem already to have been proven as fact.

Kunstler, too, objected to the tone in which the judge had read the indictment. It was, he said, "as if Orson Welles had read the Declaration of Independence," a comparison which the judge found flattering. Later, however, when Leonard Weinglass moved formally that the entire panel be dismissed because of the tone in which the indictment had been read, the judge replied angrily. He told Weinglass that he had clearly instructed the jurors to keep their minds open, and that the indictment was not evidence but a statement of unproven charges. "Do you hear me?" the judge shouted at Weinglass. "I deny your motion and I resent the insinuation. It is the first time such a charge has been leveled against me."

Judge Hoffman then asked whether anyone on the panel was related to the defendants, or to the lawyers for either side, and whether they or their relatives had ever worked for anyone involved in the case. A black man replied to this question that his wife had once worked for Mr. Foran. "In domestic service?" the judge asked pleasantly.

"No," the man replied. "As a legal secretary." Thereupon he was excused from the panel.

Prospective jurors are chosen by lot from the same lists of registered voters from which grand jurors are chosen, a process to which the defense objected since it excludes people who, for whatever reasons, choose not to vote. The judge, however, denied the motion of the defendants that the entire panel be dismissed for this reason. A federal marshal then proceeded to call out the names of twelve panel members, who took their places in the jury box. As each juror entered the box, the judge asked where he was employed, where he lived, and with whom.

Among the first jurors thus selected were the daughter of a Chicago policeman, the aunt of a policeman from a suburb, and a businessman who belonged to a policeman's social club. The defense asked the judge to disqualify these jurors on the grounds that they could hardly decide impartially, but he refused. "I do not have the right," he said, "to deprive the daughter of a policeman of her right to sit on a jury." It was enough, the judge ruled, that this woman had assured him of her impartiality, as had the other prospective jurors who remained on the panel.

Judge Gary, who presided at the Haymarket Trial, had also accepted such assurances from jurors without further inquiry. In the case of a juror who admitted his close friendship with several Chicago policemen, one of whom had been wounded in the riot itself, the judge asked, "Do you believe that you can fairly and impartially render a verdict in this case?" When the policemen's friend replied, "I believe I could," the judge admitted him to the jury. He then denied a defense request to remove this juror for cause.

In the Haymarket Trial the defense was entitled by law to 160 peremptory challenges, twenty for each defendant. These peremptory challenges entitle the defense to disqualify a juror without the consent of the judge. But when these challenges were exhausted, Judge Gary quickly seated a panel of jurors, most of whom had admitted their prejudice against the defendants. In the Conspiracy Trial the judge allowed the defendants as a group only seventeen peremptory challenges. Judge Hoffman explained that in trials involving several defendants his practice was to allow ten peremptory challenges to one defendant, and one to each of the others.

The defense, therefore, recognized that it must use its challenges cautiously. Once these challenges were exhausted, the selection of the jury would be in the hands

of the judge and the prosecutor, whose interests, the defendants felt, were identical.

As each juror was peremptorily challenged by either
side, the name of a new juror would be called out by the
marshal. This juror would then take his place in the box.
The government, provided it chose not to exercise its own
right of peremptory challenge, would then present the
entire panel of twelve to the defendants, who would huddle
with their lawyers to decide whether or not to accept. By
the time the defense had exhausted nine of its seventeen
challenges, the defendants felt that at least four of the
jurors selected so far might prove to be sympathetic. Two
of these were black women, one of them a nurse's aide who
wore a sprightly red wig, and the other a retired cook, to
whom the judge remarked genially that such servants had
lately become hard to find. The third of these jurors was
a young woman who wore a miniskirt, and the fourth was
a housewife who, the defendants noted, was carrying a
book by the black writer James Baldwin. Even though the
jury at this stage in the selection included some members
who appeared to be decidedly hostile to the defendants—
especially a huge, peroxided woman who glared out at the
courtroom through jeweled sunglasses—the apprehensive defendants decided to take their chances. To exercise their
remaining peremptory challenges would invite the government to do the same. For the defense, therefore, it was a
gambler's choice. They chose to accept the formidable blond
lady, along with several other apparently hostile jurors,
rather than risk the government's rejection of the two blacks,
the miniskirted girl, and the lady who read James Baldwin.

Thus the jury was chosen. It included ten women and
two men, one an elderly car cleaner for the Chicago Transit
Authority, and the other an unemployed house painter who
lived in a hotel on Chicago's skid row. Four alternate jurors,
all women, were also chosen.

On Friday morning, September 26, the principals in the case, together with some seventy members of the press and an equal number of spectators, gathered in Judge Hoffman's courtroom on the twenty-third floor of the Federal Building. Like the other courtrooms in the building, Judge Hoffman's is two stories high and paneled in polished wood. As the visitor enters through swinging doors he finds himself standing on a gray-carpeted aisle between two rows of wooden benches. Those on the left are for spectators, who are searched by federal marshals before they are allowed to enter. The benches to the right are for the press, though the last three rows of this section are reserved for relatives of the defendants. Since the trial had attracted considerable attention, the benches on both sides of the aisle were filled, and many would-be spectators had been turned away.

At the end of the aisle is a plush rope of the sort used at the entrances to theaters and restaurants, and beyond this rope, in a large, carpeted open space, the defendants sat around four tables arranged in a large rectangle. On the opening day of the trial, Seale, in a light blue turtleneck jersey, sat at the corner of this rectangle farthest removed from the judge's bench. On his left wrist he wore a plastic bracelet, such as hospital patients are given, bearing his name and prison number. Reclining in a black leather armchair of modern design, supported by four spherical chrome wheels, he had flung back his head. His eyes were fixed on the ceiling, which consisted of a metal grid meant to diffuse the fluorescent light. Before him on the table was the yellow legal pad on which he had written his motion the night before. Along the sides of the rectangle were ranged the other defendants and their lawyers. Abbie Hoffman wore a tan suede jacket with a Navaho design printed on the back; Hayden, his hair grown long, wore a blouse made of pennants announcing the revolutionary movement of

Berkeley High School students; Rubin was in a yellow shirt, striped in red, and bright green corduroy trousers. His hair had been cut short in jail and, like Seale, he wore on his wrist a plastic bracelet.

Opposite the defendants, at a table half the size, were seated the government lawyers. Foran, nearest the bench, Schultz directly behind him, and opposite Schultz, a pale young man named Cubbage, who represented the Justice Department. Together with these three lawyers there sat an FBI agent named Stanley. Behind the government lawyers the jury sat in its box.

At the front of the room, facing the court, is the judge's bench, elevated to form a sort of stage on several levels. On a low platform to the judge's right sits the court stenographer. Behind her, a foot or so higher, is the witness stand. At the opposite end of this stage sits a marshal in a kind of pulpit. To his left, along the wall behind the defendants' table, are folding chairs for members of the press who are unable to find seats in the regular press section. In this wall are two doors, hardly distinguishable as such, made of the same polished wood as the wall itself. The door farther from the judge's bench leads to a cloakroom, and from there to the corridor, while the one nearer to the judge leads to the lockup, one floor above. When this door was opened, the defendants could see the gray steel bars through which Seale and Rubin were led into court by the federal marshals.

On the wall behind the judge's bench are conventional portraits, chosen by the judge himself—of the Founding Fathers, of Abraham Lincoln, and three of periwigged English jurists. Above these portraits, on the upper part of the wall, is the Great Seal of the United States, and in a circular design around it are the words "United States Court for the Northern District of Illinois." The building is so designed that if this upper wall were transparent, the defendants could look up from their table and see through the Great Seal directly into the lockup on the twenty-fourth floor.

Despite his diminutive size and his curiously exaggerated bearing—at once rigid and dainty, like a masked Japanese actor—the seventy-four-year-old judge conveyed an unmistakable authority on the first day of the trial. Though he stood only five feet four inches tall, and weighed hardly more than the smallest of the formidable lady jurors, his diminished stature permitted him to enter the courtroom, from a door behind his bench, in such a way that his presence did not become known until he had materialized atop the highest of the several stages at the front of the room. On the first day of the trial, he accomplished his entrance in this manner, so that the unprepared spectators seemed startled by his magical appearance and hardly had time to rise in response to the marshal's order.

"Good morning," Judge Hoffman said to the members of the jury, who had been shown to the jury box by a United States marshal. The jurors replied in the singsong greeting of a grammar school class, "Good morning, Your Honor." The judge then introduced Mr. Schultz, who would outline the government's case.

"The government, ladies and gentlemen of the jury," Schultz began, "will prove in this case that [the defendants] planned to bring people into Chicago to protest—legitimately protest, create a situation in this city where these people would come to Chicago, would riot, and the defendants, in perpetrating this offense, they the defendants, crossed state lines themselves, at least six of them, with intent to incite this riot.

"We will prove, ladies and gentlemen of the jury, that the defendant David Dellinger, who sits right there, the defendant Rennard Davis who sits next to him, and Thomas Hayden who is standing . . ." But Hayden, in response to

Schultz's introduction, had done more than stand. He had also raised his fist to greet the jury in the Panther salute, whereupon the judge ordered the jury to leave the room.

"Who is the one that shook his fist in the direction of the jury?" the judge demanded.

"This is my customary greeting, Your Honor," Hayden replied. "It implied no disrespect for the jury."

"Regardless of what it implies," the judge warned him, "there will be no fist shaking and I caution you not to repeat it." The judge then settled back into his large black leather armchair, and stared silently for a moment from between Judge Landis' green library lamps. When he was satisfied that the room was quite silent, he asked the marshal to bring the jury back in.

Schultz continued. "In promoting and encouraging this riot, the three men I have just mentioned used an organization which they called the National Mobilization Committee to End the War in Viet Nam. They used this organization to plan these activities." Then Schultz introduced Abbie Hoffman to the jurors. As he did so, Hoffman rose and blew a kiss in their direction.

"The jury is directed," the judge warned, "to disregard the kiss thrown by the defendant Hoffman and the defendant is directed not to do that sort of thing again." Then Schultz introduced Rubin, and Weiner, "who," Schultz said, "calls himself a professor at Northwestern University." (He is, in fact, an instructor of sociology there.) Next Schultz pointed to John Froines, "standing at the far end of the table . . . an assistant professor of Chemistry at the University of Oregon."

Finally Schultz introduced Bobby Seale, who turned and waved a greeting to the jury.

"The government will prove," Schultz continued, "that each of these eight men assumed specific roles and they united and that the eight men conspired together to encourage people to riot during the convention. We will prove that the plans to incite the riot were in three basic steps. The first was to use the unpopularity of the war . . . to urge people to come to Chicago during the convention for the purposes of protest.

"The second step was to incite these people . . . against the police department, the city officials, the National Guard and the military and against the convention itself, so that these people would physically resist. . . . The third step was to create a situation where the demonstrators who had come to Chicago and who were conditioned to physically resist the police . . . so that a riot would occur.

"We will prove that in executing these plans to cause the demonstrators to meet the police . . . the defendants Dellinger, Davis, Hayden, Rubin and Hoffman made what are called non-negotiable requests and unreasonable demands upon the city of Chicago . . . for certain permits. . . . First they demanded [that] these people could sleep in Lincoln Park. At one point they were talking in terms of . . . 500,000 people who were coming to Chicago to sleep in Lincoln Park . . .

"The second non-negotiable demand . . . was for a march to the International Amphitheatre . . . although they were told that the Secret Service said that a permit could not be authorized because of the danger . . . to the President, the Vice President and the candidates . . .

"We will show . . . that while they were having these negotiations . . . the defendants were, in fact, trying to discourage the issuing of permits . . . During these negotiations . . . Rubin told the Administrative Assistant to the Mayor of Chicago . . . 'We came to fight in this city and tear up the town and the convention' . . . The defendant Hoffman . . . said 'Give us $100,000 and we will not hold our Festival of Life; we will get out of town.' . . . The defendant Dellinger . . . told Mr. Stahl [the mayor's assistant] that he, Dellinger, had just returned from the Sorbonne in France, where he studied the tactics used by the students there in riots, and that he believed in civil disobedience and that civil disobedience was part of the program which he had planned for the demonstrations in Chicago.

"The government will prove . . . that the defendants met with one another and planned their actions. The government will not prove that all eight defendants met together at the same time, but the government will prove that on some occasions two or three of the defendants would meet, on other occasions four would meet . . . and on several occasions six would meet to discuss their plans. . . . We will prove these meetings in two ways: one by the testimony of people who were present and two, by the testimony of Chicago policemen who are charged with the responsibility of surveilling, following certain of the defendants just prior to and during the convention.

"We will prove that the defendant Bobby Seale flew to Chicago. He flew here . . . on Tuesday, August 27, and he gave a speech [that] night to a crowd and he gave another on Wednesday to a crowd . . . We will prove that these speeches were intended to incite these people to attack policemen. We will prove that the defendant Rubin arranged for Seale's speech on Tuesday night . . . and that he gave a speech just prior to Seale's . . . Seale said that 'If a pig comes up to us unjustly, we should bring out our pieces and start barbecuing that pork, and if they get in our way, we should kill some of those pigs and put them on a morgue slab . . .'"

Though Seale had not used these last words in his Lincoln Park speech—nor would Pierson, the government witness, claim that he had—Seale remained silent throughout Schultz's opening speech, and seemed to pay no attention. From time to time he would write a sentence or two on his yellow pad, but most of the time, as Schultz spoke, Seale was stretched out in his chair, his head thrown back, gazing at the fluorescent ceiling.

Schultz completed his opening statement to the jury by explaining that the government would show how Weiner had planned to use Molotov cocktails to blow up the parking garage under Grant Park, and how Froines had bought a foul-smelling chemical that a group of women later dropped on the rugs in the lobby of the Hilton Hotel and in a bar in the Palmer House.

The government would also prove, Schultz said, that Hayden had told a crowd in Grant Park on Wednesday, August 28, to "make sure that if blood is going to flow, let it flow all over the city. If gas is going to be used, let it be used all over Chicago. If we are going to be disrupted and violated, let this whole stinking city be disrupted and violated. I will see you in the streets."

"In sum," Schultz concluded, "the government will prove that the eight defendants charged here conspired together to use interstate commerce and the facilities of interstate commerce to incite and to further a riot in Chicago . . . and that they took steps, they did things, to accomplish this conspiracy."

The defendants and their lawyers concluded from Schultz's opening statement that the government's case was weak. The acts and speeches that the government would attribute to them were typical of the kind of aggressive public speech and political assembly that the Supreme Court, in recent years, had come to agree was permitted under the First Amendment. Thus Kunstler in his opening statement stressed the constitutional tradition that permitted the defendants to hold their rallies and give their speeches. Though he did not attempt to challenge the constitutional validity of the anti-riot act itself, Kunstler made it clear that the defense would show that nothing the alleged conspirators said or did was beyond the protection of the First Amendment or alien to the American tradition of vigorous political protest.

On the other hand, Judge Hoffman had denied a pretrial motion to dismiss the indictments on the grounds that the anti-riot law was unconstitutional by virtue of the First Amendment. Therefore the argument that Kunstler outlined in his opening statement would be inadmissible during the trial itself. Thus, while the defendants were relieved by what they considered the triviality of Schultz's case, they were nevertheless convinced that their chances of being acquitted, under the anti-riot act and according to the rules established by Judge Hoffman, were marginal. Their only chance, they felt, lay in the possibility that the injustice of the anti-riot law itself would become apparent to the four jurors on whom they had fastened their hopes: the two black women, the miniskirted girl, and the housewife—whose name was Jean Fritz, but whom the defendants came to call Mrs. Baldwin because of the book she had been carrying. What the defense hoped was that these jurors would be sufficiently revolted by the anti-riot law to assert their own moral authority over the rules of the Court and the actions of Congress, and vote to acquit the defendants on grounds of reason and humanity.

When Kunstler finished his statement, the judge asked Tigar and Lefcourt to step forward. It was at this point that he advised the defendants that the "keys to the County Jail" were in their pockets. Then he sent the two lawyers to the lockup, where Seale and Rubin were also taken, to spend the lunch-time recess. There the other defendants and their lawyers met with Seale and Rubin to discuss what Weinglass should say in his opening statement that afternoon. Professor Tigar—who was to have lectured at UCLA that afternoon on Repression in America—sat with Lefcourt in an adjoining cell, where they were given fish sandwiches for lunch. Though Weinglass was inclined not to make a statement at all since he felt that Kunstler had said enough, he was finally convinced by Hoffman and Rubin that he should speak nevertheless. What they wanted was for him to speak on behalf of the "life style" that characterized the defendants, and especially the Yippies. Rubin and Hoffman wanted Weinglass to show that while it might be offensive to the majority for young people to behave unconventionally, there was nothing illegal in such behavior.

While the defendants were thus engaged, Judge Hoffman, accompanied by his elderly clerk and two armed marshals, proceeded across the street to the Standard Club, a club for Jewish men to which all federal judges, regardless of religion, are also invited to belong. It is Judge Hoffman's custom to take his lunch in the men's bar on the second floor of this somber and pretentious establishment, where he is usually joined by one of his fellow judges.

Upon his return from lunch, Judge Hoffman entered the elevator in the Federal Building and, according to a reporter from the Washington *Post* who was in the same elevator, said to his two companions, "Now we're going to hear this wild man Weinglass." Ten minutes later the judge had resumed his place on the bench, and Weinglass began his opening statement.

He said that the defense would prove that the defendants' demands for permits were not "non-negotiable," as Schultz had claimed; that they wanted to use only fifty or sixty acres of a public park that included 1,285 acres; and that they filed their permits in good faith not only for the use of the park, but for a march to the Amphitheatre, where the convention was to be held. What they would not accept, Weinglass said, was the city's suggestion that they meet in a different part of Chicago, where their demonstration would be irrelevant. The protest had to occur at the Amphitheatre itself to be in any way effective.

"We contend," Weinglass then said, "that the First Amendment of the Constitution gives us the right to peacefully assemble and meet—" whereupon Foran objected.

"I object," he said, "to counsel commenting on the law." Judge Hoffman sustained this objection and Weinglass apologized.

"Mr. Weinglass," the judge continued, "the function of an opening statement is to tell the jury what the evidence will be, not the law of the case. I will do my best to tell the jury what the law of the case is."

It is unlikely, however, that Judge Hoffman in fact intended to explain to the jurors the ambiguous rulings on the First Amendment made in recent years by the Supreme Court, a tangle of legal improvisation and political compromise whose complexities have recently been the subject of a lucid study, *The System of Freedom of Expression*, by Professor Thomas Emerson of Yale. Though the government case would rest almost entirely on the public speeches and private conversations of the defendants—material that is normally protected by the First and Fourth Amendments and is thus inadmissible as evidence in a criminal prosecution—the judge, throughout the trial, refused to hear arguments against the admission of such evidence, a refusal that at first puzzled many observers. There were, however, several reasons for the judge's position.

In the first place, the indictment under which the defendants were charged did not state that their speeches were in themselves criminal. These speeches were merely "overt acts" that pointed to certain alleged criminal "intentions." Under the anti-riot statute only these "intentions" are punishable. The "overt acts" themselves may or may not be criminal. It makes no difference. Furthermore, under a conspiracy indictment, the conspiracy itself is the crime, not the acts that issue from it. What the conspirators do to further their conspiracy may be perfectly innocuous, as the Poulterer's Case held. Judge Hoffman also made it clear that such fundamental questions of law as freedom of speech and assembly are not matters for a district court to decide, but should go before the higher courts. On an earlier occasion, the judge had said, "This is a criminal trial on my criminal calendar, assigned to me in rotation. It is just another brown envelope." What he meant was that he would treat the Conspiracy Trial as if it involved legal questions no more complex than those in a prosecution for burglary, in which only the facts are at issue. But even had the judge agreed to confront First Amendment questions and to let the jury consider them, he would probably have been no more capable than his superiors on the Supreme Court of sorting out for the jury precisely what freedom of speech and assembly means in America.

The First Amendment to the Constitution provides that "Congress shall make no law . . . abridging the freedom of speech, or of the press, or of the right of the people peaceably to assemble, and to petition the Government for a redress of grievances." A strict interpretation of this amendment would appear to prevent the government from indicting the defendants on the basis of any statements they might have made—no matter how violent or aggressive—before or after their arrival in Chicago. Under such an interpretation the government could not, for example, use the speeches of Seale and Hayden that Schultz mentioned in his opening statement as evidence of a crime or of criminal intentions. Instead, the government would have to show that the defendants had actually organized or taken part in a riot—not simply that their speeches might have stimulated one, or revealed an intention to do so. Under such a strict interpretation the anti-riot act would, therefore, clearly be unconstitutional. But the Supreme Court has not so far interpreted the First Amendment to mean what it literally says.

For example, the courts have always agreed that libelous speech is not protected by the First Amendment, nor are false advertising claims or fraudulent contracts. The evil consequences of speech or writing of this sort are directly apparent, and the courts have traditionally assumed the right to protect the public from whatever material damage may follow from such expressions. Furthermore, in time of war or other emergency, the Congress has passed, and the courts have upheld, laws that limit the kind of controversial or seditious speech that the amendment evidently was meant to protect.

Thus Lincoln closed the post office to "treasonable correspondence" during the Civil War. And in 1917, a federal Espionage Act was passed that made it a crime "to convey false reports" that might hinder the war effort, "promote the success of the country's enemies," or "cause insubordination, disloyalty, mutiny or refusal of duty," in the armed forces. A year later, the act was amended to cover statements critical of Liberty Bonds, the flag, the government, war production, and the Constitution itself. Under a Minnesota version of the federal statute, a man was found guilty of having told a woman that "no soldier will ever see the socks" she was knitting for the troops.

Once the First World War was over, the Supreme Court agreed to hear a number of cases in which convictions under the Espionage Act appeared to conflict with First Amendment rights. The first and most famous of these cases involved the general secretary of the Socialist party, a man named Schenck, who had been convicted for having published a pamphlet critical of the draft. Justice Holmes, who voted with the majority to uphold Schenck's conviction, ruled that no matter what the First Amendment appeared to say it did not protect all speech indiscriminately. For example, it did not protect a man who "falsely shouts fire in a theatre and causes panic." Thus Holmes concluded that "the question in every case is whether the words are used in such circumstances and are of such a nature as to create a clear and present danger that they will bring about the substantive evils that Congress has a right to prevent." In upholding the conviction, Justice Holmes felt that Schenck's pamphlet constituted such a "clear and present danger."

Under the same espionage law, Eugene Debs was sentenced to ten years in the penitentiary for having said in a speech, "You need to know that you are fit for something better than slavery and cannon fodder." This conviction, too, was upheld by the Court, and Debs stayed in prison until President Harding pardoned him, Woodrow Wilson having refused to do so.

Though the Espionage Act remained on the books, many of its provisions were repealed in 1921. However, the Smith Act, passed in 1940, made it unlawful to "advise, counsel or urge" disloyalty in the armed forces or "to distribute written or printed matter which advises or urges" such disloyalty. Throughout the World War II the Supreme Court largely avoided the First Amendment issues raised by the Smith Act, but it did reverse a few Smith Act convictions on such technical grounds as insufficient evidence. Its attitude toward the act was apparent, however, in the one decision based on the First Amendment which it did hand down during the war. This concerned two Jehovah's Witnesses who had been convicted in Mississippi under a local statute derived from the federal law. The Court ruled that the defendants had merely expressed their opinions on domestic and world affairs and should not be punished.

Though the Espionage Act and the Smith Act remained on the books, it became apparent by the 1960's that the Court would no longer uphold convictions for statements critical of American wars. In the case of Julian Bond, the Georgia legislator who had been denied his seat because of his statements against the war in Vietnam, the Court ruled that "there can be no question but that the First Amendment protects expressions in opposition to national foreign policy."

It would be wrong, however, to assume from the Bond decision that the Court had at last decided to stand on a literal interpretation of the First Amendment in cases involving political comment.

The First Amendment was drawn in response to the British sedition laws, which made it a crime to speak treasonably of the government. These laws, which had emerged in the fifteenth century and were strengthened in the sixteenth and seventeenth, despite the opposition of such powerful critics as John Milton, whose Puritan comrades were cruelly oppressed by them, were not significantly modified until 1792, when truth was declared by Parliament to be a defense against charges of seditious libel, by which was meant criticism of the government. The First Amendment was drafted in the spirit of this reform.

From the beginning, however, the amendment was subject to ambiguous interpretation. In 1789, only eight years after the last of the colonies had ratified the Constitution, Congress passed the Alien and Sedition Acts, which imposed upon the republic a version of the British sedition laws by making it a crime "to write, print or utter . . . any false, scandalous and malicious writing against the government of the United States, or either house of Congress . . . or the President, with intent to defame said government, etc., or to stir up sedition within the United States." Though this law was much disputed at the time, the Supreme Court chose not to face the issues it raised. In 1801, however, the law was allowed to expire, and it was never reenacted. Nevertheless, the Supreme Court waited until 1964 to rule that the Sedition Act had violated "the central meaning of the First Amendment."

But, while Congress refused to pass, and the Court eventually chose not to uphold, laws forbidding criticism of the government or its personnel, numerous statutes have been passed, and for a time upheld by the Supreme Court, prohibiting speech that advocates the overthrow of the government. In 1923 Benjamin Gitlow, a member of the National Council of the Left Wing Section of the Socialist Party, a forerunner of the American Communist Party, was convicted under the New York State criminal anarchy statute, which made it a crime to advocate, advise, or teach "the duty, necessity or propriety of overthrowing organized government by force or violence." Gitlow was convicted for having issued a pamphlet that advocated revolutionary socialism and urged a communist revolution based on "the class struggle" and the "power of the proletariat" through "revolutionary mass action."

The Supreme Court in 1925 upheld Gitlow's conviction and ruled that the First Amendment "does not confer an absolute right to speak or publish, without responsibility, whatever one may choose. . . . A state in the exercise of its police power may punish those who abuse this freedom by utterances inimical to the public welfare, tending to corrupt public morals, incite to crime or disturb the public peace. . . . A state may punish utterances endangering the foundations of organized government and threatening its overthrow by unlawful means." The Court, having ruled on the validity of the statute, then refused to consider whether Gitlow had actually violated it in such a way as to cause the substantive evil which the statute meant to prevent.

Justices Holmes and Brandeis dissented. "Every idea is an incitement," Holmes said, and he added that he found "no present danger" that the government might be overthrown at Gitlow's urging. He also said that the right of free speech included the right to express belief in a "proletarian dictatorship."

The Smith Act of 1940, under which many communists were subsequently convicted, was modeled on the New York State criminal anarchy statute that the court upheld in the Gitlow case. Along with its prohibition of speech tending to cause disaffection among the troops, the Smith Act also prohibits teaching or advocating the overthrow of the government by force or violence or "joining any group or assembly of persons" that has such aims.

Not only did the Smith Act thus specifically contradict the First Amendment, it also defied a considerable body of traditional opinion in America, beginning with the Declaration of Independence and including Abraham Lincoln's statement when, as a Whig member of Congress, he opposed the Mexican War. "Any people anywhere being inclined and having the power, have the right to rise up and shake off the existing government and form a new one that suits them better," Lincoln said on behalf of the Mexican residents of the disputed Texas territory. "This is a most valuable, a most sacred right," Lincoln said, "a right which we hope and believe is to liberate the world."

Many prosecutions were brought under the "overthrow" provision of the Smith Act and upheld by the Courts. The first important prosecution of this sort was that of Eugene Dennis and ten other members of the Communist party for conspiracy to overthrow the government. Though in 1948, Tom Clark, Ramsey's father, who was then Attorney General, advised against the Dennis indictment on the grounds of insufficient evidence, the indictments were nevertheless handed down a year later. Though the American Communists by this time had become a wan and toothless party, the defendants were convicted of conspiracy to advocate the overthrow of the government. Judge Learned Hand, who wrote the appellate decision affirming the conviction, admitted that the conduct of the defendants supplied no evidence that they advocated any specific or immediate acts of force or violence. However, it was enough to convict them, Judge Hand said, that they taught the doctrines of Marx and Lenin.

The Supreme Court affirmed Judge Hand by 6 to 2, but

the sense of its ruling was ambiguous. Five of the justices wrote opinions, and each produced a different theory of the First Amendment. Justices Reed, Burton, and Minton supported the opinion of Chief Justice Vinson, who ruled, in keeping with Holmes' "clear and present danger" formula, that the Court "must ask whether the gravity of the evil, discounted by its improbability, justifies such invasion of free speech as is necessary to avoid the danger." The Chief Justice agreed with Judge Hand that the eleven Communists were guilty of advocating a sufficiently grave and probable evil that the First Amendment did not protect them.

Justice Frankfurter also affirmed the conviction, but reached his decision by a different and rather more obscure route. He chose to weigh "the conflicting interests" in the case to see whether the government's interest in preserving itself counted for more or less on balance than an individual's interest in the right of free expression. Justice Frankfurter ignored the obvious objection to this method of analysis—that the only legitimate interest of the government under the Constitution is to protect the rights of individuals, including the right of free expression, except where these rights may interfere with the general welfare. He found, on the side of the government, that communism is "in the ascendency in powerful nations." The American Communist party, he learned from a magazine article, "included 60,000 members," and a Canadian Royal Commission had recently said that "the Communist movement was the principal base within which the espionage network [of Klaus Fuchs] was recruited."

On the side of the First Amendment, Frankfurter noted that "freedom of expression is the wellspring of our civilization . . . that there may be a grain of truth in the most uncouth doctrine," and that ". . . suppressing advocates of overthrow inevitably will also silence critics who do not advocate overthrow but fear that their criticism will be so construed."

Having weighed these conflicting interests, Justice Frankfurter then proceeded to reach his conclusion by a different means entirely, one that had nothing to do with balancing the "conflicting interests" involved. "It is not for us to decide," he wrote, "how we would adjust the clash of interests which this case presents were the primary responsibility for reconciling it ours. Congress has determined that danger created by advocacy of overthrow justifies the ensuing restriction of freedom of speech. . . . Can we then say that the judgment Congress exercised was denied it by the Constitution?" Though Chief Justice Marshall would have said, in keeping with his ruling in *Marbury v. Madison*, that the Court's responsibility is not to ask such questions but to answer them, Justice Frankfurter presumably meant his question to imply a negative answer. Congress had the right, Frankfurter's ruling implied, to ignore the First Amendment. Thus he agreed that the eleven Communists should go to jail.

Justice Jackson's affirmation was still more puzzling than Justice Frankfurter's. He chose not to discuss the First Amendment at all, but said simply that since "it is not forbidden to put down force and violence, it is not forbidden to punish its teaching or advocacy, and the end being punishable, there is no doubt of the power to punish conspiracy for the purpose." Thus Justice Jackson affirmed not only Learned Hand's ruling, but the corresponding rule established in the Poulterer's Case as well as the sedition laws of the same period.

Justice Black in his dissent found the indictment "a virulent form of prior censorship of speech and press." He then referred to the "clear and present danger" formula, which he said "does not mark the furthermost constitutional boundaries of protected expression but does no more than recognize a minimum compulsion of the Bill of Rights."

Justice Douglas applied the "clear and present danger"

test and found that to believe that the eleven "miserable merchants of unwanted ideas" might "endanger the nation is to believe the incredible."

Thereafter the Justice Department and the various states under statutes of their own undertook numerous prosecutions of lesser Communist party members. In 1956 the Supreme Court agreed to hear another of these cases. This was the so-called Yates Case, a state prosecution involving twelve California Communists convicted for advocating the overthrow of the government by force and violence, a case much like Dennis. The majority opinion, written by Justice Harlan, held that the trial judge had been wrong not to ask the jury to distinguish between the "mere advocacy of abstract doctrine of forcible overthrow" and "action to that end, by the use of language reasonably and ordinarily calculated to incite persons to such action. . . ." Justice Harlan concluded that the "essential distinction is that those to whom the advocacy is addressed must be urged to *do* something now or in the future, rather than merely *to believe* in something." Justice Harlan ruled that in the case of five defendants there had been no evidence that they had urged such specific actions. These the Court acquitted. For the rest the Court ordered a new trial.

Thus by 1957 the Court had begun, however tentatively, to introduce a distinction between expression and action as a means to test the limits of the First Amendment. Though in the Yates Case the Court did not go so far as to rule that all expression is protected by the First Amendment, while only specific actions are punishable, it did, at least, make a hesitant and philosophically awkward start toward a confrontation with the immensely complicated question that such a distinction raises.

The Yates decision effectively halted prosecutions under the Smith Act; but it also raised the question, more philosophical than legal—and finally perhaps imponderable—of the point at which speech leaves off and action begins, and of the area where the two merge and become indistinguishable.

In cases of libel and false advertising, it is clear that the expression itself may be a form of action, or so close to action as to make no difference. The palpable damage that follows from such expression can often be measured and rationally assessed by the court. But in the case of political advocacy the palpable damage that may result may be not only obscure but nonexistent, or the effect of such advocacy may not be damaging at all. It may be beneficial, as in the case of such a seditious document as the Declaration of Independence, though such benefits may not be apparent to the Courts at the moment of trial.

It may have been with such complexities in mind that the authors of the First Amendment boldly chose to prohibit any limitation on advocacy whatever: to let the young country take its chances with whatever political exhortation might be offered, on the assumption that to limit speech in any degree would be to expose the republic to a revival of the very sedition laws which had so offended the colonists in the first place. That the young nation was of at least two minds on the question of such broad and dangerous freedom is clear, however, from the fact that within the same generation it passed its own alien and sedition laws.

Well before the Yates decision rendered the Smith Act useless, Congress had begun to prepare a more sophisticated substitute for it. This was the Internal Security Act of 1950, the so-called McCarran Act, passed in the same heated political atmosphere that presumably afflicted the Court when it ruled in the Dennis Case.

The McCarran Act provided, among other things, for the registration of presumably subversive groups with the Attorney General, and for detention camps where suspected subversives were to be lodged during national emergencies.

Under this law the American Communist party was presumed to be "a clear and present danger to the security of the United States and to the existence of free American institutions." Members of the Communist party were further presumed to have "repudiate[d] their allegiance to the United States and in effect to have transfer[red] their allegiances to [the USSR]." Therefore, members of the party and affiliated groups were required to give the names of their officers and members to the Attorney General, to account for their funds, and to list their printing equipment. Members of subversive organizations could not apply for passports or work for the government, nor could the organizations themselves send material through the mail or make radio broadcasts unless they identified themselves as communist.

The McCarran Act also made it a crime for a person "to knowingly combine, conspire or agree with any other person to perform any act which would substantially contribute to the establishment within the United States of a totalitarian dictatorship [controlled by a foreign power]." Since the McCarran Act did not require that a defendant do anything more than conspire to accomplish such ends, it proved a more sinister expression of the spirit of the Alien and Sedition Acts than had the Smith Act, which required outright advocacy.

In 1961 the Supreme Court upheld by 5 to 4 the registration provision of the McCarran Act. Justice Frankfurter, writing for the majority, proceeded once again to weigh the conflicting interests and found, as he had done in the Dennis Case, that Congress had been within its constitutional right to enact the legislation. Justice Douglas concurred. Since communists not only make speeches but commit espionage, they should be made to register. The issue is not, Douglas said, simply one of free speech but of illegal action as well.

Justice Black dissented. "Under our system of government," he said, "the remedy [for subversive ideology] must be the same remedy that is applied to the danger that comes from any other erroneous talk, education and contrary argument. If that remedy is not sufficient, the only meaning of free speech must be that the revolutionary ideas will be allowed to prevail. . . . The Founders drew a distinction . . . which we would be wise to follow. They gave the government the fullest power to prosecute overt actions in violation of valid laws, but withheld any power to punish people for nothing more than advocacy of their views."

Despite the Court's ruling on the First Amendment question, the registration requirement of the McCarran Act was subsequently overturned by the lower courts on Fifth Amendment grounds. To require that an alleged subversive register as such, was, the Courts ruled, a form of self-incrimination. The First Amendment question, however, remained obscure. Justices Frankfurter and Douglas had ruled that Communist party membership involved not only protected speech and assembly but also included impermissible action, while only Justice Black seemed to agree with Justice Harlan's opinion in the Yates Case that a more precise definition between expression and action must be drawn than the Court had so far been able to do.

By 1967, however, Justice Douglas had come around to the position held by Justice Black. In another case involving the McCarran Act, he wrote, in a dissenting opinion, that "there is the line between action on the one hand and ideas, beliefs and advocacy on the other. The former is a legitimate sphere for legislation. Ideas, beliefs, and advocacy are beyond the reach of committees, agencies, Congress and the courts."

Though the further decline of the communist movement in the fifties and sixties rendered the McCarran Act largely useless, numerous convictions for sedition under various

state laws have recently been appealed to the Supreme
Court. Of these, the most interesting from the point of view
of the Conspiracy Trial is the case of *Brandenberg v. Ohio*.
Brandenberg, a leader of the Ku Klux Klan, was convicted
under an Ohio statute for having said, "We're not a re-
vengent organization, but if our President, our Congress, our
Supreme Court continues to suppress the white, Caucasian
race, it's possible that there might have to be some re-
vengence taken."

The Supreme Court unanimously reversed Brandenberg's
conviction. It announced "the principle that the constitutional guarantees of free speech and free press do not permit
a state to forbid or proscribe advocacy of the use of force
or law violation except where such advocacy is directed to
inciting or producing imminent lawless action and is likely
to incite or produce such action." Thus the Court, forty
years later, came to embrace the minority position held by
Justice Holmes in the Schenck Case: that the First Amendment protects all advocacy except that which directly incites and results in unlawful acts.

To Kunstler and Weinglass it appeared therefore that
the anti-riot statute must be invalid on its face, and that the
indictments must be dropped. Even if it could be shown,
as the defendants were sure it could not be, that Seale's
speech in Lincoln Park and Hayden's the following day in
Grant Park had deliberately and unequivocally incited acts
of violence, these speeches were not the basis on which the
alleged conspirators had been indicted. The charges against
them were that they had intended to advocate and incite a
riot months before the convention occurred—as long before, in fact, as April 12. How, therefore, could the speeches
and other statements they had made in this earlier period be
shown to have been the direct and unequivocal cause of the
Chicago riots?

From the government's point of view, however, such

questions as these were irrelevant. The indictment had nothing to do with freedom of speech or assembly but with certain criminal intentions, of which the defendants' speeches and rallies were merely the outward signs. The punishable crime, under the anti-riot statute, occurred within the minds of the defendants, and the Constitution says nothing about states of mind. To Foran and Schultz, therefore, the First Amendment was beside the point. Thus they persisted in their objections whenever the defense attempted to raise questions of freedom of expression or assembly. What did it matter, these objections implied, whether the Supreme Court had at last begun to draw a line between expression and action? The defendants' expressions were not at issue. It was their unexpressed intentions for which they were on trial.

The contention to which Foran objected in Weinglass' opening statement was that the defendants had the right to assemble whether or not the city had granted them permits; that their intentions therefore in assembling in Lincoln Park and elsewhere in Chicago were entirely legal. What Weinglass had in mind when he offered this point was a recent Supreme Court ruling in the case of *Shuttlesworth v. the City of Birmingham*, in which Rev. Fred Shuttlesworth of SCLC and others, including Martin Luther King, were denied a permit to demonstrate. When they demonstrated, nevertheless, they were arrested, tried, and convicted. The Supreme Court overruled the conviction and adopted an argument advanced as a minority opinion by Justice Roberts in 1939 in a similar case. The Court quoted Roberts as follows: "Wherever the title of streets and parks may rest, they have immemorially been held in trust for the use of the public and, time out of mind, have been used for purposes of assembly . . . and discussing public questions. Such use of the streets and public places has, from ancient times, been a part of the privileges, immunities, rights and liberties of citizens. The privilege of a citizen of the United States to use the streets and parks for communication of views on national questions may be regulated in the interest of all . . . but it must not, in the guise of regulation, be abridged or denied."

Under the anti-riot statute, however, the Court's ruling in the Shuttlesworth Case was irrelevant. The defendants were not on trial for having assembled illegally, but for having intended that their assembly—whether it was legal or not—should result in a riot. Since the government would not argue that the rallies in the parks had been illegal, Judge Hoffman had no difficulty in ruling that it was immaterial for the defense to argue the contrary. By granting that their overt behavior was not at issue, the government and the judge thereby denied the defendants the protection of the Constitution. In this way the sinister, if perhaps unintended, brilliance of the anti-riot statute became clear by the third day of the trial.

Faced with such a challenge, Weinglass was determined to confront the jury itself with the inequity of the law, despite Judge Hoffman's ruling that the jury would decide only on the facts, while he himself would rule on questions of law. "We of the defense do consider you," Weinglass told the jurors in his opening statement, "to be the highest authority and we will—"

At this point Judge Hoffman exploded angrily. He slapped his palm against a pile of papers on his bench, and dismissed the jury.

"Mr. Weinglass," he said, "I have repeatedly admonished you not to argue to the jury, not to tell the jurors anything other than what in your opinion the evidence will reveal. I think your persistency in disregarding the direction of the court and the law in the face of repeated admonitions is contumaceous conduct and I do find it on the record."

"Your Honor," Weinglass replied, "has tried to stop me

from speaking; however, it is the only way in which—" The judge again interrupted him.

"I'm not stopping you at this time. I am the governor of the trial under the Supreme Court's direction and you are going to do it according to the law." The jury was then readmitted to the courtroom. Weinglass completed his remarks and returned to his chair at the defense table.

Judge Hoffman then asked whether any other lawyer wanted to make an opening statement to the jury. Seale got to his feet with his yellow pad in hand, and strode coolly to the lectern. "Just a minute, sir," the judge asked. "Who is your lawyer?"

"Charles R. Garry," Seale replied. Foran then asked the judge to dismiss the jury once more, which the judge did. He then asked Kunstler whether he represented Mr. Seale.

"No, Your Honor," Kunstler replied, "as far as Mr. Seale has indicated to me that because of the absence of Charles R. Garry—"

The judge interrupted. "Have you filed his appearance?"

"Filed whose appearance?" Kunstler asked.

"The appearance for Mr. Seale."

"I have filed an appearance for Mr. Seale," Kunstler replied.

"All right," the judge said. "I will permit you to make another opening argument in behalf of Mr. Seale, if you like. I will not permit a party to a case to—"

Then Kunstler interrupted. "Your Honor," he said, "I cannot compromise Mr. Seale's position . . ."

"I don't ask you to compromise it," the judge replied, "but I will not permit him to address the jury with his very competent lawyer seated here."

"If I were to make an opening statement, I would compromise his position that he has not his full counsel here," Kunstler continued. But Judge Hoffman ignored this argument, and ordered the marshal to bring the jurors back in.

He then recessed the court briefly to permit the government to bring its first witness to the stand.

The appearance of this witness, a man named Simon who served as corporation counsel for the city of Chicago, proved to be an anticlimax. After all that had happened that day—the arrest of the lawyers Tigar and Lefcourt, the unsettled question of Seale's defense, and Leonard Weinglass' unsuccessful attempt to put the constitutional question directly before the jury—Mr. Simon's testimony made little impression on the defendants.

When Foran had completed his direct examination of Simon, the lawyers for the defense asked for time to resume their arguments on behalf of the two lawyers who were facing the weekend in jail. Judge Hoffman granted this request, but added that his clerk had just handed him an order from the Court of Appeals, which, he said, "might be helpful to counsel in discussing" this matter.

What his clerk had given him was a ruling of the Appeals Court that denied a suit by the defense—what is known as a writ of mandamus—to order Judge Hoffman to release the lawyers and postpone the trial until Garry could attend. Judge Hoffman read this order with evident satisfaction, and added that he hoped that in the future when he was to be "sued" the lawyers would tell him in advance. "I didn't know until it was decided in my favor that [a suit] had been filed . . . I like to know," he told the lawyers, "when I am being sued by a lot of people."

To this, Kunstler replied, "How sweet the victory when you don't know."

Judge Hoffman then said that he would release the lawyers only if he had an "unequivocal" statement from the defense that they would relinquish their claim to Garry's services. With a copy of the Appeals Court ruling before him, he added, "I haven't been able to get anything more than an equivocal statement from Mr. Kunstler. Even though he has filed written appearances here for people, he insinu-

ates or intimates or suggests or implies that [he has filed]
a qualified appearance. I don't want that. I want appearances
. . . at their face value [and] I want the lawyers to say it."
He then offered to read the ruling of the Appeals Court
once again and ordered that the two lawyers who had been
brought down from the lockup and were now standing
before him be held in contempt and remanded to the custody of the United States marshal. Furthermore, the judge
ordered that they be denied bail.

"Your Honor," asked a Chicago lawyer who had been
engaged to represent the two lawyers, "are they to remain
in custody for the rest of their lives? Is there no term?"

"I will determine the disposition of this case on Monday
morning at ten o'clock," the judge replied. Then he repeated, "You can give them the key to the County Jail, Mr.
Kunstler, if you want to."

"You are asking us," Kunstler replied, "to sacrifice our
Sixth Amendment rights that are of record in this case [in
order] to get them out."

"Let them be remanded," the judge ordered, slapping the
bench with his outstretched hand.

The tension in the courtroom diminished, however, when
it was learned later that afternoon that Judge Cummings of
the Seventh Circuit Court of Appeals had overruled Judge
Hoffman's decision not to grant bail, and ordered that Tigar
and Lefcourt be released on their own recognizance to reappear in Judge Hoffman's court the following Monday.

It had, nevertheless, been a trying day. In the corridor
outside the courtroom six young women, friends of the defendants, were seated on the floor against the marble wall.
Softly they chanted a phrase from the speech Bobby Seale
had made in Lincoln Park. "We're tired. We're sick and
tired. We're tired of being sick and tired."

The purpose of Mr. Simon's testimony had been to show
that the city of Chicago had had good reason not to issue

permits for the demonstrators to sleep in the parks and to march on the Amphitheatre on Wednesday, August 28, the night on which the Democrats would choose their Presidential nominee. Mr. Simon, a man in his thirties who was soon to enter private practice with Mayor Daley's son and be replaced as corporation counsel by Daley's cousin, testified that on August 8 he, an assistant named Elrod, and Mr. Stahl, the deputy mayor, had met with Hoffman and Rubin. In his testimony he explained why the mayor's office could not issue permits for the Festival of Life that the Yippies wanted to hold in Lincoln Park and which, according to its sponsors, might involve as many as five hundred thousand people. The mayor, Mr. Simon testified, had no authority to grant such permits, and Mr. Stahl advised Hoffman and Rubin to apply to the Park District, which they did.

Though the demonstration leaders followed Mr. Simon's suggestion and applied to the Park District, they also filed suit in federal court to force the various city agencies to issue the permits for which they had applied, and to which applications they so far had had no response. They based their suit on the Shuttlesworth ruling, and on August 21 and 22, appeared before William Lynch, a District Court judge who had once been Mayor Daley's law partner. Mr. Simon testified that he, too, had attended this hearing and that in Judge Lynch's chambers he had explained to Rennie Davis, who spoke for the Mobe leaders in their suit, why the parks could not be used as dormitories. He also suggested alternate parade routes, ones that would not, however, bring the demonstrators within "eyeshot" of the Amphitheatre. "I said," Simon testified, "if you are interested in what you allege in your complaint, that is, to exercise your constitutional rights of speech and assembly, then I think these rights can be afforded full protection and you can exercise them if we have a march but one that is a little more reasonable."

To this offer, Davis replied, according to Mr. Simon, "that these were all very reasonable proposals, but that he felt [they were] unacceptable if [they] didn't allow for an assembly at the Amphitheatre." As for the request that the demonstrators be allowed to sleep in the parks, Mr. Simon testified that Judge Lynch had asked, "Where in the Civil Rights law does it require that the government furnish sleeping accommodations to anyone?" Mr. Simon's response to the demonstrators was more direct. He testified that he suggested to Mr. Davis that "he seek hotel accommodations" for his followers.

But Davis could not accept this offer, according to Mr. Simon. Davis replied that "his members couldn't really be housed in hotel accommodations, that many of them didn't have money, and that what they really wanted was the use of the parks so that they could sleep there and meet all night." Then Simon testified that Davis had said, "There will be tens of thousands of people without a place to stay" if the city didn't permit sleeping in the parks. "They will go into the parks and the police will drive them out, and they will run through the streets and there will be disorder and conflict and problems and the police will fight back and there will be tear gas and mace and billy clubs . . . it will be suicide for the city not to consider our request for sleeping in the parks."

Mr. Simon's testimony suggested that the difference between him and Davis was a disagreement between reasonable men. Davis had made a request that the city could not grant, while Mr. Simon's offer was less than the demonstrators could accept. The dilemma was therefore left to the wisdom of Judge Lynch who, finding no merit in the claims of the demonstrators, dismissed their suit a week before the convention began.

On the same day that Judge Lynch issued his ruling, Director Lyons of the Intelligence Division of the Chicago

Police Department, sent the memorandum concerning the "potential problems" facing the city in connection with the convention to his superior, Deputy Superintendent Mulchrone. This memorandum included not only the warning of a Panther invasion but described the "New York Yippie leaders," who were said to include Abbie Hoffman, who "has a large, prominent nose," and Irwin Allen Ginsberg, "also known as 'La Poesia,' a self-admitted homosexual." Among the "Primary Targets" of the demonstrations, according to Director Lyons, were to be the Federal Building, the main police building, the induction center, the First National Bank of Chicago, and the Cook County Jail. Mr. Simon was not asked by the government lawyers whether he had known of this memorandum at the time he suggested to Davis that since the demonstrators could not sleep in the parks, they might arrange for hotel accommodations instead.

Having completed his direct testimony on Friday afternoon, Mr. Simon was excused until the following Monday, when he was to reappear in court for cross-examination. But on Monday the Court was distracted by news that had reached Chicago on the weekend that a District Court judge in San Francisco had found Judge Hoffman's warrants for the arrest of the other two pretrial lawyers invalid. For an arrest warrant to issue on a summary judgment of direct contempt, the contemptuous act must have been committed in the presence of the Court, otherwise a hearing is required to determine the facts. Since this had not been the case with the four pretrial lawyers, the San Francisco judge vacated the two warrants on the grounds that they failed to state an offense.

That Judge Hoffman should have committed so fundamental an error on such an elementary point of law, seemed to some of the lawyers in the courtroom that morning a sign that he had let his political convictions get the better of his judicial understanding. One lawyer, however, recalled that the judge had made the same error and had been reversed on appeal in 1950 when he had served on the Superior Court of Cook County. In this case two litigants who had just left Judge Hoffman's courtroom fell to quarreling in the corridor, and one of them assaulted the other. The judge's bailiff then brought the two men back into the court, and the judge sentenced the assailant to sixty days in Cook County Jail—a "most generous" sentence, Judge Hoffman said—for having committed contempt in the presence of the Court. The Appeals Court disagreed. The judge had not witnessed the contempt himself, and therefore had no right under the law to make a determination of the facts on his own authority. His ruling, therefore, was reversed.

The San Francisco ruling was not the only distraction to come before the Court that morning. Over the weekend some hundred fifty lawyers, from all parts of the country, had gathered in Chicago to picket the Federal Building in protest against Judge Hoffman's treatment of the four lawyers. This delegation, which was supported by thirteen members of the faculty of Harvard Law School and which included a number of other professors as well, submitted a brief, as friend of the Court, which called Judge Hoffman's actions "a travesty of justice [which] threatens to destroy the confidence of the American people in the entire judicial process . . ." By ten o'clock the angry lawyers had begun to march around the Federal Building, where they were joined by hundreds of student radicals, several Black Panthers, and a hundred or more blue-helmeted Chicago police.

Shortly before noon, about forty of the picketing lawyers carried their signs into the lobby of the Federal Building, despite the notice posted on the glass wall beside the entrance, and signed by Judge Campbell, forbidding such demonstrations within the building. Hardly had the lawyers entered, however, than Judge Campbell himself descended to the lobby, dressed in his black robes and accompanied by a marshal, a stenographer, and his court clerk. Surrounded by the angry lawyers, who were themselves encircled by a ring of police and federal marshals, the judge proceeded to hold Court then and there. He announced that unless the pickets withdrew immediately, he would charge them with contempt.

This time, he warned, there could be no question that their contempt would occur in the presence of the Court, and would thus be subject to summary punishment. No sooner had he made this announcement, however, than a voice from the throng shouted, "Fuck you, Campbell." After a moment of tense silence, followed by a cheer from the crowd and a noticeable stiffening among the police, Judge Campbell himself withdrew. Then the lawyers, too, left the lobby and rejoined the pickets on the sidewalk.

In Judge Hoffman's courtroom meanwhile, Foran, presumably embarrassed by Friday's impasse and apprehensive of further disorder, urged the judge to vacate the remaining contempt citations, which were presumably invalid, as the San Francisco judge had found in the case of the other two. To this request Judge Hoffman agreed. "It appears the defendants are adequately represented," he said in a genial tone, "and as far as this court is concerned I have no desire to damage the reputations of young lawyers. The contempt motion will be set aside and leave will be given them to withdraw." Thus Judge Hoffman's first attempt to force the defendants to relinquish their claim to Garry's services failed.

To add to Judge Hoffman's troubles, Kunstler on the following morning filed a motion requesting that the judge disqualify himself for having called Leonard Weinglass a "wild man"—the description overheard by the reporter from the Washington *Post*, who had printed the judge's remark in his newspaper over the weekend. Attached to Kunstler's motion was a copy of the reporter's article, along with a page of the trial transcript that included the judge's interruption of Weinglass' opening statement to the jury. This, Kunstler felt, proved the judge's hostility. The judge, however, denied this motion and ruled that it did "not state grounds for the relief sought."

No sooner had the judge disposed of this problem, than Foran submitted a motion for a private meeting with the defense lawyers in the judge's chambers. The lawyers for both sides then spent the rest of the morning session closeted with Judge Hoffman. The defendants, who were as puzzled as the spectators by the prolonged absence of the judge and the lawyers, concluded that perhaps something had arisen that might bring the trial to a premature end. These speculations produced an atmosphere of excitement and apprehension.

By noon, the defense lawyers had told their clients the reason for the meeting; and at a press conference the defendants explained what had happened. Identical threatening letters had been sent to two of the jurors. They were written with a felt-tip pen and said, "We are watching you." They were signed, "The Black Panthers."

The defendants told the reporters that they felt these letters had probably been inspired by the FBI in order to compromise jurors who might be sympathetic to the defense. That one of the letters had been sent to the miniskirted girl confirmed these suspicions for the defendants. "We consider our jury to be the young people of this country; the young people of the world," Hayden told the reporters. He then read a message from Bobby Seale which accused "the fascist government of doing this because they know that the rotten racist Hoffman had made them look bad." The letters, he added, "were a low-life racist attack" by the FBI "to tamper with the jury and make the Panthers look bad." As for the possibility that the Panthers themselves might have sent the letters, the defendants explained that the party does not refer to itself as "The Black Panthers," and that it would hardly be a sensible tactic "to threaten jurors like that. It just doesn't make sense."

When the defendants returned to the courtroom for the afternoon session, the morning's tension had considerably subsided. As they and the spectators awaited the judge's arrival, Rennie Davis passed a box of cakes and jelly beans around the courtroom. Once the press and spectators had taken what they wanted, he offered some to the government lawyers, who gratefully declined. Then Judge Hoffman emerged from his chambers, and the courtroom was restored to order. Kunstler told the judge of the suspicions of the defendants, and the judge irritably asked Kunstler to prove his charges "right now." Kunstler suggested that the government and the defense should conduct separate investigations of the letters. The judge rejected this proposal and ordered Kunstler to be seated. Then he asked the marshal to bring Kristi King, the miniskirted juror, to the jury box. When she had taken her seat he told the marshal to hand her the letter. Then he asked whether she had ever seen it before. She had not, she said.

"Having seen it [now]," the judge asked, "will you please tell me if you can still be a fair and impartial juror in this trial?"

"No, sir," Miss King replied. "I cannot."

Kunstler then objected. Miss King, he said, had never seen the letter before the judge had shown it to her, and thus it was the judge himself who "had led her into saying she can no longer be impartial." What had happened was that Miss King's letter had been opened in her absence by her father, who had immediately turned it over to the FBI. The FBI then presented the letter to Foran, who had given it to the judge in his chambers that morning. Thus Kunstler was correct in saying that Judge Hoffman had shown Miss King the threatening letter for the first time.

Nevertheless, the judge overruled Kunstler's objection and dismissed Miss King from the jury, to the dismay of the defendants. For Miss King's part, however, her dismissal was perhaps not such a disappointment. She had an engagement in San Francisco the following weekend and nothing, she had promised a fellow juror, would prevent her from keeping it.

The judge then called Ruth Peterson, a middle-aged housewife, to the jury box. She too had received a threatening letter and, unlike Miss King, had opened it herself. That morning she had handed the letter to Judge Hoffman's clerk. The judge asked her, as he had asked Miss King, whether she could still be impartial. Mrs. Peterson replied that she could. When the judge then asked whether she had discussed the letter with her fellow jurors, she said that she had told Mrs. Mildred Burns about having received it, but had not said what it contained.

The judge then called Mrs. Burns to the jury box. She admitted that Mrs. Peterson had indeed told her what the letter contained. Kunstler then demanded that Mrs. Peterson be removed from the jury, but Schultz replied that her "inconsistency" had been "insignificant." The judge agreed. He then replaced Miss King with Kay Richards, an alternate juror who, like Miss King, was twenty-three years old.

Having settled the matter of the threatening letters, the judge ordered that the jury be sequestered for the duration of the trial. The jurors were taken that night to the Palmer House Hotel, three blocks from the Federal Building, where they would remain for the next five months.

That evening Kunstler went to a dinner party at one of the fine houses in the vicinity of State Street on the Near North Side. There he explained that when he had been in the judge's chambers that morning, he had repeated his desire to withdraw the appearance he had filed on behalf of Bobby Seale. The judge, however, had told him that he would deny such a motion if one were made. Kunstler found such stubbornness incomprehensible and concluded that the judge could not imagine that a black man might be capable of defending himself in court. He then took from a shelf a copy of *Who's Who* and proceeded to read aloud to the other dinner guests the judge's biography to see if his personal history might help to account for his intransigence.

Julius Hoffman, Kunstler noted, was born in Chicago in 1895, the son of Bertha and Aaron. He graduated from the law school of Northwestern University in 1915, underwent no military service, and entered private practice that year. In 1928 at the age of thirty-three he married Eleanor Greenebaum, the former Miss Bensinger. The Bensinger family, one of the other dinner guests pointed out, had for years operated a pool hall on Randolph Street and had, in the course of this business, come into possession of the Brunswick-Balke-Collender Company, a billiard table manufacturer. This dinner guest also recalled that Hoffman had served as Mrs. Greenebaum's lawyer in her suit for divorce against her former husband, Moses, the scion of a family of Chicago mortgage bankers. From the time of his marriage until 1947, Hoffman served as general counsel to the billiard table company owned by his wife's family. Then Kunstler read from *Who's Who* that in 1947 Hoffman became a judge on the Illinois Superior Court. In 1953 he was appointed a Federal District Judge. The dinner guest added that his sponsor had been Senator Dirksen. Though Mrs. Greenebaum had two children by her former marriage, she and the judge had none. Among the affiliations listed in the judge's biography were the Northwestern University Alumni Association, of which he had once been president, the Republican party, the Standard, Tavern, Union League and Mid-day clubs of Chicago, the Lake Shore Country Club of Glencoe, and the Post and Paddock Club at the Arlington Heights race track.

Kunstler remarked that given this background Judge Hoffman could hardly be expected to understand the political and cultural interests of the defendants, to say nothing of the background and character of Bobby Seale.

On the following day, David Stahl, the mayor's young assistant, appeared as a government. witness. He testified that he had first met Hoffman and Rubin on March 26, 1968, when they appeared in his office, accompanied by television news cameras, to announce their plan to bring five hundred thousand demonstrators to the convention. The demonstrators would sleep in the parks, Rubin said, and they would be entertained by rock bands. Then Stahl testified that on August 2 he met Davis and other leaders of the Mobe at the Palmer House. Davis, Stahl said, advised that the city should prepare for between two and three hundred thousand demonstrators. The protest, Davis said, would be peaceful. It would include a march to the Grant Park band shell on Wednesday, August 28, and from there a march to the Amphitheatre, to coincide with the balloting for the Presidential nominee. Davis also warned, according to Stahl, that the city should try to keep the hippies away from the Negro neighborhoods, since their presence there might lead to violence. To his request for a permit, Stahl replied that the mayor's office had no jurisdiction over the parks and that Davis should apply to the Park District for permits. As for the march to the Amphitheatre, the demonstrators should try the Parade Board at the Department of Streets and Sanitation. Stahl then testified that he told Davis that an ordinance forbade sleeping in the parks and that the Secret Service had warned against a march to the Amphitheatre. Therefore, Davis should expect this application to be denied.

Stahl then testified that on August 7 Rubin and Hoffman reappeared in his office, together with several other Yippies and a photographer from *Life* magazine. Hoffman, Stahl said, explained that if the city wanted to avoid trouble it should appropriate $100,000 to sponsor the Festival of Life, but "better still, it should give [us] $100,000 and we'll leave town." Hoffman then said, according to Stahl, that the festival would include "body painting, nude-ins at the beaches, public fornication, discussions of the draft and draft evasion."

Then Stahl described the meeting on the following day, about which Simon, the corporation counsel, had also testified. At this meeting, Stahl said, Rubin had told him the Yippies were "taking over" the application for permits that had originally been filed by the Free City Survival Committee, a group of Chicago Yippies who had decided to withdraw from the convention protests for fear that the intransigence of the city and the determination of the demonstrators would lead to violence.

The government lawyers did not, however, ask Stahl to testify about a memorandum he wrote on the day following this meeting with Hoffman and Rubin. In that memorandum, which summarized his conversation with Earl Good, the writer for *Barron's* magazine, Stahl had written: "The Yippies and the National Mobilization Committee do not want McCarthy nominated . . . They will try to involve their supporters in a revolution along the lines of the recent Berkeley and Paris incidents. They propose to block the streets, send men into the Negro sections of the city to breed disorder, paint cars to look like cabs to drive delegates out of town and throw blood. They have trained people with football helmets and axe handles to converge on police lines. One of their objectives is to get someone killed to serve as a martyr. Their ideal would be a 19 year old female McCarthy supporter. Good suggested we do everything possible to control these groups as soon as they arrive in Chicago, and proposed that we mobilize public opinion against them. Good suggests that we guard the routes to the Amphitheatre very carefully."

Whether Stahl agreed with Good's warning is unclear. If he did, then he had been disingenuous not to tell the demonstration leaders that the city would not only refuse their permits, but would actively resist their efforts to assemble and protest. If Stahl did not believe Good's warning, then had he been in good faith he should have advised the leaders that such malicious reports were circulating and that they should hasten to clarify their peaceful intentions for the convention. There was, however, no way for the defense lawyers, who had seen a copy of Stahl's memorandum, to learn what his opinion of Good's advice had actually been. Under the rules of evidence, as Judge Hoffman interpreted them, an opposing lawyer could cross-examine a witness only with respect to matters that had been introduced in direct testimony. Thus the jury remained ignorant of Stahl's memorandum.

Stahl then testified that on August 10 he met once more with Davis, this time at a coffee shop on Monroe Street, where Davis told him to expect a hundred thousand members of the Mobe, and that "we should use little visible police in dealing with members of this group, as they regarded the Chicago Police as the Gestapo. . . . I told Mr. Davis once again," Stahl continued, "that he was applying to the proper place for the use of the parks by applying to the Park District, but cautioned him that he was unlikely to get a permit for his group for sleeping in the Park. I also said that the probability of obtaining a permit to march to the Amphitheatre was very slim in view of the requirements that had been imposed on security around the Amphitheatre by the Secret Service." However, Stahl said nothing to suggest that he had told Davis about the memorandum based on his conversation with Earl Good that he had written the day before.

The next meeting to which Stahl testified took place on August 12 with Davis, Hayden, Dellinger, and other protest leaders. At this meeting Dellinger said, according to Stahl, "that he had just recently returned from Paris where he had been studying street riots at the Sorbonne. He said he was studying these because he was anxious to know why they had failed, and he was interested in the whole subject of street demonstrations. He said he was, however, not interested in violence or disturbing the delegates or the convention."

The last meeting with the demonstration leaders to which Stahl testified was on August 26. At this meeting Stahl spoke to Dellinger, who warned him again that there would be trouble unless the city issued a permit for the demonstrators to sleep in the parks.

Before Stahl was asked to describe this meeting, however, Foran, as had been his custom since the trial began, interrupted to explain to the Court, ". . . at this time I would like to offer the evidence of this conversation with respect to the defendant Dellinger only." Since the government had not yet proven the existence of a conspiracy, Foran was not prepared to charge the other defendants with responsibility for Dellinger's remarks. Later in the trial, when he felt that he had accumulated enough evidence to show that a conspiracy had existed, he would ask the Court that the testimony against each defendant be applied against all the defendants. Weinglass objected to this procedure, and argued that before evidence could be introduced to show that the defendants had belonged to a conspiracy, the existence of the conspiracy itself had to be proven first.

What Weinglass had in mind was an opinion of Justice Jackson that "the prosecution should first establish prima facie the conspiracy, and identify the conspirators, after which evidence of acts and declarations of each in the course of its execution are admissible against all." The reason, according to Justice Jackson, that the prosecution must first establish that a conspiracy existed, is so that the courts may avoid what usually happens in conspiracy prosecutions in which "the accused is often confronted with a hodge podge of acts and statements by others which he may never have authorized or intended or even known about, but which help to persuade the jury of the existence of the conspiracy itself. In other words," Justice Jackson concluded, "a conspiracy is often proved by evidence that is admissible only upon the assumption that a conspiracy existed."

Judge Hoffman, however, disagreed with Weinglass, ignored Justice Jackson's opinion, and agreed to Foran's request. He instructed the jury that "the testimony which this witness is about to give is offered by the government only with respect to the defendant Derringer and to no other defendant, at this time."

Kunstler then stood up and said, "I think Your Honor meant Dellinger."

"Dellinger, that's right," the judge replied.

Foran then proceeded to ask Mr. Stahl what Dellinger had said to him.

"Mr. Dillinger," Stahl replied, "said that we should issue a permit . . ."

The judge interrupted Stahl to say, "I am going to get back at you, Mr. Witness. I mispronounced the defendant's name. But you said Dillinger. It's Derringer. We were both wrong. You mean Mr. Derringer, do you not?"

Foran then interrupted to explain that the name was Dellinger and completed his examination of the witness.

In the direct examination of a witness, the examining lawyer may not ask leading questions, but must rely upon the witness' unaided memory for the answers to his questions. The assumption is that a friendly witness needs no stimulus to testify in the interest of the lawyer who examines him. In cross-examination, however, the opposite assumption holds. Because the witness is presumed to be hostile, the lawyer is free to question him aggressively and to jog his memory by a variety of means. But the cross-examiner is not permitted in federal court to question the witness on subjects that have not arisen in direct examination. He is not, in the jargon of the courts, permitted to go outside the scope of the direct examination.

Many judges, however, recognize the necessary imprecision of this rule and the difficulty of determining the limits of the subjects raised in direct examination. Thus they apply the rule with considerable latitude. Some federal courts have gone so far as to permit cross-examination on any subject that may cast doubt on the veracity or impartiality of a witness. But many judges prefer to interpret the rule narrowly, often in the interest of clinging to the letter of the law, and thus reducing the risk of reversal in the higher courts.

Judge Hoffman, following the custom of his district, chose to interpret the rule narrowly, a practice with which Weinglass, who had tried only one case before in federal court, may have been unfamiliar. Thus when he attempted to determine in his cross-examination of Stahl whether the witness had negotiated in good faith with the demonstration leaders, Foran objected to this line of questioning. The question of whether Stahl had done all he could to help the demonstrators get their permits had not come up on direct examination, and was therefore inadmissible on cross-examination. The judge sustained Foran's objection.

What Weinglass wanted to know was whether Stahl had "ever had an understanding with Mr. Dellinger or Mr. Davis that [he] would bring before them at one meeting heads of the Park District and the Department of Sanitation and Streets for resolution of the problem."

When the judge sustained Foran's objection, Weinglass attempted a different approach. "Was it your understanding," he asked, "whether at the August 12 meeting you were to have other people there from the city who did not appear?"

Once more Foran objected and the judge sustained him. Weinglass then attempted to ask the question in still a different form, with the same outcome, and when he tried a fourth time the judge angrily dismissed the jury. Foran then addressed the Court. "Your Honor," he said, "I find it a little unusual to conduct a class in basic legal procedure, but where counsel constantly asks questions that are outside the scope of the direct examination, I cannot expect that it is for any reason except to generate some erroneous impression of the jury. . . . There is a perfectly proper way to put [into evidence] matters other than those covered on direct examination. [Foran meant that Weinglass, to refute Stahl, could later in the trial call witnesses of his own.] It is not by trying to put facts into question that if they are denied sound as if they are in the record. That is the reason that common law since the beginning of time designated a trial technique and I ask Your Honor to direct counsel to comply with what is the proper conduct of examination of a witness."

Foran's argument was open to considerable question, especially with respect to "common law since the beginning of time." To this day, British courts do not follow the rule of American federal courts restricting the scope of cross-examination, nor do many state courts in America. Nevertheless, Judge Hoffman sustained Foran and called Weinglass' attention to a ruling in the case of *Sacher v. United States*. Since Sacher had been a lawyer in the Dennis Case and was, at the end of that trial, sentenced to six months in jail for contempt of court—a sentence which the Supreme Court later affirmed—Judge Hoffman's warning was ominous. It was the second time since the trial had begun that Judge Hoffman had warned the defense lawyers of the possibility that they might be charged with contempt.

8

Chicago Is Ours

THE HERO OF Upton Sinclair's novel *The Jungle* is a
Lithuanian immigrant eager to make his way in America
and confident that he will succeed. He comes to Chicago
a few years after the Haymarket Riot, finds work in the
stockyards, but soon suffers an accident and loses his job.
Thereafter he undergoes a sequence of brutal humiliations,
including the seduction of his wife by the foreman at the
sausage plant where she works and the death by starvation
of their only child. He himself is blacklisted, beaten, and
imprisoned for his attempts to help organize a union. Disillusioned, he works briefly at stuffing ballot boxes for the
Irish political leader of the stockyards area, who is himself
a tool of the meat-packers' trust. But Sinclair's hero soon
gives up this work and, after several terrible adventures, is
converted to socialism. At the end of the novel he attends
a rally of socialist workers, where he listens to a speaker
much like Eugene V. Debs. The orator concludes his
speech to the assembled workers with the cry "Chicago
will be ours!"—the words with which the novel itself ends.

In a way that neither Sinclair nor the socialist orator
could have foreseen, this prophecy has, in part, come true.
The son of a blacklisted sheet-metal worker, Richard Daley

—who still lives in the same stockyards neighborhood that Sinclair wrote about—won the most recent of his four elections with 74 percent of the votes. Though his constituents are anything but the socialists that Sinclair's orator predicted, they are nevertheless the heirs of the immigrant workers who were brought to Chicago to work in the packing plants and harvester factories in the eighties and nineties, and who feel that, at last, they have come into possession of the city that their fathers struggled to build.

Daley became mayor in 1954, a time when Chicago was in serious economic difficulty. In the twenties and thirties, the years in which he reached political maturity, the city's political life had been dominated by an uneasy alliance of the underworld and the Catholic hierarchy, whose bishops supported and were accordingly favored by the New Deal government in Washington. By the end of the war, however, the power of the criminals and the bishops had begun to wane. A reform administration then took office, but soon found itself incapable of controlling the city's aldermen who, upon the decline of the former instruments of political centralization, had begun to run their wards as independent principalities.

The instability that resulted discouraged investment. Established companies, unable to find a reliable center of political authority, threatened to leave the city, while new enterprises were reluctant to move in. Because the warring aldermen could not agree on a location for a new airport, the convention business, on which the city's hotels and department stores depended for much of their trade, suffered, and these establishments were faced with the prospect of closing down.

Though the city's businessmen were reluctant to turn the government back to the old Democratic machine, they feared the anarchy of the wards still more. Thus, while a majority of the city's financial leaders supported the Republican candidate against the reform mayor, Martin Kennelly, many of them, including a number of liberals, backed Richard Daley, who was, at the time, clerk of Cook County. In this position Daley dispensed much of the county's patronage and became expert in the art of political obligation.

With the support of such leaders as the former Governor, Adlai Stevenson, and William Dawson, boss of the South Side ghetto, who delivered the black vote almost intact, Daley defeated the reform mayor in the primary election and easily won the general election against a Republican opponent. Soon he added to his powers as mayor the duties of party leader, and was thus able to dispense some 35,000 city and county jobs. This patronage, which Daley administered with infinite care, became the basis of his political power. By parceling out these jobs among his district leaders—together with an equal number of jobs to which he has access in private industry—Daley has been able to coerce the obedience of the fractious wards. Mike Royko, the columnist for the Chicago *Daily News*, wrote in 1968, "I don't know of any powers Daley doesn't have."

As Susan and Martin Tolchin have shown in their recent study of political patronage, one of the most effective powers possessed by a strong mayor is over the use of land: the power to affect zoning regulations, grant tax abatements, and determine the future sites of large public and private developments. Along with his other patronage powers, Mayor Daley has used this power effectively. Not only has he used the zoning power in small matters affecting the interests of local residents who must apply to their district leaders to intercede with City Hall if they want to extend a driveway or remodel a building; he has also used it in large matters. Thus he has been able to encourage developers to build the dozen or so towers of metal and glass that reflect the pompous new prosperity of the city's business district.

In this way the city has been adorned, while such speculators in real estate as Judge Campbell's wife have prospered
by the revival, under Mayor Daley, of the city's commerce.

A further effect of this revival has been that to his other
powers the mayor has added the strength and loyalty of
the construction unions, whose members are supplied with
work, while in return they agree to complete, without
striking, the projects undertaken with the approval of the
mayor. It is not, however, to this extent alone that the children of Upton Sinclair's *Jungle* have come to possess the
city of Chicago. To confirm the city's gratitude to its
workers, Mayor Daley has appointed their leaders to posts
of public honor.

As Mike Royko has noted, the chief of the city's janitors'
union sits on the Police Board, the Park District, the anti-
poverty board, the buildings' commission, and the Railroad
Terminal Authority. The head of the plumbers' union is on
the Board of Health and runs the annual St. Patrick's Day
Parade. The head of the electricians' union is on the Board
of Education, and his son is vice-chairman of the City Council. The head of the steelworkers' union and an official of
the clothing workers' union sit on the library board, while
the head of the building employees' union is on the Chicago
Housing Authority.

Among the incidental beneficiaries of the city's real
estate activity, in addition to such investors as Mrs. Campbell, is United States Attorney Thomas Foran, whom Daley
has called "one of the greatest attorneys in this country and
the finest man I have met in private and public life." In
private practice, some ten years before he assumed public
office, Foran, who had already attracted the sympathetic
attention of the mayor, made his fortune as a specialist
in the legal problems of zoning and land condemnation,
particularly in negotiations over urban renewal and slum-
clearance programs, for which the city of Chicago, through

Mayor Daley's influence in Washington, had received large federal subsidies.

His fortune made, Foran then moved with his wife and six children to the prosperous suburb of Barrington, north of the city, where he keeps a stable of horses. He lives not far from David Stahl, who had himself left a profitable real estate business to become the mayor's assistant, and whose oldest child is a playmate of Foran's youngest.

Thus, in the early days of the trial, as Foran and his assistant Schultz questioned Deputy Mayor Stahl and Corporation Counsel Simon, the future law partner of Daley's son, on the permit negotiations, it became apparent that the protestors had not so much challenged a political machine as they had intruded upon the tranquility of a rich, proud, and powerful family. "No one," Mayor Daley had said in January 1968—long before the first demonstration leaders appeared in Mr. Stahl's office to apply for permits—"is going to take over this city. No one will ever take over a single street or a political convention, now or next summer." In a private conversation shortly after he testified, Stahl amplified this remark of the mayor's. To let the demonstrators sleep in Grant Park was unthinkable; it would be like letting them sleep in "the city's living room."

In *The Jungle*, Sinclair describes a bitter strike at the packing plants, to which the employers responded by importing Southern blacks as strikebreakers. Though these inexperienced hands often drank on the job and could not perform the complicated tasks assigned to them, they succeeded in bringing the strike to an end, with the result that the immigrant white workers, fearful of blacks in any case, came to fear and despise them still more.

Blacks now make up 30 percent of the city's population and occupy the huge and dismal ghettos to the west and south of Grant Park, the park that Stahl called the city's living room. Here they languish in the shadow of the political and economic citadel that Daley and his constituents have built for themselves.

When the Weathermen came to Chicago early in October, a week after Stahl's testimony, one of their aims had been to join with the Chicago Panthers for the sake of encouraging these blacks to rebel, much as the Haymarket radicals had hoped the starving and ill-housed workers of the eighties might be encouraged to do. To the Chicago Panthers, however, such an assault upon Mayor Daley's citadel seemed suicidal. On October 9, a number of Panthers attended a rally in the Federal Building Plaza, where Fred Hampton denounced the Weathermen as "anarchistic, opportunistic and Custeristic," and warned once more against an attack on the Chicago police, numbers of whom had also gathered in the plaza.

By the second week, the trial had come to absorb the defendants almost entirely. The courtroom itself became hermetic, like a ship out of sight of land or a sealed chamber deep in the recesses of the fortress city. The details of the defense became an obsession, and though Hayden said privately that he wanted more than anything else to go home to Berkeley, he and Weinglass returned eagerly each night to the South Side apartment they had rented for the duration of the trial, and prepared their case against the government's witnesses.

With the exception of Simon and Stahl, a few high officers of the Chicago Police Department, and some television cameramen, these witnesses were undercover Chicago policemen, paid civilian informers, and agents of the FBI. When it became clear that such witnesses as these were to provide the main part of the government's case, Weinglass moved that their testimony be excluded on Fourth Amendment grounds. Such surveillance, he said, amounted to an illegal search and seizure of evidence, no different from

200 · THE GREAT CONSPIRACY TRIAL

electronic eavesdropping or the actual intrusion by an officer without a proper warrant into a private dwelling. The judge overruled this objection. "It has been common police practice for years," he said, "to observe a person's conduct in public. No court has ever suggested that this violates the right to privacy." But the judge's ruling did not go to the point that Weinglass had made. What the defense objected to was police surveillance not of public but of private conduct, for it was by means of such intimate surveillance, more than by the evidence of public behavior, that the government hoped to show the jury that the overt acts of the defendants implied the criminal intentions for which they had been indicted.

The government's case emerged mainly from the testimony of three police spies and an assistant to Jack Mabley, a Chicago newspaper columnist. These four had represented themselves to the demonstration leaders as supporters of the convention protests, infiltrated the offices of the Mobe and the ranks of the demonstrators, and taken part in the protests themselves. The first of these undercover witnesses to take the stand was Robert Pierson, the police spy who had heard Seale's speech in Lincoln Park. He began his testimony on October 8, and remained on the stand for three days.

Pierson testified that for the sake of infiltrating the ranks of the demonstrators he had let his hair grow long and gone without shaving for four weeks. He then "purchased the attire of a motorcycle gang member, which is motorcycle boots, a black tee shirt, black leather vest and a motorcycle helmet." He also rented a motorcycle and on August 23 appeared in this costume in Lincoln Park, under the name Lavin, where he joined a band of cyclists known as the Headhunters. On the following day he returned to the park with two members of this group, one known as Gorilla and the other as Banana.

By Monday, August 26, he had ingratiated himself sufficiently with the radicals gathered in the park so that he was able to meet Abbie Hoffman. He then identified Hoffman from the witness stand as the man wearing "gold pants." Pierson testified that Hoffman said to him, "Last night they pushed us out of the park, but tonight we're going to hold the park." Pierson then testified that Hoffman used a "foul word": " 'We're going to f - - - up the pigs and the convention.' " To this Pierson had replied, "You can count on me in every way in doing my best to keep [you] from getting arrested."

Pierson testified that he met Jerry Rubin, whom he identified at the defense table as the man "in a yellow and red shirt and with a black arm band." Rubin, he testified, gave him a phone number to call in case he was arrested and needed bail, and Pierson offered to serve as Rubin's bodyguard, an offer that Rubin accepted. Then he recalled that in Lincoln Park on Monday, August 26, he and Rubin walked over to where a crowd had gathered around Tom Hayden, who, with a companion, had just been arrested and was being put into a police van. Rubin, according to Pierson's testimony, "kicked the ground and said, 'We're going to get even with those f - - - - - - pigs.' " Then Pierson, Rubin, and "Rubin's girl, Nancy . . . discussed the fact that we wanted to get something to eat, so we walked over to a hot dog stand . . . and ate the food and drank the liquid." Afterward all three joined a group of "four or five hundred" demonstrators who were preparing to march to the Loop to protest Hayden's arrest. The organizer of this march, according to Pierson, was Rennie Davis, whom he identified in court as "the man with the brown and white striped shirt and [who] also has on a black arm band."

Pierson then testified that he joined the march to the Loop and, in the company of Rubin, entered Grant Park, where some marchers had climbed on the statue of John A.

Logan, a Civil War general, while others shouted, "Take the hill," where the statue stood. From the statue the demonstrators "displayed the Viet Cong flag," which Pierson described as "the red and black flag." Pierson then left the park and went to Police Headquarters, where he discussed the day's events with members of the Intelligence Division. Later he returned to Lincoln Park but did not see Rubin there.

Pierson went on to testify that on Tuesday he met "Rubin and Nancy" in the park again. "Rubin said to me that he'd heard I'd been arrested Monday night and that he had an attorney call Police Headquarters to have me bonded out." Then Nancy left, and Rubin and Pierson walked toward a group of demonstrators. "We have got to create little Chicagos everywhere . . . We've got to have riots everywhere," Rubin told these people, according to Pierson. Pierson testified that Rubin added, "We should isolate one or two of the pigs and kill them." Then the two men walked over to a group of demonstration marshals— men and women who had been assigned by the Mobe to keep order among the protesters—and, according to Pierson, Rubin said, "We've got to do more to keep the crowd active . . . we want them in the park for the Bobby Seale speech that is going to be here tonight."

At this point in Pierson's testimony, Seale rose from his chair and objected, "You know my lawyer is not here, Your Honor, and I want my lawyer here to speak when he mentions my name and testifies against me. I have asked you," he reminded the judge, "before that jury came and was put together."

The judge ordered a marshal to return Seale to his chair, told the jury to disregard what it had just heard, and said that he would "deal appropriately with the incident in due course."

Pierson resumed his testimony. He told the jurors that

Rubin promised a march on the Amphitheatre for the following night, when there would be "a special surprise for the pigs." Pierson then testified that he advised Rubin to transfer Seale's speech from Lincoln to Grant Park, "where it would really foul up traffic at that time of day." Though Rubin called Mobe headquarters and recommended this plan, the idea was rejected, Pierson said, and the speech took place in Lincoln Park after all. Pierson then described Seale's speech, but made no reference to the "morgue slabs" that Schultz had mentioned in his opening statement.

According to his testimony, on Wednesday afternoon Pierson went with Rubin to the band shell in Grant Park, where "there was a large crowd that had gathered and where Rubin spoke to Rennie Davis and Tom Hayden on the stage of the band shell or right near it . . ." Pierson then testified that Rubin told him that "he and Abbie Hoffman, Tom Hayden and Bobby Seale . . . had gone to their out-of-state people and told them to bring back to their home cities the revolution that had started in Chicago." Then Pierson testified that some demonstrators had lowered an American flag and replaced it with a red flag, and that when the police arrived, Rubin shouted, "Kill the pigs," whereupon objects were thrown by the demonstrators at the police. With this, Pierson completed his direct testimony and the court recessed for lunch.

When the court reconvened, Weinglass moved to strike Pierson's testimony concerning the Lincoln Park speeches. "In order for the government to use a man's public utterances against him," Weinglass argued, "I feel the government must first . . . show that these words . . . presented a clear and present danger to the immediate society in the speaking area."

Judge Hoffman interrupted to ask Weinglass whether he meant that "if a man mounts a public rostrum and says 'I am going to kill Leonard Weinglass' . . . and thereafter [kills him] do you mean to say to me that those words are constitutionally protected?"

To this, Weinglass replied that neither Seale's nor Rubin's speeches were instances of the hypothetical case that the judge described. Pierson did not "testify that any actions were taken against any police officers who were in the vicinity where the speech was made or that the people there committed crimes against the police."

The judge then asked Weinglass whether he meant to say that the speeches were not admissible for purposes of showing intent.

"Yes," Weinglass answered. "You are using public speeches and asking a jury to infer back from those speeches to a certain intent when a person crossed state lines. If you [do that] you are going to prevent people from speaking their minds freely once they cross state lines, because anything they might say after they cross state lines can be used against them to show what their intent may have been when they crossed state lines."

"Oh," the judge replied, "I think the lecture bureaus would go out of business if what you said were true."

Schultz replied to Weinglass' motion with evident vigor but obscure logic. "If what [Seale and Rubin] said was not illegally seized under the Fourth Amendment, then it is not suppressible under the First Amendment. So . . . there's absolutely no argument at all . . . [Weinglass] is asking for people to say anything they please, unless [he] thinks it is a clear and present danger—where he got that proposition I can't imagine. There's absolutely no authority whatever for that. If Mr. Weinglass' novel proposition is that people in public can say anything they please, the prosecution would be completely emasculated."

The judge then denied Weinglass' motion, and the court recessed for the day.

To the defendants and to many members of the press,

such rulings as this revealed not simply the judge's bias in favor of the government, but a contemptuous regard for the defense and especially for Weinglass himself, who seemed unable to gain the judge's sympathetic attention. The judge's hostility seemed also to extend to the friends and relatives of the defendants who occupied the last three rows of benches in the press section. On the morning following Pierson's direct testimony, Seale's wife and four other Panthers were admitted by the marshals to seats in these rows. But when the judge entered the courtroom and saw them there, he slapped his bench angrily to get the attention of the marshal who sat in the little pulpit to his left. He then pointed toward the blacks and ordered the marshal to remove them, whereupon the marshal walked to where the Panthers were sitting and carried out the judge's order.

"I protest you taking my wife out of here," Seale said. "She has a right to be here and I also protest you barring black people from this building . . ." What Seale meant was that the marshals who guarded the entrances to the Federal Building had been ordered not only to inspect the purses and brief cases of everyone who entered, but also to exclude whoever looked suspicious. As a result, many blacks were sent away.

When the defense protested these arrangements, the judge replied that he had no control over who came into the building or who was admitted to the courtroom itself. Such matters, he explained, were left to the chief federal marshal, who was carrying out the orders of Chief Judge Campbell. "I have had phone calls from some very prominent persons," he said, "but I have told them to stand in line [if they wanted to be admitted as spectators] like everybody else."

But on the morning Seale's wife was told to leave, there were seated in the press section four fashionable ladies, none of whom, it turned out, was a reporter or had been made "to stand in line like everybody else." One of these ladies, the wife of a Chicago publicity agent, knew the judge personally and was planning a dinner party at which he would be the guest of honor. After having visited Judge Hoffman in his chambers that morning, she and her three friends had been invited by him to take seats among the reporters. This inequity angered some members of the press who had witnessed the expulsion of Mrs. Seale, and confirmed their belief that the judge had no interest in maintaining even the show of impartiality. On the following day, a reporter circulated among his colleagues a copy of some remarks written nearly a century before by a man named McConnell, who himself had been a Chicago judge and was a contemporary of Judge Gary, the judge who presided at the Haymarket Trial.

"From the first [we] were critical of Judge Gary," McConnell had written. "We did not like his rulings or his conduct. I never was in the courtroom during the trial when he did not have on the bench sitting with him, or near him, three to five women. He seemed to treat the affair as a Roman holiday. One day my wife sat on the bench and Gary showed her a puzzle. When I heard this I was shocked at his levity, with eight men sitting there in dire peril of their lives, certain to die if he continued to rule every motion against them as he did. Judge Rogers agreed with me that Gary was making new law and ignoring every rule of law which was designed to assure a fair trial for a defendant on trial for his life."

Upon the protests of the defense against the expulsion of the Panthers, the judge, perhaps embarrassed by the presence of the four well-dressed ladies, readmitted Mrs. Seale to the courtroom. Kunstler then proceeded to cross-examine Pierson, and the morning session of the trial soon came to an end. After taking their lunch in the main dining room of the Standard Club, a room which admits the wives of members, the four ladies visited the ruins of the Haymarket statue and did not return to court again.

That afternoon the judge seemed more than usually irritable. Late in the afternoon, he angrily sent the jury out of the room in order to scold Kunstler for asking questions of Pierson to which Schultz had objected, objections which the judge had sustained. "I excused the jury, Mr. Kunstler, to say on the record that your persistent disregard of the court's directions . . . is unprofessional conduct, and I want that statement on the record."

"Your Honor," Kunstler replied, "may we argue this point now? I [have] brought the law in. You called me unprofessional and I have a right to say what I think my authority is . . . I want to do what is right and I have brought in . . ."

"You are not doing what is right," the judge interrupted. "I don't want to argue it. It is elementary . . ."

"I have got McCormick on Evidence [a standard textbook on the subject]," Kunstler replied, "I have got Judge Holtzoff. I have got Judge Learned Hand . . ."

"We have got the United States Supreme Court up here," the judge answered.

"I have the Supreme Court as well, Your Honor," Kunstler said.

"I don't want you to do it and that is the reason why I excused the jury," Judge Hoffman concluded. He then recessed Court for the day.

On the following Monday the government showed the jury a television film of Dellinger speaking to a group of ten or twelve people in Grant Park on August 26. "What will come out of this [demonstration]," Dellinger said, "is that it heightens people's political consciousness [and] . . . a consciousness which is really heightened is a consciousness which takes action. . . . Therefore we want to make it very clear that rather than back down . . . under provocation and political harassment and arrest, we [will] be all the stronger and all the more determined . . . we will try to make [our] actions as vital and militant as possible."

The film also showed Rennie Davis, who said, "The police are surrounding us [but] we're going to have many demonstrations tomorrow, which is Lyndon Johnson's birthday. We're going to be demonstrating at the Polish Embassy, at the induction center, the First National Bank, CIA Headquarters, Police Headquarters and other [places] . . . " Davis then went on to describe other events that the demonstrators had planned. "Tomorrow at 11 A.M. while the Democrats are celebrating Johnson's birthday, we will have a Johnson pavillion of our own in the Coliseum . . . where we have a kind of artistic vomiting of the politics of joy, where we will trace through art and sculpture, pictures and performances, the accomplishments of Johnson from the first election that he stole in Texas to his accomplishments in putting down revolt in the black community in the United States." Davis then pointed to the police who had gathered menacingly in the park, and told his listeners, "If you don't want a riot, you'd better move out of here. If you want a riot you can stay."

Mr. Cubbage, the pale young Justice Department lawyer who introduced these films, explained that his purpose was "to show intent and leadership capacity on the part of defendant Dellinger and defendant Davis." But while the films may have revealed something about the "leadership capacity" of the two defendants, they were hardly substantial proof that their intentions had been to incite a riot, either at the time the film was made or in the months following April 12, 1968, the date on which the conspiracy was alleged to have begun.

Thus by the twelfth day of the trial the government had

failed to produce evidence that clearly supported the charges in the indictment. From none of the testimony given so far about the overt acts of the defendants during convention week could it be determined what their intentions had been before they arrived. What the government's evidence had shown, however, was that the particular acts and statements of the defendants, though consistent with the radical convictions they had long held, were often provoked by the hostile presence of the police and the refusal of the city to grant the permits for which the demonstrators had applied.

Thus it appeared that the government would have great difficulty in establishing a strict and incriminating relationship between the overt acts of the defendants and their earlier intentions, as Representative Edwards had warned when the anti-riot bill was before the House in 1967. For the government, much depended upon its attempt to show that Simon and Stahl had dealt with the defendants in good faith, while the defendants themselves had presented demands that were "non-negotiable," for the sake of provoking a confrontation with the police. But the statements of Mayor Daley and their reflection in the behavior of the other Chicago officials suggested that if the defendants had been unwilling to negotiate, so had the mayor's office. Therefore the defendants felt that under the Shuttlesworth ruling it was the city of Chicago that had broken the law.

Thus Kunstler told an interviewer during the second week of the trial that "the wrong defendants are in the dock" and that "the real defendants would be the mayor of Chicago, certain federal officials, certain highly placed people in the Democratic party and certain state officials of Illinois, who conspired together to ensure that there would be no protest demonstrations around the convention. And when all else failed they resorted to the brutality of just clubbing the demonstrators and preventing them from doing what they came to Chicago to do, namely [hold] a peaceful demonstration to protest the war, racism and poverty in the United States."

The defendants disagreed that the trial was "just another criminal case" on Judge Hoffman's calendar. Rather, they thought it was an attempt by the government to silence a political adversary, as Mayor Daley had tried to do at the convention itself. The defendants, however, chose not to be silenced.

On October 14, they petitioned the Court for an adjournment so that they could participate on the following day in the Vietnam moratorium, a national observance to protest the war. President Nixon had denounced this protest. "To allow government policy to be made in the streets," he said, "would destroy the democratic process." Kunstler told the Court that the defendants were "deeply involved" in the peace movement and were "obligated" to fill speaking engagements on the following day. For example, Kunstler explained, Davis had been invited to speak at Yale by President Kingman Brewster and Mayor Lee of New Haven. Foran objected. He said that the defendants were using "two sympathetic causes"—the war and "the tragic human flaw of racism"—to "take it upon themselves to tear down the fabric of American society." The defendants, he said, wanted only to "corrupt" the moratorium.

Judge Hoffman agreed. He denied Kunstler's motion and said, "I have no authority to close this court. I have received no order from the President or from the Chief Judge of this district."

In reply, Kunstler said, "The defendants are asking for much the same thing now that they wanted in Chicago a year ago—a permit from the Court to allow them to protest with the hundreds of other observers of the moratorium." The Judge, however, remained adamant. He told Kunstler that he had a different opinion from the defendants of

the duties of a citizen, and that perhaps he and Kunstler
were not citizens of the same country.

The government witness that morning was a Chicago
Vice Squad policeman named Riggio who had been assigned to follow Hayden during the convention. He testified that Hayden had let the air out of the tires of his
police car on Sunday, August 25, but that he had been
prevented from arresting him at the time by the angry
crowd. He did, however, arrest Hayden on the following
day. As for Hayden's intentions before he arrived in
Chicago, Riggio's testimony clarified nothing.

At the conclusion of Riggio's direct testimony, Weinglass
and Schultz engaged in a procedural controversy, in the
course of which Weinglass mentioned the name of Bobby
Seale. "Hey, you don't speak for me," Seale interrupted.
"I would like to speak on behalf of my own self. . . . How
come I can't speak in behalf of my own self?"

"You have a lawyer of record," the judge reminded him,
"and he has been of record here for you since September
24 . . . I direct you, sir, to remain quiet."

"And just be railroaded?" Seale replied.

"Will you remain quiet?" the judge asked him.

"I want to defend myself. Do you mind, please?" Seale
answered.

After the judge had asked the court reporter to take care
that this exchange appeared on the record, Kunstler asked
permission to speak, and the judge let him. "I will let you
speak as long as you want to . . . because your appearance
is still of record."

"That is right, Your Honor," Kunstler replied, "but when
a man stands up and says he wants to defend himself—"

The judge interrupted. "That is not the law in the middle
of a trial," he said, having forgotten, perhaps, that Seale
had first attempted to defend himself before the first
witness had been called, and thus before the trial had technically begun.

"That is not the law," Kunstler replied, having himself perhaps forgotten to remind the judge that Seale had not waited until the "middle of the trial" to make his request. "The Constitution says that any man may defend himself if he wants to."

"You speak of the Constitution as though it were a document printed yesterday," the judge replied. "We know about the Constitution way out here in the Middle West, too, Mr. Kunstler. . . . We really do. You would be amazed at our knowledge of constitutional law. . . . I am getting a little weary of these thrusts by counsel and I don't want any more of them. I had occasion to admonish you before . . . bring in the jury."

"You are not letting me argue—" Kunstler said.

"No," the judge replied. "You haven't anything to say that is important right now."

At their lunch-time press conference the defendants handed the newspapermen a copy of a note written by Seale in which he referred to the judge as "a bald-headed dog of a judge." Then Hayden discussed the Weathermen. He said, " . . . in 1968 we took entirely legal actions. This year these young people think the law is meaningless." But what they don't know, he then explained privately to a reporter, "is how rough the law can be." This, he said, is because they are "upper middle class." He was referring to what the Weathermen themselves call their "white skin privilege," of which they hoped to rid themselves in their confrontations with the police. In the opinion of the Weathermen, "You have no right," a radical journalist had explained earlier, "to think that your life is worth more than a black or a brown life. You're bullshit if you think you're more sensitive and intelligent and that you have a right to bourgeois self-preservation. You've got to be as willing to die as they are and they have this mental picture of themselves as Viet Cong charging into machine guns."

As for the defendants themselves, Hayden told the reporters, "Of course we're going across the country tomorrow."

But on the following morning the defendants appeared in court, as the judge had ordered. Each of them wore a black arm band, however, as did their two lawyers, and they brought with them a large flag of the National Liberation Front and a somewhat smaller American flag, which they spread out, side by side, on the defense table. As the day's spectators were taking their seats, a marshal pointed to the Vietnamese flag and shouted, "Take that thing off the table."

"We have a right to have it here if we want to," Abbie Hoffman told him, whereupon the marshal grabbed one end of the flag, while Hoffman held the other; the two men tugged in either direction. At last the marshal prevailed and removed the flag from the courtroom.

As he did so, Dellinger rose and, in a quavering voice, began to read the names of American soldiers who had died in Vietnam. His plan was to read these names and later the names of the Vietnamese dead. But by this time the judge had entered and ordered Dellinger to sit down.

"Mr. Hoffman," Dellinger told him, "we are observing the moratorium."

"I am Judge Hoffman, sir."

"I believe in equality," Dellinger replied, still standing, "so I prefer to call people Mister or by their first name."

"Sit down," Judge Hoffman ordered. "The clerk is about to call my case." Whereupon a marshal put Dellinger back in his chair. Within a few moments the jury was brought into the courtroom.

No sooner had the jurors taken their seats, however, than Dellinger got to his feet again. "Before the witness resumes the stand, we should like to propose a moment of silence."

"Will the marshal take that man into custody?" Foran shouted, whereupon the judge excused the jury.

"We only wanted a moment of silence," Dellinger explained.

"Your Honor, I object to this man speaking out in court," Foran said, his face white with rage.

Kunstler objected to Foran's tone. The prosecutor replied, more angrily than before, "This is outrageous. This man is a mouthpiece. Look at him, wearing an arm band like his clients, Your Honor. Any lawyer who . . . acts in conjunction with that kind of conduct before the court, Your Honor, the government protests his attitude and would like to cite . . ." Then, recognizing his error, he paused, and continued, "would like to move the Court to make note of his conduct."

"Your Honor," Kunstler replied, "I think the temper and the tone of voice and the expression of Mr. Foran's face speaks more than any picture could tell—"

"Of my contempt for Mr. Kunstler," Foran interjected.

"To call me a mouthpiece and Your Honor not to open his mouth and say that this is not to be done in your court, I think violates the sanctity of this court," Kunstler pleaded, with as much passion by now as Mr. Foran had shown. "This is a word that Your Honor knows is contemptuous and contumaceous."

"Don't tell me what I know," the judge said, as angry now as the two lawyers.

"I am wearing an arm band in memorium to the dead, which is no disgrace in this country," Kunstler said, more calmly.

"Did you say you wanted to admonish me?" the judge asked him.

"No. I want you to admonish him," Kunstler said, pointing to Foran.

"Let the record show," the judge replied, "I do not

admonish the United States Attorney because he was
properly representing his client, the United States of
America." He then turned to Kunstler and said in a voice
hardly audible with fury, "Sir, you a lawyer in the United
States District Court permitting your client to stand up in
the presence of the jury and disrupt these proceedings. I
do not know how to characterize it."

"Your Honor," Kunstler answered, "we do not permit
or not permit our clients. They are free, independent human
beings who have been brought by the government to
this courtroom."

"That is right," the judge replied. "They are free but
they will conform to the law and they will conform to the
directions of the court here, sir."

Thus, on moratorium day the defendants recapitulated
in miniature within the courtroom itself the sequence of
frustrated intentions and outraged responses—responses to
which the government replied in kind—that had been
typical of convention week itself. Therefore, what Judge
Hoffman had called just another criminal trial would now
proceed, whether the judge liked it or not, as a political
confrontation between the defendants and the government.
In the courtroom on the morning of moratorium day there
stood twelve federal marshals, all armed, guarding the defense table and the rows of benches occupied by the friends
and relatives of the defendants. A reporter remarked at
lunch time that in his imagination the walls of polished wood
had begun to give way so that he could see in his mind only
the bars of the lockup behind the Great Seal of the United
States which hung over the judge's bench.

On the morning of moratorium day the second of the
four major government witnesses took the stand. He was
Dwayne Oklepek, a graduate student at the Buffalo campus
of the State University of New York. In 1968, Oklepek had

taken a summer job with the Chicago columnist Jack Mabeley, who paid him $140 a week to infiltrate the Mobe and report on its activities.

Oklepek commenced his assignment on July 24, when he presented himself at the Mobe offices dressed in "blue jeans, a tee shirt and an old denim jacket." From that day until August 30 he worked with the Mobe staff. He "typed letters, did some filing and answered the phone when it rang." He also made notes of the conversations he overheard and reported them to Mr. Mabeley, as he later did to the FBI and the grand jury.

In response to Foran's questions, Oklepek testified that on August 9 he had attended a meeting in the Mobe office with Hayden, Davis, Froines, and about a dozen others. At this meeting Davis suggested the various routes that the demonstrators might use on their march to the Amphitheatre, and explained that the Mobe was still awaiting a reply from the city to its permit application. Davis also said, according to Oklepek, that if the city did not grant permits to sleep in Lincoln Park, and if the police ordered the demonstrators to leave after the eleven o'clock curfew, the demonstrators should go to the Loop area and "tie it up and bust it up." Davis said, according to Oklepek, that they should "disrupt traffic, smash windows, run through the streets."

Someone else in the room then advised against a certain route because it passed under some viaducts from which people might "throw missiles at" the demonstrators, "and things like that." According to Oklepek, Davis replied, "We will put marshals on those things and shoot the shit out of anyone who opens up on us."

Oklepek also testified that Davis had said, "All of these marches would be submitted to the city for their consideration for a parade permit . . . and if they don't accept any of these proposals we will know that they won't cooperate and that will be a declaration of war."

When someone then asked Davis what would happen if the demonstrators could not get through the police lines in Lincoln Park, Davis replied, according to Oklepek, "That's easy. We'll just riot."

Oklepek next described an afternoon in Lincoln Park on which the Mobe marshals, along with Hayden and Froines, were practicing a Japanese snake dance.

"At the completion of this training, was there a discussion?" Foran asked the witness.

"I object," Kunstler said. "That is a leading question."

"Yes. That is leading," the judge replied. "I sustain the objection."

Foran then restated the question. "At the completion of the training, did you overhear a conversation concerning it?"

"Objection, Your Honor," Kunstler said. "It's the same question."

"I don't perceive," the judge replied, "that it is the same question. I will let him answer that one over objection."

In the conversation to which Oklepek then testified, Hayden described the function of the Japanese dance. "It was," Hayden said, according to Oklepek, "the same type of formation that Japanese students had used to precipitate riots in 1960 which prevented President Eisenhower from visiting that country . . . This formation was very good for breaking through police lines in the event of an arrest situation and would be used during convention week to break police lines and try to escape from Lincoln Park."

It then began to rain, Oklepek testified. He, Hayden, and a few others took cover under a bridge, where Hayden discussed plans for a demonstration in Grant Park opposite the Hilton. According to Oklepek, Hayden said, "The people would proceed to Grant Park in groups of two or three or four so that they could not be arrested for marching in an illegal parade. And that marshals would circulate among all the protesters in Grant Park to get a consensus of opinion as to whether or not the group wanted to march to the Amphitheatre at that time and if they did, how this march would be conducted." Hayden also said, according to Oklepek, "that it was very unlikely a permit would be granted until the last moment or perhaps not at all."

Soon after this testimony the morning session concluded. The defendants, including Rubin—who had served his sentence and was now free—but not including Seale, who was returned to the lockup, left the Federal Building and walked in a group to the Civic Center Plaza, where some five thousand people had assembled to observe the moratorium. The defendants had been invited to address this rally. In the crowd David Stahl could be seen carrying a portable tape recorder. He said he was collecting oral greetings for Richard Elrod, the assistant corporation counsel, who had broken his neck when he attempted to tackle a marcher during the Weathermen demonstration the week before and who was now in the hospital. Meanwhile, Dellinger, who was leading the defendants to the speakers' platform, found his way to the podium blocked by an angry Chicago businessman. This man was one of the organizers of the moratorium and presumably agreed with Foran that Dellinger's presence would only "corrupt" the ceremony. Another moratorium leader, however, a businessman named Gordon Sherman, took the microphone and introduced Dellinger despite the objections of his colleague. Thus Dellinger was able to speak. In the same quavering voice with which he had read the names of the dead, he told the crowd of the judge's actions in court that morning.

Oklepek completed his testimony in the afternoon, but added little to what he had said in the morning. He returned on the following day for cross-examination.

That morning, while the jury was out of the courtroom, the marshals once more removed a group of blacks from the seats at the rear of the press section. According to

Seale, "It was actually an old court matron who seemed to be the cause of it all. Every time I looked around at her she'd almost be breathing down the necks of every Black Panther and black person in the courtroom. . . . All of a sudden she told some chick to get out and another cat to get out. They weren't being noisy, but she was getting them out of the courtroom. Kunstler got up and said, 'Why are they removing black people from the courtroom?'

"I think there is a bit of racism involved myself," Seale replied from the defense table. This remark prompted the judge to write agitatedly in a ledger that he kept on his bench. Upon Kunstler's protest, however, the blacks were soon readmitted, and Seale returned to the copy of Fanon's *Wretched of the Earth* that he had been reading.

When the judge had finished writing in his ledger he turned to Kunstler and said, "Anyone who knows me knows that there is no discrimination in my courtroom." He then reminded the defendants of his decision in the South Holland case, which prompted a ripple of laughter among the reporters. Though it was not the defendants who laughed, the judge turned angrily to Kunstler. "Your clients sit there," he scolded, "and laugh at a judge of the highest trial court in the United States."

The defense completed its cross-examination of Oklepek on the following day. Kunstler managed to elicit from the witness that Davis had once told him that "there would be no dictators" among the Mobe leaders, and that these leaders would, as Hayden had suggested, according to Oklepek's earliest testimony, merely propose alternatives to which the demonstrators could respond as they liked. Oklepek also admitted under cross-examination that in his testimony before the grand jury he had described "Hayden's views as always contrary to everyone else's."

Foran, in his redirect examination—which is a further examination of the witness in response to questions that have been raised on cross-examination—asked Oklepek to read the complete statement that he had made to the grand jury concerning Hayden's contrary views. This, Foran felt, would show that Hayden's influence had not been so marginal as Oklepek's earlier testimony had made it seem. Thus Oklepek read the following sentence from the transcript of his grand jury testimony: "Mr. Hayden was considered violent by his own intimates and also extremely irrational—"

Kunstler then objected. What Hayden's intimates thought of him, he said, was "pure hearsay testimony," that is, testimony based not on what the witness himself observed but on the words of a third party who is not himself available in court for cross-examination. Because the truth of such statements cannot be tested in court, hearsay testimony is, as a rule, excluded from evidence.

"The motion," Judge Hoffman ruled, "will be denied."

But the government lawyers agreed with Kunstler that the judge was mistaken in this ruling. When Oklepek's redirect testimony was concluded, Schultz hastened to urge Judge Hoffman to correct the record. What he feared was that Oklepek's inadmissible testimony, if it remained on the record, would constitute "reversible error," that is, an improper ruling by the court which then becomes the basis for an appellate reversal of the verdict. "Mr. Kunstler," he said, "made an objection, if the Court please, that the part of the answer that was read by the witness was what other people said. [Kunstler] said it was hearsay, which, of course, it is . . . The question was asked, of course, to give the whole statement and I think it would be appropriate—"

But the judge did not wait to hear what Schultz thought would be appropriate. "That was the reason I ruled as I did. I was not considering it a hearsay matter. It was what was contained in the transcript before the grand jury."

"That's right," Schultz replied, "and the reason I bring it up is that I think it would be appropriate, if the Court please, for the court simply to instruct the jury that state- ment . . . was admitted only for the purpose of giving the complete answer, not for the truth of those statements." The judge then started to address the jury, but Kunstler had already begun his reply to Schultz.

"Your Honor," Kunstler said, "I think all Mr. Schultz has done is emphasize the fact that Your Honor has permitted hearsay to be read to a jury and I think that this attempt to clear it up is not going to be successful. The defendants have been hopelessly prejudiced by the inclusion of hear- say evidence before this jury."

"Not at all," the judge replied. "Anyone reading this transcript will know that hearsay evidence was not per- mitted. It was the reading of what was said on an occasion."

"Your Honor," Kunstler replied, "if that isn't hearsay I have never heard it. I move for a mistrial on behalf of all the defendants on the grounds that impermissible testimony has been allowed to be heard by this jury."

The judge denied the motion, but in the confusion he also failed to instruct the jury to disregard the hearsay testi- mony, as Schultz had urged him to do. Thus a serious procedural error remained on the record.

The following witness—one whom Schultz described as "one of our short witnesses" to distinguish him from such "long witnesses" as Oklepek—was a reporter for a San Diego television station. His name was Gilman and he was paid $150 a month as an informer for the FBI. For this work he also received between $30 and $50 a month in expenses. Gilman testified that on July 25, 1968, at about 8:30 P.M., he saw and heard Dellinger in Room 300 of the life sciences building at San Diego State College, where Dellinger was addressing a group of about one hundred students.

Before Gilman could tell the jury what Dellinger had said on that occasion, Weinglass repeated his objection that testimony concerning a speech by one of the defendants was inadmissible under the First Amendment. To augment his earlier argument he cited an opinion by Justice Douglas in 1966, which held that the Constitution does not permit the government to introduce speeches that did not constitute a clear and present danger in the circumstances in which they were given. On previous occasions when Weinglass had argued such motions, the judge had excused the jury, since their concern was not with questions of law but with the facts of the case. This time, however, the judge ruled that since "the question is not so complicated" the jury could remain. Weinglass thus argued before the jury that "to have undercover agents appear at public rallies and report in a later criminal prosecution the content of a speech [will] chill the desire of people to engage in public debate."

Schultz then replied, "What Mr. Weinglass is saying is that nobody can be prosecuted in public for making incriminating statements." Then he gave as an example the case of a man who says, "I am going to kill Mr. X tomorrow . . . and then tomorrow Mr. X is murdered . . . and the man who made that statement is seen in the vicinity of the murder." Weinglass, Schultz argued, would find X's statement of his intentions inadmissible on First Amendment grounds. He would say that "because we don't want to chill anybody's right to speak, people should be able to say anything they want."

But Schultz's argument did not go to the point Weinglass had made. Instead, it recalled the objection that the ACLU had made in support of Representative Edwards when the House of Representatives had debated the anti-riot bill; that is, that a logical confusion arises when a statute permits a separation in time between a defendant's stated intent and the commission of the criminal act itself. According to the argument of the ACLU, Mr. X's statement the day before the murder would contribute to evidence of his guilt only if it could also be shown that he had held these views at the time of the murder itself. Thus Schultz inadvertently suggested a further line of argument that Weinglass might have taken against Gilman's testimony. Weinglass did not, however, seize the opportunity.

Schultz's arguments often suffered from logical flaws of this sort, but he pleaded so vehemently and used his hands so meticulously to chop the air into precise geometrical segments that his words occasionally seemed to have more substance than they actually did. To Schultz's argument, Weinglass replied that if Mr. X confesses to a murder, after one has taken place, then obviously his words can be used against him, but "the government cannot in this country prosecute a man for what he is thinking or for what his ideas are." He then cited Holmes' opinion in the Schenck Case and contrasted the clear and present danger doctrine with the government's attempt in the present case "to portray through a public speech what [it] thinks Mr. Dellinger's thoughts and ideas are and then attempt to ask the jury to find in a criminal prosecution a citizen of the United States guilty for his thoughts and ideas as expressed in a public forum."

Schultz replied that it was a "misstatement" to say that the government was prosecuting Dellinger for what he had been thinking. "He is being prosecuted for his intent," whereupon Schultz drew a vertical line through the air with his outstretched hand to distinguish "intent" from "thoughts and ideas." "He is being prosecuted," Schultz insisted, "for what he was planning, what acts he intended to take."

The judge then overruled Weinglass' objection. Gilman testified that Dellinger had said, "Burn your draft cards.

Resist the draft. Violate the laws. Go to jail. Disrupt the United States government in any way you can to stop this insane war . . . I am going to Chicago to the Democratic National Convention where there may be problems." Then, according to Gilman, Dellinger shook his fist and said, "I'll see you in Chicago."

Weingless then moved to strike Gilman's testimony. Dellinger's speech was not an "open confession . . . that he was about to commit a crime," as Schultz had advised the court when he offered the analogy with Mr. X, the hypothetical murderer. "There is no mention of Mr. Dellinger's intention to commit a crime, directly or indirectly, in the city of Chicago from what I heard and so I don't think the speech as given by this witness passes muster even under the prosecutor's own test."

Schultz replied that he felt Dellinger's speech did reveal criminal intentions, and the judge agreed that Gilman's testimony should be admitted.

That afternoon an FBI agent testified that he had heard Rubin say in a speech in New York that "people should mass and cause disruptions to the election system in the United States and that thousands and thousands of people will go to Chicago to implement these disruptive tactics." Weinglass objected to this testimony, as he had to Gilman's. This time he cited the ruling of the Supreme Court in the Brandenberg Case, in which the Court had said, ". . . the mere abstract teaching of the moral propriety or even the moral necessity for a resort to force and violence is not the same as preparing a group for violent action and steeling it to such action."

Foran objected to "this argument . . . it keeps coming up over and over again." The defendants, Foran argued, were not on trial for their speeches but for their intentions. "There is nothing illegal in my saying 'I am going to kill the marshal,' " Foran said. "But to say that because I said it in public it could never be used as evidence of my intent to kill the marshal, if I did later do it, is such a sophomoric argument that it isn't even close."

Thus Foran too sank into the spongy logical ground on which the anti-riot statute rested. The defendants were not on trial for a criminal act comparable to murder, a crime in which the act of killing is the substantial evil. The prosecutor, in a trial for murder, need only show that the defendant killed someone and that his intention to do so concurred with the act itself. In such a prosecution, the defendant's statement "I am going to kill Mr. X" could be offered as evidence of criminal intent, provided that it could also be shown that he committed the murder. However, under the anti-riot statute, the defendant's acts are not in themselves the substantial evil to which the federal law is addressed. The issue instead is the defendant's intentions as he crosses state lines. His acts—that is, his speeches—are presumed innocent under the First Amendment, or, if they are actually inciteful under the Brandenberg ruling, they are still beyond federal jurisdiction. They are local crimes. Federal jurisdiction, in such cases, extends only to illegal activities that occur continuously from one side of a state line to another, revealing an unbroken criminal intention.

For example, the Mann Act forbids the interstate transportation of women for immoral purposes. Under this law, the criminal intention is the substantial evil. The act of driving a woman from New York to New Jersey may in itself be quite innocent. It is the defendant's intention to engage her in interstate prostitution that constitutes the crime. Such intentions may be revealed by the acts of striking a bargain on one side of a state line and completing it on the other—acts which in themselves are subject to local, not federal, jurisdiction. The federal crime consists in the continuous act of illegal transport commencing on one side of the state line and concluding on the other.

The anti-riot act is not, however, quite analogous to
the Mann Act, on which it was to some extent modeled.
Under the Mann Act, the illegal transport is a continuous
act, reflecting an unbroken intention. To prove a comparable crime under the anti-riot act would require the
government to show that Rubin's speech in New York
and his speeches in Chicago revealed a similar unbroken intention to go from New York to Chicago to incite a riot.
Theoretically, this would require showing an unbroken
series of inciteful statements commencing on one side of
a state border and continuing on the other. In the case of
Rubin and the other defendants, the government could
show no such continuous chain of acts—comparable to the
procurer's arrangement to transport the woman—to demonstrate the continuity of their allegedly illegal intentions.

Meanwhile, the speeches of the defendants were in themselves either innocent under the Brandenberg ruling or not
subject to federal jurisdiction. Under federal law, therefore, the speeches were innocent acts, equivalent to Foran's
hypothetical statement "I am going to kill the marshal," in
which Foran admitted there is "nothing illegal"—provided
that the speaker does not kill the marshal.

The logic of Foran's analogy was that the incitement of
the Chicago riots was equivalent to the murder of the
marshal. But the defendants were not on trial for the
incitement of these riots. They were on trial only for
their intentions. And, according to Foran, the mere statement of an intention does not become evidence of a crime
unless the act itself is performed; or unless, as the principle
of federal jurisdiction implicit in such laws as the Mann
Act holds, the statements of the defendants reflect a continuous illegal purpose. Thus Foran's argument should
logically have supported Weinglass' objection to the testimony against Rubin. The judge, however, ruled in favor
of Foran.

Throughout the trial so far, Seale, except for the few occasions on which he had spoken out to insist on his right to defend himself or complain about the treatment by the marshals of black spectators, had remained silent, and appeared to hold himself aloof from the proceedings of the Court. Usually he read his volumes of Fanon or the *Autobiography of Malcolm X*, and occasionally he made notes on the yellow legal pads that were piled beside him. Though the defendants and the two lawyers met with him in the lockup at the end of each afternoon session, he seldom joined in their conferences at the defense table, and he showed little interest in the testimony of the government's witnesses.

On the morning of October 20, while a Chicago detective named Tobin was on the stand, Seale was bent over the defense table writing on his yellow pads. Tobin's testimony was that Davis had been in front of the Conrad Hilton on Wednesday, August 28. According to the witness, Davis had pointed to a television camera mounted over the entrance to the hotel and then pointed to a line of police guarding the entrance. He told the demonstrators to kick the police in the shins because this would provoke the police to charge the demonstrators, and the cameras would record the attack. The spectators responded to Tobin's testimony with laughter, but Seale paid no attention either to the witness, the laughter, or the judge's warning that such outbursts would not be tolerated. He continued to write on his yellow pad.

When the trial resumed that afternoon, Seale handed what he had written to the judge's elderly clerk, who then announced, "There is a motion here of defendant Bobby Seale to be permitted to defend himself."

"I will hear you, Mr. Seale," the judge said.

Seale walked to the lectern and explained that ever since the arraignment in April, he had assumed that Charles

Garry could be his lawyer. "It has been my contention all along . . . that the other lawyers would appear in court only for pretrial hearings." He then read his motion.

"I, Bobby Seale, demand and move the court as follows. Because I am denied the lawyer of my choice, Charles R. Garry, I cannot represent myself as my attorney would be doing, but because I am forced to be my own counsel and to defend myself, I require my release from custody, from the bail presently in force, so that I can interview necessary witnesses, do the necessary investigating, do necessary factual research and all the other things that being in custody makes impossible:

1. The right to cross-examine witnesses and examine witnesses of my choice.

2. The right to make all necessary motions that I as a layman can think of to help my defense and prove my innocence and to argue those motions.

3. The right to do any and all other things for myself that I am forced to do because I am denied the services of my lawyer Charles R. Garry."

When Seale completed his statement Kunstler rose, walked to the lectern, and said that the other defendants would like to join in this motion. He then read from various Supreme Court decisions on the subject of legal self-defense. Kunstler told the judge that in 1942 the Court had said, "Essential fairness is lacking if an accused cannot put his case effectively in Court. But the Constitution does not force a lawyer upon a defendant. He may waive his constitutional rights to assistance of counsel if he knows what he is doing and his choice is made with eyes open." Kunstler then argued that in 1962 the Second Circuit Court of Appeals had ruled that the right of legal self-defense arises "out of the Federal Constitution and is not the mere product of legislation or judicial decision." In another case the same appellate court had said, "The right of an accused to defend himself rests on two bases: he must have the means of presenting his best defense and to this end, he must have complete confidence in his counsel. Without such confidence a defendant might be better off defending himself. And, moreover, even in cases where the accused is harming himself by insisting on conducting his own defense, respect for individual autonomy requires that he be allowed to go to jail under his own banner if he so desires and if he makes the choice with his eyes open."

Kunstler then reminded the judge that on September 29 Seale had filed a written notice with the court discharging his lawyers. Seale interrupted to say that he had done this on the twenty-seventh. But both Seale and Kunstler were mistaken. Seale had filed his notice on Friday morning, September 26, before the first government witness had been called to the stand.

Schultz then replied. "Your Honor," he said, "this is a ploy. It's just a simple, obvious ploy . . . On the first day of the trial, September 24 . . . Mr. Kunstler filed an appearance . . . to represent Bobby Seale . . . Then on Friday Mr. Seale stood up and said, 'I fire all my lawyers.' It's true that an individual has the right, if he wants, to defend himself . . . But he can't under the circumstances in this case, and that is, having a total of five lawyers—Mr. Tigar, Mr. Birnbaum, Mr. Kunstler, Mr. Bass and Mr. Garry—and then fire four of them and say 'I want this one or I won't go ahead,' and saying that after the trial has begun."

Seale had not, in fact, refused to go ahead with the trial unless Garry could defend him. On the 26th, when the judge refused to postpone the trial, Seale arose to defend himself. Neither is it clear that Seale had made his motion "after the trial [had] begun," as Schultz told the Court. Lawyers are divided on the question of whether a trial technically begins before the selection of the jury, which in the present case was September 24, or before the first

witness has been called, which was the day on which
Seale filed his motion. In Seale's case, however, this technicality was not the main issue. A defendant may choose to
defend himself whenever he likes, provided his decision,
in the Court's opinion, does not interfere with an orderly
proceeding. The judge is required to grant this right if it
seems reasonable to him that the defendant is not engaged
merely in what Schultz called a "ploy" to upset the trial.

Thus Schultz should properly have attempted to prove
that Seale's attempt to defend himself on the twenty-sixth
was intended merely as a disruption; that it was, in fact,
a "ploy." Schultz, however, could produce no evidence
to this effect, so he returned to his original theme that
"there were other lawyers representing Seale . . . and this
is why [the Court] did not grant him the right" to defend
himself, an argument which seemed inconsistent with the
appellate rulings cited by Kunstler. Then Schultz added,
"The ploy is so obvious . . . I might add, it's silly. It's
ludicrous. The defendants are trying to create error in
the record. . . . The defendants know that if Mr. Seale
were to cross-examine witnesses here and argue to the jury,
we would have a mistrial in two minutes. There is absolutely no doubt about that." But, while Schultz may have
had no doubt that the ploy was obvious, neither did he
have proof that he could offer in Court. What he may,
however, have had were transcripts of intercepted telephone
conversations between Seale in Cook County Jail and Garry
in San Francisco. Five months after the trial was over,
Schultz petitioned the Court to add to the record transcripts of Seale's telephone calls from jail. Since Seale had
called only Garry, it was these conversations that the defense assumed the government had overheard. Perhaps these
conversations suggested to Schultz that Seale and his lawyer were planning to disrupt the trial. However, the
wiretaps were clearly illegal and could not be offered in
open Court.

Schultz then argued that the defendants "know perfectly well that the Court cannot permit Mr. Seale, having been represented by five lawyers, to get rid of them in the middle of the trial by standing up and saying 'I get rid of them' and then proceed with the trial."

Seale answered that he had not made his request in "the middle of the trial. A signed statement was filed here a month before the trial began that . . . Mr. Garry would be the only one representing me . . . so this idea of a ploy and all is not true. . . . When I was taken here incommunicado for some six days and arrived here some two or three days [before the trial] and talked to my lawyer on Thursday night [September 25] on the phone from Cook County Jail, and he said that he would definitely have to enter the hospital . . . the next morning I brought my written statement here that I wrote in jail myself."

Judge Hoffman replied by reading from the trial transcript for September 24, the day on which Kunstler filed his appearance for Seale. On that day Kunstler had told the judge, "Mr. Weinglass will be representing four of the defendants and I will be representing four of the defendants."

"Have you prepared and are you ready to file an appearance in behalf of these four?" the judge had asked.

"They have already been filed, Your Honor," Kunstler had replied.

The judge then put the transcript aside and ruled that on the basis of this assurance, "The defendant Seale is now represented by competent counsel." He then proceeded to read several judicial opinions to the effect that "the right to discharge one's counsel and defend himself is not unqualified if an accused seeks to exert it after the trial has commenced." In the rulings he cited, the courts had said that judges had been right to deny such motions when it appeared that to grant them would disrupt the proceedings or delay or confuse the trial.

"I find now," Judge Hoffman ruled, "that to allow the defendant Seale to act as his own attorney would produce the same disruptive effect . . . Moreover . . . the complexity of the case makes self-representation inappropriate and the defendant would be more prejudiced were he allowed to conduct his own defense than if his motion were to be denied." The judge then called the jury back.

When the jury entered the courtroom Seale was still standing at the lectern facing the judge. "I would like to say, Judge, that you denied my motion to defend myself and you know this jury is prejudiced against me."

"I will ask you to sit down," the judge replied.

Seale continued to stand. "You know," he said, "that the jury can't go home to their loved ones and their homes, and you know they have been made prejudiced against me."

Thereupon the judge excused the jurors, who silently filed out through the door by which they had just entered. As they left, Seale said, "I should be allowed to defend myself. I should be allowed to speak so I can defend myself."

"Mr. Seale," the judge said, "I must admonish you that any outburst such as you have just indulged in will be appropriately dealt with at the right time during this trial and I must order you not to do it again."

"In other words," Seale replied, "you are going to put me in contempt of court for speaking on behalf of myself? . . . Is that what you are saying to me? I want to be clear."

"I will not argue with you," the judge answered. "You have lawyers to speak for you."

"I am my own legal counsel," Seale said. "I don't want these lawyers. The jury is prejudiced against me, and you know it because of those jive threatening letters. How can that jury give me a fair trial? I will speak for myself," Seale said. "I still want to defend myself and I know I have a right." He then turned to the defense table and said, "I just want to let him know. That racist. That fascist. You know what happens when the black man tries to get a fair trial in this country. The United States government, Nixon and the rest of them." Then he turned once more to the judge and said, "Go ahead and continue. I'll watch and get railroaded."

Two days later, on October 22, Kunstler again attempted to withdraw his appearance for Seale, and once more the judge denied his motion. Seale then arose and walked to the lectern.

"Can I speak on that?" he asked.

"Not at this time," the judge answered. "This is not your motion. This is the motion of Mr. William Kunstler for leave to withdraw as your lawyer."

"Well, this man has misconstrued a lot of things concerning my right to defend myself and he knows he did. They can jack you up and get you to sit there," he continued, pointing to the judge, "and say rotten, crazy stuff concerning my right to defend myself."

The judge then ordered the marshal to put Seale back in his chair.

"Well, I still want my right to defend myself," Seale said. "This is a railroad operation and you know it, from Nixon on down. They got you running around here violating my constitutional rights."

Later that morning an undercover policeman testified that a black demonstrator had approached Davis in Grant Park on August 28 and proposed that the revolution begin "right now." Schultz then moved that a picture of this demonstrator be entered into evidence. "We have this picture," Schultz said, "of the boy with the Black Power symbol fist on his sweat shirt . . ."

"That's not a black power sign," Seale protested. "Somebody correct the court on that. That's the power to the people sign . . . and he is deliberately distorting that and that's a racist technique."

"If the court please," Schultz interrupted. "This man has repeatedly called me a racist—"

"You are, Dick Schultz," Seale shouted. "Yes, you are."

The judge then excused the jury and said, "Mr. Seale and Mr. Kunstler, your lawyer, I must admonish you that such outbursts are considered by the Court to be contemptuous and will be dealt with appropriately in the future."

"Your Honor," Kunstler explained with exasperation, "the defendant was trying to defend himself."

"The defendant was not defending himself," the judge replied angrily.

"I was too defending myself," Seale exclaimed. ". . . I want to defend myself and ask him if he isn't lying. . . . No siree, I am going to request that you understand that this man is erroneously representing symbols directly related to the party of which I am chairman.

When the judge returned to his courtroom after the noon recess he found Seale seated alone at the defense table. The front row of the press section was occupied by a group of ten Panthers and on the benches behind them were more than the usual number of wildly clad reporters representing the underground press. When the marshals, upon the arrival of the judge, ordered the spectators to stand, the Panthers refused. The judge himself then ordered them to rise, and nine complied. The tenth refused, whereupon a black marshal dragged him from the courtroom.

"You're a pig for taking him out," Seale shouted at the marshal. The nine remaining Panthers then raised their fists in the party salute and exclaimed "Right on!" From the rear of the press section came cries of "Oink, oink," addressed to the marshal.

When the courtroom regained its calm, Kunstler told the judge that the "other defendants have purchased a birthday cake for Chairman Bobby Seale whose birthday is today [but] the marshals would not let them bring the cake into court. Since the only way the defendants can get the cake to Seale is to give it to him in the courtroom, they request permission to present him with the cake before the jury comes in."

"Mr. Kunstler," the judge replied, "I won't even let anyone bring me a birthday cake. I don't have food in my chambers. I don't have any beverages. This is a courthouse and we conduct trials here. I'm sorry."

"The cake is not to eat here," Kunstler told the judge.

"Your application will be denied," Judge Hoffman ruled.

The seven defendants meanwhile were waiting in the corridor outside the courtroom. Rubin was carrying the cake, on which was written "Free Huey. Free Bobby." No sooner had the judge denied Kunstler's motion, than a marshal left the courtroom, entered the corridor, and wrested the cake from Rubin. "That's a cakenapping," Abbie Hoffman shouted.

Davis, as he entered the courtroom, explained, "Hey, Bobby, they arrested your cake."

"They've arrested a cake," Seale replied, "but they can't arrest a revolution."

"Right on!" the Panthers cried, raising their fists, whereupon Seale turned to them.

He warned, "Don't say nothing no more brothers. Just sit in the court and observe the proceedings. O.K? All right?"

"Mr. Seale, I will issue the orders around here," the judge advised.

"They don't take orders from racist judges," Seale said. "But I can convey orders to them and they will follow them."

"If you continue with that sort of thing," Judge Hoffman warned, "you may expect to be punished for it."

"We have protested our rights for four hundred years

and we have been shot and killed and murdered and brutal-
ized . . ." Seale muttered as he turned from the bench.

The judge then ordered the court stenographer to be
sure that Seale's last remarks were on the record.

"I hope you get mine for the record too," Seale told her.
Then Dellinger spoke up. "I think you should understand
that we support Bobby Seale in this . . ." He turned to his
fellow defendants, as if to ask for confirmation. When there
was no response, Dellinger added, "At least, I do."

"I haven't asked you for any advice here, sir," the judge
answered.

"If you let me defend myself, you could instruct me on
proceedings that I can act—" Seale asked.

The judge cut him short. "Let the record show that defendant Seale has refused to be quiet in the face of the admonition of this court."

"Let the record show that Bobby Seale speaks out in behalf of his constitutional rights, his right to defend himself,
his right to speak in behalf of himself in this courtroom,"
Seale replied.

"Bring in the jury, Mr. Marshal," the judge ordered.

"Please do," Seale said.

On the following day another FBI informer appeared in
court as a government witness. This was a man named Louis
Salzberg, a photographer, who had ingratiated himself with
various radical groups in New York, and in this way come
to know Dellinger and Hoffman. For his work as an undercover agent the FBI paid him $10,000 over a period of two
years.

Salzberg testified that he had attended a meeting in a New
York church, where he heard a speech by Hayden. Schultz
asked the witness to identify Hayden at the defense table.
As Salzberg approached the table, Dellinger said to him in
a low voice, "Quite a letdown. I am really disappointed in
you, Louis." Several other defendants squealed, "Oink,
oink."

Salzberg then walked over to where Hayden was sitting and Schultz said, "May the record show that the witness has identified Thomas Hayden."

"The record," the judge agreed, "may so indicate that he has identified him by placing his finger on the defendant Hayden's back physically."

Salzberg then testified that Hayden had said in his speech that the Mobe was "hoping to get at least 200,000 people to Chicago . . ." where they "hoped to fuck up the convention."

On Monday, October 27, the government introduced the third of its major witnesses. However, before this witness was brought to the stand Schultz reminded the judge that Seale had not yet come into the courtroom.

"Oh," the judge said, "I thought he was here," whereupon he ordered a marshal to bring Seale down from the lockup. Seale arrived just as the jury entered its box.

"Ladies and gentlemen of the jury, good morning," Judge Hoffman said genially.

But before the jurors could answer, Seale turned to them and said, "Good morning, ladies and gentlemen of the jury. As I said before, I hope you don't blame me for anything."

"Mr. Marshal," the judge said with exasperation, "will you tell that man to sit down. Mr. Seale is saying something there—"

"I know I am saying something. You know I am getting ready to speak out in behalf of my constitutional rights again, don't you?"

"I will ask you to sit down, sir," the judge warned, "you have a very competent lawyer of record here."

"He is not my lawyer," Seale said calmly. "I fired him before that jury was even picked and put together. . . . What about my constitutional right to defend myself and have my lawyer?"

"Your constitutional rights—" the judge began.

"You are denying them," Seale interrupted, shouting. "You have been denying them. Every other word you say is denied, denied, denied, denied," he screamed, "and you begin to oink in the faces of the masses of the people in this country. That is what you begin to represent, the corruptness of this rotten government for four hundred years."

A marshal then approached Seale and asked him to sit down.

"Why don't you knock me in the mouth?" Seale asked him. "Try that."

"Sit down," the marshal, a towering black man, warned.

The judge then excused the jurors, and as they filed out Seale called after them, "I hope you don't blame me for those false, lying notes and letters that said the Black Panther party threatened the jury. It's a lie and you know it's a lie and the government did it to taint the jury against me . . . You got that?" he shouted as the last juror left the room. "This racist government with its superman notions and comic book politics: we're hip to the fact that Superman saved no black people."

Kunstler then stood up and addressed the Court. "I might say, Your Honor, you know that I have tried to withdraw from this and you know that Mr. Seale—"

"I don't know what you tried to do," the judge interrupted. "I know that your appearance is of record and I know I have your assurance orally that you represent this man."

"You have a withdrawal of that assurance, Your Honor," Kunstler reminded him. "You know that on September 30 . . ." he said, referring to the date on which he told the judge in his chambers of his intention to withdraw.

"You represent him and the record shows it," the judge shouted.

"Your Honor, you can't go on those semantics. This man wants to defend himself."

"This isn't semantics. I am not fooled by all this business," the judge replied, leaning across his bench, as if perhaps he too may have become aware of Seale's intercepted conversations from jail.

"I still demand the right to defend myself," Seale repeated. "You are not fooled? After you have walked over people's constitutional rights? The Sixth Amendment. The Fifth Amendment. You have done everything you could with those jive, lying witnesses up there presented by these pig agents of the government to lie and say and condone some rotten, fascist crap by racist cops and pigs that beat people's heads. I demand my constitutional rights. Demand. Demand. Demand," Seale shouted, as the huge black marshal pushed him back into his chair.

Schultz then introduced his witness, a smooth-shaven young man named Frapolly, who identified himself as a student at Northeastern Illinois State College, where he had been, since the summer of 1968, a member of the College Peace Council, SDS, the Chicago Peace Council, the Student Mobilization, and the National Mobilization. From his seat at the defense table Dellinger interrupted to say, "There are no members of the National Mobilization Committee," by which he meant that the National Mobe was not a membership organization but a steering committee. His interruption was ignored by the Court. The witness went on to explain that when he had worked with the Mobe he had worn his "hair exceedingly long," and had grown a goatee and a mustache. He then testified that he had been a member of the Chicago Police Department since 1966.

Frapolly explained that on August 9, 1968, he had attended a meeting at Mobe headquarters where he saw, among others, Rennie Davis, David Dellinger, Lee Weiner, Dwayne Oklepek, and Irv Bock, another police spy who was to be the last of the four major government witnesses. At this point the defendants muttered "Oink, oink," but the judge paid no attention. Frapolly then testified to the same conversation concerning routes to the Amphitheatre that Oklepek had described. Davis, Frapolly said, talked about plans for a "mill-in" on August 28 in which "from fifty to one hundred thousand people would go through the Loop and try to disrupt it." Davis also said, according to Frapolly, "We should use music and sex to lure the McCarthy kids, young delegates and the children of prominent people to a rock festival on August 25." He then described the same snake dance practice in Lincoln Park that Oklepek had seen. As he watched this practice, Frapolly testified, a demonstrator walked up to Davis and told him that he had seen an army jeep on whose radiator was strung a net of barbed wire. Frapolly testified that Davis had asked whether anyone knew how to cope with such a vehicle should it be used against the demonstrators, and Frapolly said that he himself proposed that "we could set up a grappling hook and a rope and throw it into the wire and that would stop it," an idea that Davis approved, according to Frapolly.

That night there was a meeting, Frapolly said, at which Davis told a group of demonstration marshals, "We know what bastards [the Chicago police are] and we can't avoid a confrontation with them—and that should be our attitude toward the police." Then Frapolly described several subsequent meetings in which Davis, Hayden, Froines, Weiner, and Abbie Hoffman, among others, outlined the demonstrations planned for convention week; for example, the unbirthday party for President Johnson in the Coliseum on August 27, and the "mill-in" in the Loop on the following day. At none of these meetings, however, did the defendants or anyone else urge that these events should result in violence, according to Frapolly's testimony. Frapolly then described a meeting of demonstration leaders in Lincoln Park on August 20. "At about 4:30," he said, "a CBS camera crew came to take pictures and everyone was supposed to go into a snake dance. We snake-danced for about fifteen minutes. The cameras photographed this. After this we did some calisthenics and two people were showing some karate and judo. They were showing kicks to the groin, judo chops to the front of the neck, the temple, the bridge of the nose and they were also showing punches to the solar plexus."

The Court then recessed for lunch. When the trial resumed that afternoon, eighteen federal marshals were poised throughout the courtroom, twelve of them standing two abreast in the aisle that separated the press benches from those reserved for spectators. Kunstler objected to "this army of marshals. It will give a false impression to the jury."

"The jury also heard what went on this morning," the judge replied.

"That was no threat to security this morning. A man made a statement trying to defend himself. That doesn't mean that seven or eight marshals—"

But Foran interrupted to say that Kunstler's statement was improper in the presence of the jury, which had just filed into its box, and the judge agreed. Frapolly then resumed his testimony. He said he had been in Lincoln Park on the night of August 27, where he "heard Jerry Rubin give a speech, Phil Ochs sang and then a person who identified himself as Bobby Seale spoke."

Seale arose, walked to the lectern, and said, "I object to that because my lawyer is not here. I have been denied my right to defend myself in this courtroom. I object to this man's testimony because I have been denied my constitutional rights."

"I repeat to you, sir," the judge said sternly, "you have a lawyer. Your lawyer is William Kunstler, who represented to the court that he represents you."

"He does not represent me," Seale answered, whereupon the judge excused the jury.

When the jury had left, the judge said to Seale, "For your

information, sir, I do not hear parties to a case who are represented by lawyers. You are represented by a lawyer." The judge extended the first vowel of the word lawyer so that it became almost a drawl, but he clipped the second vowel short with a rising inflection.

"I still object," Seale said, coolly. "You think blacks don't have a mind. Well, we got big minds, good minds, and we know how to come forth with constitutional rights. I am not going to be quiet. I am talking in behalf of my constitutional rights, man, in behalf of myself, that's my constitutional right to talk in behalf of my constitutional rights . . . Black people ain't suppose to have a mind? That's what you think. We got a body and a mind. I wonder. Did you lose yours in the Superman syndrome comic book stories? You must have to deny us our constitutional rights."

Seale paused for a moment and continued. "Taint the jury against me, send them threatening letters that I never sent, and you know it's a lie. You keep them away from their homes and they blame me every time they come into this room because they are being kept away from their homes and you did it." By this time, however, the marshals had surrounded Seale, and forced him back into his chair. The jury was readmitted.

Frapolly then resumed his testimony. He described a conversation with Froines in Lincoln Park later on in the evening of August 27. "While this conversation was going on," Foran asked, "did anything occur?"

"Yes," Frapolly replied. "Marilyn Katz showed us a group of guerrilla nails she had."

To this, Weinglass objected that statements or conduct of a third person who is not a party to the indictment cannot be used as evidence against the alleged conspirators. To support his argument he cited a concurring opinion by Judge Aldrich in the reversal, five months earlier, by the First Circuit Court of Appeals of the conviction for conspiracy in the Spock Case. Judge Aldrich had written that "the specific intent of one defendant in a case such as this is not ascertained by reference to the conduct or the statements of another, even though the conspirator has knowledge thereof."

On the basis of this opinion Weinglass argued that the government could not "show that Mr. Froines' intent was to be part of an illegal conspiracy by introducing evidence of what a third person had done or said," in Froines' presence.

Foran replied that Weinglass had misstated the Spock Case. "The Spock Case didn't have anything to do with statements made by persons in the presence of the defendants."

From Judge Aldrich's opinion, it is unclear whether he meant that an alleged conspirator may be held responsible for statements of which he has knowledge because they were made in his presence, while statements of which he learns by other means may not be used as evidence against him. That Judge Aldrich chose not to make such a distinction suggests that he may not have considered it vital to do so; that the source of the conspirator's knowledge, whether direct or indirect, is immaterial. Foran, on the other hand, appeared to think that such a distinction was crucial.

The judge apparently agreed. He turned to Foran and said, "If you will excuse the interruption [Mr. Weinglass'], conclusion was misstated. I don't think he misunderstood the language in the Spock Case, but the language is not applicable."

"That is right, Judge," Foran replied. "In this instance the defendant is present. In the Spock Case the defendant was not present. The case is clearly not applicable to this evidence."

Weinglass then offered to repeat what Judge Aldrich had

written, but the judge refused the offer. He did, however, permit Weinglass to paraphrase Judge Aldrich's opinion. Weinglass then explained that what Judge Aldrich had said was "that conduct and statements were not admissible against a defendant even if the defendant had knowledge of that statement or conduct. Now, I don't know what he was talking about," Weinglass continued, "if he was not talking about statements made in the presence of the defendant."

"Well, you would have to ask the court what it was talking about," Judge Hoffman replied. "You say you don't know. I don't know either. You are mistaken, in my opinion, Mr. Weinglass. Your objection is not well taken."

"How," Weinglass pleaded, "can the government show what the intent of John Froines was . . . through the words and conduct of a third person who isn't even named in the indictment?"

"The objection will be overruled," Judge Hoffman said with abrupt finality. Frapolly resumed his account of Miss Katz's guerrilla nails. These nails, the witness explained, are meant to be scattered on highways, where they will puncture automobile tires.

Frapolly then testified that on the following day there had been a meeting at which Dellinger said he was afraid that there would be no march to the Amphitheatre after all, but that the demonstrators might at least try to have such a march and that he would offer to lead it. Miss Katz then joined the meeting to ask for money to buy an additional supply of guerrilla nails.

At this point in the testimony Dellinger rose from his place at the defense table and asked, "Mr. Foran, do you believe a word of that?"

"May the record show," Foran replied, "that the comment was made by the defendant Dellinger."

"Yes, it was," Dellinger replied. "I asked Mr. Foran if he

could possibly believe one word of that. I don't believe the witness believes it. I don't believe Mr. Foran believes it."

The judge admonished Dellinger for this interruption, and within half an hour Foran completed his direct examination of Frapolly. The Court then recessed for the day.

When the trial resumed on the following morning there were even more marshals in the courtroom than there had been the day before. Kunstler began by presenting a motion for a mistrial. "The defendants," Kunstler said, "take the position that this being a conspiracy trial, the rights of all of them have been adversely affected" by the rulings of the court in the matter of Seale's defense.

"I will deny the motion," the judge replied wearily.

Kunstler then moved for a one-day adjournment so that he and Weinglass could fly to San Francisco and confer with Garry, who was still recuperating. The judge denied this motion, too. Then Kunstler asked whether he or Weinglass could go to San Francisco alone.

"Only on these conditions," the judge replied, leaning forward in his high-backed leather chair, "that first each and every defendant in this case stand up at his place at the defense table and agree that either you or Mr. Feinglass look after his interests."

"The name is Weinglass, Your Honor," Kunstler corrected the judge.

"Yes, Mr. Weinglass," the judge continued. "Only under these conditions," and then he said to Kunstler, "that you live up to your oral and written representation to me that you represent Mr. Seale."

Seale then stood and told the judge, "Since you say each and every defendant, I ain't going for it no way. He ain't my lawyer . . ." at which point the judge ordered a marshal to tell Seale to be quiet. Seale then sat down.

"I cannot make any such representation," Kunstler told

the judge, "because I consider myself not to be Mr. Seale's attorney." Kunstler then conferred with the defendants and, a moment later, returned to the lectern. He asked the judge, "Is the price of my going [to San Francisco] the compromising or waiving by Mr. Seale of his constitutional assertion that he wants to defend himself?"

"You do not expect me," the judge replied, "to answer a question put to me in that way, do you?"

"Why not? You expect us to answer questions," Dellinger said from his place at the defense table.

"Mr. Marshal," the judge ordered, "will you tell Mr. Derringer to remain quiet."

"The name is Dellinger," Kunstler said. The judge then denied the motion by the defense for permission to fly to San Francisco.

The morning passed without further incident as Kunstler cross-examined Frapolly. In the afternoon, however, when Kunstler had completed his cross-examination and returned to his seat, Seale stood up and said, "I would like to request to cross-examine the witness."

The judge denied this request and ordered the marshal to quiet the defendant. Despite the marshal's efforts, Seale shouted that the judge had "violated section 1892 of the United States Criminal Code. You violated title 42 of the United States Criminal Code. You are violating it because it states that a black man cannot be discriminated against in his legal defense." Seale was referring to a Reconstruction statute which grants blacks equal protection under the law.

He then addressed the witness. "Hey," he asked him, "did you see me make a speech in Lincoln Park, Mr. William Frapolly? Did you see me make a speech in Lincoln Park supposedly on August 27? Did you make some statements to the FBI that I was supposed to have made some racist statements about black people taking on white people? Did

you? Do you know a lying Robert Pierson? . . . You seem
to be very interested now. You turn your head to look this
way."

"You needn't answer any of those questions," Judge
Hoffman told the witness. "Will you sit down?" he then
asked Seale patiently.

"I would like to cross-examine the witness," Seale replied.

Dellinger then spoke: "The defendants support Bobby
Seale's right to have counsel of his choice here and affirm
that he has been denied that right."

With a sigh, the judge excused the jury for the day. He
then turned to Seale. "I admonish you," the judge said.
"You have a lot of contumacious conduct against you."

"I admonish you," Seale replied in a theatrical tone. "You
are the one in contempt of people's constitutional rights."

As Seale said these words the judge closed his eyes tightly
and stretched his mouth in the way that cats sometimes
do when they yawn. It was a grimace to which the defendants might have grown accustomed by this time. The
judge's face, especially his mouth, is highly mobile and, as
a rule, he is able to adjust his features so that they display
the emotions he means to convey. Toward the end of the
day, however—especially days as difficult for him as the
past few had been—he would occasionally lose control
of his features, and his face would either sag, expressionless,
or would seem to reveal feelings that he may not have had.
On this occasion it appeared that he was laughing, and
Hayden, who had remained silent throughout Seale's previous exchanges with the judge, called out, "Let the record
show the judge is laughing."

"Who made that remark?" the judge snapped, now fully
in control once more of his features, which he screwed into
an angry knot.

"Yes, he is laughing," Seale said.

"I am warning you now, sir," the judge said through

clenched teeth, "that the Court has the right to gag you. I don't want to do that," he added. "But under the law you may be gagged and chained to your chair."

"Gagged," Seale said, more to himself than to the judge. "I am being railroaded already."

"The Court will be in recess until tomorrow morning at ten o'clock," the judge then announced.

"Everyone will please rise," cried the marshal.

"I am not rising," Seale said. "I am not rising until he recognizes my constitutional rights."

Dellinger had not risen either, and Hayden, who had begun to get to his feet, fell back into his chair. Then the other defendants sat down.

"You advised your clients not to rise? Did you?" the judge asked Weinglass.

"I have no obligation to ask my clients to rise. They are doing nothing disruptive in this courtroom," Weinglass replied.

"I might add," Kunstler interjected, "that the clients are in protest of what you have done in their opinion to Bobby Seale's right to defend himself."

"Will you advise your clients to rise?" the judge asked Kunstler.

"Your Honor, if you direct me to, I will advise them."

"I direct you to," the judge replied.

"Then I will pass on the direction," Kunstler said, but the defendants remained seated. "They are free and independent and they have a right to do what they please," Kunstler told the judge.

"Let the record show that none of the defendants has risen," the judge shouted, and swept out of the room.

On the morning of October 29, a group of perhaps forty Panthers was searched by the marshals and admitted to the spectators' section, having waited in line since dawn outside the Federal Building. Seale recalls that as he waited in the lockup that morning before being brought down to the courtroom, a marshal came to him and said, "Bobby, you've got a lot of Black Panthers out there. I hope nothing happens."

"Well, nothing's going to happen," Seale told the marshal. "They've got a right to be there."

"Well, the judge told us to go over and sit you down, and I just don't want any of you to start anything," the marshal warned.

"They're not going to start anything," Seale reassured him. Then he said, "When you guys are pushing me down in chairs and stuff like that you're carrying out a racist judge's orders. He's making you act in a racist manner."

"Well, I'm not really a racist," the marshal, a tall, good-humored black man, replied.

Five minutes later Seale was brought into court. The judge had not yet appeared, and all the defendants, as Seale recalled, were scattered around the defense table. Schultz and Foran were at the prosecution table. Seale then turned to the Panthers and said, "Brothers and sisters in the audience, I want to say a few things to you."

He then pointed to the pictures on the wall above Judge Hoffman's bench, of Washington, Jefferson, Hamilton, and Franklin, and told the Panthers that they had all been slaveholders. Then he told them that he had been denied his right to defend himself, but that the Panthers should remain "cool" in court that day. "You've got a right to observe the trial," he told them, "but I don't want you cats out there to get upset and emotional and start doing anything that's out of the ordinary. . . . But if anybody attacks you," he told them, "you know what to do. We defend ourselves. If they make us leave the courtroom, then we just leave. But keep your cool. We're human beings and we've got a right to defend ourselves. But keep cool. Right on, brothers, O.K.? All right?"

The judge then entered the courtroom. Kunstler objected to the presence of so many marshals. Their numbers had increased since the day before. "Your Honor," he said, "we are objecting to this armed-camp aspect."

"It is not an armed camp," the judge replied. Yet there were marshals everywhere. Furthermore, the press section included a number of strangers, who the regular reporters assumed were plain-clothes police.

Abbie Hoffman stood up and said, "There's twenty-five marshals in here and they all got guns. Two of them are practically in the jury box."

"It's not right," Kunstler insisted. "It's not good and it's not called for."

"If the court please," Schultz interrupted, as he walked angrily to the lectern, "before you came into this court-room, if the court please, Bobby Seale stood up and addressed this group . . . and he told these people in the audience, if the Court please, and I want this on the record: it happened this morning, that if he's attacked they know what to do." As he spoke he jabbed his finger in the direction of the Panthers. "He was talking to these people about an attack by them," Schultz concluded.

"You're lying," Seale shouted. "Dirty liar. I told them to defend themselves. You're a rotten, racist, pig, fascist, liar. I said they had a right to defend themselves if they are attacked and I hope that the record carries that Tricky Dick is a liar and we have a right to defend ourselves, and if you attack me I will defend myself." At this several spectators shouted, "Right on!"

"If the court please," Schultz continued, "that is what he said, just as he related it."

"You're darned right," Seale answered.

"In terms of a physical attack by the people in this—" Schultz began.

"A physical attack by these damned marshals, that's what I said; and if they attack any people, they have a right to defend themselves, you lying pig."

"Let the record show," Judge Hoffman intervened, "that

the tone of Mr. Seale's voice was one of shrieking and pounding on the table and shouting. That will be dealt with appropriately at some time in the future."

Kunstler then reminded the judge that Schultz had also been shouting.

"Yes, he raised his voice," the judge answered, "and if what he said was the truth, I can't blame him for raising his voice."

Schultz then returned to his seat; Seale threw a contemptuous glance in his direction and returned to his own chair. With the Court restored to order, Judge Hoffman called in the jury.

Seated in the press section that morning, along with the other spectators, was Dr. Spock. When the jurors had taken their seats, Kunstler proposed to introduce the well-known doctor to the Court. The judge, however, declined the offer. "My children," he said humorously, "are already grown," a reference, presumably, to his wife's two sons, since the judge himself is childless.

Weinglass then proceeded to cross-examine Frapolly. When he had finished, Seale arose again and demanded that he too be allowed to cross-examine the witness.

"Take the jury out," the judge ordered.

As the jurors left, Seale pointed to the pictures behind Judge Hoffman and said, "You have George Washington and Benjamin Franklin sitting in a picture behind you, and they were slave owners. You're acting in the same manner, denying me my constitutional rights."

"Mr. Seale, I have admonished you," the judge warned again. "Mr. Kunstler has his appearance on record here as your attorney."

"He is not. He is not. He is not my lawyer," Seale replied.

"We are going to recess now, young man," the judge then told him. "If you keep this up—"

"Look, old man," Seale interrupted, "if you keep up

denying me my constitutional rights, you are being exposed to the public and the world that you do not care about people's constitutional rights to defend themselves."

"I will tell you that what I indicated yesterday might happen to you," the judge answered.

"Happen to me?" Seale asked him, "What can happen to me more than what Benjamin Franklin and George Washington did to black people in slavery? What can happen to me more than that?"

Then the judge turned to the seven other defendants. "I might add, since it has been said here that all of the defendants support you in your position, that I might conclude they are bad risks for bail—"

"I still want my constitutional rights," Seale shouted, whereupon three marshals rushed at him to force him to sit down. As they approached the defense table, however, Dellinger, holding his arms tightly against his sides, thrust his body between Seale and the marshals.

"May the record show," Schultz shouted, "if the court please, that while the marshals were pushing Bobby Seale in the chair, the defendant Dellinger physically attempted to interfere with the marshals by pushing them out of the way."

"I want my rights," Seale said.

"I tell you," the judge replied, "that Mr. Dellinger, if that is his name, has said here that they support the performance of this man . . . Now I will tell you this . . . I over the noon hour will reflect on whether they are good risks for bail and I shall give serious consideration to the termination of their bail."

Seale then got to his feet again. "You trying to make jive bargaining operations and that's different from the right I have. I have a right to defend myself whether you sit me down or not. Why don't you recognize my right to defend myself?"

Once more the marshals lunged at Seale, forcing him into his seat.

"May the record show," Schultz asked, "that the defendant Dellinger did the same thing just now?"

"Mr. Marshal," the judge said, "we will recess. Mr. Kunstler, will you ask your clients to rise?"

"If you direct me to, Your Honor," Kunstler replied; but the defendants remained seated.

"This honorable court will take a brief recess," cried the marshal who stood in the pulpit to the judge's left.

When the Court resumed its session that afternoon, the spectators' benches were filled with elderly pensioners, men who call themselves The Federal Court Buffs and wander through the corridors of the Federal Building, exchanging gossip about the various cases on trial. One of these men explained to a reporter that something "big" was going to happen that afternoon and that the Buffs didn't want to miss it. Because the marshals had let the pensioners into the courtroom before the other prospective spectators could enter, there was no room that afternoon for the Panthers.

When the judge took his seat on the bench, Kunstler read to the Court a long list of the defendants' grievances, beginning with the treatment of Ball when he presented the motion to permit Fred Hampton to visit Seale in jail. Thereafter, Kunstler said, the defendants had been denied their Sixth Amendment rights, illegal warrants had been issued for four of their lawyers, he himself and Mr. Weinglass had been threatened repeatedly with punishment for contempt, and on that very morning the judge had threatened to revoke the defendants' bail—which he had no legal right to do—as a way to coerce them to abandon their support for Seale's claim to his rights under the Sixth Amendment.

Foran answered these contentions at equal length, saying

that if Seale's rights had, in fact, been violated, the appeals courts would correct the error. When he had finished, the judge once more reminded Kunstler of his decision in the South Holland Case, and repeated that Ball had attempted to impose a forgery upon him; that, furthermore, "He had got me out of bed on a Saturday afternoon."

The judge then ordered that the jury be brought back in.

"What about section 1982, Title 42 of the Code," Seale asked him, "where it says that the black cannot be discriminated against in any court in America?"

"Mr. Seale, do you know what is going to happen to you?" the judge asked.

"You just got through saying you observed the laws," Seale replied. "That law protects my right not to be discriminated against in my legal defense. Why don't you recognize that?"

"Hold the jury, Mr. Marshal," the judge ordered. "We will take a recess." Then, turning to a group of three marshals who stood poised beside Seale at the defense table, he said, "Take that defendant into the room in there and deal with him as he should be dealt with."

Within eleven minutes Seale was returned to the courtroom, his hands and feet chained to a gray metal chair. A gag of muslin passed through his mouth and was tied at the back of his neck.

The judge then turned to him and explained gently, "Mr. Seale, not only your Sixth Amendment rights but all your constitutional and statutory rights have been and will be preserved in this trial. . . . If you assure the court that you will be respectful, I am willing that you resume your former place at table and in the same physical condition that you were in prior to now. Will you?"

"I can't speak," Seale shouted in a muffled voice through his gag. "I have a right to speak. I have a right to be heard for myself and my constitutional rights."

"Give me your assurance," the judge pleaded with Seale.

"Give me your assurance that you will let me defend myself," Seale said angrily.

"Mr. Marshal," the judge said, "I don't think you have accomplished your purpose with that contrivance. We will have to take another recess." Whereupon Seale was carried out on his metal chair and returned to the lockup on the twenty-fourth floor.

Ten minutes later Seale was brought back into the courtroom, chained as before, but this time with his mouth covered by adhesive tape.

The jurors were then readmitted. Jean Fritz, the woman whom the defendants called Mrs. Baldwin, looked across the room at Seale, fell into her chair, and turned her head away. Kay Richards, the young juror who had replaced Kristi King, allowed her head to slump onto her chest, while the heavy-set, peroxided woman, whom the defendants called Mrs. Wallace after the Alabama governor, stared blankly at the judge.

The judge explained to the jurors that "the steps taken here are to insure a fair trial." The reporters laughed at this, more from tension, perhaps, than from the incongruity of the remark. The judge paused menacingly and continued.

"I direct you, ladies and gentlemen of the jury, not to hold it against any of the other seven defendants. When these measures are taken against Mr. Seale, they indicate no evidence of guilt or lack of guilt of the charges contained in the indictment." As the judge spoke his name, Seale rattled his chains against the metal arms of his chair, and the jurors averted their eyes from the bench.

Soon court recessed for the day. In their conference with Seale immediately thereafter, the defendants debated what further protests they should take against the judge's actions. Rubin and Hoffman thought that all the defendants should wear gags to court the following morning. Seale disagreed. He said that the defendants as a group were "in a fight to win," and he urged that they maintain "revolutionary discipline," rather than indulge in Yippie antics. The political issue was his own right to defend himself, Seale said. He wanted nothing to call attention away from Judge Hoffman's irresponsible denial of this right and from the cruel and unusual punishment that he had imposed when he continued to demand it.

Judge Hoffman found the legal authority for chaining Seale in a recent ruling of the Seventh Circuit Court of Appeals. This court had reversed the conviction of a bank robber named Allen because the trial judge, having found Allen's behavior in court intolerable, excluded him from the proceedings. The Appeals Court ruled that the trial judge had thereby deprived the defendant of his Sixth Amendment right to confront his accusers. What the trial judge should have done instead, the Appeals Court said, was to bind and gag the defendant. In this way, he could remain in court, but would be unable to create further disturbances. It was upon this recommendation of the Appeals Court that Judge Hoffman ordered Seale gagged and shackled.

But Seale's case was not comparable to Allen's. In the first place, when Allen asked to defend himself, the judge agreed, provided the defendant accept the assistance of a court-appointed lawyer to "protect the record." Nevertheless, Allen became unruly, tore apart his file of legal papers, and threatened the judge's life. He then shouted, "There's not going to be no trial here . . . I'm going to start talking and I'm going to keep on talking all through the trial." For these reasons the judge sent him out of the courtroom for the duration of the trial. Seale, however, had neither threatened the judge's life nor vowed to disrupt the trial. His remarks in every case were addressed to the question of his legal self-defense, and though his language was often intemperate, his claims were always consistent with this demand. Nothing that he said or did gave evidence that his aim had been to cause an uproar, nor did he interrupt the proceedings, except when his name was mentioned by a government witness or lawyer, or when black spectators were interfered with by the marshals.

Shortly after the Conspiracy Trial itself had come to an end, the Supreme Court reversed the appellate ruling in the Allen Case. Not only did the trial judge have the right, as the Seventh Circuit Court had ruled, to shackle Allen, he also had the right, the Supreme Court said, to exclude him from the courtroom.

The courts are "palladiums of liberty" and cannot "be treated disrespectfully with impunity," Justice Black wrote, on behalf of the majority of the Justices. Justice Douglas dissented. Though he agreed that a courtroom is "a hallowed place," and that trials must be conducted with dignity, he also felt that Allen might have been "a mental case," and that defendants whose disruptive behavior may have a more rational basis should not be bound by a ruling derived from such an example.

Since it was apparent that the Court's ruling in the Allen Case, so soon after the completion of the Conspiracy Trial, may have been intended to support Judge Hoffman's treatment of Bobby Seale, Justice Douglas added to his dissenting opinion a reflection of his own on the Chicago trial. He quoted at length from an account of the trial of William Penn, who in 1670 had been indicted in London, along with a fellow Quaker, for conspiracy to incite a riot. Under the Conventicle Act, which forbade unauthorized preaching, the Quakers had been denied the use of their meeting house in Grace Church Street. Therefore they held their meeting in the street itself. Penn and a fellow Quaker, a linen draper named Mead, were then arrested, charged with conspiracy, and brought before the mayor of London to be tried. The testimony against them was given by two policemen who had mingled with the crowd, but who were unable to tell the Court what the defendants had said in their speeches. Thus the prosecution could produce no evidence that the defendants' speeches had led to the alleged disturbance. Penn then argued in his own behalf.

"I design no affront to the Court," he said, "but to be heard in my just Plea, and I tell you that if you deny me an account of the law [under which I am being tried], you do at once deny me an acknowledged right, and evidence to the whole world of your resolution to sacrifice the privileges of Englishmen, to your sinister and arbitrary designs."

"Take him away," the prosecutor said. "If you take not some course with this pestilent fellow to stop his mouth we shall not be able to do anything tonight."

"Take him away," the judge ordered. "Take him away. Turn him into the baledock."

"Is this justice, or true judgement?" Penn asked. "Must I therefore be taken away because I plead for the fundamental law of England?"

"Be silent there," the judge ordered.

"I am not to be silent in a case wherein I am so much concerned, and not only myself but many ten thousand families beside," Penn replied.

The jurors refused to find Penn guilty of inciting a riot, a verdict which infuriated the Court. "Gentlemen," the judge said to the jurors. "You shall not be dismissed until we have a verdict that the Court will accept; and you shall be locked up without meat, drink, fire and tobacco. You shall not think to abuse the court. We will have a verdict, by the help of God, or you shall starve for it."

When Penn objected to this treatment of the jury, the judge ordered, "Stop that prating fellow's mouth, or put him out of the court"—the same expedient that Justice Black recommended three centuries later.

Nevertheless, the jury persisted in its refusal to find Penn guilty. Thus Mead, his alleged co-conspirator, was found to be innocent too, since, as he argued, he could hardly have conspired alone. "I am sorry," the judge told the jurors, "you have followed your own judgement and opinions, rather than the good and wholesome advice which was given you." Thereupon the judge found the jurors, along with the two defendants, guilty of contempt of court and sent them all to Newgate.

"The next day," Seale recalled, "they strapped me to a wooden armchair, put a lot of padding in front of my mouth and tied a large rag around it. Another rag came up under my chin." The marshal who had strapped Seale's legs to the feet of the chair asked, "Is that too tight?"

"No," Seale replied. Then, as Seale recalls, the marshal made the straps tighter. A few minutes later another marshal loosened the straps, but when the first marshal saw what had been done, he tightened the straps on Seale's legs, as well as those holding his arms. This affected the circulation of Seale's blood, so that by the time he was carried on his chair into the courtroom—the ends of his gag projecting above his head like rabbit's ears—his left arm had begun to hurt him. With a vigorous shake of his head he managed to indicate that he was in difficulty. A young black woman, a law student who assisted the defense and whose particular responsibility was to help Seale, took the chair next to him at the defense table to see what the trouble was. She placed a pencil between his fingers, and held her own hand over his to help him write a note to explain his problem. Schultz noted this gesture and later objected to it as an attempt to win the jury through a display of affection. Weinglass also observed Seale's difficulty and addressed the Court.

"If Your Honor please," he said, "the buckles on the leather strap holding Mr. Seale's hand are digging into his hand and he appears to be trying to free his hand from that pressure. Could he be assisted?" The judge agreed that the marshals might look into the problem. He then excused the jury and declared a brief recess. At this point, however, Seale had managed by himself to loosen the straps around his left hand, and when the marshal who had tightened them earlier that morning saw what Seale had done, he lunged toward him at the defense table. Two other marshals joined him, and in the confusion Seale's chair fell backward into the press section. The marshals and Seale, still strapped and gagged, then fell into a heap, knocking over some of the reporters. "Your Honor," Kunstler shouted, "when are we going to stop this medieval torture? This is a disgrace."

Meanwhile, Rubin had turned in his own chair to help Seale. "This guy," he cried, "is putting his elbow into Bobby's mouth and it wasn't necessary at all."

"This is no longer a court of order, Your Honor," Kunstler pleaded. "This is a medieval torture chamber."

Seale meanwhile had managed to pull his gag off. "Don't hit me in the balls," he shouted at the marshals, who continued to struggle with him.

"Your Honor," Kunstler cried, "this is an unholy disgrace."

"Created by Mr. Kunstler," Foran screamed.

"You fascist dogs, you rotten, low life son of a bitch," Seale shouted at the marshals. "I am glad I said it about George Washington used to have slaves . . ."

"Somebody go to protect him," Dellinger called out from the far side of the defense table, where he himself was being held by a marshal.

"May the record show," Foran shouted again, "that it was the defendant Dellinger saying someone go to protect him."

"May the record show that Foran is a Nazi," Rubin hollered.

"Everything you say will be taken down," the judge replied.

"I feel so utterly ashamed to be an American lawyer at this time," Kunstler said.

"You should be ashamed of your conduct in this case, sir," Judge Hoffman replied.

Seale was then removed from the courtroom and taken out to the lockup, where the marshals loosened his straps and replaced the gag. Soon thereafter, he was carried back in, and the jury was readmitted. Weinglass, however, refused to continue with his cross-examination of Frapolly. Instead, he asked the Court to poll the jury so as to determine whether the jurors could continue to hear the evidence impartially. No sooner had Weinglass offered this motion than the judge angrily sent the jurors back out of the courtroom.

"That statement of counsel," Foran said, "was the worst attempt to corrupt the jury that I have ever seen."

"If the court please," Schultz added, "Mr. Weinglass' conduct in this case is a shameful thing! A shameful thing!"

"Mr. Weinglass," the judge added, "you have made a vile . . ."

"I plead with this court," Weinglass interrupted, "to cite Mr. Foran the canon of ethics which Your Honor knows about, which admonishes attorneys in an adversary proceeding to refrain from making a personal attack on the opposing attorney. Not only have you permitted it, you have added to it with your own intimidation of me personally—"

"That wasn't intimidation, sir . . . and again I caution you not to repeat your conduct . . . " the judge said menacingly.

By this time, however, it had become evident that the possibility of decorum had been lost irretrievably for that morning, and Judge Hoffman soon declared a recess until the afternoon session. As Seale was being carried out through the door to the lockup, he shouted through his gag, "Cruel and unusual punishment. You're a fascist dog, Judge."

The afternoon session passed quietly. When the government had completed the direct examination of its next witness, a policeman named Healy, Weinglass read to the court a statement that Seale, whose bonds had been loosened by the marshals, had managed to write with the assistance of the black woman who sat next to him, and of whose presence Schultz continued to complain. Seale's statement was "I object. I want to see the matters that the government is trying to hide to railroad me." What he wanted to see were the minutes of Officer Healy's grand jury testimony, material which the government must, by law, turn over to the defense.

The judge then told Weinglass that he could have Seale's note numbered for identification as a defense exhibit, but he warned Seale, who had begun to make muffled sounds through his gag, to remain quiet. "What is the number [of the exhibit] Mr. Weinstein?" the judge asked, then corrected himself, "Mr. Weinwer . . . Weinberg . . ."

"Weinglass, Your Honor," Weinglass said.

By 4:15 the defense had completed its cross-examination of Healy, and Seale through his gag said that now he wanted to examine the witness. The judge dismissed the jury and calmly warned Seale that he would have to be quiet or the Court would deal appropriately with him. Just what this meant, however, was unclear, nor did the judge attempt to explain. Thus when the court recessed for the day the defendants were left to wonder what further restraints the judge had in store for tomorrow. That evening a reporter who had attended the trial from the start noted that the afternoon session had been "a slow volley." Tomorrow, he felt, would prove more decisive.

"The next morning when they tried to gag me," Seale recalls, "I thought I was going to die. . . . I was in the lockup before court convened and they said, 'Sit in the chair.'"

" 'Don't tighten those things too tight on me,' " Seale

told the marshals. " 'We're not going to,' " the marshal answered, " '. . . but we've got to put something in your mouth.' "

" 'No, you're not putting a damn thing in my mouth,' " Seale replied.

" 'Well, we have to put something in your mouth,' " the marshal said. " 'The judge has ordered it, and that's what we're going to do.' " Seale, who was being treated at Cook County Jail for tonsilitis, was worried about his throat, and he threatened to bite the marshals' fingers if they tried to force a gag into his mouth.

" 'Grab his head,' " a marshal ordered, and "one of the marshals," as Seale recalls, "put his hands on top of my head . . . he had rubber gloves on and was holding a wad of rag that was wrapped up . . . He was going to jam this junk down my mouth. I was shackled down. Legs, arms, everything. He grabbed my nose . . . and was going to wait until I needed some breath, and when I opened my mouth he would move real fast and jam the rag into it."

" 'You rotten dogs,' " Seale shouted. Then he felt that he was about to faint and this "cat was pushing, pushing, pushing against my mouth."

"So I pushed with my feet," Seale recalled. "I pushed real hard. I was about to pass out. I thought about Eldridge and I thought about the struggle and everybody in the party and I was thinking about Nat Turner even . . ."

Finally the marshals abandoned their attempts to stuff Seale's mouth, and instead wrapped an elastic bandage tightly around his head. Then they carried him into the courtroom. This bandage, which is the sort worn by athletes to support a weakened knee or ankle, grows tighter as one moves, and soon it had begun to affect the circulation of blood to Seale's head. When Seale's six-year-old son, Malik, who had been brought to court that morning, greeted his father, Seale appeared to be too weak to reply.

"Your Honor," Weinglass asked, "Mr. Seale is having difficulty. He is in extreme discomfort . . . would it be possible to have those bandages loosened."

The judge ruled that if Mr. Schultz agreed, the marshals might loosen the elastic bandages. Since Schultz had no objection, the bandages were loosened. Once it appeared that Seale had recovered, Kunstler proposed that Court be recessed for the rest of the day so that he and Hayden could fly to California and consult with Garry. Perhaps in this way, Kunstler explained, a solution to the impasse could be found. Kunstler also moved that another solution might be for the judge, at last, to permit Seale to defend himself. This, Kunstler said, "would stop any disturbance in the courtroom."

"The record does not indicate that I could stop Mr. Seale," the judge replied, to which Kunstler answered that Seale had never asked for anything but the right to plead his own case.

"Mr. Seale," the judge said, "is being treated in accordance with the law."

"Not in accordance with the Constitution of the United States, Your Honor. He has a right to defend himself," Kunstler answered.

"I don't need someone to come here from New York or wherever you come from," the judge replied, "and tell me there is a constitution in the United States. . . . Read the books. You will find that the Court has the authority to do what is being done and I will not let this trial be broken up by his conduct."

Kunstler then pursued his motion for an adjournment. "It is impossible," he said, "for white men to sit in this room while a black man is in chains."

"I wish you wouldn't talk about the distinction between white and black men in this courtroom," the judge replied. "I lived a long time and you are the first person who has ever suggested that I have discriminated against a black man. Come into my chambers and I will show you on the wall what one of the great newspapers of this city said editorially about me in connection with a school desegregation case."

Nevertheless, the judge granted the adjournment. He did, however, propose a condition. He did not want Hayden to appear on television while he was in California and "vilify" him. "I don't want to be lying in bed peacefully looking at television and suddenly see him calling me a 'blackmailer,' " he said.

To this Hayden replied, "The purpose of my going to see Mr. Garry is to explore with him the crisis that has developed in this courtroom. I am sorry if anyone thinks I'm going to appear on television. But I will not preclude the possibility of my speaking in California. One gag is enough."

The judge let Hayden go nevertheless, and Court recessed for the weekend.

On Monday, Seale appeared in court neither gagged nor bound. Since the visit to Garry had produced no more than a statement by Garry denouncing Judge Hoffman's rulings and demanding that Seale be allowed to defend himself, there was much speculation among the reporters concerning the judge's intentions. This curiosity was partly satisfied when Schultz later that morning said, "To be candid about it, we don't think it helps the government in the eyes of the jury," for Seale to be bound and gagged. Nevertheless, Schultz continued to complain of Seale's "ploy," to which Weinglass replied, "A citizen has a constitutional right to defend himself and that is not a 'ploy.' "

On the following day, Seale appealed to the judge once more to be permitted to defend himself. "I don't know all of these formalities," he explained, but "I could easily learn it if you would coach me and allow me to defend myself and cross-examine the witnesses and ask pertinent questions that directly relate to these charges against me, because I am very well aware of these charges." The judge, however, denied this request and told Seale that he resented having been called a pig.

"I wasn't shackled because I called you a pig and a fascist, which I still think you are—a pig and a fascist and a racist; but because I was denied my constitutional rights. When a man is denied his constitutional rights—"

"Will you sit down please," the judge cut him short, and ordered the marshal to put him in his chair.

". . . you will still be considered a pig," Seale continued as he was forced by three marshals into the chair, "and a fascist and a racist. You still denied me my constitutional rights."

The judge reacted calmly to these remarks and asked the reporter to be sure that she had recorded them.

Weinglass then arose to argue once more on behalf of the seven other defendants that Seale be granted his constitutional rights. To this argument Foran responded that Weinglass had made a "two-faced, phony" statement.

Kunstler arose in defense of his colleague. "I have heard these remarks directed at my co-counsel . . . You know it is not right to call a man two-faced and a phony. [Yet] you don't say anything and you countenance the remark."

"For your information," the judge replied, "the word phony is in the dictionary."

"So is the word pig, Your Honor," Kunstler answered.

Late that afternoon, Bill Ray, the San Mateo County Deputy Sheriff who had seen Seale buy the airplane ticket in the San Francisco Airport, was called to the stand, and on the following morning when Kunstler had completed his cross-examination of this witness Seale arose and said, "Well, I think I have a right to cross-examine."

"No, you have no right in the circumstances of this case," the judge replied.

"Why did you follow me? Could you please tell me, Mr. Witness," Seale persisted.

"Mr. Seale," the judge interrupted. "I ask you to sit down."

"Have you ever killed a Black Panther party member?" Seale continued.

"Mr. Seale, I will have to ask you to sit down, please," the judge repeated.

"Have you ever been on any raids in the Black Panther party offices or Black Panther party members' homes?" Seale went on.

"Mr. Seale, this is the third time I am asking you to sit down as courteously as possible." But Seale refused to sit down and the judge then said, "We are going to recess this court now, young man. If you keep this up—"

"Look old man," Seale replied, "If you keep up denying me my constitutional rights, you are being exposed to the public and the world that you do not care about people's constitutional rights to defend themselves."

The judge then called a recess until two o'clock. At lunch, Rubin and Dellinger sat with a group of reporters and debated the appropriate tactics to pursue in the face of such injustice as they felt the court had committed. "I'm going to spend ten years in jail anyway," Rubin said. "The least I can do is call the judge a pig." Furthermore, he said, such language "builds a sense of community."

"You can build a movement in the short run with such tactics," Dellinger replied, "but not for the long run, because your movement won't be based on sensitivity to people or thought. It would turn into Stalinism. Words like that lead to mob spirit; the way the police like to call people reds."

"Well, we need some mob spirit now," Rubin replied, and then he predicted that in ten years America would have a student movement like Japan's. The Weathermen, he said, were the harbinger of this tendency in America.

"I think it would be a tragedy," Dellinger said, "if the Weathermen became popular. You're never going to storm the United States by throwing rocks at policemen. The problem is how to get beyond mass demonstrations to something more effective, something to paralyze the machine. Perhaps strikes and other disruptions of 'business as usual.' That's something to think about."

"But I want action first," Rubin answered, "and thinking later."

A few minutes after two-thirty Judge Hoffman re-entered the courtroom. "There is a matter," he said, "that I wish to take up before we proceed further with this trial." He then explained, "As everyone who has attended the various sessions of this trial must, if he is fair, understand, the Court has done its best to prevent efforts to delay and obstruct this trial which, I think, have been made for the purpose of causing such disorder and confusion as would prevent a verdict by a jury on the issues presented by the indictment."

He then proceeded to read aloud from a long document excerpted from the trial transcript that listed Seale's various outbursts. He read from this document for nearly two hours. When he finished he found Seale guilty of sixteen separate acts of contempt and sentenced him to consecutive three-month sentences for each such act, or a total sentence of four years in prison. Thus, he sentenced Seale to three months for having asked to cross-examine Oklepek, and for arguing with the Court when this request was denied. He also sentenced him to three more months for his attempt that same morning to cross-examine Ray. When the judge had finished reading, but before he imposed sentence, he invited Seale himself to speak.

"How come I couldn't speak before?" Seale asked.

"This is a special occasion," the judge replied pleasantly. Then he explained to Seale that he was free to address the Court on the question of his punishment.

"Punishment?" Seale asked. "You've punished black people all your life. If what you're talking about is putting me in jail or prison or hanging people, and all that stuff, I have nothing to say about that. I have something to say about the fact that I want to defend myself still. I want my rights to cross examine witnesses." But the judge would not hear Seale on this question, and ordered him to prison. He also severed his case from the trial of the seven other defendants, and ordered that he be brought to Court on April 23 to stand trial alone.

"I demand an immediate trial right now," Seale said.

The judge paid no attention and recessed the Court.

"I still want an immediate trial," Seale demanded. "You can't call it a mistrial. I'm put in jail for four years for nothing?" Then as the marshals dragged him through the door into the lockup he looked back at his chair and noticed that he had left something behind. "I want my coat," he called out as the lockup door closed behind him.

"Free Bobby! Free Bobby!" cried the spectators. The voice of the marshal announcing a recess for the day was lost in the shouting.

The sentence that Judge Hoffman imposed upon Seale has no precedent in recent history. Professor Dershowitz of Harvard Law School told a reporter that, in fact, he "recalled no case in the entire history of Anglo-American jurisprudence in which a sentence of this length had been handed out for contempt." Yet there have been harsher sentences: for example, the one imposed by an English judge in 1631 upon a defendant who had thrown a brickbat at him. The brickbat missed, but the judge ordered that his assailant's right hand be cut off immediately and nailed to the gibbet. Once this had been done the defendant was hanged in the presence of the Court.

From a procedural point of view, the English judge, rash though he was, revealed a firmer grasp of the law of contempt than Judge Hoffman showed in sentencing Seale. A judge's summary power to reach a finding of guilt upon the evidence of his own sense in a case of direct contempt —that is, contempt committed in the judge's own presence —and to impose punishment without a determination of the facts by a jury, is meant to assert the authority of the court as swiftly as possible, and to insure an orderly proceeding thereafter. The essence of the punishment is its swiftness, and its sting is meant to coerce an immediate response from the offender. For this reason, and this reason only, Anglo-American Courts have permitted punishment for direct contempt without trial by jury. In 1965 the Supreme Court ruled that summary punishment for direct contempt may be imposed only when "swiftness is a prerequisite of justice." Thus summary punishment for direct contempt is not retributive in the ordinary sense, but is a form of restraint, a barbed admonition meant to coerce respect for the Court. Zealous as he was, the English judge observed the spirit of the law of contempt by imposing summary punishment within moments of the contemptuous act. In this way he immediately asserted the power of the court and forced the defendant to recognize, no matter how briefly, that his behavior had been inappropriate.

Judge Hoffman, on the other hand, punished Seale retroactively, long after most of the alleged contempts had occurred and the damage to the dignity of the Court had been done. Thus the sentence imposed by Judge Hoffman did not serve the only purpose for which the power of summary punishment is appropriate. The judge may himself have been sensitive to the possibility of error on this account, for later he explained that to have "halted the trial upon each instance of misbehavior and imposed punishment . . . at that time . . . would merely have compounded the disruption . . . and the trial would have undergone even more delay than [had been] caused by the conduct itself."

Though this argument is not unreasonable as far as it goes, it does not go far enough. By appropriating to himself the powers of judge, prosecutor, and jury, Judge Hoffman deprived Seale of the protection of due process, the very protection that an orderly trial is meant to guarantee. He thus raised, but failed to explore, a most subtle and ambiguous question of law.

From its origins in the twelfth century the contempt power has served the purpose of coercing respect for the law. But in the United States the law itself serves to protect the rights of a sovereign people. Though these rights cannot reasonably include a license to disrupt the Courts, they do require that the Courts observe due process of law; that is, a presentment by a grand jury, followed by adversary proceedings and a determination of the facts by a trial jury, followed, in the event of conviction, by an appeal. The Courts have long recognized that an orderly proceeding is essential to the fulfillment of these rights, hence the summary contempt power for the direct and immediate purpose of maintaining order and coercing respect. But the courts have also recognized that this power must be used with the greatest care; otherwise its exercise defeats the principle of due process that the contempt power was meant to protect.

The Courts have yet to establish clear limits over the severity of sentences that judges may impose in cases of direct contempt. Lately, however, the Supreme Court has begun to approach this complicated question, and later in the Conspiracy Trial, Judge Hoffman attempted to justify his actions in the case of Seale by reference to a recent Supreme Court ruling on this question. He cited the case of *Bloom v. Illinois,* in which a lawyer had presented to the Court a forged will—a clear case of contempt committed in the presence of the Court, and for which the judge imposed summary punishment. Bloom appealed on the grounds that he had been denied trial by jury, but the Illinois Supreme Court affirmed his sentence, ruling that a criminal contempt is an offense against the Court and not a violation of the law in the usual sense; hence trial by jury is not available. The United States Supreme Court disagreed with the Illinois judges. It ruled that "criminal contempt is a crime in the ordinary sense," but it added, "It is an old law that the guarantee of jury trial found in Article III [of the Constitution] and in the Sixth Amendment does not apply to petty offenses." For this reason, a trial judge may impose a summary sentence of up to six months without a jury trial. On the basis of this ruling, Judge Hoffman confirmed that Seale's individual contempts had been "petty offenses," each punishable by a light sentence.

He then added to his citation of the Bloom Case an observation of his own. "There is nothing," he said, "in Bloom which would preclude each contumacious act to be separately cited by the Court." Thus he attempted to defend his imposition of a four-year cumulative sentence for sixteen "petty offenses." That the Bloom ruling says nothing about consecutive sentences for repeated offenses does not, however, supply the justification that Judge Hoffman claimed. Bloom had committed only one contempt. Therefore, the Court's silence on the question of separate citations meant only that the question of punishment for repeated contempts had not been relevant to its deliberations in that case.

On the same day, however, that the Court ruled in Bloom, it also ruled in *Duncan v. Louisiana*, another case in which a defendant demanded trial by jury on a charge of direct contempt. In this ruling the Court addressed itself to the maximum sentence that may be imposed without due process of law. The Court wrote that the seriousness of an offense may be determined retroactively by the severity of punishment. In conformity with Bloom it ruled that

"Crimes carrying possible sentences of up to six months do not require a jury trial, if they otherwise qualify as petty." But, the Court added, "the penalty authorized for a particular crime is of major relevance in determining whether it is serious or not, and may, if it is serious enough, subject the trial to the mandates of the Sixth Amendment," that is, trial by jury. Furthermore, the Court ruled in the Bloom Case itself that "we are to look to the actual penalty imposed as the best evidence of the seriousness of the offense." Then, in 1968, the Court expressed itself unequivocally on this point. In the Frank Case it ruled that a sentence of six months or more cannot be imposed without trial by jury.

The question that Judge Hoffman failed adequately to explore in his partial reference to the Bloom ruling and in his failure to consider the Duncan and Frank rulings at all was whether Seale had, in fact, committed sixteen separate "petty offenses" or whether he had been guilty of a single, continuous contempt—one that may have amounted to a serious crime, requiring trial by jury, as the four-year sentence suggests. By ruling, without further inquiry, that Seale had committed a series of separate "petty offenses," Judge Hoffman not only evaded this question but put himself at odds with the requirement that summary punishment must be imposed "swiftly" as each such disruptive act occurs. For the judge to have allowed such offenses to accumulate and then to have imposed punishment retroactively at a later time defeats the purpose of the summary contempt power, which is to restore order immediately. The punishment then becomes retributive and does not serve its intended purpose of swift coercion.

Thus the expedient by which Judge Hoffman attempted to evade the six-month limit imposed by the Frank ruling forced him into a logical dilemma. To impose summary punishment upon Seale retroactively for sixteen separate crimes offends the rule that punishment for contempt must occur swiftly. But for the judge to regard Seale's contempt as a continuous act which at last became intolerable and justified a summary sentence of four years in prison, put him at odds with the rulings in Bloom, Duncan, and Frank concerning the maximum sentence that can be imposed without trial by jury. Thus Judge Hoffman's attempts to circumvent the Court's ruling by imposing consecutive three-month sentences violated the letter of the old tradition as well as the spirit of the recent rulings.

His decision may also have violated both the spirit and the letter of another recent Supreme Court ruling, one that addressed itself directly to the question of repeated contempts. This ruling arose from a subsidiary question in the Yates Case, the case that was tried under the California version of the Smith Act. The defendant had refused on eleven separate occasions to answer questions put to her by the prosecutor. For each such refusal she was found in contempt and sentenced to eleven years in jail. The Supreme Court reversed this conviction and found that her refusals represented a single contempt. To find the defendant guilty on separate counts not only raises the question of double jeopardy, the Court ruled, but invites the prosecutor to repeat his questions endlessly, thus subjecting the unwilling witness to an indefinite term in jail.

In the Yates Case the defendant's contempt arose from her own failure to respond. In Seale's case, it was the defendant's repeated initiatives that were the source of the contempt citations. Thus the question of repeated contempt in Seale's case raises a somewhat novel question upon which the Supreme Court will, perhaps, eventually have to rule.

Judge Hoffman's ruling on Seale's contempts raised still another question concerning the power of judges to impose summary sentences for contempt. In a dissenting opinion in the Sacher Case—the case to which Judge Hoffman had ominously referred Weinglass during the early days of the trial—Justice Frankfurter objected to the six-month sentence for contempt imposed by the trial judge upon Harry Sacher, a defense lawyer in the Dennis trial. Frankfurter warned against the power of trial judges to sit as judge, prosecutor, and jury in cases of contempt that occurred in their presence and in which their personal feelings might interfere with their capacity for disinterested judgment. "Men who make their way to the bench," Justice Frankfurter wrote, "sometimes exhibit vanity, irascibility, narrowness, arrogance, and the other weaknesses to which human flesh is heir"; therefore, they should leave the determination of guilt in cases of direct contempt to other less interested judges. Rule 42 (b) of the Federal Rules of Criminal Procedure requires in cases of indirect contempt—that is, contempts committed not in the presence of the judge—that "If the contempt charge involves disrespect to or criticism of the judge, that judge is disqualified from presiding at the trial or hearing except with the defendant's consent." Justice Frankfurter's opinion seems to have been that rule 42 (b) should extend to cases of direct contempt as well, which would, in effect, terminate the ancient power of judges to impose summary sentences for contempts committed in their presence.

Two days after he had been sentenced, Seale reappeared before Judge Hoffman accompanied by a San Francisco lawyer named McTernan, a partner in Garry's firm. McTernan moved that Seale be granted bail pending an appeal of his four-year sentence. The judge denied this motion and said, "You don't call the judge a pig or a fascist . . . We are not running a country store here . . . By his words," Judge Hoffman concluded, Seale "seeks to destroy and overturn the American judicial system . . . His shouting in open court, his insulting characterizations of the presiding judge . . . mean he is a dangerous man. If he is a dangerous man as I have ruled, it would be a gross error for him to be free pending bail."

McTernan attempted to remind the judge that "We are dealing with a black man, who comes out of a black ghetto." He then tried to explain that ghetto blacks do not necessarily intend violence when they use strong language. But the judge cut him short.

"I don't want to hear another thing about a black man," he said. "You don't know me, sir, but I'm as good a friend of the black man as they have in this community and if you don't believe it, read the books. I have known literally thousands of what we used to call Negro people . . . and I never heard that kind of language emanate from the lips of any one of them . . . I never did."

As the judge spoke Seale kept shaking his head. That afternoon he was returned to the Cook County Jail, and from there he was taken by airplane to the San Francisco jail, where he would await the outcome of extradition proceedings in connection with his forthcoming trial in New Haven. Thus the Chicago Eight became, for the remainder of the trial, the Chicago Seven.

9

The Government Rests

With Seale's departure the tension in the courtroom
slackened, and the days grew dull. For another month the
government case wore on, but it produced no new evidence to show what the intentions of the defendants had
been before they came to Chicago. Instead, the testimony
concentrated on the defendants' overt acts: what they had
done during convention week itself. Thus the stories of
Hayden's arrest and Davis' alternate routes to the Amphitheatre came to be told over and over. Fewer reporters
attended—seldom more than a dozen. The defendants no
longer held daily press conferences in the press room that
had been assigned them on the second floor of the Federal
Building, but talked to reporters individually. Only once
or perhaps twice a week would they all assemble in the
press room, either to make an announcement that they considered of special importance or to introduce an interesting
or distinguished visitor to the trial. On November 10 they
announced their plan to subpoena Lyndon Johnson, Richard Daley, Eugene McCarthy, and J. Edgar Hoover to
testify as witnesses for the defense. At the same press conference, Abbie Hoffman described the defendants' plan to
picket the Justice Department on November 15—the day

of the forthcoming Mobilization rally in Washington—
to demand an end to the trial.

However, the spectators continued to fill their section
of the courtroom. Each morning, shortly after dawn, fifty
or more high school and college students would line up
on the sidewalk alongside the green glass wall of the Federal Building, wrap themselves in blankets, and wait for
the marshals to admit them to the twenty-third floor, where
they would line up once more and wait for the courtroom
to open. Some of them may have been disappointed by
what they found once they were admitted. Much of the
testimony seemed aimless and petty. Often Hayden and
Hoffman slept at the defense table. Weiner read for hours
at a time from a volume of Lao-tse, and on the few occasions when he put this book aside he would turn to his
girl friend, who sat in the front row of the press section,
and exchange a few words with her by means of a sign
language they had developed. Dellinger—whose habitual
brown tweed jacket and green shirt had come by now to
seem as remarkable for its modesty as Hoffman's and Rubin's costumes were for their flamboyance—sat before his
opened brief case and busied himself with preparations for
the November 15 antiwar rally, of which he was a chief
organizer. From time to time during the recesses Abbie
Hoffman would repeat to the occupants of the courtroom
his invitation to picket the Justice Department. On November 12 he extended this invitation to the judge himself. "We
think you ought to come to Washington this Saturday and
protest this trial," he urged. The judge ignored the suggestion.

Shortly after ten each morning a marshal delivered mail
addressed to the defendants in care of the Federal Building.
By lunch time these letters and their torn envelopes, together with the day's newspapers and scraps of yellow
legal notepaper would clutter the defense table and over-

flow the wastebasket beneath it. Weinglass—whose orange shoes had turned over at the heel and whose reddish hair had grown long and wild in the manner of the defendants —persisted in presenting constitutional arguments to the Court, which the judge as doggedly brushed aside. At the government table Foran sat hour after hour, his head cradled in his left hand, sketching the heads of horses and bars of music on his yellow legal pad. Though winter was upon the city, the courtroom itself, concerned as it was with the events of late August, retained the sleepy atmosphere of a long summer's day.

Each afternoon, shortly after three, Mr. Kratzke, the elderly cleaner for the Chicago Transit Authority, would begin to nod, abruptly awaken himself, gaze thoughtfully for a few moments at the witness, and then fall back to sleep again. Mr. Nelson, the unemployed housepainter, who had originally come to court in a worn, short-sleeved work shirt and cotton trousers much too large for him, had bought some new suits and shirts with the twenty-five dollars that he was paid for his service each day as a juror, and thus acquired the air of a man of substance. At the end of each afternoon session, the jurors were returned in a yellow school bus to the Palmer House, where they were served a communal dinner, chosen for them by the marshals. Later they watched films, which the marshals also chose. Thus before the trial ended, they had seen all the films based on the adventures of James Bond, the manly undercover agent who infiltrated and destroyed great international conspiracies. They were not, however, permitted to watch television or listen to the radio. Nor could they read newspapers or magazines. Every Sunday each juror was allowed a single visitor, but a marshal joined their conversations to see that no news of the outside world was brought to the sequestered jurors.

Though relations among the jurors were generally harmonious, occasionally they would squabble at the dinner table. Several jurors later admitted that by this time factions had begun to form among them. One group was composed of Mrs. Fritz, whom the defendants called Mrs. Baldwin; Mrs. Seaholm, a widowed bookkeeper; Mrs. Robbins, a clerk for the gas company; and Mrs. Butler, the black woman who was a retired cook. The other group included the two men; Mrs. Burns and Mrs. Bernacki, who attended Roman Catholic services together; Mrs. Evelyn Hill, the black lady who had worn a red wig on the first day of the trial, and who had since bought a blond one with her earnings as a juror; Mrs. Miriam Hill, the heavyset woman whom the defendants called Mrs. Wallace; and Mrs. Peterson, the woman who had received one of the threatening letters. Kay Richards, the young juror who had replaced Kristi King, attached herself to neither group, but tried to ingratiate herself with both. However, Mrs. Fritz and her friends had grown mistrustful of her, and their suspicions grew darker once they learned that Miss Richards' fiancé worked in City Hall. When he came to visit on Sundays they felt that the marshals did not monitor his conversations with her as assiduously as they did those of the other jurors and their visitors.

On November 12, Irwin Bock, the last of the four major government witnesses, took the stand. He testified that since 1967 he had been a member of the Subversive Unit of the Chicago Police Department. In this capacity he had joined the Veterans for Peace in Chicago. He later became a member of its executive committee, a position he continued to hold as of the time he took the witness stand. He also represented the Veterans for Peace on the Chicago Peace Council, and served on the steering committee of the New Mobilization Committee to End the War in Viet Nam, the group of which Dellinger was chairman, and which was making plans for the November 15 rally in Washington.

Bock testified that on July 18, at a meeting of the Chicago Peace Council, he heard Davis say that if any trouble arose at the convention it would come from the bitterness of Eugene McCarthy's followers over the nomination of Humphrey. Then Bock testified that on July 27 he attended another meeting, at which Davis said that some twenty-five or thirty "movement centers" would be opened in Chicago on August 24. There members of various protest groups, such as the Yippies and SDS, might gather to meet their friends and learn of the demonstrations planned for that week. Davis also announced the plans for President Johnson's un-birthday party, and for training 2,500 marshals "in the event of a direct action with the police."

At this point the witness announced that his memory of the July 27 meeting was exhausted, but Schultz prodded him, as he was to do repeatedly whenever Bock lost the thread of his testimony. Kunstler objected to this tactic on the grounds that a friendly witness on direct examination should have to rely upon his own memory and not be coached by his lawyers. The judge overruled Kunstler's objection and warned him not to question Schultz's integrity. Bock then recalled that Davis had also announced a rally for August 28 at the Amphitheatre. "He said that this was not to disrupt the convention," Bock testified, "but it would show the world that there would be war in the streets until there is peace in Vietnam." Then Bock testified that at a meeting on August 1, Davis had said, "If permits were not granted [for the march to the Amphitheatre] . . . that the dissident McCarthy students . . . would return to the Loop, flood the Loop with demonstrators . . . and he said, the Loop would fall."

On August 4, Bock attended a meeting at which Dellinger spoke. According to Bock, Dellinger said, "We haven't come here to disrupt the Democratic convention, nor have we come here to support any candidate to that convention." Bock testified that Dellinger then introduced Davis, who said, "We would test the police on [August 25] to see what reaction they would have toward the demonstrators, to see whether or not they took a hard stand or a soft stand." Bock also testified that Davis had announced a "mill-in" in the Loop for August 28 that would close down the banks, the draft boards, the Federal Building, and police headquarters.

When the August 4 meeting adjourned for lunch, Bock joined Hayden and Davis. According to his testimony he overheard Hayden tell Davis, "We have the formula for Mace and if we place this in the squirt type bottle, the demonstrators could use that against the police."

Then Bock testified that he attended a meeting at the Mobe office on August 9 at which Dellinger, Davis, Hayden, Weiner, and Hoffman were present. This was the same session that Oklepek had described.

At this meeting, according to Bock, "Hayden said that he, Davis and Hoffman had been making plans for diversionary tactics to take place while the main march was going to the Amphitheatre." These tactics were to include "the breaking of windows, pulling of fire alarm boxes, the setting of small fires," and they had two purposes: to divide the police and to require the presence of the National Guard. Bock then testified that Hayden said, "If the South and West Sides would rise up as they did in the April riots, the city would have a lot of trouble on their hands." Hoffman, according to Bock, agreed. "It would," he said, "be like another Chicago fire."

Bock then described the same snake dance practice on August 15 that had been observed by Frapolly and Oklepek. Three days later, he attended a meeting at which Froines, who had been appointed chief marshal, explained how the marshals were to be trained. In his speech, Froines discussed "guerrilla tactics." Bock then testified that Froines later explained that this term meant "the same as mobile tactics . . . the breaking of windows, pulling of fire alarm boxes, setting fires . . ."

Bock's direct testimony continued throughout the afternoon session. Since he had so far described meetings that included all the defendants except Seale and Rubin, the purpose of his testimony evidently was to provide the final elements necessary to support the conspiracy charge, as well as the substantive charges against the individual defendants. At around four o'clock, Bock testified to a meeting that he had attended in Lincoln Park, at which Rubin too was present. When Schultz asked him to identify Rubin at the defense table, it became apparent that Rubin was not in Court. He had left, Kunstler expalined, to get to the airport in time to fly to New Jersey, where he was scheduled to speak that night at Rutgers University.

Judge Hoffman turned to his clerk and said, "Mr. Clerk, let a bench warrant issue for the arrest of the defendant Rubin. Let his bail bond be terminated." This news reached Rubin over the radio of the taxi that he had taken to the Chicago airport, and he immediately returned to the city, where he surrendered to an agent of the FBI. He spent that night in Cook County Jail and on the following morning was brought to court in the custody of the marshals.

That morning, before Bock resumed his testimony, Kunstler argued for Rubin's release, explaining that his early departure the day before was the result of a "misunderstanding." The defendants had assumed that if they agreed to waive their rights to be present at the trial they could, from time to time, take leave. Accordingly Rubin had signed such a waiver, given it to Kunstler and left at four o'clock to catch his plane. The judge replied that there had been no such "misunderstanding" on his part and that the defendants could not leave his courtroom whenever they felt like it. Kunstler then explained that the purpose of Rubin's trip was to help raise money for the defense by means of the lecture fee he expected to receive. "These fees," Kunstler explained, "are all the defendants have, plus some contributions . . . and even though they have no legal fees to pay in this case . . . [since] their counsel serve without fee, they do have the costs of transcripts . . . of [traveling] to interview [defense] witnesses, and they have the problems of phones and rent and living that are necessitated by the fact that all but two of them are not from Chicago."

Kunstler then referred the judge to a ruling by the Supreme Court in a similar case. The Court said that bail may be revoked only "when the defendant's conduct presents the danger of significant interruption with the trial . . ." The Court added, "The record, in this case, shows only a single brief incident of tardiness . . . In these circumstances, the trial judge's order of commitment, made without hearing or statement of reasons, had the appearance and effect of punishment rather than of an order designed solely to facilitate the trial."

Kunstler then asked if Rubin could speak on his own behalf, and the judge agreed.

"As to yesterday, Your Honor," Rubin explained, "I felt that it was sufficient to sign a statement stipulating that I would withdraw my constitutional right to be here. I did not know the witness on the stand, had never seen him and did not expect him to testify about me. I did not intend to defy you or the Court . . . and I did not know I was doing anything wrong. I did not walk out on the trial . . . I like being here. It is interesting—"

"That is the best—" the judge interrupted.

"Let me finish," Rubin said.

But the judge continued. "That is the best statement I have heard here during the trial. You said you enjoyed being here."

"It is good theater, Your Honor," Rubin replied.

The judge then reinstated Rubin's bail, and Bock resumed the stand. He identified Rubin as the defendant wearing a shirt with pink and blue stripes and green corduroy trousers. Bock then testified that in Lincoln Park on the evening of August 26 he saw Davis, Rubin, Froines, and Weiner. They had been discussing Hayden's arrest and Davis said, "We should have a wall-to-wall sit-in in front of the Conrad Hilton," and that when the police come, the people should form small bands and cause disturbances in the Loop. Rubin added that they "should start fires in the Loop," and Froines said that they might use ammonia against the police. Then Bock described a meeting at Mobilization headquarters on August 28, at which Dellinger, Hayden, Davis, Froines, and Weiner were present. At this meeting, according to Bock, Dellinger said that "the city would not allow permits" for the march to the Amphitheatre. Then Hayden said, "If the city doesn't give in to our demands there would be war in the streets and there should be." Bock testified that Dellinger said there were "two alternatives for actions" that he would propose later that day at a rally at the Grant Park band shell. The demonstrators could either disperse or they could "march to the Amphitheatre without a permit," and when the police stopped them they could "sit down and practice the old form of nonviolent resistance." Some of them, however, Dellinger added, according to Bock, might decide to become "more militant"; this would be a "third alternative."

Later that afternoon Bock went to the Grant Park rally, where he saw Froines and Weiner. According to Bock, Weiner said, "A good mobile tactic would be to pick a target in the Loop and bomb it." The target that Weiner suggested, according to Bock, was the underground garage in Grant Park. This, Weiner said, "would draw the police away from the Loop" so that the demonstrators could carry on their other actions more easily. With this, Bock's direct testimony was concluded.

The cross-examination of Bock lasted for five more somnolent days, during which the personnel of the trial became increasingly irritable. The defendants complained that Bock's testimony had been so superficial as to exclude all reality. They said that it reflected the same crude mentality that produced the indictments themselves. What angered the defendants most was that Bock, presumably with Schultz's coaching, had represented their rhetorical statements and their tentative suggestions for this or that activity as if they were the equivalent of action itself. Though the defendants continued to read their books and newspapers throughout most of Bock's testimony, occasionally they would respond to his replies with an exaggerated groan or gasp, or with laughter. The judge warned them not to persist in this behavior, but Dellinger replied, on one such occasion, "We are not ashamed to laugh . . . [Bock] is a vaudeville actor."

Though the judge followed the examination attentively and marked certain passages in his ledger, he too had begun to reveal signs of strain. On the afternoon of November 17, he interrupted the examination to scold Kunstler for resting his elbow on the lectern.

"Mr. Kunstler," he said, "there is a great architect, Mies van der Rohe, who recently left us. He designed that lectern as well as this building and it was a lectern, not a leaning post. I don't permit lawyers to lean on that thing. I don't want you to do it. That was put there by the government, designed by Mies van der Rohe, and I want you to use it for that purpose."

"Perhaps I am tired, Your Honor," Kunstler replied. "What is wrong with leaning on it?"

"I will not permit you to . . ." the judge answered. "Since

you are tired we will take a recess and you can sleep for the rest of the afternoon." Thereupon he adjourned the court. As soon as the jury had left, he warned the defendants that he would not tolerate any further laughter from them. "You can't use this courtroom as a circus," he told them.

On November 24, Weinglass presented a motion to stop the trial. He repeated his earlier argument that the government's use of the defendants' lawful speeches as evidence of criminal activity violated their First Amendment rights. In support of his argument he cited a ruling made by the Supreme Court in 1965 in the case of *Dombrowski v. Pfister*. In this case, members of the Southern Conference Education Fund were indicted on the evidence of their speeches and writings under a Louisiana sedition statute. The Federal District Court, however, forbade the prosecution on First Amendment grounds, and the Supreme Court agreed. The Justices added that the prosecution had no basis in law and therefore may have been intended only to harass the defendants by putting them to the expense of a trial. The effect of such frivolous prosecutions, the Court ruled, would be to "chill" the expression of dissenting opinion on the part of others who might fear an ensuing legal involvement.

Weinglass then cited a recent ruling of the Seventh Circuit Court of Appeals, which elaborated on the Dombrowski doctrine. "When a significant chilling effect on free speech is created by a bad faith prosecution," the Court ruled, "the prosecution will thus, as a matter of law, cause irreparable injury regardless of other outcome. . . . Speech is an evanescent thing. . . . That is why a mere prosecution may destroy it. . . . If there is any right asserted by private parties, the preservation of which amounts to a compelling national interest, it is the right of free speech."

Foran then replied. "Your Honor," he said, "of course

this is, I think, the third rehash of this same concept." Then he explained that the First Amendment protects only the right to assemble "peaceably." The testimony so far had shown, Foran argued, that the intentions of the defendants had not been peaceable. The Founding Fathers, he said, did not mean to protect the speech of "two bank robbers" who meet in the open and discuss the division of loot that they hope to acquire in a forthcoming robbery. Therefore, the question is, "Have these men been participating in legal activities or are those [illegal] activities with which they are charged in this indictment—which are traveling in interstate commerce to incite a riot and with the intention to participate in one and to aid and abet other people who are participating?"

Thus Foran raised the fundamental legal question of the trial. Were the defendants' speeches in fact inseparable from a subsequent criminal act, and thus equivalent to the conversation of the two robbers? Had the evidence, in other words, shown that their speeches revealed a continuous and unbroken intention to come to Chicago for the unequivocal purpose of inciting the riots that occurred there? Foran evidently felt that the evidence had shown such an uninterrupted intention, in which case the objection raised by Representative Edwards and the ACLU against the anti-riot act might not apply in the present case; for the intention to incite and the incitement itself would then be simultaneous, even though the origins of the defendants' intentions could be traced far back in time. If the testimony had revealed such a continuous intention, then perhaps the speeches of the defendants could be offered as the direct and deliberate cause of the attacks by the demonstrators upon the police. Thus, Foran argued, it is up to the jury to decide whether the evidence has revealed such an unbroken chain. "The First Amendment," Foran concluded, "does not permit people to travel in

interstate commerce with an intention to incite a riot . . .
or to teach and demonstrate the making of incendiary
devices or to interfere with police in their lawful duties
nor to do any of the other things with which these people
are charged in this indictment."

Weinglass replied that the question is not one of facts
but of law. Before the jury may deliberate, the Court must
decide what is "advocacy of action and what is criminal
speech." Again he cited the case of *Brandenberg v. Ohio*
in which the Supreme Court had decided that the defendant's angry words were not in themselves criminal. The
Court had ruled, Weinglass said, that Brandenberg had not
told his audience, "Let's you and I go down to march,"
but instead had suggested a future action, one that never,
in fact, occurred. Though the riots in Chicago had actually
occurred, Weinglass continued, the government had not
shown that they were the direct result of the speeches made
by Dellinger in San Diego, or Rubin in New York, or even
of the speeches that the defendants had made in Chicago
itself. The government had not, Weinglass' argument implied, demonstrated the unbroken chain of cause and effect
that Foran had presupposed when he introduced the analogy of the two bank robbers; thus there was no evidence
that the defendants' speeches had been the clear and present
cause of the riots. Since the speeches were not unequivocally part of a criminal act, they could not, Weinglass
argued, go before the jury as evidence of the defendants'
guilt. How, Weinglass asked the Court, could the jury use
the evidence of the defendants' speeches to make a determination of guilt unless the Court itself first determined
that the speeches were constitutionally admissible as proof
of criminal activity?

The judge evidently agreed that this was an important
question, for he interrupted Weinglass' argument to ask,
"Who is the one to decide whether the language might

incite a person to commit mayhem? Who is the one to decide?"

Weinglass replied, "In the Brandenberg Case . . . the United States Supreme Court . . . [said], in effect, that [it] was a matter which a jury should not properly consider; that those words were not so inherently inflammatory and the judge should not have submitted them to the jury."

"They were not sufficiently inflammatory," the judge agreed, "but suppose the trial judge should reach the conclusion that as a matter of law, he must submit the case to the jury for their determination in that regard?"

Weinglass replied that before the jury could deliberate, the judge must first determine that the government has produced evidence showing "imminent peril, clear and present danger . . . [but] I don't think the government has once tried to demonstrate that a [given] speech created an immediate peril to the safety of the persons in the area. . . . If they would bring in a police officer," Weinglass continued, "who would testify that 'I was standing there. I heard Bobby Seale speak on the 27th. What he said placed me in immediate peril. That crowd was ugly and they were about to march on me . . .' that would be enough. But I asked the police officer who testified that he had heard Seale speak, 'What was that crowd like?' 'Oh, they were peaceful and quiet.' 'What did the crowd do after Mr. Seale finished? Did they march on anybody? Did they attack anybody?' 'No they got up and left the park.'" Therefore, Weinglass concluded, the government had not shown that the defendants' speeches—of which he felt Seale's was the most inflammatory—had constituted a clear and present danger. Thus, as a matter of law, these speeches could not, he argued, be submitted to the jury as evidence of guilt, so the trial should now be stopped.

The judge replied that he had never before heard a motion to stop a trial, and that, furthermore, Foran had been right when he said that much of what "Mr. Weinrob" had argued had already been dealt with in earlier rulings. Therefore he denied the motion.

Schultz then presented a motion on behalf of the government. The motion was ". . . to admit the evidence—only as to certain defendants to be admitted as to all the defendants . . . because it is our contention that we have established a prima facie conspiracy so far in our proof."

The evidence of conspiracy that Schultz then summarized began with the attempt by Rubin and Hoffman on March 26 to apply to Deputy Mayor Stahl for a permit. Then on August 2 Davis also negotiated with Stahl, and on August 7 Rubin and Hoffman met with Stahl again. On the following day, Rubin and Hoffman submitted their application once more, and on August 10 Davis met with Stahl a second time. Then on August 12 Dellinger, Davis, and Hayden "again contacted Stahl, showing a joint operation, a joint attempt," Schultz emphasized, holding his outstretched hands apart and then bringing them together, the fingers intertwined.

Then on August 9 Davis, Weiner, Dellinger, Hoffman, Hayden, and Froines attended the meeting to which Frapolly, Oklepek, and Bock had testified. At this meeting, Schultz reminded the Court, "they discussed a march to the Amphitheatre. They discussed a mill-in where they were going to disrupt traffic, run through stores and streets, blocking streets, setting off false alarms, setting off small fires, tie up the Loop, bust it up, shut down Chicago, the Chicago Loop. They discussed dividing the police. Hoffman said it might be like another Chicago fire." Though none of these disasters, in fact, occurred, the defense could not object. Under conspiracy law, as the Poulterer's Case established, the crime consists in the plot, not in its outcome.

Schultz summarized the government case at length, recounting the various meetings at which the defendants were present, and which had been described to the Court by the government witnesses. At last he paused and turned to the judge. "I think," he said, "that at this point the evidence is not simply prima facie, but the evidence is beyond a reasonable doubt that a conspiracy was formed." He then asked the judge to instruct the jury accordingly. Judge Hoffman, however, reserved his decision until the following day, when he would hear Kunstler's reply to Schultz.

The next morning Kunstler replied to Schultz's motion. The meetings with Stahl were not, he said, proof of criminal intent on the part of the defendants, but an innocent attempt to conform to the laws and regulations of the city of Chicago. If the permit negotiations did give rise to suspicion of conspiracy, Kunstler argued, then the conspirators must have been the city officials and not the defendants, for the defendants had negotiated in good faith.

Then Kunstler attacked the testimony of the undercover agents. At the August 9 meeting, for example, Bock said that he had seen Weiner, Davis, Hayden, Froines, Hoffman, and Dellinger. Oklepek, however, had seen only Davis, Hayden, and Froines, while Frapolly had seen Davis, Dellinger, and Weiner. Kunstler then proceeded to show similar inconsistencies throughout the rest of the government's testimony. Furthermore, he argued, the defendants had no criminal intentions. "Everything possible, the evidence indicates, was done to avoid violence by the demonstrators. They didn't want to go into black neighborhoods where there might be violence," Kunstler argued. "They were afraid of hostile white neighborhoods. The marshals were told to try to negotiate and protect them from hecklers . . . The training," Kunstler concluded, "was defensive."

He then referred to the appellate reversal in the Spock Case in which the Court had written, "The intertwining of illegal and legal aspects, the public setting of the agreement and its political purposes and the loose confederation of possibly innocent and possibly guilty participants raise the most serious First Amendment problems. . . . There is a danger that one in sympathy with the legitimate aims of [an] organization but not specifically intending to accomplish them by resort to violence might be punished by his adherence to lawful and constitutionally protected purposes because of other and unprotected purposes which he does not necessarily adhere to."

To these arguments Schultz replied, "Mr. Kunstler has spent well over an hour and I think except for about five or seven minutes that he devoted to legal analysis he has wasted our time—"

"But you will admit," the judge interrupted, "that I did my best to stop him."

"Yes, you did," Schultz replied, an acknowledgment that throughout Kunstler's long and complicated argument the judge had frequently interrupted to ask that he conclude his remarks quickly. Then Schultz added that as for himself, he would not "waste any time of the court replying to the nonsense of Mr. Kunstler except that he has given no reason whatever why the instruction that we have presented should not be given to the jury."

The judge then granted the government motion that a prima facie case of conspiracy had been established and could therefore go before the jury at the conclusion of the trial for a determination of the facts.

That afternoon, the government played a tape recording that had been made by a Naval Intelligence Officer at the Grant Park band shell on Wednesday afternoon, August 28. Though the Mobe had at last secured from the city a permit to hold this rally, the police nevertheless ringed the 10,000 demonstrators who attended it. Dozens of plainclothes men mingled with the crowd. Dellinger, who was chairman, stood at the microphone on the stage of the faded blue band shell. The first speaker he introduced was

Jerry Rubin, whose voice could be heard on the tape telling the audience, "We are going to take the same risks that blacks take. If the cops are going to beat on blacks they are going to beat on us too. And if anything happens to Huey Newton they're going to have to do something to us." He then said, "Many of us were born in relative wealth, but we are rejecting wealth because we don't believe in the value of money or the profit system. The hell with property . . ." He concluded by saying, "Just one more thing . . . It has been shown that white people are going to take to the streets to become fighters to try to take the country away from the people who run it and that's how we are going to join the blacks, by joining them on the streets. See you on the streets tonight," he concluded.

Dellinger then introduced several other speakers, who addressed the crowd in the same militant vein. By the time the third speaker came to the microphone, a disturbance had broken out between the spectators and some of the police, and the uproar could be heard on the tape. Though Dellinger had no way of knowing at the time what the trouble was, a voice could be heard shouting that the police had released tear gas, and that a fight had begun near the flagpole to the right of the band shell, about two hundred feet from the stage. What had happened, Dellinger soon learned, was that a young demonstrator had climbed to the top of the pole and lowered the flag to half-mast. Another group standing at the base of the pole then lowered the flag the rest of the way, and one of these people hoisted a red cloth to the top of the pole. At this point, the police attacked and some of the demonstrators fought back.

"All right, everybody," Dellinger's voice could be heard over the uproar. "Everybody stay where you are. The marshals are at their sites and we will hear from them later. Everybody please sit down and leave it to the marshals . . . This is being done for the whole world to see. Let them see who is committing the violence here. We will have a report . . ." He then read a message from the marshals that only fifty police were involved in the incident. "Don't listen to rumors," he shouted. "Stay in your seats . . . What the police want to do is create a disturbance here. Our marshals are handling it. We will not let the police provoke a riot here." Though by this time several spectators had been hurt, and others arrested, most of the crowd followed Dellinger's instructions, and soon the police abandoned their attack.

Then Dellinger proposed the "alternatives" to which Bock had testified. "Now there are going to be three different ways in which people will want to act," he said. "In a moment I'm going to call on someone to talk about one of them. But one of the ways is that some of us, including myself . . . will assemble peacefully, approximately eight abreast. We will be prepared to march to the Amphitheatre. We've got to go! But this will be . . . a nonviolent march to the Amphitheatre. . . .

"Secondly, there will be some people, and you will hear this explained to you in their own words . . . who believe that it is important to get away from here and to regroup and take other actions.

"Thirdly, there will be people who want just to sit quietly here while one group is forming for the nonviolent march and the other group is forming for their regroupment and action."

Dellinger then introduced a speaker named Tom Neuman, who presented the second option. "We have decided," Neuman said, "to move out of this park in any way we can and to defend ourselves in any way we can." What Neuman was suggesting was the potentially violent option that Dellinger, a pacifist, could not support, but which he could not, as spokesman for the coalition of autonomous radical groups that formed the Mobe, condemn.

After Neuman spoke, Rubin brought a pig to the stage and introduced it as the only candidate that could beat Nixon. "This pig," Rubin announced, "demands a debate with Hubert Humphrey Hog, Richard Milhous Pig and George Piggy Wallace in a four-pig debate on national television."

Then Dellinger took the microphone and said, in his quavering voice, "I want to inform the people who are going on the nonviolent march to the Amphitheatre that it will be led by Veterans of the Vietnam War, by people from the Poor People's Campaign, by Allen Ginsberg, Jean Genet, William Burroughs, myself and others . . . Hold your cool, move slowly, and we will begin to take our positions."

Hayden took the microphone next, and made the speech to which Schultz had referred in his opening statement to the jury. He began by saying that Davis was in the hospital with "a split head," the result of a blow by the police. Therefore, Hayden told the crowd, "if blood is going to flow, let it flow all over the city . . . if the police are going to run wild, let them run wild all over the city of Chicago and not over us in the park . . . if we are going to be disrupted and violated, let this whole stinking city be disrupted and violated. Begin to find your way out of here. I'll see you in the streets."

Soon thereafter, Dellinger's march proceeded to leave the park, but was immediately stopped by the police and troops of the National Guard who were posted at the exits. In the confusion, the demonstrators scattered. Many eventually found their way out of the park and onto Michigan Avenue, across from the Conrad Hilton. By eight o'clock, the terrible riot of Wednesday night at the corner of Michigan and Balbo had begun. Hundreds of police battled the thousands of aimless, angry, and bewildered demonstrators and bystanders who filled Michigan Avenue. "There is little doubt," according to the Walker Commission Report that was issued shortly after the convention disturbances, that while it was not "a one way street . . . the preponderance of violence came from the police." Foran himself, a week after the trial ended, admitted, ". . . the police moved in and got even for what they had been taking from the demonstrators for three days. After that the police felt great. They were smiling and waving and you could see that it was a great psychological thing for them."

But during the trial it was the government's claim that this violence had been the deliberate plan of the alleged conspirators, a plan that had originated on April 12, the date on which the indictment declared the conspiracy to have commenced; that Dellinger's speech in San Diego, Rubin's in New York, the various negotiations for permits, the meetings at Mobe headquarters, the marshal training, and so forth represented a coherent chain of deliberate preparations meant to incite the confrontations between the demonstrators and the Chicago police that culminated in the violence on Michigan Avenue on Wednesday evening, August 28. Of this riot, Dellinger, according to Schultz, had been "the principal architect." Thus the recording that the prosecution had played to the jury on November 25 served as the climax of the government's case; it revealed the culminating overt act to which all the others were merely the prelude and from which the jurors might infer what the intentions of the defendants had been during the preceding five months.

On the following day, the defendants, aware that the government's case was now nearly complete, petitioned the Court for a writ of habeus corpus in order to bring a man named John Sinclair to Chicago to testify for the defense, which would begin the following week. The writ was necessary because Sinclair, a white radical from Detroit, was serving a nine-and-a-half-year sentence in a Michigan prison for possessing two marijuana cigarettes.

Kunstler argued on behalf of his motion that Sinclair was

a "key defense witness," who had helped the Yippies arrange their Festival of Life in Chicago. Thus his testimony would clarify the intentions with which Hoffman and Rubin had come to the convention. "The jury," Kunstler argued, "has been told much about Yippies and about the language employed by Mr. Hoffman and Mr. Rubin. We want to call Mr. Sinclair, who is an expert on youth culture, to explain to the jury what The Youth International Party is, what its purposes are, its aims, how it began, and to place in the proper context Mr. Rubin's and Mr. Hoffman's words and speeches."

The judge then asked why Sinclair was in prison and Kunstler explained that he had been sentenced for possession of two marijuana cigarettes. "I don't believe," Kunstler said, "by any stretch of the imagination that that makes a man dangerous." Kunstler's reassurance on this point was gratuitous; the defense in a criminal trial is normally free to subpoena any witness whose testimony, it feels, might be helpful.

"Oh, I can stretch my imagination to this point," the judge replied, "that I don't think any judge in this building would sentence a man to nine years . . . for the possession of two marijuana cigarettes. . . . It would seem to me that the presentence report, if there is one [must have], indicated some previous encounters with law enforcement agencies. [Therefore] I will decline this petition," the judge concluded. "Furthermore," the judge said, "Sinclair is not an essential witness. Many others were in Chicago at the time who could testify just as effectively."

The defendants were enraged. "This man is a key witness to our defense," Kunstler argued. "Your Honor has made a decision in your discretion not to let us have this key witness."

"Aw Jesus. Fascist," Dellinger exclaimed as he rose to his feet.

"Who is that man talking?" the judge demanded.

"That is Mr. David Dellinger," Dellinger replied, "and he is saying it is an arbitrary denial when you say who is key to our defense."

"Mr. Marshal," the judge replied, "make that man sit down."

"I think it is acting like a fascist court," Dellinger continued, "like Mr. Seale said when you made decisions that deprive us of our witnesses."

"Why don't you gag all of us?" Davis asked.

"Who said that?" the judge snapped.

"Bobby Seale said that," Davis replied.

"The defendant Davis said that, Your Honor," Schultz said.

The defendants were by now in great and obvious turmoil. Abbie Hoffman turned to the judge and said, "We are very confused about this. Is the government going to present our defense as well as our prosecution?"

"What is the name of that defendant speaking?" the judge asked.

"Just Abbie. I don't have a last name, Judge. I just lost it," Hoffman replied. "We can't respect this court when it's a tyranny."

A week later the government rested its case. It had presented fifty-three witnesses and fourteen television films, filled more than 9,000 pages of transcript, and provided the occasion for Seale's confrontation with the judge, in order to show that eight radicals—and not the city of Chicago or the federal government—had been responsible for the Chicago riots. Thus Representative Cramer's bill had had its day in Court, and Chief Judge Campbell and Mayor Daley had had theirs.

Weinglass felt that a defense was not necessary and might even be damaging. The government case, he told the defendants, had been so superficial that at least some of the

jurors—Mrs. Fritz, for example—would be unlikely to accept it. Thus the chance for a hung jury at this point was
considerable and would not necessarily improve if the sequestered jurors had to sit through two or three months of
further testimony. Furthermore, a defense would be expensive. It would mean several more months in Chicago and it
would also mean that money would have to be found to
bring witnesses to the trial and house them while they were
there. All of this would cost many thousands of dollars beyond what had already been spent. To make matters worse,
the defense had only three witnesses on hand for the first
day of their presentation. Once these had testified, the defense might find it difficult to find others in time to continue their case. Should it happen that the defendants could
not produce a new witness, the judge would probably order
them to rest then and there.

Despite these arguments, Dellinger said that he wanted
a defense not only so that he and the others could vindicate
themselves in Court, but because they wanted to present
their political arguments to the public as well. Hayden was
even more committed to a defense. "We are on trial for
our identity," he had said. Thus the defendants rejected
Weinglass' advice and decided to present their case. They
felt that they could easily refute the government's evidence,
and that they would also seize the opportunity to explain
who they really were. Since it was their identity, as Hayden
had said, that was on trial, they would call witnesses not
only to give their version of what had really happened in
Chicago, but to tell the jury and the world what this identity
actually was. Thus they would attempt to use the Court as
a forum for the generation that they claimed to represent.
Furthermore, they would try to show that the ideals to
which, in their opinion, this generation subscribed were the
true and ancient ideals of the republic, ideals that had been
corrupted by the usurping politicians who had, in the

opinion of the defendants, indicted them in order to justify their illegitimate control of the nation's destiny and the cruel and greedy imposition of their debased civilization upon the people of the world.

10

Natural Law

THE SUPPORTERS of Eugene McCarthy, upon whose disaffection, according to Bock, the defendants had been counting, had come to Chicago for the purpose of reforming the
Democratic party. Their candidate had promised to end the
war in Vietnam, and though he offered his followers no
more than this, many hoped and some believed that if he
were elected President he would at last undertake the programs of domestic reform that had been promised by John
Kennedy in 1960, but which had been forestalled by the
struggle in Asia. Though the silence of their candidate on
domestic matters suggested to some that he may have been
indifferent to the misery of the blacks and the poverty of
the cities, others believed that once the Asian war was over,
the Democrats would proceed to fulfill the long-awaited
promises of their party, if only because these promises had
been so long outstanding. To this end, the silence of a withdrawn and reflective President would, they felt, be no ob-
stacle, if only the war would end.

The defendants, however, saw no hope for reform in the
American political system as it had come to be. The Asian
war and the brutality of domestic life were not, in their
view, the work of a few wilful and misguided men who,

having seized the party of American progressivism, had thrust themselves upon a benign and trusting people. Instead, the evils of American life were, they believed, the inevitable product of the native culture itself, a profound and probably incurable disease that had destroyed the hopes and dignity of the people, and of which Lyndon Johnson, Richard Daley, and Hubert Humphrey were not the accidental but the essential expression. Thus the defendants and their followers, having concluded that the country had lost its claim on the faith of the people, became a diffuse party of radical adversaries, split among many factions but all opposed not only to the American political system but to the cultural processes from which, in their view, the system came.

Though they hated the war and the presumption of racial superiority that they felt sustained it, they hated still more the political economy that fed the root of these evils, together with the moral system that attempted to justify them. Though they seldom lingered over such grand generalizations, what offended some of them most deeply was the Puritan tendency within Christian history itself: the claim that a single rule of moral conduct should govern all the world's people—a rule which had come to hold that the successful extraction of profit from men and nature is the proof of virtue, that money measures everything, and that industrial progress is a self-evident good.

Thus they lost confidence in much of the historical ground on which, as white Americans, they stood. As a consequence, many of them experienced what theologians call a crisis of faith, and psychoanalysts call a crisis of identity. To survive this crisis some of them sought to create for themselves a new identity derived from alternate values to which they could attach their faith. Thus their aim at Chicago had been not to reform a political party or even a political system, but to make a new society. "We shall not defeat

Amerika," Hoffman had said, "by organizing a political party. We shall do it by building a new nation." In this way, they would remake themselves as well. This is what Hayden meant when he said that the defendants were on trial for their identity, and what Judge Hoffman perhaps inadvertently affirmed when he said, at the pretrial hearing on September 9, that "the substance of the crime is a state of mind."

"The New Left in this country has been very reluctant to become revolutionary," Hayden had told the House Un-American Activities Committee in December 1968. "Like many young people, I was given a good deal of hope by the 1960 presidential campaign of Senator Kennedy. I felt, and many other young people at the time felt, that the Cold War and the arms race were . . . poisonous to a democratic system. [Thus] the Peace Corps represented an alternative.

"[But] we saw the Peace Corps become wedded to American foreign policy. Its more decent programs [were] ways to brighten up the more brutal and exploitative patterns of [that] policy. [So] we dropped out of the Peace Corps.

"The major issue that shaped our political outlook, however, was not foreign but domestic policy and particularly the problem of civil rights in the South, which came to the attention of the Northern students in 1960. Working in the South brought us face to face for the first time with the reality of the police state. Civil rights workers were arrested by the thousands, beaten by the hundreds, killed on one occasion, and terrorized by the police constantly. The crucial discovery of that experience for many students, however, was that the South was not an isolated and backward region but an integral part of the whole country. . . . The federal government and the Democratic party could not and would not offend Southern officials."

Like the early Christians, whose fears and scruples had turned them against the corruption of a cruel and dying empire, many of the young people who had shared the experience that Hayden described undertook, once they had broken with their historic surroundings, to create, from whatever scraps of doctrine they could find, a new place to stand; to discover new political and moral bearings.

For the early Christians there had been the solace and imperative of the Hebrew God, along with the powerful example of a zealous and ambitious priesthood, eager to inherit the residual power of the dying empire. For the Haymarket radicals there had been the promise of militant communism and the immediate, if ambiguous, example of the Paris Commune, which offered the hope, if not the proof, of the revolutionary power of the working class. But for the radicals of Hayden's generation who considered themselves revolutionaries, there was neither religion nor ideology in the usual sense; nor did the experience of most of them confirm that the American working class was a likely revolutionary ally. There was left to them only the idea of revolution itself and the hope that from the radical conversion of individual consciousness and a continuing struggle with the dying culture, something better and more humane would emerge. Thus many of them attached themselves to the example of the militant blacks and the revolutionary Cubans, Algerians, and Asians.

Unlike the black radicals, however, who considered themselves a captive colony within the "mother country," or the third world revolutionaries who had literally been colonized, these white Americans were the sons and daughters of the "mother country" itself. For them, therefore, revolution was not simply a political or military struggle—a matter of defeating and breaking loose from an alien oppressor— but also a spiritual and psychological enterprise in which they would have to purge their own corrupt inheritance as well as contend with their despised rulers.

Though the white revolutionaries occasionally borrowed the language of Marxism, the revolution that they actually awaited involved more than turning the engines of society over to a new class of men. It also meant breaking away from the habits of their tribe and starting over. Thus many of them welcomed drugs, celebrated an emancipated sexuality, deplored the nuclear family and the virtue of remunerative work; they let their hair grow long, discarded the traditional costume of their elders, danced to a new music, and spoke an obscene language. By means of this "life style" they hoped not only to regain their own souls but perhaps eventually, if enough of their generation followed them, to make the country itself conform to their example. "The world we have known is passing," said the late A. J. Muste, the pacifist leader who had been Dellinger's mentor. "Mankind has to find the way into a radically new world. Mankind has to become a 'new humanity' or perish." Though Dellinger himself came to court in his brown tweed jacket, green shirt and tie, was often accompanied by his wife and daughters, and generally exemplified the older "life style," he did not disagree with Hoffman and Rubin, who made a political principle of the new style, that the traditional culture, having denied for so long its more decent values, had grown foul and become a menace. Though neither Dellinger nor the others could say clearly what form the revolution should take, much less what tactics to apply against their still powerful, if dying, adversary, this did not keep them from sharing with Muste the view that a radically new world was essential to human survival.

On the day that the defense case began, Hayden told the reporters that he and the other radicals on trial had come to Chicago "as participants in the creation of a new society in the streets . . . with its own natural laws, structures, language and symbols." The defense, he said, will argue that a revolution is necessary in order to dispossess the "dinosaurs controlling an obsolete system." In the previous December he had told HUAC, "Our identity as a generation is what has become criminal in your eyes and your laws are merely convenient devices to punish and exterminate that identity. We disrespect your authority. You cannot stand it." Thus he told the reporters a year later that "the jury will be invited to commit civil disobedience against the judge's instructions. Chicago, 1968, will be recreated in the courtroom." What he meant was that he and the others on trial would attempt to convert the jurors to the new faith toward which they themselves were groping.

Concerning the demoralization of the Romans after the reign of Augustus, Gibbon observed that "the people when they discovered their deities were rejected and derided by those whose rank or understanding they were accustomed to reverence, were filled with doubts and apprehensions concerning the truth of those doctrines which they yielded the most implicit belief. The decline of ancient prejudice exposed a very numerous portion of mankind to the danger of a painful and comfortless position. A state of skepticism and suspense may amuse a few inquisitive minds," Gibbon added, "but the practice of superstition is so congenial to the multitude that, if they are forcibly awakened, they still regret the loss of their pleasing vision."

In their defense, Hayden and the others would undertake deliberately to exacerbate the doubts and fears of what Gibbon called the multitude—or at least of the majority of the jurors. By revealing their own loss of faith in America to the jury, the defendants hoped to remain true to their convictions, but they also knew that they would frighten and offend the only people who stood between them and prison. Though the other defendants shared Hayden's commitment —and Hoffman may have exceeded it—Hayden himself, who felt that it was among the duties of a revolutionary to keep out of jail, had calculated the situation of the jurors from still another, more cautious, perspective. He knew that while a candid defense would surely antagonize some of the jurors—especially the woman they called Mrs. Wallace, and probably Mr. Kratzke too—their antipathy would perhaps, in Hayden's term, "polarize" the jury so that the more sympathetic women would support the defendants with even more determination.

Though the resolve of the defendants was firm enough in itself, it had been considerably stiffened by the example of Seale. It was further strengthened, two days before Hayden's interview with the reporters, by the death of Fred Hampton, the Illinois Panther chairman. Early on the morning of December 4, fourteen Chicago police, on orders from the office of the state's attorney, entered Hampton's apartment in the West Side ghetto and killed the Panther leader in his bed. Mark Clark, another Panther, was killed at the same time. Though the Chicago newspapers supported the account of the police that they had been fired upon first, the defendants took the word of the surviving Panthers that this had not been so. Hampton and Clark, they believed, had been murdered by the police in keeping with the Justice Department program to destroy the Panther party. By the following May, a federal grand jury confirmed the suspicions of the defendants. Neither the FBI nor the Chicago police had been able to show that more than a single shot of the more than eighty bullets that had been fired came from Panther guns. Thus the seven surviving Panthers who had been found in the apartment and who had been held by the Chicago police on charges of attempted murder were released. But the federal grand jury, under the supervision of Jerris Leonard, Chief of the Civil Rights Division of the Justice Department, returned no indictments against the fourteen officers. However, Deputy Superintendent Mulchrone, the chief of inspectional services for the Chicago police, was demoted and his salary reduced from $27,500 to $19,000. This was the same man to whom Director Lyons had passed on the FBI reports, in the summer of 1968, that the Panthers, encouraged by the "communist" Hayden, were planning to make trouble at the convention. According to the federal grand jury, the raid on Hampton's apartment had also been inspired by a report from the FBI to the Chicago police that guns were being stored there.

Despite what Hayden told the reporters, the first defense witnesses were uncommonly respectable: a Chicago man who worked in a candy factory, a young Quaker girl with austere braids, a woman member of Parliament, another woman who had recently received a doctorate from Cornell, and a fourth woman who was an elderly habitué of entertainments presented at the Grant Park band shell. All of these witnesses testified that the police and not the demonstrators had provoked whatever violence they had seen during convention week. Furthermore, they had all been injured by the police, the MP and the woman from Cornell most seriously.

Though the sobriety of these witnesses perhaps impressed the jurors favorably, they may also have noticed a degree of awkwardness among them compared with the cool and practiced manner of the police witnesses who had testified for the government. Thus when the judge asked Mrs. Kerr, the MP, how he should address such a personage as herself, she replied, "Just call me Anne." When the judge rejected this opportunity, she replied, "Well then, my lord, you may call me the honorable member from Rochester and Chatham," an exchange that may have seemed to some jurors frivolous and perhaps snobbish. Mrs. Fritz, however, put her fist to her mouth and laughed silently.

While Weinglass and the other members of the legal staff were occupied with finding witnesses who could testify to the misbehavior of the police, Hoffman and Rubin were arranging for the appearance of witnesses who could convey to the jurors the "life style" of the defendants and especially the Yippies. What they wanted to expose to the jurors was the meaning of their "alternative culture," a culture whose principles were described in a pamphlet that had been distributed during the convention, and which had antagonized not only the Chicago officials but the members of the congressional committee that had questioned Hayden a year earlier.

"Disobey your parents," this pamphlet had urged. "Burn your money. You know life is a dream and all our institutions are man-made illusions, effective only because you take the dream for reality. Break down the family, church, nature, city, economy, turn life into an art form and theatre of the soul. What is needed is a generation of people who are freaky, crazy, irrational, sexy, angry, irreligious, childish and mad. People who burn draft cards, burn high school diplomas, college degrees. People who say 'to hell with your goals.' People who lure the youth with music, pot, and acid. People who redefine the normal, people who break with the status-royal-title-consumer game. People who have nothing material to lose but their flesh and finally, the white youth of America who have more in common with Indians plundered than they do with their own parents. Burn your houses down and you will be free."

At the HUAC hearing, Representative Watson of South Carolina, a supporter of the anti-riot bill, had read this pamphlet to Hayden and asked him is "this, in your judgment, the way to have a better America?"

"I think that beautiful sentiments are expressed in that statement," Hayden replied, "and I wish that you could understand them, Mr. Watson."

"Fine," Representative Watson concluded. "That wraps it up real well."

The poet Allen Ginsberg was the eleventh witness to testify for the defense, and the first who would attempt to describe the defendants' life style. He entered the courtroom in tennis shoes, a leather vest, and jeans, and walked, slightly slouched but with a bouncing, catlike gait, toward the witness stand. From a sling over his left shoulder there hung a large woven purse. Facing the bench, as he stood between the spectators and the press, he paused, pressed his palms together, touched his fingertips to the bottom of his wiry, black beard, and made an elegant little oriental bow in the direction of the defendants, as well as toward the diminutive judge, who stared down at him through his golden spectacles from his high-backed, black leather chair. Ginsberg then took his seat and began to explain, in response to Weinglass' questions, how he had traveled to India to study the religions of the East, whose mantras and other chants had been known to calm large assemblies of people. Weinglass' aim was to qualify Ginsberg as a witness who not only spoke out of deep religious convictions but whose spiritual specialty was the pacification of turbulent souls. Foran, however, soon tired of this discourse and upon his objection, sustained by Judge Hoffman, Ginsberg then began to explain how he had first heard from Hoffman and Rubin about their plan to stage the Festival of Life in Lincoln Park during convention week.

He testified that in February 1968 he and Hoffman had discussed the forthcoming Chicago convention, and Hoffman had said to him that "politics has become theatre and magic . . . that the manipulation of imagery through mass media . . . was confusing and hypnotizing the people in the United States and was making them accept a war which they did not really believe in; that people were involved in a life style which was intolerable to them, which involved brutality and police violence as well as a larger violence in Vietnam and that we ourselves might be able to get together in Chicago and invite teachers to present different ideas of what is wrong with the planet, what we can do to solve the pollution crisis, what we can do to end the Vietnam war, to present different ideas for making the society more sacred and less commercial, what we could do to improve the whole tone of the trap that we all felt ourselves in as the population grew and as politics became more and more violent and chaotic."

Then Weinglass asked Ginsberg if he could recall a speech he had made at a meeting in New York on March 17, 1968, at which he, Hoffman, Rubin, and several others had attempted to explain the purpose of the Chicago demonstrations.

Ginsberg replied, "My statement was that the planet earth at the present moment was endangered by violence, overpopulation, pollution, ecological destruction, brought about by our own greed, that the younger children in America and the other countries of the world might not survive the next 30 years, that it was a planetary crisis that had not been recognized by any government and had not been recognized by our own government, nor by the politicians who were preparing for the elections; that the young people of America were aware of that . . . and that we were going to gather together to manifest our presence over and above the presence of the more selfish elder politicians who were not thinking of what their children would need in future generations or even in the generation immediately coming or even for themselves in their own generation and were continuing to threaten the planet with violence, with war, with mass murder, with germ warfare; and we were going to invite them [to Chicago]; and that the central motive would be a presentation of a desire for the preservation of the planet and the planet's form, that we do continue to be, to exist on this planet, instead of destroy the planet, it was manifested to my mind by the great Mantra from India to the preserver God Vishnu whose Mantra is . . ." At this point in his testimony Ginsberg's voice rose and contracted, as if he had been gathering breath, and then suddenly he burst forth in the chant, "Hare Krishna, Hare Krishna, Krishna, Krishna, Hare, Hare, Hare Rama, Hare Rama, Hare, Hare."

Ginsberg's loud musical voice filled the courtroom and startled the spectators. One of the marshals reached inside his jacket as if to get his gun, but when the witness at last fell silent, the courtroom remained still. The marshal grinned with what appeared to be embarrassment and relief.

"Now, in chanting that," Weinglass asked, as if nothing had happened, "did you have the accompaniment of a musical instrument?"

Foran, smiling tightly, arose and objected. The question, he said, was immaterial.

The judge, however, ignored Foran's objection and said, "I don't understand it. I don't understand it because the language of the United States District Court is English." Then he too drew his lips back and smiled.

"I know," Kunstler told him, "but you don't laugh at all languages."

"I didn't laugh. I didn't laugh," the judge protested. "I didn't laugh at all. I wish I could tell you how I feel. Laugh? I didn't even smile. All I could tell you is that I didn't understand it because whatever language the witness used . . ."

"Sanskrit, sir," Ginsberg said.

"Sanskrit?" the judge replied.

"Yes," said Ginsberg.

"Well, that is one I don't know. That is why I don't understand it."

As this dialogue proceeded, Weinglass handed Ginsberg an object in the shape of a large shoe box, made of wood and painted red. This proved to be a kind of harmonium or small organ, which Ginsberg then began to play, though Weinglass had asked him to do no more than identify it.

"All right," Foran shouted. "Your Honor, that is enough.

I object to it. Your Honor, I think it is outrageous for counsel to—"

But the judge interrupted to scold Weinglass. "You asked him to identify it and instead of that he played a tune on it."

"It adds spirituality to the case," Ginsberg suggested from the witness stand, whereupon Court was recessed for the day.

Ginsberg returned to the stand the following morning and testified that Hoffman had told him of his difficulties with Stahl over the matter of permits. Therefore, he himself agreed to see Stahl on the chance that his intervention might be of some use. He testified that he visited Stahl in the mayor's office, where he chanted the Hare Krishna Mantra "as an example of what was intended by the Festival of Life," but to no avail.

Ginsberg then described the scene in Lincoln Park on the night of August 24, shortly before the eleven o'clock curfew. "There were several thousand people gathered, waiting late at night. There were some bonfires burning in trash cans. Everybody was standing around, not knowing what to do. . . . Then there was a sudden burst of lights in the center of the park and a group of policemen moved in fast to where the bonfires were and kicked over the bonfires. There was a great deal of consternation and movement and shouting and I turned, surprised, because it was early. . . . I turned . . . and said, 'The police are not supposed to be here until 11 o'clock.' "

Weinglass then asked Ginsberg what he had done next and Ginsberg replied, "I started to chant O-m-m-m-m-m, O-m-m-m-m-m," which he recited in Court as he had presumably done in the park, his voice like a giant cello or organ. Once again the courtroom was filled with sound, but the spectators remained calm.

"What was occurring in the park at the time you began your Om chant?" Weinglass then asked.

"A great deal of swift and agitated motion in many different directions, without any center and without any calm," Ginsberg replied. "But when we began chanting, there was one central sound and one central rhythmic behavior vocalized by all the people and a slow quieting of the physical behavior of all the people, slowly moving out of the park, away from the police, calmly, without running and without physically agitated behavior."

Ginsberg then testified that he returned to the park on the following day, when John Sinclair and his Detroit rock group were performing. Ginsberg asked Sinclair whether he could do a little "chanting on the microphone," and soon he began to chant the Hare Krishna Mantra for "about fifteen minutes." Then, Ginsberg testified, he "chanted a poem of William Blake in order to calm the crowd and advise those who were of a violent nature—"

"Objection, Your Honor," Foran interrupted.

"I sustain the objection," the judge replied. "The reference of the witness to his having spoken or chanted a poem of William Blake may go out and the jury is directed to disregard it."

"Could you just state, without chanting, the poem of William Blake?" Weinglass then asked, despite the judge's ruling. Thereupon Ginsberg recited, in a bravura voice, "The Grey Monk," a poem of nine quatrains that includes the lines, "But vain the sword and vain the Bow/ They never can work war's overthrow/ The hermit's prayer and the widow's tear/ Alone can save the World from fear/ For a tear is an intellectual thing./ And a sigh is the sword of an Angel King."

Weinglass then asked Ginsberg to describe the events in Grant Park on the afternoon of Wednesday, August 28, the afternoon on which Dellinger announced that he would lead the march to the Amphitheatre. "I went down off the platform into the crowd," Ginsberg explained, "and saw Mr.

Dellinger. He looked me in the eye, took my arm and said, 'Allen, will you please march up front in the line with me?' . . . and I said, 'Well, I am here with William Burroughs, Jean Genet and Terry Southern,' and he said, 'Well all of you together, can you form a front line and be the first of the group of marchers?' "

"Then," Ginsberg continued, "we came to a halt in front of a large guard of armed human beings in uniform who were blocking the way, people with machine guns, jeeps, police, and what looked to me like soldiers on our side and in front of us. . . . The march stopped and we waited, not knowing what to do. I heard Dave Dellinger saying, 'This is a peaceful march. All those who want to participate in a peaceful march please join our line. All those who are not peaceful, please go away and don't join our line—' "

"Did you go over with him," Weinglass asked, "or did you remain behind?"

"Yes. I went over with him, took his arm for a moment and also brought a little armful of flowers that had been given us as we left the band shell."

"And what did you do with the flowers?" Weinglass then asked.

"Mr. Dellinger and the city agents and police officials were talking together, negotiating, and whenever they seemed to me to be agitated, I took the flowers and put them in between their faces, shook them around a little."

"Then what, if anything, did you do?" Weinglass asked.

"I got up to walk away from the march with Mr. Dellinger," Ginsberg replied. "I think Mr. Dellinger announced that the march was over and had been victorious inasmuch as the government had simply forced us to abandon our citizen's rights to have a peaceful assembly for redress of grievances and there was nothing we could do about it at that point. We had not offered ourselves to be arrested and so we were going to disperse and move on. Mr. Dellinger declared the march to be over."

"Where did you go when you left?" Weinglass asked.

"I started walking north past the bridges [between the park and Michigan Avenue] but I wanted to get out onto Michigan Avenue by the hotels but couldn't because all the bridges were blocked by soldiers. So I kept going further and further north until I ran into tear gas. There was gas on the street and in the park even though nothing was happening and people were just trying to get out. I was blocked and couldn't leave the area and lost Mr. Dellinger."

With that, Ginsberg completed his direct examination. It was now shortly after noon and Foran asked the judge if the Court might recess early. "I have to get some materials to properly carry out my cross-examination of this witness," he said. "It will take some time to go downstairs and get them."

But Kunstler objected to an early recess. He told the judge that the defense had a witness waiting to testify who had to leave the country on the following morning and a delay in the trial might mean that he would be lost to the defense forever. Furthermore, Kunstler pleaded, "We asked for a five-minute recess two days ago and you refused to give it to us."

"You will have to cease that disrespectful tone," the judge warned.

"That is not disrespect; that is an angry tone, Your Honor," Kunstler explained.

"Yes it is. Yes it is," the judge shouted, as angrily as Kunstler had spoken to him. "I will grant the motion of the government."

"You refused me five minutes the other day," Kunstler persisted.

"You are going to have to learn," the judge replied.

"I am trying to learn," Kunstler answered.

"I will not sit here," the judge then said, "and have you assume a disrespectful tone to the Court."

"This is not disrespect," Kunstler explained.

"Yes it is," the judge said. "You are shouting at the Court."

"Everyone has shouted from time to time," Kunstler replied, "including Your Honor."

"I have never shouted at you during this trial," the judge said.

"Your Honor, your voice has been raised," Kunstler said, imploringly.

At this point, as Kunstler argued while the judge scolded and there seemed no likely way for the controversy to end, Ginsberg, from the witness chair, began to chant, "O-m-m-m-m-m-m-m, O-m-m-m-m," whereupon the courtroom fell silent.

"Will you step off the witness stand?" the judge ordered Ginsberg.

"He was only trying to calm us down," Kunstler explained.

"Oh no. I needed no calming down," the judge said angrily, and swept out of the courtroom.

The materials that Foran needed for his cross-examination proved to be several volumes of Ginsberg's poems. During the morning session, as Ginsberg had given his direct testimony, Special Agent Stanley of the FBI, a burly, smooth-faced man with large, soft eyes and a jaw so tense that it seemed paralyzed, could be seen at the government table, where he had sat throughout the trial, examining some of these volumes. Presumably Foran felt that the prosecution needed others as well.

When the trial resumed after lunch, Foran's tactic became clear. He began by asking Ginsberg to recount the details of his religious training in India. Then he asked him whether he considered his own poetry to partake of his religious beliefs. Ginsberg said that he did. Foran then asked him to read a poem that he had written in 1946, called "Night Apple," whereupon Ginsberg read the following verse: "Last night I dreamed/ of one I loved/ for seven long years,/ but I saw no face,/ only the familiar/ presence of the body/ sweat skin eyes/ feces urine sperm/ saliva all one/ odor and mortal taste."

"Could you explain to the jury what the religious significance of that poem is?" Foran asked, politely.

"If you would take a wet dream as a religious experience, I could. It is a description of a wet dream, sir," Ginsberg replied, in a serious tone.

Foran then asked Ginsberg to read another of his poems, one that began, "I walked into the cocktail party/ room and found three or four queers/ talking together in queer talk . . ."

When Foran asked whether he could explain "the religious significance of that poetry," Ginsberg replied, "Actually, yes." Then he undertook a thoughtful and lengthy account of his poetic method, to which Foran listened attentively and then thanked him.

Finally Foran asked Ginsberg to read his "Love Poem on a theme by Walt Whitman," which begins with Whitman's line, "I'll go into the bedroom silently/ and lie down between the/ bridegroom and the bride . . ."

When Ginsberg had finished his recitation of this poem Foran asked if he could explain its religious significance too. Ginsberg replied, "As part of our nature we have many loves, many of which are suppressed, many of which are denied, many of which we deny to ourselves. [Whitman] said that the reclaiming of those loves . . . was the only way that this nation could save itself and become a democratic and spiritual republic.

"He said that unless there were an infusion of feeling, of tenderness, of fearlessness, of spirituality, of natural sexuality, of natural delight in each other's bodies, into the hardened, materialistic, cynical, life-denying, competitive, afraid, scared, armored bodies, there would be no chance for spiritual democracy to take root in America—and he defined that tenderness between citizens as adhesiveness, a natural tenderness, flowing between all citizens, not only men and women, but also men and men, as part of our democratic heritage, part of the 'adhesiveness' that would make the democracy function: that men could work together not as competitive beasts but as tender lovers and fellows.

"So he projected from his own desire and from his own unconscious a sexual urge which he felt was normal to the unconscious of most people, though forbidden for the most part.

" 'I'll go into the bedroom silently and lie down between the bridegroom and the bride,' " he repeated Whitman's line.

"Walt Whitman is one of my spiritual teachers and I am following him in this poem, and projecting my own unconscious feelings of which I don't have shame, sir, which I feel are charming, actually."

"I didn't hear that last word," the judge interrupted.

"Charming, sir," Ginsberg replied, soberly.

With this testimony, Foran completed his cross-examination and returned to the government table. As he reached his seat he turned to Schultz and said, in a voice that could be heard in the press section, "Goddamned fag," and sat down.

Weinglass then undertook his redirect examination. He asked Ginsberg if he could recite from his poem, "Howl." This Ginsberg did. When he came to the lines "Moloch! Moloch! Nightmare of Moloch! Moloch the loveless! Moloch, the heavy judger of men!/ Moloch the crossboned, soulless jailhouse and Congress of sorrows! Moloch whose buildings are judgment! . . ." he wheeled in his chair, pointed an outstretched finger at the judge and, in a booming voice, completed the passage, "Moloch, the vast stone of war! Moloch, the stunned government! Moloch whose ear is a smoking tomb! Moloch, whose blood is running money!"

and so on. Startled at first, the shriveled judge recoiled in his high-backed chair, but then in what was clearly a deliberate gesture, flung his skeletal hands, like the bare branches of an apple tree, up to his face, in the style of the old Yiddish theater, and succeeded, if not in matching the poet's performance, at least in reminding the courtroom that political theater is not the exclusive province of the defendants and their witnesses.

There was another side to the revolutionary identity that the defendants hoped to reveal. A week later there appeared on the stand a young woman from Berkeley named Linda Morse, who testified that she had attended a Quaker school in her native Philadelphia, where she had won a Kiwanis award for decency. She had come to the Chicago convention a pacifist. What she saw of the police there convinced her, however, that pacifism would not do. "We had to defend ourselves or be wiped out," she testified.

What Miss Morse meant by self-defense emerged in Schultz's cross-examination. "My ultimate goal," Miss Morse told Schultz, "is to create a [free] society where everyone is fed, where everyone is educated, where everyone has a job, where everyone has a chance to express himself artistically, politically and religiously."

"And you are prepared, aren't you, to kill and die [for such a society]?" Schultz asked.

"Yes," she replied. Then she added, "In self-defense."

"And this is part of the reason," Schultz continued, "why you are learning how to shoot your M-1 rifle?"

Miss Morse replied that there were two reasons for her rifle practice. One was to protect herself from sexual assaults and the other was to protect herself from the police —who had been harassing her in Berkeley, who had attacked the Black Panther office in Los Angeles the week before, and who had killed Fred Hampton in Chicago two weeks earlier.

Schultz then asked Miss Morse, "Isn't it true that on a prior occasion you have said that the more you realize society is sick, the more you want to tear it from limb to limb?" What Schultz meant by a "prior occasion" was an interview that Miss Morse gave *Playboy* magazine, shortly after the convention, in which she said that lately she felt like "tearing the country limb from limb." As he questioned the witness Schultz displayed a copy of this magazine as a warning to her that she could not now repudiate her earlier statements. The warning, however, was not necessary. Miss Morse replied affirmatively to Schultz's question. Then he asked her whether she had also practiced karate in order to take part in guerrilla warfare on "the streets of American cities."

"I still don't know whether I could ever kill anyone," the former pacifist replied. "I haven't reached that point yet."

Then Schultz asked whether she had ever said that she found the McCarthy campaign "revolting."

"I don't think 'revolting' is the correct word," she replied, whereupon Schultz thrust the copy of *Playboy* into her hands and asked whether this "refreshed [her] recollection." "No," Miss Morse replied. The word "revolting" was incorrect. What she had actually told the interviewer, she explained, was that "McCarthy's campaign was an attempt on the part of the system to bring back the young people who had been protesting the war and the draft back into the system, and to offer them an alternative which in my opinion was just not real, because I felt that even if McCarthy would be elected, he would not have the power to stop the war, if certain people wanted it to continue."

In his redirect examination Kunstler asked Miss Morse what her political views had been before the Democratic convention.

"I believed [then]," she replied, "that the system had to be changed, but the way to bring about that change was through nonviolent means and political organizing. I felt that we could reach policemen and the government by holding nonviolent sit-ins and demonstrations, by putting our bodies on the line and allowing ourselves to be beaten and showing that we could create a different kind of society, a society of love [which would] change the policemen's attitudes and the government's attitudes by loving them."

When Kunstler asked Miss Morse what had made her change her mind, she replied, ". . . the actions of Mayor Daley in refusing to give us permits, in violating the Constitution, the actions of the police and the National Guard in beating demonstrators, and what I saw on television of what was going on inside the convention which convinced me that the democratic political process had fallen apart; that the police state that existed outside the convention also existed inside the convention and that nonviolent methods would not work to change that. We had to defend ourselves or we would be wiped out."

The fundamental legal question that the trial raised was the relation of intention to act; that is, the degree to which a defendant can be held responsible for having contrived and pursued an evil or dangerous plan, even though he may not have pursued this plan to its outcome. The political question was similar but more complex. Ginsberg's plea for universal sexual communion as the basis for true democracy; the Yippie command to kill your parents and burn your houses; Hayden's provocative speech in Grant Park; and Linda Morse's rifle practice—all of these statements and gestures may have foreshadowed, but were not equivalent to, the actions that they urged or implied. Under the literal interpretation of the First Amendment toward which the Supreme Court has lately moved, such expressions are constitutionally protected, and attempts by the government to punish them are correctly seen as acts of political repression. The constitutional requirement of legal forbearance does not, however, follow from an assumption that such expressions are inconsequential, but that their effects are obscure.

The position of the Court rests, as does the First Amendment itself, upon a somewhat arbitrary distinction between expression and action, a distinction more appropriate to the luminous philosophical simplicity of the Enlightenment than to contemporary understanding. That speech is itself a form of action is self-evident and the Court has never denied as much. Not only had Holmes observed that shouting fire in a crowded theater is a criminal act, but Justice Douglas recently argued that in cases of picketing, for example, speech and action are indistinguishable. The picket may even use his sign as a club. But even in less extreme cases the same is true. Meaningful speech is never without more or less palpable consequences. A doctor's prescription, a recipe, a general's command, an act of Congress, a political speech, a declaration of war or love, a jury's verdict, a judge's sentence—all such expressions affect events, more directly in some cases than in others. Though formally they are expressions; in substance, they are acts, and like all acts they have consequences, from which certain responsibilities attach to their authors. The distinction that the law attempts to make between expression and action is seldom clear in everyday life.

In permitting a broad range of political expression, the authors of the First Amendment evidently meant to permit a certain breadth of political action as well; for it is unlikely that they meant to protect only speech that has no effect, that is meaningless. Thus the First Amendment is itself not only a kind of political expression, but a most consequential political act as well; one that encourages almost unlimited political action—provided such action takes the form of speech—and, as the Supreme Court has come to interpret the amendment, provided the consequences of such speech are sufficiently remote so as not to constitute an immediate and obvious criminal danger.

The demoralization of the Romans, according to Gibbon, owed as much to the despair of Cicero and the wit of Lucian as to the rebellions in Gaul and the mischief of the bishops—maybe more. "The contagion of these skeptical writings," he wrote, "had been diffused far beyond the number of their readers. The fashion of incredulity was communicated from the philosopher to the man of pleasure or business, from the noble to the plebian and from the master to the slave who waited at his table and who eagerly listened to the freedom of his conversation." Thus Rome learned of its decline and imminent fall. In Gibbon's view, the power of the bishops, the conversion of Constantine, and the foundations of the Christian empire owed less to the force of Christian arms, which was negligible, or to the moral example of the church, which for Gibbon was even less substantial, than to the misery and dismay of a credulous people who, having lost their ancient faith, hastened to acquire a new one. To the dissolution of Roman authority, from which wreckage the Christian empire grew, the letters of Cicero, Gibbon felt, made a considerable contribution. John Adams made a similar point about the American Revolution, which was not, in his view, so much a matter of armed struggle as of altered consciousness. "The revolution," he said, "was effected before the war commenced. The revolution was in the hearts and minds of the people. This radical change in the principles, opinions, sentiments and affections of the people was the real American Revolution."

The First Amendment arose in response to the hated sedition laws that England had imposed upon her colonies, but it also reflected the confidence of its authors that the new nation could survive and benefit from the skepticism of an enlightened and critical people; that the letters of a new Cicero or the satires of another Lucian could not destroy and might advance the interests of the country, as the writings of Jefferson and Paine had done. Though the authors of the Alien and Sedition Acts evidently lacked this confidence, the optimism implicit in the Bill of Rights prevailed, and the possibility of a continuing American revolution remained fixed as a foundation of American law, if not of American political life.

For nearly a century, as the country expanded to its natural borders, this principle survived (perhaps because it was so seldom challenged) with only a single significant exception. This was Lincoln's suspension during the Civil War of habeas corpus. But, as Lincoln explained in a letter to Erastus Corning, who had objected to so violent an abridgment of the Constitution, here was "a case of rebellion—a clear, flagrant and gigantic case of rebellion; and the provision of the constitution that 'the privilege of habeas corpus shall not be suspended unless, when in cases of rebellion or invasion, the public safety may require it,' is the provision which specifically applies in the present case." Once the rebellion was ended, Lincoln promised, "the right of public discussion, the liberty of speech and the press, the law of evidence, trial by jury and habeas corpus," would be restored, "throughout the indefinite peaceful period that I trust lies before them."

Though the constitutional guarantees stopped short, as Lincoln observed, of armed rebellion—and thus nullified the claim of the Declaration of Independence that the people are free to alter or abolish a government that destroys their right to life, liberty, and the pursuit of happiness—nevertheless, these guarantees permitted such political expression as had led to the rebellion itself. The Southern leaders, and many Northerners, felt themselves free under the Constitution to demand the nullification of the same compact from which they derived their freedoms.

And even Lincoln himself, in 1848, had urged, as a Congressional opponent of President Polk's invasion of Mexico, "that any people anywhere being inclined and having the power have the right to rise up and shake off the existing government and form a new one that suits them better." Furthermore, Lincoln added, "any portion of such people that can may revolutionize and make their own so much of the territory as they inhabit."

In his first Inaugural Address, which he delivered only two years before he wrote his letter to Erastus Corning, Lincoln returned to these sentiments, but on this occasion he expressed them with misgivings. "This country with its institutions belongs," he said, "to the people who inhabit it. Whenever they shall grow weary of the existing government, they can exercise their constitutional rights of amending it or their revolutionary right to dismember or overthrow it." But, as President, he warned against such extreme actions. "Secession is the essence of anarchy," he said. "The only true sovereign of a free people is a majority held in restraint by constitutional checks and limitations, and always changing easily with deliberate changes of popular opinion and sentiments." Thus he concluded his Inaugural Address with a call for "patient confidence in the ultimate justice of the people . . . [who] have given their public servants but little power for mischief, and have with equal wisdom provided for the return of that little to their own hands at very short intervals."

But then, as Edmund Wilson has observed, Lincoln ended with a curiously contradictory sentiment. It was not upon the moral authority and inalienable rights of a free people that he finally rested his case, but upon the "chorus of Union," swelled by "mystic chords of memory, stretching from every battlefield and patriot's grave to every heart and hearthstone on this broad land." Thus Lincoln in 1861 subordinated the theme of popular sovereignty

328 · THE GREAT CONSPIRACY TRIAL

—what he had called the "ultimate justice of the people"—
to the idea of Union, whose bloody origins were mystically
linked to the hearts of all Americans.

That Lincoln was sensitive to the paradoxical nature of
his commitment to the principle of revolution and his determination in the present case to nullify it is clear from
the anguish of his Inaugural speech. Lincoln was a conservative, in fact, a Whig before he became a Republican.
His advocacy of rebellion derived not from a preference
for chaos but from a desire for order, the order that arises
from the sensible pursuit of their own interests by responsible citizens, bound by contract, and interfered with as little
as possible by abstract authority. For Lincoln, the right of
rebellion was the necessary means by which an enlightened
people might limit the power of their government. It was
not a means to dispense with government altogether in
order that individuals might enjoy unlimited personal satisfaction or economic advantage at the expense of the common good—as the Secessionists, in his view, demanded.

Thus Lincoln's contradictory attachments, to the mystical idea of Union on the one hand and the right of rebellion
on the other, flowed from the same Whig preference for
responsible liberty. As Wilson argued, the confusion of
these contrary attachments was unsettling to Lincoln and
portentous for the country. It implied that he had little
confidence that the Secessionist parts of the nation were
any longer capable of governing themselves under the Constitution, that the people of the South and the territories
needed the protection of a central government to guarantee
their political freedom: a government that would impose
upon them a reverence for constitutional decorum that they
might not otherwise be inclined to observe. Since the Constitution presupposes a system of self-government in which
the people are presumed capable of protecting their own
rights and choosing their own political forms, Lincoln's

dependence upon the idea of Union suggests that by 1860 he had begun to lose faith in "the ultimate justice" of at least some of the people.

In such a case, the dilemma for a Whig must have been intolerable, for the government must then be turned into the most powerful institution of all, more powerful than all the people combined. While it may have been Lincoln's genius to foresee this event, and his wisdom to regret it, he had no power to avert it. Within thirty years of his first Inaugural, and a century after the ratification of the Bill of Rights, the Haymarket radicals would be persecuted for having advocated what Lincoln himself had proposed as a Congressional opponent of the Mexican War in 1848. Hereafter, Americans would assail their increasingly powerful institutions at their peril.

The Whig principles to which Lincoln adhered are embedded in the history of Anglo-American political liberty and are a main source of the freedoms guaranteed by the Constitution. But, like the Constitution itself, these principles were themselves derived from violent rebellion against the arbitrary power of kings. Thomas Macaulay, the great Whig historian, wrote that in Plantagenet times the king was "not wise who presumed far on the forbearance of the English people. They might sometimes allow him to overstep the constitutional line: but they also claimed the privilege of overstepping that line themselves, whenever his encroachments were so serious as to excite alarm. If, not content with occasionally oppressing individuals, he dared to oppress great masses, his subjects promptly appealed to the laws, and, that appeal failing, appealed as promptly to the God of Battles.

"Our forefathers might indeed safely tolerate a king in a few excesses," Macaulay added, "for they had in reserve a check which soon brought the fiercest and proudest king to reason, the check of physical force." Macaulay then observed that in the one hundred and sixty years that preceded the union of the Roses, "nine kings reigned in England. Six of these nine kings were deposed. Five lost their lives as well as their crowns." From this the kings of England learned to limit their royal authority. Prudently they installed between themselves and the people a Parliament and a constitutional form of government.

Macaulay then acknowledged how difficult it must be for a modern Englishman to understand how swiftly and with what force the English people had once been able to attack an unjust king. In our own day, Macaulay wrote, "a few regiments of household troops are sufficient to overawe the discontented spirits of a large capital . . . [but] in the middle ages," when the kings had no such standing regiments, "resistance was an ordinary remedy for political distempers, a remedy which was always at hand, and which though doubtless sharp at the moment, produced no deep or lasting ill effects."

It was from this remedy, according to Macaulay, that the governments of England and America derived their traditions of limited and divided public authority. "As our ancestors had against a tyranny a most important security which we want, they might safely dispense with some securities to which we justly attach the highest importance." The ease, in other words, with which they could resort successfully to violence reduced their strict dependence upon a given constitution. But, Macaulay added, "as we cannot, without the risk of evils from which the imagination recoils, employ physical force as a check on misgovernment, it is evidently our wisdom to keep all the constitutional checks on misgovernment in the highest state of efficiency."

Thus constitutional government substitutes for the armed strength of a free people by reproducing the power of their swords and spears in the form of a political contract. In this sense, Macaulay appears to have anticipated the opinion of Mao Tse-tung that morality comes from the barrel of a gun; for the political morality of England and America flowed, in Macaulay's view, from the armed interference by a free people with the tyranny of kings, while only the strict observance by government of constitutional decorum assures and justifies the abstinence of the people from their ancient remedy.

The genius of the First Amendment is that it preserved the power of the people in the form of speech, while recognizing the impropriety of armed rebellion. The constitutional power of a free people to denounce their rulers —to run a pig for President, if they like—is, in this Whiggish view, equivalent to the power of an armed people to kill the king. As Huey Newton had discovered on the streets of Oakland, the power of the people against illegitimate authority resides in the Constitution.

The theoretical distinction between expression and action implied by the doctrine of clear and present danger is meant to distinguish protected speech from punishable crimes, and thus to guarantee the right of the people to attack their government and other institutions, short of armed rebellion. This was the basis for Justice Black's dissent in 1952 in the case of the Communist-front organizations that had failed to register under the internal security provisions of the McCarran Act, and the source of his opinion that "under our system of government, the remedy for [the advocacy of revolution] must be . . . education and contrary argument. If that remedy is not sufficient, the only meaning of free speech must be that the revolutionary ideas will be allowed to prevail." When Black wrote this opinion the country had been seized by the fear of communism, confused by the loss of its atomic monopoly, and intimidated by the sullen power of the Soviet Union. Perhaps for this reason Black was alone in his dissent. But as the country regained its confidence, so did the Justices regain their courage. By the time the radicals had gathered in Chicago, the Court had ruled unanimously in the Brandenberg Case, and the right of revolutionary dissent was restored as a principle of law.

The voice of the Court is not, however, equal to the force of an armed government, despite Justice Marshall's opinion in *Marbury v. Madison*; nor does the confidence of the Justices in the good sense of a free people so easily overcome the preference of a frightened people for the mystical chords of Union. Thus President Johnson and Richard Daley mustered their armies and readied their prisons against the divisive speeches and demonstrations of the radicals. In their view, the arrival of the demonstrators was a case much like the one Lincoln had faced when he suspended habeas corpus: a case of flagrant and gigantic rebellion. That the weapons of the rebels were to be pamphlets, speeches, and parades made no difference. The political leaders were frightened, the right of speech and assembly was suspended, and the streets were lined with soldiers.

"I live in Woodstock Nation," Abbie Hoffman announced when he took the stand on December 29 to testify in his own defense.

"Will you tell the court and jury where [this place] is?" Weinglass asked him.

"It is a nation of alienated young people. We carry it around with us as a state of mind in the same way as the Sioux Indians carried the Sioux nation around with them," Hoffman replied. "It is a nation dedicated to cooperation versus competition, to the idea that people should have better means to exchange property than by means of money; that there should be some other basis for human interaction."

"Just tell us where it is," the judge interrupted. "That is all."

"It is in my mind and in the minds of my brothers and sisters . . . It does not consist of property or material but rather of ideas and certain values," Hoffman repeated.

"This doesn't say where Woodstock Nation, whatever that is, is," Schultz objected.

"Your Honor," Weinglass replied. "It is a state of mind. He has the right to define that state of mind."

"No," the judge ordered. "We want the place of residence, if he has one, and the place of doing business, or both . . . Nothing about philosophy or India, sir."

"Can you tell us your occupation?" Weinglass then asked.

"I am a cultural revolutionary," Hoffman replied, and then added, "Well, I am really a defendant."

"What do you mean by the phrase, 'cultural revolutionary'? " Weinglass continued.

"Well," Hoffman answered, "it is a person who tries to shape and participate in the values and customs of a new people who eventually become the inhabitants of a new nation and a new society, through art and poetry, theater and music."

When Weinglass then asked about his background, Hoffman explained that he studied psychology at the University of California in 1960, returned the following year to his home in Massachusetts, where he worked as a psychologist at a state mental hospital and became a campaign manager for a Harvard professor who ran for Congress on an antiwar platform. Thereafter he became publicity director for the NAACP branch in Worcester, Massachusetts, and later, chairman of the local chapter of the Congress of Racial Equality. He then became field secretary for the Student Non-Violent Coordinating Committee, the organization of which Stokely Carmichael was soon to become the leader.

In 1964 and again in 1965 he went South, where he worked in McComb, Mississippi, in a freedom school and in Americus, Georgia, where he worked with the Southern Christian Leadership Conference. He also worked for the Poor People's Corporation of Mississippi, where he helped set up a cooperative owned and run by blacks who manufactured handbags, dolls, and dresses that were sold in "Freedom Stores" in the North. In these endeavors, he was often beaten by the police, but when Weinglass asked him to explain the circumstances of these beatings, Schultz objected and the judge sustained him.

Hoffman then testified that in the summer of 1966 he left his "$18,000 home in Worcester" and "his lawn mower" and moved to the Lower East Side of New York, where, he explained, "I reside today." There he opened Liberty House, a store that sold the goods made by the Mississippi cooperative. This store, Hoffman explained, "was more or less a training ground to train black people in business matters."

But that winter Hoffman broke with SNCC, which had come to dominate the black radical movement. "SNCC decisions," he wrote at the time, "have hurt the chance of seeking the radical kinds of changes in this system which most of the New Left wants. It has turned its back on the concept of class struggle . . . and instead, substituted a kind of racism that even Malcolm X in his last few months had turned his back on . . . I am interested in fundamental changes in American society, in building a system based on love, trust, and brotherhood and all the other beautiful things we sang about. Trust is a sharing thing, and as long as Stokely says he doesn't trust any white people, I personally can't trust him."

In the summer of 1967 Hoffman left Liberty House and

became involved in a "new community that was commonly referred to in mass media as the Hippie Movement . . . I was an activist in that movement," Hoffman testified. "We established bail funds to get people out of jail . . . We helped set up crash pads for the tremendous number of young people—some as young as twelve and thirteen—who were running away from society and family life and coming to the Lower East Side . . . and we fed and clothed and sheltered these people. . . . We also had tremendous festivals . . . mass gatherings of communities of people who felt that the values of the country were falling apart and they wanted to come together and experience a new sense of joy and creativity . . .

"At this time, I was employed by the City of New York in the Youth Board Program," he testified, "and the money I got from that job I threw out over the floor of the Stock Exchange in Wall Street . . . because we wanted to make a statement that we weren't doing it for the money and that money should be abolished. . . . The attitude was to take property and destroy it and turn it into art. Art would be the thing in which people would have some hope. It would be something that maybe they would be willing to die for, a work of art. Little kids would say, 'Ours is the block with the big five-foot mural on it.' We live on that block. We like it.' "

Throughout this part of Hoffman's testimony Schultz repeatedly objected that Weinglass' questions and Hoffman's extended answers were irrelevant to the charges specified in the indictment. The judge sustained these objections as often as Schultz made them, but Weinglass would repeat his questions in slightly different form and Hoffman would attempt to answer before Schultz and the judge could stop him. Moreover, Weinglass denied that his questions were irrelevant. They were meant, he said, to reveal the defendant's state of mind, and this, he reminded the Court, was how the judge himself had described the nature of the alleged crime at the pretrial hearing on September 9. Nevertheless, Judge Hoffman continued to sustain Schultz's objections, and it was only with the greatest difficulty that the witness was able to describe his personal history.

The judge did, however, permit Hoffman to explain how he had first met Rubin. In the summer of 1967 Rubin had come to New York from Berkeley, where he had been active in the Free Speech Movement, and told Hoffman that he "was going to be project director of a peace march in Washington that was going to march to the Pentagon on October 21 . . . He asked me if I had any ideas for this march and I said that the Pentagon was a five-sided symbol and many religions considered [such symbols] evil and it might be possible to approach [the march] from a religious point of view . . . If we got large numbers of people to surround the Pentagon, we could exorcize it of its evil spirits. There would be a lot of magic involved and we had to have a certain amount of fantasy and theater. . . . So Jerry asked me if I would go around the country talking to different groups and getting them involved . . . rock groups and performers and people like that."

"Now in exorcizing the Pentagon," Weinglass asked, "were there any plans for raising the building up off the ground?"

"Yes," Hoffman replied. "We wanted a permit to raise [the Pentagon] 300 feet up in the air, and [the police] said 'how about 10?' So we said 'OK.' But they threw us out of the Pentagon and we went back to New York and had a press conference . . . where we introduced a drug called 'Lace' which when you squirted it at a policeman it made him take his clothes off and make love; a very potent drug." Schultz objected that this testimony was frivolous and irrelevant, but Weinglass replied that in that case the trial should end immediately, for the Yippies' intentions at Chicago were no less frivolous, and the city of Chicago should never have taken them seriously in the first place. Judge Hoffman ordered that the testimony continue.

Hoffman then testified that a month later he and Rubin organized a demonstration in New York to announce that the war was over. This demonstration was so successful, Hoffman explained, that Rubin and he decided to organize others like it. At a meeting in his apartment during the first week of December 1967, they "talked about the possibility of having such a demonstration at the Democratic National Convention in Chicago . . . Jerry said that it would be a good idea to call it the Festival of Life in contrast to the Convention of Death and to have it in some kind of public place, like a park or something, in Chicago.

"One thing that I was very particular about," Hoffman continued, "was that we didn't have a concept of leadership . . . We had to create a kind of situation in which people would become their own leaders and I described how this could be done by creating a number of imageries that would conflict, that when added up meant that the people were on their own to do whatever they felt it was necessary to do . . . This would go along with our philosophy that people were basically good, that they had innate potential for creativity and for love if we just created the kind of situation in which these potentials could come to the fore—[if we could] create a society in which everyone was an artist—and so we devised certain methods for communicating that idea."

It was at this meeting that the term Yippie was coined to describe the political movement that Hoffman and Rubin had begun to evolve. "Anita [Hoffman's wife] said at the time that although 'Yippie' would be understood by our generation, straight newspapers and the government wouldn't take it seriously unless it had some kind of formal name, so she came up with the name 'Youth International Party' . . . Everybody would think that this was a huge international conspiracy but actually it would be the kind of party you had fun at," Hoffman explained.

"I said that fun was very important," Hoffman continued. "It was a direct rebuttal of the ethics and morals that were part of the religion of the country; that the Protestant ethic was designed to keep people working in a rat race, that people couldn't get into heaven, they were told, unless they kept working, unless they tried to keep up with the Joneses—that work had lost its joy and that there was a whole system of values that told people to postpone their pleasure, to put all their money in the bank, to buy life insurance, a whole bunch of things that didn't make any sense to our generation at all and that fun actually was becoming quite subversive.

"Jerry said that because of our action at the Stock Exchange when we threw out the money, they had actually enclosed the whole Stock Exchange in bullet-proof glass that cost something like $20,000 because they were afraid we'd come back and throw money out again.

"He said that at the Pentagon, the sight of armed, helmeted, bayoneted troops guarding the Pentagon against unarmed, hairy-looking freaks was quite devastating to the image of American military power around the world, that young kids, every time they looked at the Pentagon that would be up in the air vibrating, and they would picture generals and bombs falling out of the Pentagon; and that if they couldn't take these institutions seriously that they would start to develop institutions of their own." Hoffman then testified that Rubin had suggested that the Yippies run a pig for President. At the same meeting it was decided to distribute throughout the country an announcement of the Yippie festival to be held at the forthcoming Chicago convention.

"Join us in Chicago in August," this announcement read, "for an international festival of youth, music, and theater. Rise up and abandon the creeping meatball. Come all ye rebels, youth spirits, rock minstrels, truth seekers, peacock freaks, poets, barricade jumpers, dancers, lovers and artists.

"It is the summer. It is the last week in August and the National Death Party meets to bless Lyndon Johnson. We are there! There are 500,000 of us dancing in the streets, throbbing with amplifiers and harmony. We are making love in the parks. We are reading, singing, laughing, printing newspapers, groping and making a mock convention and celebrating the birth of free America in our own time.

"A new spirit explodes in the land. Things are bursting in music, poetry, dancing, movies, celebrations, magic, politics, theater and life styles. All these new tribes will gather in Chicago. We will be completely open. Everything will be free. Bring blankets, draft cards, tents, body paint, Mrs. Leary's cow, food to share, music, eager skin and happiness. The threats of LBJ, Mayor Daley and J. Edgar Freako will not stop us. We are coming! We are coming from all over the world!

"The life of the American spirit is being torn asunder by the forces of violence, decay and the napalm-cancer fiend. We demand the politics of ecstasy. We are the delicate spores of the new fierceness that will change America. We will create our own reality. We are free America! And we will not accept the false theater of the Death Convention.

"We will be in Chicago. Begin preparations now! Chicago is yours! Do it!"

On March 22, Hoffman flew to Chicago to attend a meeting called by the Mobe. "The meeting was held," Hoffman testified, "at a place called Lake Villa, about 20 miles outside Chicago." He arrived at the meeting dressed as an Indian, the costume in which he had flown from New

York. There he met Rennie Davis for the first time, as well as Hayden and Dellinger, whom he had known before.

"At that meeting," Weinglass asked, "was any decision reached about coming to [the convention]?"

"I believe that they debated for two days about whether they should come or not to Chicago and there was a vote taken and I think it was 48 to 52 or something very close. I can't remember whether they decided to come or not, but they decided to have more meetings."

On March 25, Hoffman and Rubin and a group of Chicago Yippies drafted their first application for a permit to hold their festival in Grant Park. On the following day they presented this application to the Chicago Park District. "The festival," the application explained, "will be entirely free . . . More than 100 entertainers have already agreed to participate . . . Those attending the festival will need to sleep in the park . . . We are asking the city to provide portable sanitation facilities. In addition, our emphasis will be on food-sharing, and we will ask the health department to cooperate with us in setting up kitchens in the park. We look forward to your response. For Fun and Freedom." To this application, however, the Yippies received no reply.

On the same day the Yippies presented a copy of their application to the Park District to Deputy Mayor Stahl, who said, according to Hoffman, "that we had followed the right procedure and the city would give it proper attention and things like that." Thereupon Hoffman and Rubin returned to New York.

On April 30, Hoffman received a call from Abe Peck, a Chicago Yippie, who told him that "they had their first Yippie meeting about a week previously and that they had advertised and sent out leaflets for it; they had the first organizational meeting at someone's house, about 80 people came, and that the police raided the meeting; they threw people against the wall, ripped up the whole apartment and arrested 21 people . . . Abe said that the police had become particularly vicious in Chicago, that there were rumors that we weren't going to be allowed to hold the festival and that I should get in touch with the city officials and perhaps come to Chicago again for a meeting. I told Abe," Hoffman continued, "that because of a new federal law this conversation was probably illegal anyway."

Hoffman testified that he then called Stahl and asked whether it was true that the Yippies could not use the park. Stahl said, according to Hoffman, " . . . that [the permit application] was being processed and that those things took time. I asked him whether there was any truth to the rumor that we were not going to be allowed to use Grant Park and he said, 'When you invite visitors into your home you don't have them sleep in the living room.' I asked him whether this meant a definite no on Grant Park and he said that it might be wise to look at other parks."

Hoffman then described "a mini-Festival of Life" that took place in Lincoln Park on May 13, Mother's Day. "There were marriages taking place there," he explained, "and everybody had pies; apple pies and cherry pies, and they were going to march to the police station to present the police who were on duty on Mother's Day with the pies."

"Objection," Schultz shouted. "Marching to the police station on Mother's Day with pies is irrelevant. I object to his continuing with Mother's Day pies, yes sir."

The judge sustained Schultz's objection and Weinglass remarked that if the witness had said "they were going to the police station carrying bombs, that would be relevant." But the judge persisted in his decision, and Hoffman went on to describe a meeting in New York two weeks later at which Abe Peck told about a further conversation with Stahl. At this meeting there appeared to be "general agreement that Lincoln Park would be used," Hoffman testified.

Weinglass then moved to admit into evidence two articles that Hoffman had written that summer explaining the Yippie program for the Festival of Life. In these articles Hoffman anticipated that the permits would probably be granted, but perhaps only at the last minute. Schultz, however, objected to Hoffman's articles as "self-serving," and therefore inadmissible. Such writings, Schultz argued, are admissible for purposes of impeaching, that is, discrediting a witness on cross-examination, not on direct examination. What appeared to bother Schultz was that Hoffman's articles contradicted the government's claim that the defendants did not really want the permits for which they had applied, that they wanted a confrontation instead, and thus that their visits to Stahl were disingenuous.

"Mr. Schultz," Weinglass replied, "claims that only statements made by these defendants that could be used for impeachment—in other words, that showed their guilty intent—can be admitted to the jury. Any statement therefore, indicating their peaceful intent is, I assume, inadmissible. If that is the rule by which we are to proceed, it is impossible to prove that they had anything but guilty intent."

"The self-serving statements of a defendant," Schultz replied, "are not admissible for the reason that they are self-serving. The defendant can explain his intent. This defendant is attempting to do so on the witness stand. But a self-serving statement of a defendant is not admissible." Thus Schultz confirmed Weinglass' gloomy observation.

The judge sustained Schultz' objection.

"I don't understand that," Hoffman said from the witness stand. "That was the only thing I wrote about Chicago. Oh man! It figures."

The principle that statements made by a defendant may not be offered in his own defense, "seems to have originated as a counterpart," according to Charles T. McCormick, the author of a standard work of reference on the law of evidence, "of the rule, now universally discarded, forbidding parties to testify. When this rule of disqualification for interest was abrogated by statute, the accompanying rule against 'self-serving' declarations should have been regarded as abolished by implication. . . . If made under circumstances of seeming sincerity [such statements] should come in [to evidence] to show the state of mind of the accused. . . . The courts which exclude [such evidence] assume that because made by a party and offered on his behalf, the declarations are so likely to be dishonest as not to be worth hearing. This is the same discredited assumption that interested testimony is to be purged, not weighed, on which rested the ancient rule that parties could not testify." Judge Hoffman did not agree with McCormick's interpretation, and Hoffman's statement about the permit negotiations did not go before the jury.

Weinglass was, however, allowed to put in evidence a second permit application that the Yippies had submitted on July 15 for the use of Lincoln Park. This application too went unanswered, according to Hoffman's testimony.

Then on August 5, Abe Peck called Hoffman in New York and described a further meeting with Stahl. Peck, according to Hoffman, was "shocked" that Stahl "didn't know we wanted to sleep in the park," and that he was using this as "a stalling technique." Peck told Hoffman that in view of Stahl's behavior and their fear of the police, the Chicago Yippies were thinking of abandoning the Festival of Life. Hoffman and Rubin therefore went to Chicago on August 7 and on the following day met once more with Stahl. "Mr. Stahl," Hoffman testified, "made it clear that these were just exploratory talks; that he didn't have the power and the mayor doesn't have the power to issue permits. . . . I pointed out to him how it was in the best interests of the city to have us in Lincoln Park, ten miles away from the convention hall. I said we had no intention of marching on the convention; that I didn't think politics in America could be changed by marches and rallies and that we were presenting an alternative life style. I said that the city ought to give us a hundred grand to run the festival and then I said, "Why don't you just give me two hundred grand and I'll split town.' . . . I told him that we were going to submit a new permit application the following morning and that the city was just trying to ignore the fact that loads of people were coming there . . . I also said that our right to assemble in Lincoln Park and present our kind of society was a right that I was willing to die for, that this was a fundamental right."

Hoffman then described his telephone call to Ginsberg and Ginsberg's subsequent and fruitless efforts to negotiate further with Stahl. Hoffman next told of the meeting at the Mobe office on August 9, when it was decided that the Yippies and the Mobe should work together on their various plans for demonstrations during convention week. One result of this agreement was the plan to file a suit against the city of Chicago in federal court on August 19.

On August 22, Hoffman appeared before Judge Lynch, the former law partner of Mayor Daley. "There was a fantastic number of guards all over the place. We were searched, made to take off our shirts, empty our pockets. . . ."

"That is totally irrelevant," Schultz interrupted. "There happened to be threats at the time and when there are threats that is the safe thing to do."

"He is right," Hoffman said. "I had 20 that week." Then Hoffman continued his account of his day in court. "It was a room similar to this," he said. "Wall-to-wall bourgeois, rugs, and neon lights . . . The judge said that our dress was an affront to the court." Judge Lynch then recessed the hearing until two o'clock, by which time Hoffman had learned of the judge's association with the mayor and decided to withdraw his suit. "I said to Judge Lynch that we had as little faith in the judicial system of this country as in the political system. He said, 'Be careful, young man. I will find a place for you to sleep.' I thanked him for that, said I had one, and left."

Thereafter, Hoffman testified to the events of convention week itself. By the time Court recessed on the afternoon of December 29, he had completed his version of the police attack that occurred in Lincoln Park on Sunday, August 25. On the following morning, he resumed the stand, but before the testimony commenced Kunstler announced that Ramsey Clark would soon be called as a witness for the defense. The judge replied that Mr. Clark's father was a "dear, dear long-time friend," but that he was not otherwise interested in the plans of the defense to call witnesses. Such matters were not, he said, properly his business.

Kunstler then raised a second point. A long line of young people had been waiting in the cold outside the Federal Building that morning for places in the courtroom. Many of them had arrived as early as 4 or 5 A.M. Some of these early arrivals had been arrested by the Chicago police for curfew violation. Kunstler asked the judge to order the police to stop this practice. Such arrests, Kunstler said, were unconstitutional, especially as they were made on federal property. The judge replied that this too was none of his business, and the testimony resumed.

On Sunday night, according to Hoffman, the police had driven some six or seven thousand young people out of Lincoln Park. At two o'clock on Monday morning Hoffman called Stahl at his home and "again pleaded with him to let people stay in the park the following night. There were more people coming and there would be no place for them to sleep. The hotels were all booked up and the young people were getting thrown out of hotels and restaurants and that he ought to intercede with the police . . . I told him that his boss, Daley, was totally out of his mind; that I had read in the paper the day before that they had 2,000 troops surrounding the reservoirs in order to protect them against the Yippie plot to dump LSD in the drinking water. I said there wasn't a kid in the country, never mind a Yippie, who thought such a thing could even be done. He said that he knew it couldn't be done but that they weren't taking any chances. I thought it was about the weirdest thing I ever heard and Stahl said, 'We're doing the best we can. This is a very difficult situation,' things like that."

Weinglass then asked Hoffman whether the Yippies intended to join the Mobe march to the Amphitheatre on Wednesday, August 28. Schultz, however, objected to the leading form of this question, and though Weinglass then restated it in a variety of forms, the judge continued to sustain Schultz's objections. The question "is so obviously bad as a matter of form," the judge ruled, "that you must know it." Weinglass then asked the question in still a different form, but this time Schultz objected on the grounds that the question was irrelevant. The judge sustained him, and Weinglass was finally forced to abandon this line of inquiry.

Hoffman then described the police raid in Lincoln Park on Monday night in which he had been "coughing and spitting because there was tear gas totally flooding the air, canisters were exploding all around me and I moved with the majority of the people out of the park, trying to duck, picking up people that were being clubbed, getting up off the ground myself a few times. The police were just coming through in this wedge, clubbing people right and left and I tried to get out of the park."

Early the next morning Hoffman went to North Beach at the edge of Lake Michigan, where he found Allen

Ginsberg and "about 150 other people kneeling in the lotus position, chanting and praying and meditating. There were five or six police cars on the boardwalk and there were police surrounding the group. Dawn was breaking. It was very chilly. People had blankets wrapped around them . . . I went and sat next to Mr. Ginsberg and chanted and prayed for about an hour."

"Do you recall what was said at that time?" Weinglass asked.

"I said," Hoffman replied, "that I was very sad about what had happened in Chicago. I said that what was going on at the beach was very beautiful, that that wouldn't be in the evening news, that the American mass media were a glutton for violence. I said that America wouldn't be changed by people sitting and praying, that that was an unfortunate reality that we had to face, that we were a community that had to learn how to survive, that we had seen what had happened the last few nights in Lincoln Park. We had seen the destruction of the festival and I said that I would never again tell people to sit quietly and pray for change."

Hoffman then testified that he returned to the Free Theatre, "a building," he explained, "with a huge courtyard. There were perhaps two or three hundred young people in small groups in the courtyard huddled around campfires with blankets over them. Many people had bandages on their heads with blood showing through. Many had bandages wrapped around their feet. People were roasting hot dogs and things over the fire. Some people had guitars and were singing folk songs, and there were people in white coats going around trying to mend up some of the people. Many people were just stretched out, totally unconscious, it seemed to me. There were police, going through the area kicking out fires . . . I told the people that it looked like Valley Forge."

Later that morning, Hoffman attended a press conference, where he said, "I had seen the birth of a new society in Lincoln Park, a revolutionary youth culture dedicated to love. I had seen that society brutally attacked by the police who had gone crazy. I said that the Yippies had become the new minority group; that we were being treated the way black people had been treated for hundreds of years in this country . . . I said that the Democratic party was a facade of democracy but underneath was a brutal system bent on destroying any way of life that challenged the way of life in power."

Later that morning, Hoffman met with some of the ministers who were planning to meet in Lincoln Park that night to protest the actions of the police. Schultz objected that this testimony was immaterial, and the judge sustained him. However, when Weinglass then asked Hoffman to describe a conversation that he had had on the same day with a member of the Blackstone P Nation, one of Chicago's black youth gangs, Schultz did not object.

Weinglass commented on the discrepancy and Schultz then attacked Weinglass. "Either he doesn't know how [to examine a witness] or he doesn't care," Schultz said, "and that is the reason this examination has gone on for over a day and a half, a bunch of hearsay, miscellaneous thoughts, going back and forth, because he doesn't know how to examine a witness."

Kunstler objected to this attack on his colleague, but the judge ordered Weinglass to proceed with his examination and took no note of Schultz's remarks. At this point Dellinger rose and faced the jury. "I am a little upset," he said, "by the dishonesty of the court's process—"

"That man's name is Dellinger, Miss Reporter," the judge interrupted.

"Yes, my name is Dellinger, and they are not interested in the truth. They just want one side of things to go into evidence. Even made-up things, but they won't allow the real truth."

"Mr. Dellinger is continuing to speak, Miss Reporter," the judge commented in a serene voice.

"Darned right," Dellinger replied. "And I hope the jury understands that too."

"This is unfair to the government," Schultz objected.

"The government will go to jail for ten years, I suppose," Dellinger replied.

Schultz then attempted to respond, but the judge, in the same serene voice, advised him not to "underestimate anybody's intelligence," and that he knew that "Mr. Dellinger had spoken out."

"We have to speak up," Dellinger replied, "because you won't give our lawyers a fair chance."

"Perhaps you can give him four years like you gave Bobby Seale," Froines said.

"You may continue with the direct examination of this witness," the judge interrupted, his voice suddenly sharp.

Weinglass resumed and once more asked Hoffman about his meeting with the ministers.

"I object," Schultz said.

"I sustain the objection," the judge replied.

Hoffman then testified that on the following morning, Wednesday, August 28, while he was eating breakfast in a restaurant, the police arrested him. "They said they arrested me," Hoffman explained, "because I had the word 'fuck' on my forehead. They said it was an 'obscenary.'"

When Weinglass asked him how the word came to be on his forehead Hoffman explained that he had put it there because he was "tired of seeing my picture in the paper and I know if you got that word, they aren't going to print your picture in the paper and it also summed up my attitude about what was going on in Chicago. But I like that four-letter word. I thought it was kind of holy, actually."

Hoffman spent the day in jail and was not released until ten o'clock that night, when he went to Grant Park. There he found a group of about 3,000 people gathered, in the aftermath of the police attack at Michigan and Balbo some two hours earlier. He made a speech in which he thanked "Ho Chi Minh for bringing medical supplies and Mayor Daley because without his help none of this would have been possible. I said that America was in the last stages of a dying empire. I compared it to the Babylonian empire and I said that in Babylon they had an emperor named Nebuchadnezzar who was the Richard Daley of his day and his last act was to resurrect a god called Moloch and summon all the people to bring forth their children and throw them into a fiery furnace as a sacrifice for their salvation."

Soon thereafter, Weinglass concluded his direct examination of Hoffman and Schultz proceeded to cross-examine him. "The Yippie myth," he asked, "was created to get people to come to Chicago, isn't that right, Mr. Hoffman?"

"That's right, Mr. Schultz," Hoffman replied warily.

"And a liberated area [according to the Yippie myth] is a place where people can do whatever they want to do, isn't that right?"

"Yes, more or less," Hoffman replied.

"And a liberated area is part of your revolutionary movement?" Schultz continued.

"We use the word differently, Mr. Schultz," Hoffman replied.

"And you use entertainers, do you not, to bring your people from all around the United States to the various demonstrations which you have, isn't that right?"

"Entertainers, as you call them," Hoffman replied, "are the real leaders of the cultural revolution. But I would not say that we have control over them."

"And you knew that you could get many [young people] to come by having a rock festival in Chicago, isn't that right?"

"Yes," Hoffman replied.

"Then, in this area where you thought you were going to have over 500,000 young people, you were going to have a liberated area where people could do what they wanted. Right? And they would be free from the city control; city and state laws?"

"Not of all the laws," Hoffman answered. "If somebody pulled a gun and started to shoot people, I assume he would be arrested and taken away."

"And you told Mr. Stahl that you were going to have nude-ins in your liberated zone, didn't you?"

"A nude-in?" Hoffman replied. "No, I don't believe I would use that phrase."

"You told him you were going to have public fornication?" Schultz continued.

"I may have told him that 10,000 people were going to walk on the waters of Lake Michigan, something like that," Hoffman answered.

"And part of your Yippie myth," Schultz continued, "was that 'We'll burn Chicago to the ground,' isn't that right?"

"No," Hoffman answered.

"And there was LSD to your knowledge in both the honey and the brownies [that they were eating in Lincoln Park]?"

"I would have to be a chemist to know that for a fact," Hoffman replied.

"Didn't you state on a prior occasion that Ed Sanders passed out from too much honey?" Schultz persisted.

"Sure," Hoffman replied. "Is that illegal? It must have been strong honey."

"The last observation of the witness may go out," the judge ordered, "and the witness is directed not to make gratuitous observations."

Throughout the afternoon session Lee Weiner had busied himself at the defense table with a pile of posters, each of which he rolled into the form of a scroll and sealed with a postage stamp. When he had accumulated a supply of these scrolls he would carry them out of the courtroom and deposit them across the corridor in the witness room assigned to the defendants. These scrolls proved to be New Year's greetings that consisted of a large photograph of Weiner and his girl friend, both naked and in a kind of seated embrace. The message was "Make a New Year's Revolution."

At 4:30 the Court recessed for the afternoon and on the following morning, December 31, Hoffman resumed the witness stand.

"Good morning, colonel," Hoffman greeted Schultz.

"The fact is," Schultz resumed, "that what you were trying to do was to create a situation where the state and the United States government would have to bring in the army and the national guard during the convention in order to protect the delegates so that it would appear that the convention had to be held under military conditions. Isn't that a fact, Mr. Hoffman?"

"You can do that with a Yo-Yo in this country," Hoffman answered. "That's easy. You can see just from this courtroom. Look at all the troops around," he said, gesturing toward the marshals posted throughout the room.

"It was your Yippie myth, Mr. Hoffman," Schultz persisted, "that people would among other things in Chicago smoke dope and fuck and fight the cops, was it not?"

"Yes. I wrote that as a prediction," Hoffman replied, "and so did Norman Mailer."

"It was also part of your myth, wasn't it," Schultz asked, "that people should fuck all the time anyone, whoever they wish?"

"Your Honor," Kunstler interrupted, "are we ever going to reach the end of this prurient interest in sex?" But

Schultz replied that his interest was not prurient. He simply
wanted to show that the city government had had good
reason to deny permits to such irresponsible applicants.

Weinglass attacked this point. "If the city had written
this organization and said 'We don't like your morals'
that would have been a different situation. But the city
never took any action to this day. The permit hasn't been
withdrawn. It is still pending."

The judge ignored this argument and overruled Kunstler's
objection to Schultz's sexual inquiries. Schultz resumed the
cross-examination. "Was it part of your Yippie myth," he
asked, "to practice punches through people's solar plexus?"

"No," Hoffman replied.

"Was it part of your myth to practice judo chops, Mr.
Hoffman?" Hoffman replied that he did not know how to
inflict "judo chops," but he did admit that it was part of
the Yippie plan to practice self-defense.

Schultz continued in this vein, and at last directed the
witness' attention to the meeting on August 7 with David
Stahl. "When dealing with city officials did you tell the
city, Mr. Hoffman, that the Yippies' statement that they
were going to burn Chicago to the ground was just a
myth, a joke, and to pay no attention to it? Did you tell
that to the city?"

"It never came up," Hoffman replied.

"And did you ever say that it was just a myth that we
will fuck on the beaches and that they should disregard
it and pay no attention?"

"It never came up," Hoffman said.

"So the answer is no," Schultz persisted.

"No," Hoffman replied. "I don't believe that that came
up at the negotiations with the city. I know I didn't say
it. No."

Kunstler rose to say that if the city was interested to
know Hoffman's real intentions, Stahl might have asked

him. Nevertheless, it was apparent that Schultz's questions had raised a troubling point for the defense.

"You [thought] you had scared the city officials pretty good, didn't you, Mr. Hoffman?" Schultz continued.

"They were scared and confused, yes," Hoffman answered.

Kunstler then objected again. Schultz replied that if Hoffman had, in fact, negotiated for permits in good faith, he would have told the city not to believe the exaggerated accounts of the Yippie program that had been appearing in the papers. Kunstler repeated that if the city had been inclined to take these myths seriously, Stahl should have asked Hoffman whether they were true or not. The judge, however, supported Schultz, and the cross-examination continued.

"Mr. Hoffman," Schultz asked by way of summary, "while you were negotiating with city officials, you were secretly attending meetings and planning for spontaneous acts of violence during the Democratic National Convention. Isn't that right?"

"How do you plan for spontaneous acts of violence? I would have no idea how to do that," Hoffman answered, but it was clear from the air of satisfaction with which Schultz received this answer that he felt he had scored a major point. He had forced Hoffman to admit that the Yippies had done nothing to reassure Stahl that their intentions, were, in fact, harmless.

Schultz was also aware that at least one of the jurors might by now have decided to reject the government's case. On December 18, Davis had made a speech at Northern Illinois University, where a young woman in the audience had announced that her mother was one of the jurors at the Conspiracy Trial. Her mother had told her, she said, that she did not believe the defendants were guilty. A Chicago newspaperman had heard of this episode and gone to Foran with the story. Foran, in turn, turned the matter over to the FBI. Since the judge had repeatedly warned the jurors not to discuss the case among themselves or with members of their families, it appeared that the sympathetic juror might not only be dismissed from the jury but that perhaps, if her daughter's statement could be proven true, she would have to face contempt charges as well.

After the lunch recess on December 31, Foran told the Court that his investigation of this incident was now complete and that two campus police had corroborated what the reporter had told him. Foran did not, however, move to dismiss the juror. The statements of the police were not enough, he said, to support the assumption that the juror had violated the Court's orders, and the matter should therefore be dropped. Some reporters assumed that Foran was apprehensive that an attempt by the government to dismiss Mrs. Fritz, whose daughter had made the statement, would result in bad publicity, especially in view of the Kristi King episode.

The defendants were greatly relieved. They knew that it was Mrs. Fritz's daughter who had spoken during Davis' speech. Thus the possibility of a hung jury, for which they had long hoped, was now distinct, provided the daughter had been telling the truth and that during the rest of the trial nothing happened to cause Mrs. Fritz to change her mind. What the defendants did not know, however, was that Mrs. Fritz had by this time begun to suffer the symptoms of phlebitis, a painful affliction of the arteries of the leg. Her doctor had warned her that her life might be in danger if she continued to sit on the jury. She felt it was her duty to remain, however, and refused to leave the jury.

Schultz continued his cross-examination throughout the afternoon and resumed, after the New Year's recess, on January 2. He continued his effort to hold Hoffman to the literal meaning of his fanciful and extravagant language so as to show that it had been the defendants and not Stahl who had made the permit negotiations impossible. "Mr. Hoffman, did you say 'We are going to wreck this fucking society. If we don't the society is going to wreck itself?' "

"Yes," Hoffman replied. "I said that the institutions in America were crumbling and that ours was a politics of being. All we had to do was sit there, smile and laugh, and the whole thing would come tumbling down because it was basically corrupt and brutal."

"Did you say you were going to wreck the society?" Schultz persisted.

"Well, just by doing what I did wrecks the society. You don't need anything else. You don't need armed troop carriers."

"So the answer is yes," Schultz insisted, and in this vein soon completed his cross-examination.

In his redirect examination, Weinglass attempted to show that Hoffman had, in fact, attempted to acquaint Stahl with the Yippies' use of excessive rhetoric. "When you met with city officials," Weinglass asked, "did you make any attempt to acquaint them with Yippies and yourself and Rubin and what your intentions were?"

Schultz, however, objected that this question was beyond the scope of his cross-examination and the judge sustained him.

"Your Honor," Weinglass pleaded, "there was extensive cross-examination [on this point]—" but the judge interrupted to say that he would nevertheless sustain the objection. Weinglass, however, persisted in his argument: "On August 7 [Hoffman] brought a scrapbook with all of his newspaper articles—" but again the judge interrupted to remind Weinglass that he had sustained the objection and would not change his mind.

Weinglass then attempted to ask the question differently.

"What, if anything, did you do during the entire period of time to acquaint the city officials with Yippies?"

"Objection," Schultz said. "Out of the scope of my examination." Since the subject of Weinglass' question had been not only within the scope of Schultz's cross-examination but was addressed directly to its major theme, Schultz's objection elicited a gasp from the press and spectators and sighs from the defendants.

"I sustain the objection," the judge replied. Weinglass' further attempts to pursue this inquiry were similarly defeated, and the redirect examination of Hoffman soon ended.

If, as Schultz had attempted to show, the Yippies had requested permits not simply for their followers to sleep in Lincoln Park and attend rock concerts there, but to break the city's drug laws as well, then perhaps the city had been prudent to deny not only Hoffman's application but the Mobe's too. To grant a permit to one of these groups would, in effect, have opened the city to all such unreliable elements. Thus Schultz tried to show that the defendants' applications were not serious because they knew that the permits could not possibly have been granted; that what they really wanted was to embarrass the city while covering their evil intentions with a show of good faith.

On the other hand Kunstler and Weinglass argued that the city had made no effort, so far as the testimony revealed, to determine the actual intentions of the various applicants. Moreover, the city had not only refused to grant the permits for which the defendants applied, it had refused even to specify the conditions on which such permits might be granted, provided the applicants agreed in advance to conform to them. Furthermore, the city had also refused a permit to the Committee for an Open Convention, a moderate group of antiwar Democrats that included a number of delegates and other elected officials. This group had no desire to sleep in the parks, much less to use drugs. It wanted only to hold a rally in Soldiers Field, but its application for a permit was ignored, and Judge Lynch upheld the city's inaction.

Thus if there was a question of bad faith or irresponsibility on the part of the defendants, there was a corresponding possibility that the city too may have acted in bad faith and irresponsibly. Though the city surely had the right to arrest drug users and sexual exhibitionists, it had no right under the First Amendment to abridge the freedom of the demonstrators to assemble, on the unexamined assumption that their meetings would not be peaceable.

To explore the question of the city's intention, and for theatrical reasons as well, the defendants called Mayor Daley himself to the stand on January 6.

Daley, a short, solid man in a dark blue suit entered the courtroom—which was once again packed with federal marshals, augmented on this occasion by the mayor's own bodyguard—and walked to his seat with expressionless composure. The spectators' benches were filled as usual with long-haired, carelessly dressed young men and women, but in their midst was seated a housewife whose hair could be seen rising above the heads of her neighbors in a kind of golden pyramid. This woman proved to be Foran's wife. She was surrounded by her several expensively dressed children. Near her sat Schultz's wife, a thin, dark woman with the concave features of a *demoiselle d'Avignon*. Her two young daughters sat next to her. The two families conveyed an air of pride and expectation as if they had come to a graduation or parade.

Daley spoke in a low, somewhat constrained voice. In reply to Kunstler's questions he said that the Department of Streets and Sanitation and the Police Department were responsible for issuing parade permits. But when Kunstler attempted to show that the officials in these departments were appointed by the mayor and were in some cases his personal friends, Foran objected. These were leading questions he said, and they were also irrelevant. "Let's get to the Democratic convention. That's what we're here for," he said. The judge sustained Foran's objections and referred Kunstler to the law of evidence which, he said, was "too simple to require argument."

"Your Honor," Kunstler explained, "one of the chief defenses in this case—"

"Did you hear what I said?" the judge warned. "There will be no argument."

Kunstler then asked if the mayor knew Judge Lynch, but Foran objected again. Once more he was sustained. "Certainly that question is improper," the judge ruled.

"But Judge Lynch refused a permit," Kunstler pleaded.

"I direct the jury to disregard the statement of Mr. Kunstler," the judge ordered, but his words were lost in the sound of a scuffle at the rear of the courtroom, where a number of courtroom officials could be seen struggling with some spectators.

"Ouch. Ow. Don't step on me, please," someone shouted.

"He isn't doing anything. She didn't do anything," someone else cried as the marshals continued to flail the spectators.

"You're hitting Frank in the face!"

"I have confidence in the Chief Marshal of this court," the judge said, over this tumult, "and he is under orders to preserve dignity." The mayor sat expressionless in the witness chair. Foran's children stared straight ahead. Schultz's daughters squirmed in their seats to see what was happening.

Kunstler, who had gone to the back of the room to investigate, returned to the lectern and explained to the judge that it was not, in fact, the marshals who had been hitting the spectators. It was the mayor's bodyguard. The judge ignored this information and ordered that the examination of the witness continue.

But as often as Kunstler asked a question, Foran objected. These were leading questions, he said, and inappropriate on direct examination. He argued that only on cross-examination, according to the law of evidence, can a lawyer confront a witness with questions that may embarrass him or may imply the answers that the lawyer hopes to elicit. Under the law, he may not attempt to discredit his own, presumably friendly, witness, Foran insisted. Thus Kunstler moved that the mayor be declared a hostile witness, a common procedure in civil cases and occasionally in criminal ones when a lawyer wants to question a partisan of the opposing side.

"Why, the mayor has been a most friendly witness," the judge said. "I deny the motion." At that, Kunstler asked that the jury be dismissed so that he could argue his motion before the judge. To this the judge agreed. Kunstler cited several cases in support of his position. "It is familiar law," he quoted the Supreme Court, "that when a witness discloses in his testimony that he is adverse in interest and feeling to the party calling him, the latter may change the character of his examination from a direct to a cross-examination."

The judge, however, ruled against Kunstler. "When you call a man as your witness, he is your witness until he is proved hostile," the judge said. The mayor had not so far been proved hostile.

Kunstler replied, ". . . the only way we are ever going to get to the truth in this matter is by being able to ask cross-examination questions of the mayor . . . I am using the criteria of the courts to get to the heart of the matter."

But there had been nothing in the witness' manner to indicate hostility, the judge said. "His manner has been that of a gentleman."

The jury was then readmitted and Kunstler resumed his direct examination. He asked the mayor whether he was familiar with the proceedings of the federal grand jury that had indicted the defendants, but once more Foran objected. "Your Honor," he said, "a federal judge doesn't have anything to do with the federal grand jury. He has nothing to do with it at all until the time of the return [of the indictments]." Presumably Foran anticipated that Kunstler wanted to reach the question of whether Daley and Judge Campbell had discussed a federal indictment of the demonstrators. The judge sustained the objection and the matter was dropped. Once more the defendants sighed, and from the spectators' benches a voice called out, "Tell that to Judge Campbell."

Kunstler then asked whether the mayor had talked to the president of the Park District about the permit application.

"I gave him the same instructions I gave every other department: to cooperate with everyone that wanted permits and to try to be as helpful as they could to them in our city."

"Are you familiar with the fact that the Youth International Party requested permits from both the Park District and the Department of Sanitation?" Kunstler then asked.

"Object to the leading form of the question," Foran said.

"I sustain the objection," the judge replied. The Court then recessed for lunch.

Shortly before Court resumed for the afternoon session the mayor entered and took his seat. Abbie Hoffman entered next, saw the mayor, and in a mock swagger walked to within a few feet of him and said, with a shake of his shaggy head, "Why don't we just settle this right here?" The mayor laughed aloud and settled back in his chair.

Throughout the early afternoon Foran persisted in his objections, and soon it became clear that Kunstler would be unable to continue. Therefore he asked that the jury be dismissed so that he could make an offer of proof, that is, a statement for the record of what might have been proven had the mayor been allowed to answer his questions.

The judge agreed and the jury was dismissed. Kunstler then proceeded to read from a long document that charged a conspiracy between the mayor and the Administration of Lyndon Johnson to crush any demonstration that might occur in Chicago in opposition to the war, racism, imperialism, and in support of alternative cultures; that members of this conspiracy used whatever means they could—including planned inertia in processing permit applications—in order to deter the demonstrators; that the mayor maintains his power through a corrupt political machine; and that he has brutally repressed people who seek alternative solutions to America's problems.

Furthermore, Kunstler charged the mayor and his co-conspirators with having attempted to shift the blame for the convention riots onto the demonstrators by procuring indictments against the radical leaders. Finally, he charged that Mayor Daley and his administrators have for years harassed, intimidated, and terrorized young people who have adopted life styles of which he disapproves, including the wearing of long hair and unconventional clothing.

Throughout Kunstler's offer of proof the mayor, the judge, and the prosecutors sat expressionless. Their manner suggested not only the majesty of potentates indifferent to their despised and powerless enemies, but the incomprehension of men assailed in a foreign language or by an alien species.

The political opposition implied by Kunstler's offer of proof—as by the trial itself—arose from something deeper than conflicting vanities: it arose from conflicting views of history and man's nature. It was a war not between rival states or factions competing for wealth and power, but between the servants of different gods, who were contending out of their deepest convictions for their country's soul. This struggle, therefore, had the form and often borrowed the language of religious conflict. Thus it reflected struggles far older than the present controversy, and far deeper ones than could be settled, as Hoffman proposed to Daley, "right here." The struggle in Judge Hoffman's courtroom was rooted in disputes that attended the birth of America itself and perhaps even the birth of civilization.

The pilgrims who settled the Plymouth Plantation in 1620 had broken with the national Church of the English Puritans and come to America, from their exile in Holland, as refugee members of a dissenting faction. The cause of their grievance was their choice of a local, or Congregational, form of church government, rather than the national, or Presbyterian, model of the Puritan majority. But this Puritan majority had itself only recently broken with the Church of England, the Church that Henry VIII had established when he expelled the Church of Rome.

Thus the pilgrims came to America as the separatist faction of a radical sect that had itself formed a faction against the original Church of the English Reformation. But within the Plymouth Plantation there soon arose a still further sectarian division, led by a man named Morton, a resident of Mount Wollaston, which was in fact a small hill that he renamed Merry Mount. In 1638 upon this hill Morton declared himself a sort of Lord of Misrule and maintained, according to Governor Bradford, who recorded these events in his *History*, a "school of Atheism." He set up a Maypole, and with his followers, spent his time "dancing and frisking together, like so many Furies or fairies, as if they had anew revived and celebrated the feasts of the Roman goddess Flora and the beastly practices of the mad Bacchanalians." Morton also wrote poems, some "tending to lasciviousness," which he hung upon his Maypole. Soon, however, Captain Endicott arrived from England to enforce order in the colony, and sent Morton away. Thereupon the name of Merry Mount was changed to Mount Dagon, after the Philistine god.

Today, Merry Mount, as it is once again called, is an industrial slum near Boston surrounded by used-car lots and a polluted river. But two centuries after Morton danced upon it, its spirit was still sufficiently alive to suggest a short story to Nathaniel Hawthorne, who described the Maypole as "a pine tree that had preserved the slender grace of youth . . . dressed with birchen boughs and others of the liveliest green, fastened by ribbons that fluttered in fantastic knots of twenty different colors, but no sad ones."

Around the Maypole there danced "a wild throng." Could it be, Hawthorne asked, "that the fauns and nymphs, when driven from their classic groves and homes of ancient fable, had sought refuge as all the persecuted did, in the fresh woods of the West?"

He then described the dancers. "On the shoulders of a comely youth uprose the head and branching antlers of a stag: a second had the grim visage of a wolf, a third . . . showed the beard and horns of a venerable he-goat. There was the likeness of a bear erect, brute in all but his hind legs, which were adorned with pink silk stockings." There was even a real bear, "lending each of his forepaws to the grasp of a human hand . . . Many of this strange company wore foolscaps, and had little bells appended to their garments, responding to the inaudible music of their gleesome spirits . . .

"Within the ring of monsters appeared the two airiest forms that had ever trodden on any more solid footing than a purple and golden cloud. One was a youth in glistening apparel, with a scarf of the rainbow pattern crosswise on his breast . . . His left hand grasped the fingers of a fair maiden, not less gaily decorated than himself. Bright roses glowed in contrast to the dark and glossy curls of each. Behind this lightsome couple . . . stood the figure of an English priest, decked with flowers in the heathen fashion . . . By the riot of his rolling eye, and the pagan decoration of his holy garb, he seemed the wildest monster there . . ." This priest or monster was about to perform a marriage.

But "there were men in the new world of a sterner faith than these Maypole worshippers. Not far from Merry Mount was a settlement of Puritans, most dismal wretches, who said their prayers before daylight and then toiled in the forest or the cornfield until evening made it prayer time again. Their weapons were always at hand to shoot down the straggling savage . . . Woe to the youth or maiden who did but dream of dance . . . if they danced, it was round the whipping post, which might be termed the Puritan Maypole.

"A party of these grim Puritans, toiling through the difficult woods, each with a horseload of iron armor to burden his footsteps would sometimes draw near the sunny precincts of Merry Mount . . ." where the revellers ". . . sang ballads and told tales for the edification of their pious visitors; or preplexed them with juggling tricks; or grinned at them through horse collars; and when sport itself grew wearisome they made game of their own stupidity and began a yawning match.

"In due time a feud arose, stern and bitter on one side and as serious on the other as anything could be among such light spirits as had sworn allegiance to the Maypole. The future complexion of New England was involved in this important quarrel. Should the grizzly saints establish their jurisdiction over the gay sinners, then would their spirits darken all the clime, and make it a land of clouded visages, of hard toil, of sermon and psalm forever. But should the banner staff of Merry Mount be fortunate, sunshine would break upon the hills, and flowers would beautify the forest and late posterity do homage to the Maypole."

Endicott prevailed. Mingling one night with the Maypole dancers, his soldiers surprised them at their games. " 'Bind the heathen crew,' " Endicott ordered, " 'and bestow on them a small matter of stripes, as earnest of our future justice.' " Some he promised to put in jail as soon as they could be brought to a settlement. Others would be branded and their ears cropped. The dancing bear was killed.

" 'And shall not the youth's hair be cut?' asked Peter Palfrey, looking with abhorence at the lovelock and long glossy curls of the young man.

" 'Crop it forthwith,' " Endicott ordered, " 'and that in the true pumpkin shell fashion.' "

Thus Hawthorne concluded his story, ". . . as the moral gloom of the world overpowers all systematic gayety, even so was their home of wild mirth made desolate amid the sad forest."

More than the "future complexion of New England" was involved in the "important quarrel" on Merry Mount; nor was the outcome decided once and for all by Captain Endicott's soldiers, as events in Lincoln Park some three centuries later, and their aftermath in Judge Hoffman's courtroom, made clear. Though the roots of this reverberating controversy are as obscure as its branches are complex, evidently they touch the deepest sources of the culture itself. Thus they penetrate to the remote parts of the human, or at least the western, mind: the recesses where Freud discovered or imagined a continuing and ultimately tragic struggle between the institutional processes—the "laws" of our psychological "nature"—and the internalized demands of civilization that this "nature" be curbed.

The dispute on Merry Mount was an exemplary episode in this perennial warfare. But more narrowly it reflected a particular split within the English reformation and revolution of the sixteenth and seventeenth centuries.

The English revolution of 1640 was a further development within the process that had begun, more or less, with Henry VIII's assault in the preceding century upon the Church of Rome. It reflected the efforts of Englishmen to reclaim for a new class the inherited privileges of the Norman aristocracy, to cast off the alien weight of European feudalism, and to transform the treasure of the monasteries into the capital required by an expanding economy. Thereafter, English history was marked by a continuing, but hardly concerted, struggle to dispel the remaining emblems and encumbrances of the medieval past—the legacy of the Norman conquest, of which the Arthurian legend and the myth of Camelot were examples.

The progress of this revolution followed, roughly, two paths, or sprang from two opposed states of mind. One of these looked toward the European Reformation itself and the modernizing tendencies that accompanied and shaped it. These included the Calvinist doctrines that harmonized traditional Christian faith with the interests of a rising commercial and manufacturing class—a class transfixed by the promise of a new technology, the discovery of new resources and the growth of new markets. For these Christians, nature had lost its innocence in the Fall. To subdue nature—to cut it down, dam it up, and dig it out—served not only a pecuniary purpose but a divine one as well. The profitable exploitation of nature, accompanied by individual self-restraint—the suppression of one's own nature—would be the method and proof of salvation. Meanwhile, the language and methods of the new science would replace the old magic as the means to transform or subdue the natural world. Scientific reason would eventually become the means to tame wanton nature and reduce it to manageable, efficient, and profitable order.

The other direction in which the English revolution

looked was toward the past—to the presumed simplicity of Saxon times, before the Conquest, and even beyond this to the time of man before the Fall. "We would derive from the Conqueror as little as we could," wrote Sir Edward Coke, the great seventeenth-century interpreter of the English common law. "The grounds of our common laws," he said in 1621—the year that Governor Bradford and his fellow Pilgrims arrived in Plymouth—"are beyond the memory or register of any beginning." These grounds were, in other words, the simple and sensible relations that Englishmen had established among themselves before the violent imposition of Norman custom. The common law, therefore, was not to be established by the creation of new codes but by the scholarly recovery of ancient precedent. Coke's reverence for the Saxon tradition of personal and political independence was the approximate counterpart in law of the preference of Puritan theologians for bare Scripture, unmediated by Papal authority.

From the modernizing tendency, with its Calvinist suspicion of nature, there eventually emerged the form of economic development that celebrated profit as the proof of good works. This emphasis on profit represented a departure in Christian tradition from the mere accumulation of treasure or necessary household goods—the primitive forms of acquisition that feudal Christians shared with mankind generally. Profit was not a commodity but an index of successful investment. It revealed itself not in storehouses of gold and barns of grain, or pairs of shoes, but numerically as a rate of return on invested capital. It was in the sixteenth century that William Perkins, a Calvinist preacher at Cambridge, justified the practice of Christian usury, thus altering the tradition that flowed from Aristotle's condemnation of usury as "the most hated form of wealth-getting because it makes a gain from money itself and not from the natural object of it." "Money," Aristotle said, "was intended to be used in exchange, but not to increase at interest." Aristotle condemned usury as the most "unnatural" way of getting money. But by the seventeenth century, when a follower of Perkins contemplated a forest, he was likely to see neither a sacred grove nor a place to live or hunt in, nor even an accumulation of trees that someday might provide warmth and shelter. He saw a capital asset to be invested for a future capital gain. He saw not a forest but money—not trees, but a number.

The natural world offered these people not an inn but a hospital: a place to suffer while awaiting the inevitable kingdom of God. Yet for all the chaos of nature and human society, the natural world was ultimately part of a self-correcting mechanism ruled by God. Within this divinely ordained system, only the fittest—what Calvin called the elect—were saved. Profitable investment was a sign of salvation. Except in the case of the virtuous poor—whose piety and good works revealed their good intentions—poverty was worse than misery; it forseshadowed damnation.

By the end of the nineteenth century in America, this doctrine had reappeared in the form of Social Darwinism, in which the terms of the old Calvinism were transposed into the language of evolution. The Calvinist idea that of all the world's people some were mysteriously elected for salvation, while the rest were to be extinguished, attached itself to the Darwinian idea of natural selection, according to which only forms of life that successfully adapted to the hazards of the physical world survived. The difference between the two doctrines were mainly terminological. Both the old Calvinism and the new Social Darwinism celebrated efficiency, order, and the aggressive search for new means to subdue hostile nature in the interest of a higher good. This search often involved the destruction of natural resources and the harassment and murder of native populations. Dissent from these pursuits was regarded by the more extreme Calvinist types—of whom Captain Endicott was an example—as the proof of sin and, therefore, as justification for wars of suppression. By the eighteenth century, Lord Jeffrey Amherst permitted his generals to infect the Algonquins with smallpox in order to quell the conspiracy of Pontiac, the bitter and doomed Indian uprising against the Westward expansion of British settlement. At the heart of this Christian passion to dominate a fallen and riotous nature, and to evangelize or destroy a world of wayward pagans, was the imperative of a single and all-powerful God, under whose harsh judgment all men fell.

From Coke's backward glance, on the other hand, there arose the tradition of political liberty based on the imagined ideal of Saxon independence—an independence that rested, according to Coke, on the absolute security of property. A man's home was his castle, which even the king could not violate. The idea that property was inviolable conflicted with the capitalist investor's subordination of property to the extraction of profit—an activity that often results in the careless waste of resources and the destruction of property—for the sake of a greater return on investment. Among Coke's heirs was Macaulay, who found in the history of Saxon independence, and its reflection in the regicide of Plantagenet times, a source of constitutional government.

But the Saxon past also inspired more radical visions than Coke's and Macaulay's, of which the revival of pagan ceremony in the woods of Merry Mount was an example. While the Calvinists hoped to enter heaven after a life of toil, prayer, and successful investment, these Maypole dancers wanted their heaven in nature itself—a heaven in which their days would be "bound each to each," in Wordsworth's phrase, by nothing more than "natural piety," as Adam's days had been before the Fall and as Saxon days had been before the Norman Conquest, according to this theory. Implicit in this pagan view was a considerable tolerance of diverse ethical and cultural forms. It was this tolerance that Gibbon celebrated, a century later, as the sublime essence of Roman polytheism, but which fell, to his great regret, before the chill monotheism of the Jews and Christians.

The political expression of this natural religion was the theory of natural rights advanced by the English Levellers of the seventeenth century, for whom the institution of property was a consequence of man's Fall. In Eden the natural world had no owners. Unlike Coke, who thought that the law should be left to judges, these Levellers wanted to leave the administration of justice—and thus the distribution of property—to the wisdom of the people themselves. Questions of law, as well as those of fact, would be answered by "twelve men chosen out of every hundred," who would make their decisions according to their own consciences. Thus the absolute security of property that Coke demanded would be subordinated to the interest of equitable distribution, as the "people" saw fit. If Coke's heirs included Macaulay, the Levellers' included the author of the slogan "to each according to his needs."

At his trial in 1649, one of these Levellers, William Lillburne, told his jurors that "those who call themselves judges are no more but Norman invaders and indeed, and, in truth, if the jury please [you], are no more but Cyphers to pronounce their verdict." Thus like the defendants on trial in Judge Hoffman's courtroom, he asked his jurors to make the law themselves.

The idea that men inherit certain inalienable rights—whether from Anglo-Saxon common law, as Coke and his Whig progeny believed, or from nature itself, as the Levellers and their still more radical contemporaries, the Diggers, felt—became, by way of Thomas Jefferson and Tom Paine, a foundation of American constitutional liberty. For Paine, George III was no more legitimate than his Norman predecessor. "A French bastard," he wrote in *Common*

Sense, "landing with an armed banditti and establishing himself in England against the consent of the nations, is in plain terms a very paltry, rascally original."

But together with the idea that nature was the source of certain inalienable rights, there was planted in America the Puritan idea that nature was corrupt; that paradise could not be regained by efforts to recreate the state of man before the Fall. Countless peculiarities have followed from the simultaneous imposition upon the New World of these contrary visions. Among the strangest is that the radical tradition in America derives from a backward glance toward simpler times and more "natural" forms of social organization, while the conservative tendency is often dominated by an obsession with the new, together with the idea that nature is something to be overcome: that its variety should be subordinated to a single principle of moral judgment for the sake of some future benefit. Lincoln's mystic chords of Union were, in fact, rather like the old monotheism in political form.

Yet the distinction was hardly so clear in practice. These two attitudes often merged in America. Occasionally they complemented each other. Their outlines, never sharp to begin with, were blurred still more. They appeared in a variety of subsidiary and derivative forms. They borrowed and then disputed the possession of each other's terms so that the words liberty, equality, and democracy came to be suffused with a hopeless ambiguity. But, at bottom, the conflict between these two cultures was unreconcilable. It produced a two-party government in which the divided and distinguished tendencies within the revolution of the seventeenth century would be permanently, if often obscurely, at odds.

Thus the anomalous passage of the Alien and Sedition Acts in the same historic breath as the ratification of the Bill of Rights was, in fact, not such a curiosity as it might seem, but rather a further and typical reflection of the struggle between "natural" diversity and Puritan unity that was fought on Merry Mount. So too was John Marshall's assertion of the supremacy of the Court over the diverse interests of the separate states, an assertion of centralized power that Jefferson feared, though were he alive in our time, he would, no doubt, feel differently. Similarly, the attempt by President Madison to annex Canada in the War of 1812, and Polk's invasion of Mexico, to which Lincoln responded by advocating rebellion, aroused much the same fears of concentrated Presidential power among advocates of diversified political authority that the Vietnam war does today.

But while the proponents of concentrated power had come to occupy the high places to which their interests and ambitions inevitably led them, the country was vast, the frontier was open, and a vigorous people, convinced that no man was their superior, were not easily governed. To the popular and natural desire for liberty, there were added a taste for adventure and the temptation of wealth. On the frontier, the ideal of independence merged with the fear of the wilderness and the desire for profit; the result was a Western empire that generated an expedient law and politics of its own, more violent and less equitable than the popular justice that Lillburne and the Levellers had had in mind.

To control such formidable energies was beyond the means of a government whose power was unequal to the vigor and ambition of the people. By Jackson's time the party in office could hardly govern, except by accommodating itself to the lawless spirit of the expanding frontier. However, by submitting to this popular will, Jackson discovered the means to strengthen, consolidate, and perpetuate his party. By dissolving the Bank of the United States he offended the interests of the established and propertied classes. But the termination of the Bank generated the broader and cheaper capital that the new men of the West and in the growing cities demanded. In place of the concentrated power of the Bank and the class whose interest it reflected, he thus established upon a far broader foundation the concentrated power of his own government and party. In the same spirit he frustrated the efforts of the Southern planters to nullify a federal tariff that would advance the interests of the new manufacturers, while it would deplete the profits from the old and overused land of the old South. Against the claims of nullification Jackson asserted the demands of union and spoke, he said, for all the people.

Hawthorne's story of Captain Endicott's victory foretold the shape of things to come. Though by the time of the Mexican War Thoreau preached civil disobedience and celebrated a life of natural simplicity, and Emerson predicted the ultimate victory of the Transcendentalist "movement," to use his term, over the Unitarian "establishment" of zealous New England investors, the Jeffersonian ideal of constitutional liberty had begun to fade. The nullification of federal power, whether from Thoreau's perspective or from that of the old Southern planters, remained an obsession, but it became a fantasy as the country expanded and its growing power became concentrated in the hands of ambitious men.

The slavery question briefly and perversely transformed the dream of nullification into the hope of secession. But the freedom to exploit human property was hardly the issue on which to defend the Jeffersonian principle of limited federal power. Rather, it was the ultimate perversion of the constitutional ideal of freedom by the obsession with profit. Jefferson himself had submitted to the Continental Congress a denunciation of African slavery to be included in the Declaration of Independence. The king, he wrote, ". . . has waged cruel war against human nature . . . Violating its most sacred rights of life and liberty in the persons of a distant people who never offended him, captivating and carrying them into slavery in another hemisphere . . . this piratical warfare, the opprobrium of infidel powers, is the warfare of the Christian king."

Jefferson's paragraph was stricken from the final document. "The Clause," he later wrote, "reprobating the enslavement of the inhabitants of Africa, was struck out in complaisance to South Carolina and Georgia . . . Our Northern brethren also, I believe, felt a little tender under these censures; for though their people have very few slaves themselves, yet they had been pretty considerable carriers of them to others."

Though the Northern victory moderated the convention by which human beings were invested as capital goods, slavery was an insult to the Constitution that permanently damaged the country. "It is still in our power," Jefferson wrote in 1785, "to direct the process of emancipation and deportation peaceably and in such slow degrees that the evil will wear off insensibly. . . . If on the contrary, it is left to force itself on, human nature must shudder at the prospect."

Though Jefferson deplored slavery, he saw no place for blacks in a white society. The Africans, he felt, should be colonized. "Why not retain and incorporate the blacks into the state . . . ?" Jefferson asked. "Deep rooted prejudices," he explained, "entertained by the whites; ten thousand recollections by the blacks of the injuries they have sustained; new provocations; the real distinctions which nature has made . . . will divide us into parties, and produce convulsions, which will probably never end, but in the extermination of one or the other race." Furthermore, Jefferson added, there are physical differences that argue for separation. The whites are more "beautiful," he said, ". . . while the blacks have less hair on the face and body. They secrete less by the kidneys and more by the glands of the skin, which gives them a very strong and disagreeable odor . . .

They seem to require less sleep." For these reasons, among others, Jefferson concluded that the two races should be kept apart. Lincoln too declared in 1858 that "if the State of Illinois had [the power to confer citizenship upon Negroes] I should be opposed to the exercise of it."

While the Civil War ended the "peculiar institution" of slavery, it also imposed, once and for all, the bonds of Union. Thus the possibility of a separate black colony was no longer even to be seriously imagined. Hereafter, all Americans would be bound to a single country, whether nature intended it that way or not.

By the 1880's, the frontier was closed and the patterns of economic, and hence political, concentration became permanent. The accumulated power of the trusts and the concentrated capital of the Eastern banks supported by a strong central government ended the possibility—though they revived the spirit—of rebellion. But by this time, the revolutionary impulse was no longer divided along the relatively simple lines that had distinguished it two centuries earlier. The more extreme American radicals borrowed the ideas of European Marxism, found themselves in Judge Gary's Court or others like it, and soon formed a party of American socialists whose principles derived partly from libertarian ideas of natural community and partly from the quite opposite idea of "scientific" social organization. It was a party that could not, given these contradictory origins, last—even had it been able to earn the loyalty of a competitive people more interested in their own advancement than in the socialist ideal of brotherhood.

The less radical opponents of economic centralization attached themselves to the various populist tendencies, whose principal theme was the claim of the common man against the power of the industrial monopolists and the social plutocrats. Most populists did not want to overthrow the system. They simply wanted a substitute for the opportunities that had been lost to them when the frontier closed. Thus cheap capital—free silver—to supplement scarce gold became their demand, as it had been the demand of the Jacksonian opponents of the National Bank.

But by this time the national government identified itself with the interests of a new monied class descended from the beneficiaries of Jackson's favors. This proved to be a more powerful, if less numerous, constituency than the people themselves, and the government acceded to the demands of the populists grudgingly, when it acceded at all.

Among these populists was Aaron Hoffman, an immigrant furrier, who had wanted to name his son after William Jennings Bryan, the Populist party candidate for President in 1896, and the hero of the free silver movement. Aaron's wife, Bertha, objected; perhaps because Bryan did not, after all, represent the respectable element. The parents compromised. They named their infant Julius Jennings Hoffman.

The Espionage Act of 1917 effectively, if temporarily, restored the Alien and Sedition Acts and suspended constitutional freedoms. President Wilson's aim was to unify the country in time of war, as the implicit aim of the war itself was to unify the world; to make it safe for American democracy, which had long since begun to expand beyond its own borders. In the name of this unity Wilson's government terrorized the Socialists, thousands of whom were sent to jail. Their newspapers were suppressed. There remained, however, a stubborn and radical Marxist fringe, most of whose leaders had emigrated from Europe. This fringe preserved itself by going underground to await the collapse of the American system and the start of the revolution. With the great collapse of the 1930's, these Marxists reemerged as the Communist party. Soon the Communists attracted a following among American radicals, some of whom hoped to create from the wreckage of the Depression an ideal community of brotherhood and cooperation. Most

Communists, however, looked for a more "scientific" and up-to-date alternative to capitalism. The Communist leaders had no interest in the native root of constitutional liberty that nourished the radical tradition in America. Instead, they attached themselves to the socialist experiment in the Soviet Union, much as the English Calvinists of the seventeenth century had looked to the Reformation in Europe. These puritanical Communists welcomed a stern and "scientific" political discipline, oriented toward the future, contemptuous of personal liberty, and bleakly suspicious of natural diversity. Before long the libertarian elements were purged from the party and denounced as romantics, anarchists, and counterrevolutionaries.

By the 1950's, military victory, along with an extravagant and largely trivial technology had restored the appearance, if not the reality, of power to America, whose energetic people had now thrust themselves into most of the world's corners, and bitterly resented that they were not welcome in them all. The American Communists, who had flourished in the disaster of the 1930's, lost their revolutionary function and their power in the prosperity of the 1950's. By the time the McCarran Act was passed, there was hardly a party left to persecute. Attracted by American power and ambition, many former Communists transferred their fierce loyalties from Russia to America, and joined their fellow citizens in a patriotic struggle against their former comrades for the possession of the future. The Cold War became the occasion for the further centralization and expansion of American political power, and what Macaulay called the "constitutional checks on misgovernment" were widely neglected. Once more the libertarians were denounced as nonconforming misfits, anarchists, and agitators who had abandoned themselves to a false ideal of political primitivism.

As Macaulay had warned, the rebellious spirit revived, largely among the young. This rebellion, Hayden told the

Congressmen on the House Un-American Activities Committee, was first inspired by the South, where constitutional neglect was at its worst. Soon, however, it appeared to many radicals of Hayden's generation that an indivisible union could not be corrupt in one branch and whole in another. Thus the spirit of rebellion spread, and moderate man sensibly shuddered, as Jefferson had foreseen two centuries before.

At last, it appeared to many Americans that the earth itself, as Ginsberg had testified, was in jeopardy, not simply from the terrible threat of war, but because a rapacious technology, committed to profit and indifferent to the safety of the natural world, had wasted its resources. Accordingly, nature too seemed to rebel against an economy that had for centuries despised and humiliated it—that had regarded nature not as a habitation but as a source of profit. The rivers withheld their freshness, the air became deadly, fish disappeared from the sea, and people became wary of the food they ate and the water they drank. The environment of the American eagle, scientists said, had been destroyed by chemical poisons; the national bird was on the point of extinction.

Yet the extravagant enthusiasm for profit persisted among businessmen. In the spring of 1969, Senator Long encouraged a partisan of the oil industry to testify before his Senate Finance Committee that further taxation of oil profits would be disastrous. Such taxes, this spokesman said, would "remove all business incentive and lead to Thursday to Tuesday weekends, wife swapping and drinking." Without the lure of profit, work would thus become meaningless. Americans would become pagan again and evils would prevail much like those that had inflamed Captain Endicott three centuries earlier.

Offended by the abuse of their natural rights, and fearful of the destruction of nature itself, the partisans of nature, as they sometimes thought of themselves, descended upon Chicago, a city whose heart, they believed, was made of money. Armed with the Constitution, the sacred vessel of the natural law, they petitioned that the city's parks become a "liberated zone," much like the one the Maypole dancers had made on Merry Mount and the one the Viet Cong, from whom they borrowed their term, were attempting to create against the intrusion of American civilization in their own country. Inevitably the city refused them the rights they demanded and explained its refusal by the fact, as Schultz forced Hoffman to admit, that the applicants had done nothing to show that their intentions were a joke. Moreover, the presence of the demonstrators, the authorities felt, would be bad for business. In the winter of the trial, the Grand Dragon of the Pennsylvania Ku Klux Klan announced, "There are two armies choosing up sides for a war; the forces of chaos and anarchy against the forces of law and order. A revolution was brewing and the vat had already begun to boil."

The final weeks of the trial were bitter. The parties were exhausted. The judge and the defense lawyers quarreled repeatedly. On January 20, the judge warned Weinglass that he would soon need a defense for himself. "Our Court of Appeals," he said, "has required trial judges to admonish counsel when they are engaging in contumacious acts or using contumacious language." Weinglass' behavior had, in fact, been decorous, though his defense had been vigorous. What might have bothered the judge, therefore, was not Weinglass himself, but his clients, for whose increasingly disrespectful manner he held the lawyers responsible. "Have a look on the expression on the face of Mr. Hoffman directed at me," the judge complained to Weinglass.

"Well, Your Honor, if your rulings are being affected by the expression on my clients' faces," Weinglass replied, "that is precisely what our problem is. I say this respect-fully. The court is allowing its ability to judge this case to be influenced by the way my clients appear in court."

The judge cut Weinglass short. "Mr. Fultz—Mr. Schultz, please continue with your examination."

The final defense witnesses included a number of folk singers and balladeers: Judy Collins, Arlo Guthrie, Pete Seeger, and Country Joe. Country Joe took the stand on January 19. He wore long hair, purple boots, a green silk shirt, and red trousers. He was a slight, sandy-haired young man who carried himself gracefully. As he stood to take the oath, his jaws were working rhythmically.

"You will remove your gum, sir," Judge Hoffman's aged clerk ordered.

"What gum?" the singer asked, his jaws continuing to work.

"The gum that you are chewing on," the clerk replied.

The singer paused, cast a glance over his shoulder as if to see whether the clerk might not have been speaking to someone else, and drawled, "I'm afraid I don't have any gum."

"You may be seated, sir," the clerk said with resignation.

Country Joe then testified that he had first discussed the Festival of Life with Hoffman and Rubin at a meeting at the Chelsea Hotel in New York. "My [singing] group was very influential with young people in America," he explained, "and it was important that we try to say some-thing in Chicago which would be positive, natural, human and loving, in order to let people know that there are Americans who are not tripped out on ways of thinking that result only in oppression and fear, paranoia and death . . . Abbie Hoffman wanted to know what the song was that I was going to sing and so I sang: 'And it's one two three, what are we fighting for?/ Don't ask me. I don't give a damn./ The next stop is Viet Nam/ And it's . . .' "

"No No No Mr. Witness," the judge interrupted. "No singing."

"Five—six—seven . . ." the singer continued.

"Mr. Marshal," the judge ordered an officer named Gracious who stood beside the witness stand. Without further instruction the marshal clapped his hand over the singer's mouth and stifled the rest of his song.

On January 20, a former Justice Department official named Roger Wilkins testified for the defense. He explained that he had served under Ramsey Clark as Director of the Community Relations Service, a bureau that assists communities "in settling racial and other disputes." Wilkins testified that on July 17 he came to Chicago, where he spoke to Rennie Davis in a bar near the Mobe office. He told Davis, ". . . the closer [your] relationships with law enforcement authorities in preparing for demonstrations, the more likelihood there was of averting violence." He then offered to help set up such a relationship with the Chicago authorities. Davis agreed to cooperate and explained, Wilkins testified, "that he [too] felt very strongly that there should be the closest kind of cooperation between the New Mobilization and the city officials if violence was to be averted. And he said that [the Mobe] had attempted to make such communications and had been unsuccessful . . . He asked me to do what I could to help . . ."

Wilkins then testified that he returned to Washington, where he prepared an eight-page memorandum for Ramsey Clark, based on his conversation with Davis. But Schultz objected that this document should not go before the jury because ". . . it was what the witness testified to on direct [examination] . . ." Oral testimony is admissible, Schultz said, ". . . not what he wrote down."

Weinglass replied that parts of the document had not been covered in the witness' direct testimony and that it was only these passages that he wanted to place before the jury.

Nevertheless, the judge sustained Schultz's objection. The document, he said, had "no probative value." He did, however, permit Weinglass to present the document, out of the presence of the jury, as an offer of proof.

Wilkins wrote to Clark that he had found Davis an "honest, intelligent man, who was candid with me in our conversation; that large-scale violence in Chicago would be a national disaster and a national disgrace; that such violence is possible and that our best chance of averting [it] is to develop the closest possible working relationship between the Chicago authorities and the Mobe." He then urged that the President and the Vice President be told of the Mobe plans and that "they be urged to adopt the assumptions listed above as their point of view . . . that one of them or someone clearly acting in their behalf call Mayor Daley to apprise him of that point of view, and that the mayor be advised that I am coming to Chicago next week to inform him of the Mobilization's plans . . . and set up a continuing working relationship between the city officials and the Mobilization."

After Weinglass had read this passage, he argued that had Wilkins' memorandum been allowed into evidence, the jurors might have had a better grasp of the defendants' intentions at the time of Wilkins' visit, but Schultz continued to object to this "so-called offer of proof," and the judge sustained him.

Wilkins then testified that on July 25 he returned to Chicago with Wesley Pomeroy, another Justice Department employee, who had been given the task of coordinating police protection at both the Republican and Democratic conventions. The two men sat with Mayor Daley and David Stahl for about half an hour, and then met with Tom Foran. That afternoon, Wilkins, Pomeroy, and Foran met with Davis in the Pinch Penny Pub near the Mobe offices. Wilkins testified that he told Davis at this meeting about his discussion with the mayor that morning. He then asked Davis to tell Foran the Mobe's plans. Davis did so, and Foran said he would be seeing the mayor later in the day and would tell him of the conversation. Wilkins then returned to Washington and made no further visits to Chicago.

When Wilkins had completed his testimony late that afternoon, Pomeroy (who had himself testified the day before), told the reporters that the meeting in Daley's office had been unproductive. "It was like two different languages," he said. Daley kept talking about "outside agitators." Pomeroy told the reporters that as they left the mayor's office he had said to Wilkins, "It's too bad one of you wasn't speaking Urdu. Then you'd know you had a communications problem."

On January 23, Rennie Davis took the stand. Except for Hoffman, he was the only one of the seven defendants to testify. He attempted to explain the intentions of the Mobe leaders, as Hoffman had done for the Yippies. On the witness stand Davis revealed the manner and skills, and perhaps also the character, of a bureaucrat. Though he too had begun to wear his hair long, the style seemed hardly appropriate to someone whom Hayden had called the "organization man" of the movement. His polite and earnest testimony, his innocent and cautious manner, and his effort to convey an air of simple candor recalled the style of the government witnesses, especially Stahl and Simon. For this reason, presumably, Foran called him "two-faced," and scorned him for trying to seem like "the boy next door."

Davis testified that when he was in high school he belonged to a 4-H Club and won a poultry judging contest. In 1967 he worked with the poor whites of Appalachia. Then he became national coordinator of the Mobilization Committee to End the War in Viet Nam.

He testified at length about planning the conferences for

convention week that were held in the winter and spring of 1968. These meetings were attended by Hayden and Dellinger, among others. They culminated in the meeting at Lake Villa on the weekend of March 22—the same meeting that Hoffman attended in his Indian costume and that the police spy, Irv Bock, attended as an officer of the Mobe. At this meeting, Davis and Hayden submitted to the assembled delegates a memorandum they had written called "Movement Campaign, 1968: An Election Year Offensive."

Foran objected that this document should not be placed in evidence. "It contains in it," he said, "a number of broad summary statements that are not supported by facts and data. It is merely an opinion of someone, totally unsupported by any evidence or fact." Furthermore, much of its contents, Foran argued, were irrelevant to the charges, and the document as a whole was "self-serving in nature and the law is clear that a self-serving declaration is inadmissible."

Weinglass replied by reminding the Court of McCormick's views of self-serving documents, as well as the views of Professor Wigmore, an earlier and equally formidable authority on the law of evidence.

Wigmore had said that the rule excluding self-serving documents rests on a presumption of the defendant's guilt. Therefore, this rule is contrary to the presumption of innocence on which Anglo-American law is founded. "If you assume that the defendants are guilty," Weinglass said, paraphrasing Wigmore, "if that is your beginning premise . . ."

But the judge interrupted. "Do you mean that offensively?" he asked. Presumably he felt that Weinglass intended the singular, not the plural, form of the second person pronoun.

"I mean that the way Professor Wigmore meant it,"

Weinglass replied, "that the whole theory of self-serving documents—"

"Professor Wigmore," the judge interrupted again, "was my teacher and employer, but he never thought I was offensive." The judge sustained Foran's objection.

"Has Your Honor read the document?" Weinglass asked.

"I have looked it over," the judge replied.

"You never read it. I was watching you," Davis said from the stand. "You read two pages," he added in a cool and reasonable tone. The judge made a note of this in his ledger, but did not otherwise respond.

That afternoon, Weinglass submitted the Lake Villa statement, out of the presence of the jury, as an offer of proof. The document began with the words "The campaign should not plan violence and disruption against the Democratic National Convention. It should be non-violent and legal. The right to rebellion is hardly exercised in an effective way by assembling 300,000 people to charge into 30,000 paratroopers. [Such] deliberately planned disruptions will drive away people who are worried about arrests or violence and thus sharply diminish the size and political effect of the mobilization. Little would be served except the political hopes of Johnson, Nixon and Wallace by a Chicago action that would be seen (as Max Lerner sees it in his fantasy already) as a gathering of 'every crackpot group, protest group and every disruptive, violent force in America that thinks it has the pipeline to absolute truth.' We must demonstrate the opposite; that the government is the real source of crackpot thinking and violence . . . We believe the demonstrations can be orderly and directed. Certainly there will be police and various incidents of violence. But they need not change the overall character of our common protest."

"That was written," Weinglass told the Court, "by Rennie Davis and Tom Hayden and delivered on March 22 to 24, four months before the convention. I submit that this writing is very clear evidence of the defendants' intent. Unfortunately, the jury will not have the benefit of this document." Weinglass then asked the judge to reconsider his ruling.

"No argument. No further argument," the judge replied. "I never hear any arguments after I ask a lawyer to make an offer of proof."

The defendants' speeches before the convention and their similar statements at the convention itself might, to some jurors, have seemed at first glance to imply an unambiguous intention to cross state lines for the purposes of inciting a riot, as the government charged. But the Lake Villa statement of Hayden and Davis, like the article by Abbie Hoffman, might, had the judge let them go before the jury, have raised a reasonable doubt in the minds of the jurors that these presumed intentions were as criminal as they may have seemed to be.

Judge Hoffman's decision to exclude these documents angered the defendants, depressed their lawyers, and further convinced a majority of the reporters that the judge was unfair.

On January 25, Kunstler, Froines, and Hayden met with Ramsey Clark at his home in Falls Church, Virginia, where they discussed their plan to call him as a defense witness the following week. The defendants were counting heavily on Clark's testimony. "If the Attorney General at the time of the convention," Hayden later wrote, "did not seem to consider us criminals, then the whole prosecution would be exposed as a purely political affair, and might cause 'reasonable doubt' of our guilt in the minds of the jurors."

The former Attorney General asked that two members of the present Justice Department attend this meeting. According to Hayden, these officials urged Clark not to testify, but Clark replied that he felt it was his duty to give what testimony he could. He also told Kunstler and Hayden that he had strongly objected to Daley's "shoot to kill" order, that his staff had been impressed by Rennie Davis, that he had opposed sending federal troops to Chicago at the time of the convention, that he had turned down FBI requests to tap the defendants' phones, and that he had opposed the investigation of the demonstrators by Judge Campbell's grand jury.

Clark appeared in Court on Wednesday, January 28; but before he came to the stand Schultz objected. He told the judge that he had heard from Mr. Morrell, one of the Justice Department lawyers who had attended the Falls Church meeting, and urged that the judge "make a determination whether anything [Clark] has is admissible." He also asked that this determination be made without the jury present. If the Attorney General were to appear before the jury "the defendants would just make a spectacle, as they have done in the past." The judge agreed and the jury was excluded.

Schultz then argued that from what Morrell had told him, Clark had nothing relevant to say. He would testify, Schultz said, that he had called Mayor Daley, as Wilkins had urged. But it adds nothing, Schultz said, for Clark to testify that he "picked up the phone and made a telephone call and spoke to Mayor Daley." Nor was it relevant, Schultz continued, for Clark to testify that he had attended a meeting in the White House, "where everyone [incuding President Johnson] thought that there was going to be a holocaust in Chicago . . . and everyone but Ramsey Clark" thought troops should be sent there. Furthermore, the defendants planned to qualify Clark as an expert witness, Schultz said, and ask him his opinion of the anti-riot statute. The former Attorney General will testify, Schultz told the judge, "that he advised the President that the anti-riot law was not unconstitutional on its face but that it could lend itself to unconstitutional abuses."

NATURAL LAW · 389

Finally, Schultz quoted a passage from the Code of Federal Regulations, which said that a former employee of the Justice Department shall not, "in response to a demand from a court or other authority, produce any materials contained in the files [of the Department] or disclose information relating to [this material] . . . without the prior approval of the Attorney General."

"That would obviously mean the Attorney General who is the Attorney General at this time, which is Attorney General Mitchell," Schultz said. Even though Clark himself "promulgated this very rule," Schultz explained, he would need Mitchell's permission to testify. Schultz then asked the judge to permit Clark to take the stand out of the presence of the jury so that the defense attorneys could question him. In this way, the Court could determine whether any of his testimony was likely to be relevant in itself or admissible under the federal regulations. The defendants, he added, had persisted in asking inadmissible questions of other witnesses "solely for their effect" on the jury, and "if they try to create impressions with this man before the jury that are erroneous because the questions are improper, they will have seriously prejudiced the government's case."

Throughout Schultz's argument the defendants were in great agitation, clutching their heads in mock exasperation and sighing aloud in genuine despair. "I wish Davis, who was such a gentleman on the stand, smiling at the jury and pretending he was just the little boy next door, would stop whispering and talking to me when I am talking," Schultz protested.

"You are a disgrace, sir. I say you are a disgrace," Davis replied in disgust. "I really say you are a disgrace."

"Yes, yes," the other defendants said.

"I think [Davis] has a split personality, like a schizophrenic," Schultz replied.

Kunstler argued that the federal regulation concerning former members of the Justice Department did not apply in the present case, as it had not applied in the cases of Wilkins and Pomeroy, who had also been employed by the Justice Department. The defense, he said, was not interested in questioning Clark about the confidential matters that the regulation was meant to protect. He wanted only to ask such questions as whether Clark had ever called Daley. This was "a perfectly proper question," Kunstler argued. "What [the government] is trying here," Kunstler said, "is to keep the jury from knowing that a former Attorney General is here and ready to testify. This is absolutely unheard of and has never occurred in any Federal Court in the United States."

"You must have done a lot of research before you came in this morning," the judge remarked.

"I have looked up this point," Kunstler answered, "and I defy the government to show a single case where a witness who was willing to testify was denied the right to testify, subject to objection, because the opposing party wanted to keep him off the stand." Furthermore, Kunstler argued, it would be a "horrendous precedent" were the opposing side able to force its adversary to expose its witnesses on voir dire, that is, to determine their competence out of the presence of the jury. This would give the government a chance to test its objections on the Court in advance so that it would, in effect, "be getting a double shot. If Your Honor grants this motion, you will be the first federal judge in the United States to [do so] . . . I've never heard of a willing witness being prevented from taking the stand or made to testify in the vacuum of a court without a jury."

"Is it not discretionary with the Court," the judge asked Kunstler, "as to whether a witness may be brought to the stand?"

"Absolutely not," Kunstler replied. "The defense in a criminal prosecution, where a defendant's liberty is at stake, has the absolute right to bring anyone to the stand it wishes. All that can stop a person from coming to the stand is if he himself moves the court to quash his subpoena, and then the court may grant the motion to quash.

"The government is motivated by the fear of letting the jury see the Attorney General of the United States . . ." Kunstler continued. "That is what is at the root of this. Not law. Not ethics. Just plain, ordinary fear that he will testify on behalf of the defense . . . Mr. Schultz says 'it will prejudice our case.' Of course it may. What are we putting him on for? For the betterment of their case?"

Schultz replied, "It is absolutely irrelevant that [Clark] made a call to the mayor. But they want to get [Clark] here to pull the stunt in front of the jury, and we are objecting to it. They are not going to make this trial the mockery that they are trying to make it . . . We are asking Your Honor not to let them parade people before this jury and create false impressions, knowing their conduct is contumaceous, but not caring, but willing to practice civil disobedience, to prove to their clients that they are in the fold, they are in the movement." Then Schultz told the judge that "the Attorney General himself said to Mr. Kunstler that he didn't think anything [he had to say] was admissible."

"That is not true," Hayden said from the defense table.

"Mr. Morrell," Schultz asked the Justice Department lawyer who had been at Clark's house, "will you tell the Court, please, what the Attorney General said about admissibility?"

"Have him sworn," Kunstler added. "I was there and I heard. Have him sworn and I will question him."

"I don't like that attitude," the judge scolded him. "Please don't order me around, Mr. Kunstler. You assume

a respectful attitude toward the court. I have been respectful to you. I have tried awfully hard throughout this trial."
The angry judge, however, had forgotten about the question that Schultz had asked Mr. Morrell, and neither Schultz
nor Kunstler had the temerity to remind him.

That afternoon the judge ruled on Schultz's motion. The
defense, he said, had called the mayor "with much fanfare
but he was able to give no evidence that was material to
this case. Because of past experience of that nature, I am
concerned that additional witnesses will be called that are
unable to give material testimony [and] will needlessly
delay this trial." The judge then admitted that "the defendants have a right to compulsory process to obtain witnesses
in their behalf under the Sixth Amendment." However, he
denied that such compulsory process applied in the present
case. "The determination of whether to allow a witness to
take the stand is a matter within the discretion of the trial
judge." He explained this apparent contradiction by offer-
ing the opinion that "where the defense has attempted to
introduce substantial extraneous matter into the case, the
Court is justified in" asking for such a voir dire as Schultz
had proposed. Clark therefore, was sworn in outside the
presence of the jury and Kunstler, under protest, commenced the examination in the "vacuum of a court without
a jury."

Clark testified that Wilkins had indeed spoken favorably
to him of Davis. He also testified that after he had spoken
to Wilkins, the President called him. Schultz, however, objected to further questions on the subject of this conversation. National security was involved, he said. Furthermore,
the conversation was inadmissible for reasons of hearsay.
Since the former President was not himself on the stand, his
version of the conversation could not be verified by cross-
examination. Schultz also objected, again on national security grounds, to Kunstler's questions about the White

House meeting concerning the possible need for troops in Chicago.

Kunstler then asked Clark whether, in his opinion, the Code of Federal Regulations prevented him from testifying in the present case.

Clark answered that the regulation means only "that the Attorney General cannot, as a practical matter, give prior approval" to the use of FBI files in criminal cases in which Justice Department officials are asked to testify. What happens in practice, Clark explained, is that the Court subpoenas such material "and generally we would wire the Court permission."

Kunstler asked whether this meant that the code prohibited Clark from answering such questions as Kunstler had already asked him. Schultz, however, objected to this question and the judge sustained him.

Then Clark testified that he had called Foran on August 30 and "told him that he wanted to investigate the occurrences during that week concerning the national convention in the manner that we had developed the investigation of civil rights cases, which is essentially through lawyers, as distinguished from a grand jury; and that that was the way we would proceed in this situation." Clark also asked Foran to check on a report that Car 100 of the Chicago Police Department had been ordered to "sweep the streets" late on Wednesday night around the Hilton.

Kunstler then asked whether "It was your understanding or your intention that the events surrounding the Democratic National Convention were to be investigated without the convening of a grand jury?" Schultz objected to this question and the judge sustained him.

When Kunstler had completed his examination, Schultz rose to object that most of the questions had been "immaterial" and that they had no "probative value." The few questions that were admissible were "cumulative," that is, they covered matters that had been dealt with in earlier testimony, so these too were inadmissible. Thus Schultz asked the judge not to "permit the former Attorney General of the United States to appear before the jury because he cannot present to them any testimony which would assist them in making a determination of guilt or innocence in this case."

Kunstler replied that the Attorney General had been in a position to assess the intentions of the defendants as well as those of the city officials, and that his testimony would therefore be relevant. But Schultz argued that "when Mr. Daley testified he was abused horribly" by Kunstler, and he implied that Kunstler could not be depended upon to observe the rules of evidence in his examination of Clark.

The judge then ruled that he had had "the strong feeling" that morning "that this witness could not testify to anything material or relevant [but] I concluded that I should give the defendants, as I did, the opportunity to ask the witness questions that they proposed to ask him if he were permitted to testify before the jury. It is my conclusion that I have given the defendants every opportunity here to demonstrate that this witness could make a relevant or material contribution. They have failed so to demonstrate." Thus he sustained the government's objection to the testimony of Ramsey Clark.

That Friday, the defense rested its case. But before he recessed the Court for the weekend the judge announced that he had a statement to make. "I wanted to say to counsel for the defendants and to the defendants themselves, if they will listen, that it has been brought to my attention that there was a speech given in Milwaukee discussing this case by one of the defendants. I want to say that if such a speech as was given is brought to my attention again, I will give serious consideration to the termination of bail on the person who makes the speech. I think he would be a bad risk to continue on bail."

"I made the speech," Dellinger said. "Was there any-thing in that speech that said I won't show up for trial the next day or was it just that I criticized your conduct of the trial? Why are you threatening me with revocation of bail for exercising my freedom of speech?"

"Free speech is not involved here," the judge replied.

"We all made that speech!" Abbie Hoffman shouted. The judge ignored this remark and recessed the Court.

Though Kunstler had rested the defense case on Friday, he petitioned the Court on the following Monday to permit one last defense witness to take the stand before the govern-ment began its rebuttal case. Ralph Abernathy, a co-chair-man of the Mobe and Martin Luther King's successor as head of the Southern Christian Leadership Conference, had flown from Atlanta that morning and was ready to testify about what he had known of the Mobe plans. He would, Kunstler explained, have been called to testify earlier, but he had been out of the country. The judge, however, re-minded Kunstler of his promise on Friday to rest the case for the defense, and refused to let Abernathy testify.

Kunstler replied that the judge's ruling was "the most outrageous statement I have ever heard from the bench, and I am going to say my piece right now and you can hold me in contempt right now if you wish to. You have violated every principle of fair play when you excluded Ramsey Clark from that witness stand. I am outraged to be in this court . . . You took the whole day from us on Thursday by listening to this ridiculous argument whether Ramsey Clark could take that stand. I am trembling because I am so out-raged. I want to say this now and I want you to put me in jail if you want to. I feel disgraced to be here; to say to us on the technicality of my representation [on Friday] that we now cannot put Ralph Abernathy on the stand. He is the co-chairman of the Mobe. I know that doesn't mean much in this court when the Attorney General walked out of here with his lips so tight that he could hardly breathe, and his wife informed me that he never felt such anger at the United States government as at not being able to testify on that stand . . . I am going to turn back to my seat," Kunstler continued, "with the realization that everything I have learned throughout my life has come to naught; that there is no meaning in this court, that there is no law in this court and these men are going to jail by virtue of a legal lynching."

The government then called Chief Lynskey of the Chicago Police Department to the witness stand as its first rebuttal witness. No sooner had the examination of this officer begun, however, than Abernathy entered the courtroom and took a seat in the rear. When Kunstler saw him, he walked quickly to where he was sitting and embraced him in the presence of the jury.

"The damage has been done," Schultz said. "The spectacle of bringing Mr. Abernathy into court is more prejudicial to the government than any testimony Mr. Abernathy could have given. The only way this prejudice can be unwound," Schultz continued, "is to bring Mr. Abernathy to the stand." Thereupon the judge agreed to let Abernathy testify on the following day. But the witness had urgent business in Atlanta that night, and therefore was unable to testify for the defense.

11

The Trial Ends

WEINGLASS HAD WARNED that Schultz and Foran would probably save their most damaging witnesses for their rebuttal case. The defendants were worried that a genuine radical—not a police spy—might be brought to testify against them, presumably in exchange for immunity from federal prosecution. But most of the government's final witnesses proved to be much like their previous ones: policemen who repeated and embellished the familiar accounts of violence during convention week.

Nevertheless, the defendants were frightened, angry, and exhausted as the ordeal of the trial approached its end and the terror and mystery of their inevitable imprisonment rose up before them. Though Abbie Hoffman had said that the bright ceiling lights made the courtroom a "neon oven," the atmosphere in these final days was gloomy. The courtroom had come to seem no more than an entrance chamber to the federal prison system.

On February 4, James Rioradan, a deputy chief of the Chicago police, took the stand. He testified that on Wednesday, August 28, he saw Dellinger leave the band shell in Grant Park and walk "with the head of the group that were carrying the flags."

"Oh, bullshit," Dellinger said, in a flat, somewhat reflective voice, as if the idea of the witness' duplicity had taken him by surprise. The word seemed to tumble from his lips of its own volition.

"Did you get that, Miss Reporter?" the judge asked.

"That is an absolute lie," Dellinger added, with somewhat more vigor, the quavering impediment catching at his words.

"Did you get that, Miss Reporter?" the judge asked again.

"Let's argue about what I stand for and you stand for, but let's not make up things like that," Dellinger said to the witness.

"All of these remarks were made in the presence of the Court and the jury by Mr. Dellinger," Judge Hoffman said to the reporter.

"Sometimes the human spirit can stand so much," Kunstler pleaded from the lectern, "and I think Mr. Dellinger reached the end of his."

"The judge replied, "I have never, in more than a half century at the bar, heard a man using profanity in this court or in a courtroom. I never did."

That afternoon, after the judge had dismissed the jury for the day, he asked the defendants and the lawyers to stay. The spectators also remained. "I have some observations to make here, gentlemen," he said. "I have demonstrated great patience during this trial in trying to insure a fair trial for both the government and for the defendants. . . . Time and again, as the record reveals, the defendant Dellinger has disrupted sessions of this court with the use of vile and insulting language. Today again he used vile and obscene language. I propose to try to end the use of such language if possible and such conduct by terminating the bail of this defendant."

The judge then admitted that ". . . it has been said by some that the purpose of bail is to insure the attendance of a defendant at the trial. That is one of the purposes." But he added that a judge may also revoke bail if a defendant's behavior, in or out of the courtroom, jeopardizes the fair administration of justice. The case he cited was that of *Carbo v. United States*, in which the defendant was suspected of having threatened the lives of government witnesses.

Kunstler rose to reply, but the judge cut him short and remanded Dellinger to the custody of the United States marshal.

"Your Honor," Kunstler pleaded, "is there not to be any argument on this?"

"No argument," the judge replied.

But Kunstler persisted. "Your Honor's act is completely and utterly vindictive . . . There is no authority that says because a defendant blurts out a word in court—"

"I won't argue this," the judge repeated.

"This court is bullshit!" Davis called out from the defense table.

"Everything in this court is bullshit!" Rubin shouted.

"I associate myself with Dave Dellinger," Davis said, "completely 100 percent. This is the most obscene court I have ever seen."

"Take us all!" Rubin shouted. "Show us what a big man you are."

"Your Honor," Schultz interrupted, "I ask that you do not do them the favor that they ask." What Schultz presumably feared was that the jurors who sympathized with the defense would be all the more sympathetic if all seven of the defendants were to be put in jail. "Don't do them that favor," Schultz insisted.

"You don't think that I would," the judge replied.

By now, several spectators had stood up. Some stood on the benches to get a better view. Some began to shout indignantly. Six marshals rushed into the courtroom from the corridor outside to augment the twenty or so who were already there. A reporter whispered, "My God! Someone's going to get killed in here!"

"You can jail a revolutionary," Davis shouted over the turmoil, "but you can't jail the revolution!"

"You are a disgrace to the Jews," Abbie Hoffman yelled at the judge. "You would have served Hitler better," but his words were hardly audible over the din in the spectators' section, where the marshals were struggling with the friends and relatives of the defendants. "You little prick!" a woman cried out, shaking her fist at the judge, as a marshal dragged her through the swinging doors at the rear of the courtroom.

"Clear the court," the judge shouted, banging his palm on the bench. The marshals then ejected the last of the unruly spectators and led Dellinger through the door to the lockup.

That evening, Hoffman and Rubin argued with the four other defendants that they should all do whatever they could on the following day to disrupt the trial. They felt, Hayden later explained, "that if all the defendants were jailed together, it would help Dellinger get out. It would also create the right image to mobilize people for action at the trial's end." As for himself, however, Hayden said that "of all the defendants I probably advocated the most careful behavior in the courtroom." His reason was that he wanted to "cultivate support within the jury of middle class Americans." He had a further reason as well. The principle of "moral witness" and guerilla "theater, at the root of the pacifist and Yippie politics . . . can expose institutions, but they can never prevent repression and punishment. . . . We would strip away the court's authority but not its power. So it seemed," Hayden concluded, "a senseless sacrifice to accumulate prison time for spontaneous outbursts."

At three-thirty that morning, Dellinger, like the other

prisoners who were to be taken that day to federal court, was awakened in Cook County Jail. Then, as he later described the routine, he was "led through a series of way stations. Everywhere you go, you stand and wait . . . And then you wait another twenty minutes or a half hour. At last you're taken to the pump room, which is so jammed with humanity that after I'd been there ten minutes I looked around to see if anybody was suffocating. And then you move from there to the next station. Everytime you leave, you're stripped. Your anus is examined. 'Lift your right foot. Lift your left foot. Spread your cheeks. Turn around. Jump up and down. Stick your tongue out.' "

Finally he was put in a van with the other federal prisoners, driven some five miles across the city, and deposited in the lockup on the twenty-fourth floor of the Federal Building. Dellinger remarked that for the first time he knew what Seale had been put through each morning before his arrival in Court.

Soon after Court convened that morning, Weinglass petitioned the judge to hear arguments on the question of Dellinger's bail. "You are keeping a man in custody," he said, "and you are not permitting a lawyer to make arguments for his freedom. This is unheard of. That is unprecedented in law."

"I have considered the matter carefully," the judge replied.

"You have not considered it," Weinglass said, "because you have not heard the argument."

"Mr. Marshal," the judge ordered, "will you ask that man to sit down?"

"You put him in jail because you lost faith in the jury system," Hoffman shouted at the judge. "That's why you're throwing us in jail this way. Contempt is the tyranny of the court and you're a tyrant. *Schtunk!*" he screamed.

"Black robes of death!" Rubin added.

"We should have done this long ago when you chained and gagged Bobby Seale. Mafia-controlled pigs," Hoffman said.

"Mr. Marshal," the judge asked, "will you have Mr. Hoffman remain quiet, please. Order him to remain quiet."

"Order us?" Hoffman replied. "You got to cut our tongues out to quiet us, Julie."

Later that day the judge decided that he would, after all, hear a motion by the defense to restore Dellinger's bail. Weinglass argued that the Carbo Case concerned a defendant with a long criminal record. In an earlier trial of the same defendant, the chief government witness was murdered before he could testify. In the trial in question, the chief government witness had received more than a hundred threatening phone calls. It was for these reasons, Weinglass argued, that Carbo had been denied bail. Moreover, the judge in the case had said that he had no faith Carbo would appear in Court unless his bail were revoked. Even so, Weinglass added, the Appeals Court reversed the trial judge.

Judge Hoffman, however, did not respond to the legal argument that Weinglass made. Instead, he said he had ". . . beseeched you and Mr. Kunstler throughout this trial, beginning with the Seale episode, to please try and get your clients to behave in this courtroom. At no time did you lift a finger or speak a word to any of them."

Weinglass, returning to his legal argument, replied that the Court could use its contempt power to punish Dellinger for what he had said, but that it had no power to revoke bail.

"I have more power than that," the judge interrupted. He added, "I don't like the word 'power.' I never use the word 'power' if I can avoid it." Then he explained that bail is "a privilege," not an "absolute right."

"That is called justice?" Rubin asked.

"Your Honor is not going to hear my argument?" Weinglass asked over the uproar that had once again broken out in the courtroom.

"I deny the motion—" the judge said.

"My argument—" Weinglass tried to say.

"That will be all, sir," the judge ordered.

"This is disgraceful!" Kunstler shouted. The judge asked the reporter to be sure to make a record of Kunstler's remark.

"Of course I said it," Kunstler said angrily. "How can I say anything but that?"

"My argument—" Weinglass persisted.

"Mr. Marshal," the judge ordered, "please have that lawyer sit down." Then he turned to Weinglass and Kunstler and said, "I ask you to sit down and there will be no further argument."

"Your idea of justice is the only obscenity in this room!" Hoffman shouted at the judge. "You *schtunk!*" Then he accused him in Yiddish of behaving disgracefully in the presence of gentiles.

"Julius Hoffman equals Adolph Hitler," Rubin added.

Above the shouting, Kunstler asked the judge to instruct the jury that Mr. Dellinger was now in custody. "We would like an opportunity," he added, "to tell the jury exactly why the defense considers him held in contempt."

"You will not have that opportunity," the judge replied.

"And will the defendants and the defendants' attorneys be instructed," Schultz asked the judge, "to make no reference to this in the presence of the jury? That's right!"

"You know you can't win this fucking case!" Hoffman shouted at Schultz. "The only way you can win is to put us away for contempt. We have contempt for this court and for you, Schultz, and for this whole rotten system."

"I order the defendants and their counsel to make no reference to this motion made," the judge shouted over the din.

"And the reason," Rubin said, "is because it is a hung jury and you know it. You know you are losing the jury trial, but you've got to get us in jail, because the people will decide that we're not guilty, so you are going to railroad us into jail."

Soon thereafter, when it appeared that the other defendants would not continue to join in their attacks, Hoffman and Rubin subsided. The jury was then admitted.

"Ladies and gentlemen of the jury, good morning," the judge said pleasantly.

"Good morning, Your Honor," the jurors replied.

"Good morning," Dellinger added.

On the following day, the Seventh Circuit Court of Appeals denied a motion by the defense to reinstate Dellinger's bail. In a conversation with a reporter, Weinglass said that the appellate judges were wrong to have upheld Judge Hoffman. "Bail," he said, "cannot be revoked for punitive reasons. But the appellate judges probably felt that they had to protect the dignity of Judge Hoffman, their man in the field, against the insults of Abbie and Jerry." They could not, Weinglass explained, add their rebuke to the tirades of the defendants.

On February 9, the testimony of the government's rebuttal witnesses came to an end, and on the following day Schultz presented his closing argument to the jury. Except that his account now referred to the testimony of government witnesses, it added little to what he had said in his opening statement. He did, however, tell the jury that the real aim of the defendants had been to establish an arm of the Viet Cong in America.

That afternoon, Weinglass replied for the defense that the trial was staged in order to shift the blame from the police to the demonstrators for the riots during the convention. Chicago, he said, "had to find a scapegoat." As for the intentions of the defendants, the government, he argued, had proven nothing. The question of their intentions, he told the jurors, was implicit in the negotiations for permits. If the jurors believed that the defendants had negotiated in good faith, while the city had been obstructive and dilatory, then the defendants must be found innocent. He then attacked the government witnesses. Undercover agents and police spies, he said, are deceitful by profession. Furthermore, they don't speak the same language as the defendants. Thus they had been unable to understand what the defendants' speeches had actually meant. He asked the jurors to imagine how a Chicago police spy would interpret the words of Jesus in the Gospel according to Matthew: "Think not that I am come to send peace on earth. I come not to send peace but a sword. For I am come to set man against his father, and the daughter against her mother, and a man's foes shall be those of his own household."

Weinglass then quoted from Lincoln's speech opposing the Mexican War and advocating rebellion. "Lincoln was so vilified for this speech," he explained, "that he had to resign temporarily from politics. But history vindicated him, and it will vindicate these defendants," he said. He added that he hoped the jury would spare history the trouble.

To these analogies from history, Kunstler added still others. He compared the defendants to Eugene Debs and Susan B. Anthony, as well as to Harriet Tubman and Martin Luther King. When Kunstler had finished, Hoffman turned to a group of reporters and said, despairingly, "Screw the war. Screw racism. The big issue now is prison reform."

Foran's summation was the most aggressive of the four.

"There are millions of kids," he told the jurors, "who resent authority, who are impatient for change. And there is another thing about the kid," he added, "his attraction to evil. Evil is exciting." He paused for a moment, his gaze fixed on Mr. Kratzke. "It is knowledge of kids like that," he resumed, "that these sophisticated, educated psychology majors know about. They know how to draw kids together and maneuver them, and use them to accomplish their purposes.

"Kids in the system are disillusioned. They feel that John Kennedy went; Bobby Kennedy went; and Martin Luther King went and the kids feel that the lights have gone out in Camelot, the banners are furled and the parade is over." He paused again and shifted his gaze to Mrs. Fritz.

"These guys," he continued, "take advantage of them—personally, intentionally and evilly—to corrupt those kids. They use them for their purposes and their interests.

"What has happened to us?" Foran asked the courtroom at large. "The bad people are the policemen, the FBI agents. The bad people are the ones who give their lives to government. You are only a good guy if you like the homosexual poetry of Allen Ginsberg. We can't let people use our kids like that. What they want is to stand on the rubble of a destroyed system of government. . . . And these men would have you believe that the issue in this case is whether or not they really wanted permits—so that they could fuck in the grass and smoke dope. I don't like to use language like that," he apologized to the jurors, "but that's what Hoffman said." Then his voice grew sharp. "Public authority couldn't give them permits to use that park; and these men," he said, pointing now toward the defense table, "are sophisticated. And they are smart and they are educated. And they are as evil as they can be."

Again Foran paused. Then he said, "We have got a crazy age on us now. We have got a time when a man can achieve the most he has ever been able to in all the world; and at the same time he is creating instruments of destruction that could destroy the world in a moment. We will have a guy actually walking on the moon and instead," he paused again, turned and faced the defendants, "they burrow downward toward the primitive, in obscenity, vulgarity and hate.

"They would have us believe that their revolution is in a lofty cause, and so they can break the laws to achieve it. The consequences of that thinking is the legitimation of violence and it would destroy this country.

"The First Amendment is not now and never was intended to protect those who violate the law. When a protest becomes a violent, deliberate and forcible assault on public order, it never can be excused or tolerated. . . . To permit factions to resort to force when they feel a particular law or policy is wrong would be to renounce our own experience and the experience of our forefathers. True freedom and substantial justice don't come from violent altercation and incendiary dissent.

"The First Amendment," Foran continued, "permits advocacy, not incitement. You can't," he explained, "[say] fight the police. To incite is not protected by the law.

"These men have named St. Matthew and Jesus and they have named Lincoln and Martin Luther King. Can you imagine these men supporting these men? . . ."

"Yes, I can!" a young woman shouted from the front row of the spectators' benches. "I can imagine it because it is true."

"Remove those people, Mr. Marshal," the judge ordered.

"That's my daughter!" Dellinger cried as the marshals pounced on the young woman. She hooked her arms over the back of the bench and vigorously kicked at the marshals who were trying to pry her loose.

"I don't have to listen to any more of these disgusting lies," another young woman shouted.

"That's my other daughter!" Dellinger cried out again. "Thank you. Right on! Right on!" Meanwhile the marshals continued to struggle with the first daughter, who persisted in kicking at them defiantly.

"Don't hit my daughter that way," Dellinger shouted. "That man hit her on the head for speaking the truth in here."

"The marshal will maintain order," the judge reassured Dellinger.

"Yes, but they don't have to hit a thirteen-year-old girl who knows I was close to Martin Luther King," he replied.

"Isn't it interesting?" Foran cried out over the turmoil that had engulfed the courtroom once more, "that these believers in free speech do not believe that the United States Attorney has the same right?"

Soon the marshal succeeded in removing the young Dellingers, along with several other spectators who had joined the shouting, and Foran concluded his remarks. "If this country should ever reach the stage where any man or group of men by force or violence, or with the threat of force, can long defy the commands of our law, then no citizen will be safe or his neighbors.

"The lights that Camelot kids believe in need not go out," he said. "The banners can snap in the breeze again. The parade will never be over if people will remember what Jefferson said: 'Obedience to the law is the major part of patriotism.'

"These seven men," he concluded, "have been proven guilty beyond any doubt. Do your duty."

Foran's summation recalled the government's final argument in the Haymarket Trial. "You stand now," the prosecutor had said in that case, "between anarchy and law. The police have done their duty. Let the jury have the same courage [so that the police] can indeed rest in peace. The flowers of spring shall bloom upon their graves, moistened by the tears of a great city. Outraged and violated law shall be redeemed and in their martyrdom, anarchy shall be buried forever."

On the following day, Saturday, February 14, the judge read his instructions to the jurors, who then left to commence their deliberations. As soon as the jurors were gone, the judge proceeded to sentence the defendants for contempt. He began with Dellinger, whom he found guilty of thirty-two separate contemptuous acts.

Before the judge passed sentence, however, Kunstler rose and attempted to argue the law of contempt. The judge said he would not hear such arguments, but Kunstler persisted, and finally the judge permitted him to make his case. "The Bloom decision," Kunstler argued, "held that the power of summary contempt should not be exercised after a trial; summary contempt is only a method of preventing disturbances during a trial; after the trial a man is entitled to a jury."

Then Kunstler quoted the decision of the Supreme Court in Bloom. "We are not persuaded," the Court ruled, "that the additional time and expense possibly involved in submitting serious contempts to juries will seriously handicap the effective functioning of the courts. We do not deny that serious punishment might sometimes be imposed for contempt, but we reject the contention that such punishment must be imposed without a right to jury trial."

"I do not share your view," the judge told Kunstler simply. He then asked Dellinger if he had anything to say before sentencing. Dellinger rose and said that the first contempt citation against him had to do with his attempt to read the names of the dead on moratorium day. The second, he reminded the judge, had to do with his support of Bobby Seale. So war and racism were once more the issues. The judge refused to hear Dellinger further on this subject. "I hope you will excuse me, sir," he requested politely. "You are not speaking strictly to what I gave you the privilege of speaking to. I ask you to say what you want to say with respect to punishment."

Dellinger insisted that his remarks were relevant to his punishment, whereupon the judge ordered him to be seated. Nevertheless, Dellinger continued to speak.

"You want us to be like good Germans, supporting the

evils of our decade," he told the judge, "and now you want us to be good Jews and go quietly and politely to the gas chamber while you and this court suppress freedom and truth. The fact is, I am not prepared to do that. You want us to stay in our place like black people—"

"Mr. Marshal," the judge commanded, "I will ask you to have Mr. Dellinger sit down."

"This is a travesty on justice," Dellinger continued, "and if you had any sense at all you would know that the record that you just read condemns you and not us. I am an old man and I am just speaking feebly and not too well, but I reflect the spirit that will echo—"

"Take him out," the judge ordered, and the Court once more erupted in turmoil and shouting.

"Tyrants! Tyrants!" spectators cried as the marshals began to drag people from the courtroom.

"That's what you have done, Judge Hoffman. That's what you have done," a woman cried as the marshals tugged at Dellinger's daughters.

Rubin meanwhile had jumped up from his chair at the defense table and marched rigidly toward the judge's bench, his right arm held stiffly out. "Heil Hitler! Heil Hitler! Heil Hitler!" he screamed. "I hope you're satisfied."

Hayden slouched deep in his chair and glanced balefully at Schultz, who was smiling broadly.

Kunstler rushed to the lectern and fell upon it, his forehead, for a moment, touching its surface. "My life has come to nothing," he wept. "I am not anything any more. You have destroyed me and everybody else. Put me in jail now, for God's sake, and get me out of this place. Come to mine now, judge, please. I beg you. Come to mine. Do me, too. I don't want to be out."

The judge sat impassively throughout this outburst. When Kunstler had returned to his chair and the marshals had restored order, he began to read the sentences for each of Dellinger's contempts. For reading the names of the dead on moratorium day, he sentenced Dellinger to six months. For saying "bullshit," he sentenced him to five months. Altogether he sentenced Dellinger to twenty-nine months and thirteen days.

He then proceeded to deal with Davis, whom he sentenced to twenty-five months and fourteen days on twenty-three counts of contempt. For calling Schultz a disgrace, Davis was sentenced to three months. For failing to restrict his replies on cross-examination to the scope of the government's questions, Davis was sentenced to six months. Before he passed sentence, the judge asked Davis to speak on the question of his punishment. Davis began by saying that he and the other defendants had come to Court hoping to win their case, even though they knew the law was unconstitutional. But the judge would not hear him on this point and ordered him to address himself only to the question of punishment. "Judge," Davis said, "you represent all that is old, ugly, bigoted and repressive in this country, and I will tell you that the spirit at this defense table is going to devour your sickness in the next generation." Davis was then taken by the marshals though the door to the lockup, where he was placed in a cell with Dellinger.

The judge next sentenced Hayden to fourteen months and fourteen days for eleven separate contempts. For rising to object that Bobby Seale "should not be put in a position of slavery" he was sentenced to three months. He was sentenced to four months for saying in the presence of the jury that the marshals were beating Seale. He was sentenced to six months for saying loudly enough for the jury to hear him that Ramsey Clark had not been allowed to testify. When Hayden rose to speak he told the judge that American youth had turned its back on the system represented by the Court. "Before your eyes," he said, "you see the most vital element of your system collapsing."

412 · THE GREAT CONSPIRACY TRIAL

"Oh, don't be so pessimistic," the judge replied in a good-humored voice. "Our system isn't collapsing. Fellows as smart as you could do awfully well under the system." Hayden seemed to pay no attention. He was staring down at the defense table.

"We don't want a place in the regiment, Julie!" Hoffman called out.

"What did you say?" the judge asked. "Your turn's coming up."

"I'm being patient, Julie," Hoffman answered.

"He thinks that annoys me," the judge said, turning to the spectators and smiling, "addressing me by a name . . . he doesn't know that years ago when I was his age or younger that's what my friends called me."

Hayden asked if he could say one or two more sentences. "The point I was trying to make," he said, "is that I was trying to think about what I regretted most about punishment. I can only state one thing that affected my feelings, and that is that I would like to have a child." With this Hayden began to sob.

"That is where the federal system can do you no good," the judge replied, in his most genial voice.

"Because the federal system can do you no good," Hayden replied defiantly, "in trying to prevent the birth of a new world."

With that, the judge imposed sentence, and Hayden too was led through the door to the lockup, where he joined Dellinger and Davis.

Abbie Hoffman was then found guilty of twenty-four counts of contempt, but he was sentenced to only eight months and six days. For saying that he could not respect the law when "it's a tyranny," and for adding that he no longer used his last name, he was sentenced to four months. But for speaking up in defense of Seale he was sentenced to only two months, whereas Hayden, for his part in the same episode, received four months. The judge offered no explanation of this apparent discrepancy, and a few reporters assumed that perhaps the lengthy recitation of the preceding contempt citation had exhausted him, so that he misread the sentences in Hoffman's case. Others, including some of the defendants themselves, thought that the judge had a special affection for Hoffman.

Hoffman's statement on the question of his punishment was restrained. "The only dignity that free men have," he said, "is the right to speak out . . . when the law is tyranny, the only order is insurrection." Then he too was led away. Once he was gone, the judge recessed the Court, leaving Rubin, Fronies, Weiner, and the two lawyers to be charged and sentenced on the following day, Sunday.

Though Rubin was found guilty of only fifteen acts of contempt—nine fewer than Hoffman—he was sentenced to twenty-five months and twenty-three days. He received a sentence of six months for complaining aloud when the marshals took his wife from the courtroom. He received another six months for saying to the judge, "Take us all. Show us what a big man you are." When he was asked to speak, he said, ". . . by punishing us you are going to have ten million more." He too was led away.

Weiner was sentenced to two months and eighteen days for seven counts of contempt. Froines received five months and fifteen days for ten counts. Weiner was sentenced to a month for saying of Schultz, after the prosecutor had called Davis "schizophrenic," "Now he's a psychology student." For suggesting to the judge that he might sentence Dellinger to four years, as he had sentenced Seale, Froines was sentenced to a month.

Finally the judge came to the citations against the two lawyers, who were now sitting alone at the defense table. He began by saying he had never held a lawyer in contempt "and only on one occasion did I hold someone who was not a lawyer in contempt." This was not true. He had held the four pretrial lawyers in the present case in contempt until his warrant had been found defective. There was also the case in 1950 in which he had incorrectly imposed summary punishment for the indirect contempt committed by one of the disputants who fell to quarreling outside his courtroom. Moreover, in 1966, he had sentenced a juror to three years in jail for having read and discussed a magazine article concerning a pending trial. In 1968, Judge Hoffman had sentenced a woman named Shirleen Janata to three months in jail for calling him a "son of a bitch." Finally, there was the case of Bobby Seale.

Judge Hoffman sentenced Kunstler to three months for calling the Court a "medieval torture chamber" when Seale was being beaten by the marshals. For arguing "in an angry tone" at the conclusion of Ginsberg's direct testimony that Court should not be recessed early, as Foran had requested, Kunstler was sentenced to three months. For asking Mayor Daley "eighty-three questions that were objectionable" he received six months. In all, Kunstler was sentenced to four years and thirteen days in prison for twenty-four counts of contempt.

Kunstler then walked to the lectern and read from a prepared statement. "I am sorry if I disturbed the decorum of the courtroom, but I am not ashamed of my conduct in this Court, for which I am about to be punished.

"I have tried with all my heart faithfully to represent my clients in the face of what I considered and still consider repressive and unjust conduct toward them. If I have to pay with my liberty for such representation, then that is the price of my beliefs and my sensibilities.

"I can only hope that my fate does not deter other lawyers throughout the country who, in the difficult days that lie ahead, will be asked to defend clients against a steadily increasing government encroachment upon their most fundamental liberties. If they are so deterred, then my punishment will have the effect of such terrifying consequences that I dread to contemplate the future domestic and foreign course of this country. However, I have the utmost faith that my beloved brethren at the bar, young and old alike, will not allow themselves to be frightened out of defending the poor, the persecuted, the radicals and militant, the black people, the pacifists, and the political pariahs of this, our common land.

"To those lawyers who may, in learning of what may happen to me, waver, I can only say this: stand firm, remain true to those ideals of the law which, even if openly violated here and in other places, are true and glorious goals, and above all, never desert those principles of equality, justice and freedom, without which life has little, if any, meaning.

"I may not be the greatest lawyer in the world, Your Honor, but I think that I am this moment, along with my colleague, Leonard Weinglass, the most privileged. We are being punished for what we believe in.

"Your Honor, I am ready, sir, to be sentenced, and I would appreciate it if I could be permitted to remain standing at this lectern, where I have spent the greater part of the past five months, while you do so. Thank you."

The spectators began to applaud and cheer. The judge ordered the marshals to remove them, and then said, "I approach my responsibility here just as unhappily as you indicated you are," though Kunstler did not seem unhappy as he spoke. Then the judge said that he was going to make "a rather unorthodox statement. First of all," he began, "there is a lot of crime. I know because I have a lot of criminal cases to try. I am one of those who believes that crime, if it is on the increase . . . is due in large part to the fact that waiting in the wings are lawyers who are willing to go beyond professional responsibility . . . in their defense of a defendant, and the fact that a defendant or some defendants know that such a lawyer is waiting in the wings, I think, has a rather stimulating effect on the increase in crime.

"I have literally thousands of editorials," the judge continued, "back there in my chambers—I know you won't believe this—that are complimentary about decisions I have made over the years. But as for you, to have sat through that Bobby Seale incident and not lifted your arm or a chair, not spoken a word, and he could have been spoken to, and your appearance was on file as his lawyer, you spoke for him as a defendant, even if I were wrong, if I were wrong, even if the many times he called me the vile names that he called me . . . I don't know how it could be proven that a man of my faith was a pig," he said plaintively, ". . . but for you . . . never to have made an attempt to say something like this to him, 'Bobby, hush. Cool it. Sit down now.' But you let him go on. . . . He was your client. Even in the way you describe it, he was your client at one time, and you made no effort to have him keep from calling a judge of the United States District Court a pig, a fascist pig, a racist pig. . . . The only reason I mention the Seale episode is that I didn't want anyone here to get the impression that I was obtuse and didn't know what was going on. I didn't want the ladies and gentlemen of the press to get the impression that I didn't know what was really the time of day."

"Your Honor," Kunstler said, when the judge had finished, "I am glad Your Honor spoke, because I suddenly feel nothing but compassion for you. Everything else has dropped away."

The judge then turned to Weinglass, whom he sentenced to twenty months and nine days for fourteen counts of contempt. Weinglass received four months for repeatedly asking questions of David Stahl after the judge had ruled that such questions were beyond the scope of the direct examination. He was sentenced to five months for continuing to argue after the judge had ruled that he could not question Davis about Ralph Abernathy's relation to the Mobe.

When the judge had completed his charges, Weinglass rose to say that this was his first trial in a federal court. Yet he felt that he had done his best. As for the contempts with which he had been charged, "each and every one," he said, "had occurred in the course of a legal argument. I have been called in the course of these legal arguments—and Your Honor will recall those words—phony and two-faced." But he said that he did not hold these insults against Mr. Foran or Mr. Schultz. "This has been a long, difficult, highly contested proceeding in which all of us, at one time or another, have lost their sense of professional control and judgment.

"What the court has chosen to label as direct contempt, I cite as nothing more than argument of counsel in the heat of battle . . . I confess that at times I should have stopped. [But] if Your Honor looks through this record with a balanced eye . . . you will see that on a number of occasions our adversary counsel argued after rulings in several instances. They were even asked to cease their arguments by the court for the very same reason and if counsel are not permitted that small leeway in the conduct of a defense, then I think you do a disservice to the profession and you unbalance the balance in the adversary proceedings—"

The judge interrupted to say that he disagreed that he had been unfair, and told Weinglass that he deserved more respect than the defendants and their lawyers had shown him.

Weinglass replied, "With respect to our different understandings of respect, I was hopeful when I came here that after twenty weeks the court would know my name and I didn't receive that which I thought was the minimum—"

"Well, I am going to tell you about that," the judge interrupted. "I have got a very good friend named Weinruss and I know nobody by the name of Weinrob, and somehow the name Weinruss stuck in my mind . . ."

Weinglass said nothing about the fact that his name was not Weinrob, any more than it was Weinruss. Instead, he told the judge, "My natural instincts are and have always been to avoid a protracted fight. I am not as strong a man as Bill Kunstler and I think I am more vulnerable to what I perceive as intimidation . . . and I have had to fight that instinct here in court, not only because I thought that the rights of other men were involved but because the inspiration I drew from Bill Kunstler—"

"Did you ever feel like tapping one of those defendants," the judge interrupted, "when they were assailing me with vile epithets to say, 'Hey, hey, be quiet'?"

"Does Your Honor really believe," Weinglass replied, "that what was in conflict here in this courtroom could have been dissipated by an admonishment from Bill Kunstler or myself?"

"I judge your whole attitude toward the Court by your omission to do that," the judge replied.

Weinglass concluded his remarks by saying that he had "come to this city as a stranger. But I say to this court that [the people from Chicago who have worked with the defense] have been sleeping on the floor of my apartment . . . have been receiving a sum of $20.00 a week for their maintenance and no more; have worked until three and four o'clock in the morning, and have given up all the opportunities that are available to them, and, like the defendants, America's best was before them. They only had to seize it."

"I think I would have paid out of my own pocket," the

judge interrupted, "for a good bed in a respectable place if you had set them a good example by at least trying to get these men to refrain from the personal epithets hurled at the court."

The judge then passed sentence and Weinglass returned to his place at the defense table, which was now deserted except for Kunstler. The two lawyers were granted bail until April. This would give them time, the judge told them, to file appeals for their clients. As for the defendants, the judge, as was his custom, denied them bail.

In the courtroom, no one spoke. A few reporters stood silently beside the defense table as Kunstler and Weinglass gathered up their papers. The spectators drifted out into the corridor. The judge returned to his chambers. It was a frozen Sunday afternoon. The streets outside the Federal Building were deserted except for a line of young pickets who moved slowly past the Federal Building with caricatures of the judge on their signs. They chanted, "Two-four-six-eight. Jail Hoffman. Smash the state." Across the street, a police car waited, its blue beacon slowly turning. In a room on the twenty-third floor, the jury was deliberating for the second day, unaware that the seven defendants and their lawyers had already been sentenced to a total of fifteen years and five days for contempt.

Judge Hoffman had prepared his charge to the jury carefully. On Saturday morning he had spent two hours reading it to the jurors before he sent them out to deliberate. He explained that a defendant charged with conspiracy need not have known every detail of the alleged plot in order to be found guilty. It is enough that the government prove that each defendant was "aware of the common purpose," and that he joined the plot willingly and knowingly. Moreover, the government need not prove that the purpose of the plot had been achieved.

The judge then attempted to explain to the jurors the extent to which the First Amendment protects a defendant's speech. "The law," he said, "distinguishes between mere advocacy of lawlessness . . . and advocacy of the use of force or illegality where such advocacy is directed to inciting, promoting, or encouraging lawless actions. The essential distinction," he explained, is between advocacy that urges people "to do something now or in the immediate future, rather than merely to believe in something." Thus Judge Hoffman appeared to base his charge on the opinion of Justice Harlan in the Yates Case, rather than on the later Brandenberg decision.

Then, to the surprise of the defendants, he instructed the jurors in the principle established by the Shuttlesworth ruling. "It is a constitutional exercise of the rights of free speech and assembly," he told them, "to march or hold a rally without a permit where applications for permits were made in good faith . . . and the permits were denied arbitrarily or discriminatorily."

The defendants were also pleased that the judge told the jurors not to be "influenced by any possible antagonism you may have toward the defendants or any of them because of their dress, hair styles, speech, reputation, courtroom demeanor, personal philosophy or life style."

Thus instructed, the jurors began their deliberations at twelve-thirty in the afternoon on St. Valentine's Day. From the beginning, they were divided. Eight wanted to convict the defendants on all counts, and four wanted to acquit them on all counts. One of the jurors felt that the police should have shot the demonstrators in Lincoln Park at the time of the convention and thus spared the government the cost of the trial. Mrs. Peterson, ignoring the judge's instructions, complained that the defendants had put their feet on the government's furniture and that they needed a bath. Mrs. Fritz also ignored what the judge had said. She argued that the law was unconstitutional. But Kay Richards, who was in favor of conviction, reminded her that the jurors were not supposed to consider the law; they must confine themselves to questions of fact.

Mrs. Fritz, however, was adamant. Not only were the defendants innocent in her opinion, but she agreed with them that the government had placed itself above the law. "I came to fear our government for the first time," she later admitted, a view that she shared with Shirley Seaholm, another juror who stood for acquittal. Mrs. Seaholm had been bothered by the heavy police guard that accompanied Mayor Daley to Court on the day he testified. "It frightened me," she said after the trial, "that the mayor of my city felt that he needed such security." Mrs. Robbins, another juror who believed that the defendants were innocent, had also been troubled by the mayor's day in Court. She noticed that the marshals brought him his drinking water in a glass rather than in the paper cups that the other witnesses used. Mrs. Robbins was reminded by the trial of the persecution of innocent people by the Nazis and she was angry that such injustices were now committed in American Courts. Mrs. Butler, the fourth juror in favor of acquittal, felt that the defendants were probably guilty of something, but not what they had been indicted for.

Like Mrs. Robbins, Mrs. Fritz was alarmed by the undercover activities of the police. "What was frightening to me," she later said, "was that there are young people who will go to college and let their hair grow long and then report back. What is happening in our country when your roommate in college may be reporting back to the government?" she asked John Schultz, a Chicago author who interviewed her several months after the trial. What does it mean, she asked, "when the government can tap anybody's phone? Or do anything it wants to do?" Mrs. Seaholm told John Schultz that she had never understood why Seale had not been permitted to defend himself. Often throughout the trial she had wanted to ask the judge, "Why can't Bobby Seale defend himself?"

By Sunday, February 15, the deadlock seemed to be immovable. Thus Mr. Kratzke, who had been elected foreman—because, as Mrs. Robbins later explained, he was a man—sent a notice to the judge that the jury was hung. The judge, however, ignored this information, as he did a similar message that was sent to him by the jurors on the following day. Mrs. Fritz recalled, in her interview with John Schultz, that after this second message had been submitted but had elicited no response, a marshal explained that "the judge can keep you here as long as he wants." Thereafter, the jurors did not deliberate but sat together in bitter silence. By Monday evening, the two factions adjourned to separate rooms at the Palmer House, and Kay Richards began to consider the possibility of a compromise verdict on which both factions might agree.

Meanwhile Mrs. Fritz was convinced that if there were a hung jury, the defendants would inevitably be retried. She feared that the jury in the second trial might not include members who favored acquittal. Mrs. Fritz had served as an alternate juror in a trial that had concluded in a hung jury a few days before the Conspiracy Trial had begun, and she recalled having seen in a newspaper that this trial had been rescheduled for October 8, 1969. Presumably she concluded from this that any trial that ends in a hung jury is retried automatically. In fact, such decisions are at the discretion of the government. And while it was likely that the case would be retried, it was by no means certain. "If we had known that the government would not try this case again, or if we'd known about the contempt proceedings, we would still be in that deliberating room to this day if that was the way Judge Hoffman had wanted it," she explained to Schultz.

Kay Richards was also apprehensive of a hung jury. "I felt as a responsible juror," she later explained, "that I had to come up with a solution. So I became the negotiator. At first I had been a hard liner," she said. But to avoid a hung jury, she "went soft." Of all the jurors, Mrs. Peterson was the most reluctant to compromise. The defendants, she said, "needed a good bath and a hairwash. They should have respected their elders. They should have respected the judge who is so much older and wiser than them or us." Nevertheless, she agreed at last to compromise, "because we hated to see all that money gone and time wasted. Most of us," she later admitted, "would have found all of the defendants guilty on both counts, but we didn't want a hung jury." So finally she too agreed that "half a chicken is better than none." Then she added that if it had not been for Kay Richards, "we'd still be there deliberating."

But Mrs. Fritz later admitted that the four jurors who favored acquittal "felt funny about Kay from the beginning. We didn't trust her and we didn't know why." Mrs. Robbins, however, felt Miss Richards' fiancé, who worked for City Hall, may have influenced her against the defendants.

The compromise that Kay Richards proposed became the verdict that the jury submitted on Wednesday morning, February 18. All the defendants were acquitted of conspiracy. Froines and Weiner were found innocent of teaching and demonstrating the use of incendiary devices. The other five defendants were found guilty of the substantive charges that they had crossed state lines with the intention to incite a riot. Except for Miss Richards, none of the jurors was content with the compromise. According to Mrs. Fritz, the jurors who favored conviction believed that the defendants were "evil," as Foran had argued, and that they had no right to come into Chicago's "living room." Mrs. Fritz later admitted, "What we did—and this I'll never get over—we gave in to ourselves. We compromised with ourselves. Kay didn't have anything to do with our decision. You might say that we used her as much as she used us. We didn't know if it was a hung jury that they wouldn't be tried again."

By Tuesday night, the compromise had been agreed upon. On Wednesday morning, Kunstler stood before the judge to argue for a mistrial on the ground that the jury was deadlocked. Like Kunstler, the defendants were convinced that Mrs. Fritz would hold out indefinitely. Thus the defendants, who had been brought to Court from Cook County Jail to be present at the motion for a mistrial, were in a confident mood when Kunstler approached the lectern. But before Kunstler could begin his argument, a marshal entered the courtroom to announce that the jury had reached its verdict. The defendants were taken by surprise. So were the government lawyers. But Schultz had prepared himself for such an event. He proposed to the judge that the defendants' relatives be excluded from the courtroom when the jury gave its verdict. They could not be depended upon, Schultz argued, to behave properly in Court. The judge agreed and the spectators, including the defendants' relatives, were removed.

As she was taken from the courtroom, Abbie Hoffman's wife shouted, "The ten of you will be avenged. They will dance on your grave, Julie, and on the grave of the pig empire."

As soon as the verdicts were rendered and the jurors had returned to the jury room, Mrs. Fritz and the three other women who had favored acquittal broke down and wept. "I went to pieces," Mrs. Fritz recalled. "I started to cry, and I couldn't stop. I kept saying over and over again, 'I just voted five men guilty on speeches I don't even remember.'" Kay Richards and a federal marshal attempted to comfort the four sobbing women. "I don't see how you could have done anything else," the marshal told them.

As soon as the jury had left, the judge announced that

he would deny the defendants bail. "I have heard the evidence here. I have watched all of the defendants . . . From the evidence and from their conduct in this trial, I find they are dangerous men to be at large."

Kunstler then moved to poll the jurors to determine whether they had reached their verdict by compromise and not by a finding of guilt beyond a reasonable doubt.

"I deny that," the judge ruled.

"There may be a question of compromise here," Kunstler insisted.

"I order the defendants and their counsel not to talk to them," the judge replied.

"But, Your Honor, one of the appellate points may be that the jury reached a compromise, that some members wanted to hang the jury. . . ."

"I order you not to do it and that's that," the judge answered.

The judge then adjourned Court until Friday, February 20. On that day he delivered his ruling on the wiretap motion that the defendants had filed the summer before and that the judge said he would not hear until the trial was over. This was the motion in which the defendants had asked to examine the illegal wiretaps withheld by the government for reasons of national security. In the same motion they had also asked the Court to determine whether the illegal wiretaps that had been revealed by the government had "tainted" any of the evidence submitted against them.

On the twentieth, the judge denied the motion of the defense to examine the withheld taps. Attorney General Mitchell had argued that these taps should not be revealed because they had been "employed to gather foreign intelligence information or to gather intelligence information concerning domestic organizations which seek to use force and other unlawful means to attack and subvert the existing structure of the government." The judge admitted that the Alderman decision obliged the government to turn over to the defense all wiretaps for which valid warrants had not been issued. But he also observed that the Supreme Court had not gone so far as to say that its ruling applied to taps that had been made in the interest of national security. To the defendants, the Court's silence on this point suggested that the Alderman ruling was meant to apply to all illegal surveillance, but Judge Hoffman read the intentions of the Court differently. He ruled that ". . . the matter of when electronic surveillance is reasonably necessary . . . to protect the national security is a matter not suitable to judicial determination, but is rather best left to the . . . President or to the Attorney General. I conclude that the electronic surveillance in national security cases is not subject to the warrant requirements of the Fourth Amendment."

The judge then denied the further defense motion that a hearing be held at some future time to determine whether the government's evidence had been tainted by the taps that had not involved national security. With respect to these taps, the judge ruled that the burden was on the defense to demonstrate "taint," and that it was up to the appellate Court to make the final determination based on the defense showing.

Once he had disposed of this matter, the judge announced his intention to pass sentence on the five defendants whom the jury had found guilty. The defendants were once more taken by surprise. Kunstler objected that the judge had allowed himself no time to consider reports from the probation service that might help him determine appropriate terms for the guilty defendants. "The whole purpose of pre-sentence reports [by the probation service] is to indicate what the sentence shall be," Kunstler argued. "You are not even using the facilities of the court to determine that."

"I shall have to do without the services of our wonderful probation department in this case," the judge replied.

Kunstler then pleaded that "the defendants had no way of knowing they are going to be sentenced today. Their families are not even present, which would seem to me in common decency would be permitted."

"The reason they were kept out," the judge replied, "is that my life was threatened by one of the members of the family. I was told they would dance on my grave last week."

"Your Honor," Kunstler asked, "are you serious?"

"Yes I am, sir," the judge replied. He then sentenced each of the five defendants to the maximum term of five years in jail and a fine of $5,000. Furthermore, the defendants were to pay the costs of the prosecution and "to stand committed until the fine and the costs have been paid." Though the sentences were the maximum permitted under the law, and the imposition of the applicable costs of the prosecution —a sum estimated to be about $40,000—was a burden the defense had not expected, the judge was merciful to the extent that the sentences he imposed under the anti-riot statute were to run concurrently with the sentences for contempt.

In their speeches before sentencing, the defendants repeated substantially what they had said when they were sentenced for contempt. Dellinger compared the present proceedings to the Moscow purge trials, but he admitted that he found the judge "spunky," if misguided. "I only wish," he concluded, "that we were all not just more eloquent. I wish we were smarter, more dedicated, more united. I wish we could reach out to the Forans and the Schultzs and the Hoffmans and convince them of the necessity of revolution." Foran and Schultz were sitting with their backs to the defendants. The judge, his eyes shut, was slouched in his chair. A reporter whispered to a colleague, "What revolution?"

Davis said that he looked "to the jury that is in the

428 · THE GREAT CONSPIRACY TRIAL

streets. My jury will be in the streets tomorrow all across this country and the verdict from my jury will keep coming in over the next five years that you are about to give me in prison. Davis then added that in 1977, when he gets out of jail, he is going to move next door to Foran. "I am going to be the boy next door and we are going to turn the sons and daughters of the ruling class into Viet Cong."

Though Hayden promised to make a short statement, he spoke for more than half an hour. It was the police and the FBI, he said, who had made heroes and martyrs of the defendants. "We were invented. We were chosen by the government to serve as scapegoats for all that they wanted to prevent happening in the 1970's." He then said that for four of the jurors to have believed in the innocence of the defendants, despite the efforts of the government lawyers and their police witnesses, "is the testimony of the ability of people to wake up from the nightmare of American life." But it was a "tragedy," he added, that the four jurors "do not yet know how to hold out, and probably never will—do not know how to fight to the end." He then asked why, if the government had not wanted to make martyrs of the defendants, it had indicted them. "If you wanted to keep it cool, why didn't you give us a permit? If you had given us a permit, very little would have happened in Chicago . . . And you know that if this prosecution had never been undertaken, it would have been better for those in power. It would have left them in power a little longer. You know by doing this to us, it speeds up the end for those people who do it to us."

When Hoffman spoke he addressed himself to the pictures on the wall behind the judge. "I know those guys on the wall," he said. "They grew up twenty miles from my home in Massachusetts. I played with Sam Adams on the Concord Bridge. I was there when Paul Revere rode right up on his motorcycle and said, 'The pigs are coming. The pigs are coming.' I know Sam Adams. Sam Adams was an evil man. So was Thomas Jefferson. He called for revolution every ten years. He had an agrarian reform program that made Mao Tse-tung look like a liberal.

"Hamilton?" he continued. "Well, I don't dig the Federalists. Maybe he deserved to have his brains blown out. . . . As for Lincoln, if he had given his first inaugural speech in Lincoln Park, he would be on trial right here in this courtroom, because that is an inciteful speech."

He then described conditions in Cook County Jail. The food, he said, was inedible. "There's no light. It's not a nice place for a Jewish boy to be, with a college education." The judge smiled. Hoffman continued, "So they shave your heads and tomorrow morning they take our hair. They can have it. It's just hair. And they will go outside the prison walls and they will sell it. Sell our hair."

Rubin offered the judge an inscribed copy of his new book, which had been published that day. On the flyleaf he had written, "Dear Julius, the demonstrations in Chicago in 1968 were the first steps in the revolution. What happened in the courtroom is the second step. Julius, you radicalized more young people than we ever could. You're the country's top Yippie."

When Rubin returned to his chair, the judge imposed sentence. When he told Hoffman that his fine would be $5,000, Hoffman said, "Five thousand dollars, Judge? Could you make that three-fifty?"

"Five thousand," the judge repeated.

"How about three and a half?" Hoffman asked again, but the moment was solemn, and the judge continued without further interruption until the last defendant had been sentenced.

On the following day, as Hoffman had predicted, the defendants' hair was cut. A day later Sheriff Woods of Cook County displayed a photograph of the shorn defendants before a rally of the Elk Grove Republican Organization. "This is just to show you that we Republicans get things done," Sheriff Woods told his cheering audience.

In Washington on the same day some two thousand demonstrators descended upon the apartment house where Attorney General Mitchell lived, and six hundred police were required to disperse them. Five thousand marched in Boston. In Chicago three thousand demonstrators assembled in front of Cook County Jail. Through their lawyers, the defendants urged these demonstrators to avoid violence. They feared that a riot at the jail would jeopardize their appeal for bail.

On February 23, the American Civil Liberties Union had filed a brief with the Seventh Circuit Court of Appeals, arguing that Judge Hoffman's denial of bail violated the First, Fifth, Sixth, and Eighth Amendments to the Constitution. Among the lawyers who signed their names to the ACLU brief were Ramsey Clark and Burke Marshall, a former head of the Civil Rights Division of the Justice Department under President Kennedy.

By Friday, February 27, the appeals court had overruled Judge Hoffman and denied the argument of the government that the defendants and their lawyers are "a danger and a threat to the community." The appellate decision was withheld, however, until Saturday the twenty-eighth. The appellate judges did not want to interfere with a celebration attended by Judge Hoffman and Mayor Daley, among others, on Friday in the Federal Building to honor Judge Campbell on his retirement.

Thus the defendants were released on the following day. At first their plan was to perpetrate themselves as The Conspiracy and become a permanent revolutionary party. Though, by the spring, their divergent interests had forced them to abandon this scheme, they nevertheless agreed to come together in New Haven on May 1 to protest the forthcoming trial of Bobby Seale, who had been taken to Connecticut, and was being held on the charge that he had taken part in the murder of Alex Rackley. On May 1 the defendants, along with some five thousand other demonstrators, gathered in New Haven with the implied approval of Yale's president, Kingman Brewster, who had said that he was no longer sure that a black radical could be fairly tried in the United States. With the cooperation of the police and the city officials, together with the Panthers, who helped to maintain order among the demonstrators, the rally passed peacefully.

Judge Hoffman, once the trial was over, went to Palm Beach, where his sojourn was interrupted by an invitation to visit the White House. There he attended a breakfast prayer meeting led by the evangelist Billy Graham. On the previous evening he had been an honored guest at the Gridiron Club banquet, an illustrious event sponsored by the Washington press corps. On this occasion, the judge was cheered by the correspondents and the politicians, who regard it an honor to be invited to the annual Gridiron celebration. Among the entertainments that evening was a sketch that included the observation that it hardly mattered if the country ignores the First Amendment; there are still twenty-three left. For the final entertainment of the evening President Nixon and Vice President Agnew put on a sort of minstrel show in which the Vice President assumed the accent of a Southern politician as he played Dixie on the piano. The two men concluded their performance by singing "God Bless America."

A week after the trial Tom Foran told a parents' meeting at Loyola High School in Chicago that the nation's children are being lost to "a freaking, fag revolution. . . . The only one I didn't think was a fag," Foran said of the defendants, "was Bobby Seale," whom the other defendants used as "grossly and callously" as if "they were masters of the plantation. . . . We have lost our kids to this fag revolution," Foran said, "and we've got to reach out for them. Our kids," he concluded, "don't understand that we don't mean anything by it when we call people niggers. They look at us like we're dinosaurs when we talk like that."

A week later, Foran, chastened perhaps by the adverse reactions of the press to his unkind reference to homosexuals, made a second speech in which he referred to a "Fagin revolution."

During the same week that Foran spoke at Loyola, Kunstler spoke at the Santa Barbara campus of the University of California. On the night he arrived, a riot had broken out among the students. In the course of their rampaging they set fire to a branch of the Bank of America. This act had been incited, according to Governor Reagan, by Kunstler's speech. The riot, however, had been in progress before Kunstler spoke. Thus, though Kunstler's speech was aggressive, the Governor's charges did not have sufficient basis to warrant an indictment under the anti-riot act.

Twelve of the Weathermen who had come to Chicago on October 8 were, however, indicted under the anti-riot act. They were ordered to appear in April for arraignment before Judge Hoffman, who had been assigned their case. But by April the Weathermen had gone underground. They did not appear for their arraignment, and only one of them could be found by the FBI. Meanwhile, they claimed credit for bombing New York City Police Headquarters. They were also presumed to be responsible for several other bombings throughout the country. In New York two Weathermen were killed as they assembled dynamite bombs in the cellar of a Greenwich Village town house.

The eight policemen who had been indicted by Judge Campbell's grand jury for interfering with the civil rights of the demonstrators were all found innocent. One was discharged from the force. The others were temporarily suspended. All seven eventually were reinstated. Throughout the spring a grand jury in Chicago had been investigating the death of Fred Hampton. By June the grand jurors had concluded that there was insufficient evidence to show that the occupants of Hampton's apartment had fired upon the police. Ballistics evidence indicated that of the eighty or so shots fired, only one had come from a Panther gun. Thus the seven Panthers who had been charged with having attempted to murder the police were released. The grand jury did not, however, go so far as to indict the police on the grounds that they may have killed Hampton without provocation. There was "absolutely no evidence," Foran said, that the police had killed Hampton and Clark intentionally. Foran, who by this time had been replaced by a Republican as United States Attorney and had entered private practice in partnership with Richard Schultz, nevertheless criticized the police who had taken part in the raid on Hampton's flat. "Where [they] went goofy is when the raiders broke in the back door and began shooting" at the police who had come in through the front door. But Foran said it would be impossible to indict the police because there was no way to prove that they intended to kill anyone. It would be "a waste of time," he said, to investigate the case further.

By the summer, as the attorneys for the defense prepared their appellate briefs, Rubin was back in Cook County Jail. Of the eight defendants, he was the only one to have been charged under state as well as federal law for his part in the convention disturbances. To these state charges he pleaded guilty. His sentence was sixty days in jail.

About the Author

JASON EPSTEIN is a Vice-President of Random House and a frequent contributor to the *New York Review of Books*. He lives in New York City and Sag Harbor, Long Island, with his wife, Barbara, and his children, Jacob and Helen.